Thame Remembers

the fallen

Compiled by

David Bretherton and Allan Hickman

with contributions from

Mike Dyer and Ian Jones MBE

Thame Remembers Project
Thame Museum
79 High Street
Thame
OX9 3AE

01844 212801
e-mail: info@thamemuseum.org
Visit our website: thameremembers.org

Published by   Daal Publishing
               8 Berkeley Road
               Thame OX9 3QT

© Text and images Copyright Thame Museum

ISBN 978-0-9539331-5-0

All rights reserved. No part of this publication may be reproduced, stored in a retrieval system or otherwise, in any form, or by any means, electronic, mechanical, photocopy, scanning, recording or otherwise without the express written consent of the publishers except for personal use.

The authors acknowledge that in the production of this work we have used pictures and words from other publications and have attributed those where applicable. Where appropriate we have attempted to gain the relevant copyright permissions and have not knowingly breached any copyright.

Front Cover picture: Lancashire Fusiliers, Ypres 1914
Back Cover picture: Troops Leaving Thame Station 1914

Front Cover Picture Band (left to right):
2nd Lieutenant Eric Rose MC, Lancashire Fusiliers.
Lieutenant Noel Alexander Target, Durham Light Infantry.
Stoker Wilfred Harry Clarke, Royal Navy, HMS Formidable
Lieutenant Stanley Hugh Winkley, Royal Air Force
Private "Mickie" Wells, Royal West Surrey Regiment
Sgt Bertie Parker, New Zealand Army Service Corps
Company Sergeant Major Cecil Amos Witney, Oxf & Bucks Light Infantry

Back Cover Picture Band (left to right):
Lieutenant Richard Tuckey Hewer, Berkshire Yeomanry
Midshipman William Cecil Hoadley, Royal Navy
2nd Lieutenant Willis Janes, Kings Own Scottish Borderers
Corporal Ernest Edward House, Canadian Infantry
Lieutenant Colonel Donald Patrick Shaw, Dorsetshire Regiment
Private Frank Chowns, Kings Royal Rifle Corps
Captain Richard J P Hewetson, Loyal North Lancs Regiment

Contents

Foreword	5	Northern Europe: RAF	187
Introduction	7	Italy	195
The Project	9	Malta	199
Thame War Memorials	15	North Africa	203
The Research	21	Singapore	211
		At Sea	213

World War One

Other Conflicts

Thame	25	South African War	223
Britain	31	Korean War	227
Belgium	37	Cyprus Emergency	229
France	61		
Gallipoli	123		

Afterword

Greece	127	The Steering Group	232
British Army in India	129	Acknowledgements	234
New Zealand	133	The Thame Cross	235
Palestine	135		

Addendum

Tanzania	137	Those Remembered	239
At Sea	139	Names on the Memorials	242
Other Names	154	Names to be Added	246

World War Two

		Thame Servicemen of WW1	249
Thame	159	Poems and Quotations	261
Britain	163	Bibliography	262
Northern Europe: Army	173		

To those servicemen
from Thame
who did not return

> NEVER SHALL THY MEMORY FADE
> SWEET THOUGHTS EVER LINGER
> WHERE THOU ART LAID

Gravestone epitaph A H Pollicott

Foreword

Lest We Forget

The words of Rupert Brooke, the English poet and Royal Naval Volunteer Reserve sub-lieutenant who died en route to the Gallipoli battlefront, 'If I should die, think only this of me /That there's some corner of a foreign field /That is for ever England' reminds us all that members of the armed forces on land, at sea and in the air have sacrificed their lives in the service of their country and for our freedom quite literally across the globe. This has not only been during the two World Wars and, since 1900, conflicts like those with the Boers in South Africa, in Korea, The Falklands and Iraq, but in a multitude of costly campaigns during the inter-war period on the Indian sub-continent and since 1945 in such trouble spots as Malaya, Kenya, Cyprus, Bosnia, Northern Ireland and Afghanistan. Figures such as 19,240 killed among 57,470 casualties in a single day on the Somme 1st July 1916, three survivors from HMS Hood's ship's company of 1,421 after its duel with the German battleship Bismarck on 24th May 1941 and the loss of 95 bombers and their crews in a raid against Nuremberg on 31st March 1944, in their starkness make grim reading. Appalling as they are, there is a further disturbing, personal hinterland.

Each statistic represents the loss of someone precious to a family and a community. Some years ago, I visited the Menin Gate, an impressive tribute to those with no known grave who fell in its vicinity. In an alcove was a small cross, with an attached poppy and a brief poignant note: 'To my father, whom I never knew'. Lawrence of Arabia movingly wrote that each death was like a pebble tossed into a pond from which 'a ripple of sorrow' spreads outwards to touch not only an immediate family, but distant relatives, school friends, and especially for conscripts, former workmates, social and sporting acquaintances.

This admirable and ambitious project to locate the far flung resting places of the sons of Thame and leave a Thame Remembers Cross 'wherever in the world that might be' gives dignity and substance to Rupert Brooke's 'foreign field'. It is a tangible and touching reminder that 'at the going down of the sun and in the morning, we will remember them'.

John Sweetman

Dr John Sweetman is a distinguished military historian and author.

Went the day well?

Went the day well?
We died and never knew.
But, well or ill,
Freedom, we died for you.
Went the day well?
When you go home,
Tell them of us and say,
For your tomorrows,
These gave their todays.

John Maxwell Edmonds
(1875-1958)

Thame Remembers

Introduction

The Thame Remembers Project has exceeded all our expectations. It has been embraced by the community and taken to their hearts. Many who have delivered crosses have said how moved they were by the experience and how grateful they were for the opportunity to have taken part. Privileged is a word that we heard said many times.

The Project was itself ambitious, even to research all the names on the War Memorials in depth would take most of the time that the Project had to run. We could not have carried this Project forward alone and we must pay tribute to Mike Dyer, who was often leading the way. We must also thank the Project Steering Group without whom we would not even have started.

When we began, we had no intention of producing this book as a record of the Project. We considered that the legacy of the Project on the website, the video record and the many delivery reports would be sufficient. The aim of the Project was to visit every grave or in the case of those with no known grave, a memorial and to deliver a Thame Cross for every service man from Thame who made the ultimate sacrifice, wherever they are in the world. However it was essential to carry out a great deal of research so that when undertaking the visit there was a full understanding of the sacrifice that each one of the men had made. As more and more records became available on the internet we were able to add to the information that we had found and thus in many cases expand the man's story.

The reports created for each delivery were themselves limited in space and so a new method of recording the research had to be found. We reconsidered our initial reluctance to produce a book about the Project and we were encouraged to do so by the many participants who requested that we should create a record in this more traditional format. Therefore in November 2016 we set about creating this legacy, even though we had not yet completed all the research or deliveries. We felt that if we waited until all that was achieved we may never get round to producing a finalised version.

We would like to thank the other members of the Project Steering Group who have contributed to this publication in their various ways but their contributions are not individually recorded.

Although this book is not intended to be a bedtime read, we hope that you will enjoy the many stories of the heroic men of Thame who all gave their lives in defence of their country.

Allan and David

For the Fallen

With proud thanksgiving, a mother for her children,
England mourns for her dead across the sea.
Flesh of her flesh they were, spirit of her spirit,
Fallen in the cause of the free.

Solemn the drums thrill: Death august and royal
Sings sorrow up into immortal spheres.
There is music in the midst of desolation
And a glory that shines upon our tears.

They went with songs to the battle, they were young,
Straight of limb, true of eye, steady and aglow.
They were staunch to the end against odds uncounted,
They fell with their faces to the foe.

They shall grow not old, as we that are left grow old:
Age shall not weary them, nor the years condemn.
At the going down of the sun and in the morning
We will remember them.

They mingle not with their laughing comrades again;
They sit no more at familiar tables of home;
They have no lot in our labour of the day-time;
They sleep beyond England's foam.

But where our desires are and our hopes profound,
Felt as a well-spring that is hidden from sight,
To the innermost heart of their own land they are known
As the stars are known to the Night;

As the stars that shall be bright when we are dust,
Moving in marches upon the heavenly plain,
As the stars that are starry in the time of our darkness,
To the end, to the end, they remain.

Lawrence Binyon

(1869-1943)

The Project

The Thame Remembers Project was originally conceived in early 2014 as a means of marking the centenary of World War One and honouring the men from our small Oxfordshire market town of Thame who had given their lives in conflict – not only during 1914/18 but in all conflicts from the Boer War to the present day. The Project launch was set to coincide with the centenary of the outbreak of World War One but, inevitably, some preparatory work was required beforehand. Principally, this involved gathering together the names of the 182 men from Thame who are remembered in the town, on two War Memorials, Church Memorial Boards and at Lord Williams's School. Secondly, we secured the necessary funding to support the Project with grants from Oxfordshire County Council, Thame Town Council and the Heritage Lottery Fund, plus a smaller donation from a local history research group which helped to provide seed funding for expenditure prior to the official launch. This enabled us to produce promotional leaflets and set up the launch event itself. Thame Museum Trustees gave their support and made Thame Remembers a Museum project.

The challenge was that people from Thame, all volunteers, should visit graves and memorials in 23 countries, across four continents, to commemorate 182 men (now 212) from the town who had made the ultimate sacrifice during times of conflict.

The launch event took place on 3rd August 2014 at St Mary's Church in Thame. A press release was circulated to local media and it was featured in local newspapers, radio stations and on the BBC website. An evocative report of the event, written by an independent journalist, was featured as the front page of our first Project newsletter and records both the first of our cross deliveries and the involvement of young members of the community. We also launched a promotional video, filmed locally in Thame, on our website and on YouTube.

> One hundred years ago World War One was declared and hundreds of Thame's young men left home, many of them leaving from Thame railway station, to join the fighting, some never to return from a war that killed millions.
>
> On Sunday, August 3rd the people of Thame joined in a collective act of remembrance, and witnessed the launch of the Thame Remembers Project, beginning the ambitious challenge to deliver a special Thame Remembers cross to the grave or memorial of each and every person named on a War Memorial in Thame, wherever in the world that may be.
>
> The programme began with a service at St Mary's Church, packed with local people of all ages, who heard Churchwarden, Helena Fickling, read Wilfred Owen's moving poem, 1914, which begins with the heart-searing words: "War broke: and now the Winter of the world, With perishing great darkness closes in."
>
> Pastor Paddy Harris, of Thame's Cornerstone Church, read the Reflection and Cllr Nick Carter read W W Gibson's poem, The Messages, which contains the devastating chorus of: "I cannot quite remember.....There were five dropped dead beside me in the trench – and three whispered their dying messages to me...."
>
> Afterwards, the congregation filed out of the church processing behind a lone piper who led them through the churchyard, passing several grave stones marked with a fluttering scarlet ribbon. The ribbons marked a war casualty whose grave or memorial would soon receive a special 'Thame Remembers' cross to start the long, world-wide, journey towards achieving the aims of the challenge.

> *What looked like a tented encampment from across Church Meadow included an exhibition of military weaponry, uniforms and artefacts; an exhibition about the tunnels and trenches that are still being explored today by the Durand Group, of which local ex-army Major and military historian Ian Jones is an active member; a refreshments tent, and an exhibition and video about the project. Rifleman Tom Bowen, a serving soldier who lives in Thame, was just one of many uniformed representatives of the modern fighting forces, most of whom themselves, like Tom and Ian, have lost colleagues and friends in conflicts around the world.*
>
> *Then came the most poignant and significant part of the evening. As a bugler played Reveille the names of 31 of Thame's fallen who are buried or remembered in St Mary's churchyard, were read out, recalling when and where they died. As each name was spoken, a relative or an invited local dignitary, accompanied by a young person, often a Scout or Guide, processed to that particular graveside or memorial where they spoke a few words of recognition of his great sacrifice, before laying a small Thame Remembers cross in front of the headstone. Once all the crosses had been delivered the evocative sound of the bugle playing the Last Post was the signal for a minute's silence before the cross parties returned to the gathering, some remaining to join a vigil in the church."*
>
> (based on an original article in 2014 by local reporter Sonja Francis; www.thame.net)

Research

This has been a consistent background feature to the Project, involving volunteers from Thame Museum, the archivist and Old Tamensians' Association at Lord Williams's School and others in the community. This research has utilised all of the relevant online archives including regimental war diaries as well as personal visits to a number of public and media archive centres. In addition to researching the stories of the men, we also managed to trace photographs of many of them and, in a few cases, have established contact with living descendants. As a result, we have been able to accompany every cross delivery with the story of the casualty.

The research revealed some unexpected results including :
- A name on the Thame War Memorial, Joe Hinder, who did not actually die in conflict but lived for another thirty years.
- An additional 30 names of men who are not remembered on Thame War Memorial but whose names will be added at a future date.
- An approach by the Commonwealth War Graves Commission (CWGC) with a request to add our research findings to their information database.

Public Awareness

The major key to the success of Thame Remembers has been public awareness and community engagement, which we have achieved from the outset.

Publicity

Print media coverage commenced with our efforts to publicise the launch event. These were rewarded in July 2014 by a dedicated two page feature in the Oxford Mail as well as shorter pieces in other local publications. Both the Oxford Mail and the Thame Gazette have continued to cover the Project with regular updates. Other notable items of press coverage have been a two page feature in Family Tree magazine in December 2014 and a two page feature in Gulf Weekly (the community newspaper of Bahrain) in November 2015. We have had reports, though no evidence, of coverage in other publications outside our immediate area and as far away as Australia and New Zealand.

Broadcast media have proven extremely successful following a direct pitch to local BBC management at the commencement of the Project. BBC Radio Oxford has featured Thame Remembers on a regular basis through both studio and telephone interviews on air. BBC South (local TV news) has also broadcast numerous features. The first was broadcast a few days after the Project launch and then, early in 2015 when planning our Battlefield Tour, we suggested that they send a reporter with us for four days to France and Belgium. Much to our surprise they agreed, with the result that as well as live radio interviews during the tour, four separate TV features were broadcast over consecutive days during November 2015. This BBC feature series was also nominated for, and won, a Royal Television Society award for the reporter, Victoria Cook. They also accompanied us on our visit to Portsmouth Naval Memorial in 2017.

It was not possible to track the spread of publicity through **web-based media,** but Thame Remembers has featured regularly in The Town Council's e-newsletter and on the independent ThameNews.Net and a Google Search will reveal our website and many other websites that have shared our Project.

Throughout the Project we have given a number of **talks and presentations** to local groups such as U3A and the local Masonic Lodge but, most significantly, to special assemblies of seven different year groups (ages 11-17) at Lord Williams's School in Thame, taking the Project to around 3000 young people in our community. Each of these presentations lasted forty minutes and included a showing of the Project video, a full introduction to the Thame Remembers challenge, a reading of 'In Flanders Fields' by a sixth form pupil in full World War One infantry uniform and an opportunity for students to discuss the Project. This is covered in more detail under Education.

Thame Remembers have taken part in many **local events,** with stalls at Thame Show, the Thame Christmas event and the Thame Food Festival. We have also played our part at Thame's Remembrance Day events 2014 -2018, including a 2.5 metre x 1 metre display in the shape of the Thame Remembers Cross.

Two events which particularly stand out, have been in collaboration with Thame Players Theatre. Firstly, Thame Players put on a production of Journey's End in which Thame Remembers played an integral advisory role and also screened a rolling credit naming all Thame's World War One casualties. The second, a one-off performance on 1st July 2016, was a commemoration in narrative, verse and archive film of the first day of the Battle of the Somme, produced entirely by the Thame Remembers Project Team but with free use of the theatre and technical assistance with sound, video and lighting provided by Thame Players. Both events were pronounced as successes. We will follow this up with a further production in November 2018 telling the story of "Ten Tommies from Thame" who joined up together in August 1914.

Cross and Wreath Deliveries
The aim of the Thame Remembers Project was, of course, to deliver a cross or wreath to the grave or memorial of all the men from Thame who died in conflict, wherever that may be in the world. That covers 212 men in 23 countries across three continents and has certainly been ambitious but our confidence in the people of Thame was well-founded and we have achieved above our initial target, which we thought would be about 95%.

The first twelve crosses to be delivered were to war graves in the local churchyard at St Mary's Church, Thame and added a particularly poignant significance to the launch event on 3rd August 2014. The first overseas delivery was made in September 2014 and by that Christmas we had already achieved thirty cross deliveries as far afield as Malta, Tanzania, New Zealand, India and Singapore. By July 2016 we had achieved nearly 70% (145) of the targeted deliveries, adding Korea and Bahrain as well as many European locations.

The Heritage Lottery Fund requirement was that up to the end of July 2016 Thame Remembers should have undertaken at least fifty visits to World War One memorial and burial sites of those men who were commemorated in Thame. Our actual achievement over that period was 79 separate visits, during which we placed crosses or wreaths in remembrance of 106 World War One casualties. In addition, the Project achieved 37 visits to World War Two cemeteries, remembering men from Thame, plus visits to Pusan (Korea) and Bahrain (Cyprus conflict) in honour of two more men from Thame.

The total for the Project is visits to 102 cemeteries and 31 memorials in 23 countries, by over 300 different people and over 150,00 miles travelled. Every delivery has been carried out by someone from Thame or on behalf of someone from Thame, whether on vacation, a business trip, or in some cases as a dedicated mission. It was a recurrent theme that people have commented on the impact that it made on them. What could be taken as a form of tokenism invariably turned into a profound and life enhancing experience for all those involved. Some even recorded their feelings for publication on our website and in our newsletters.

We recognised that there were only two locations which we were highly unlikely to get the opportunity to visit and we utilised memorials at the National Memorial Arboretum and CWGC HQ to substitute for the actual grave. We also placed crosses at the National Memorial Arboretum for the two men whose resting places we have been unable to locate.

Family Contacts

From the outset it was always hoped that the Project would put us in touch with living family members of some of Thame's casualties. We decided that we would not intrude into people's lives, but instead hope for them to make contact with us. There are many examples where this has occurred, whether local people talking to us at our many events, contacts made through our website, those who have seen the TV features and email contact from as far afield as New Zealand and Australia.

Wherever possible it was the family members themselves who delivered the crosses, two of these being featured in the BBC coverage. These family contacts have also been a rich source of extra material, including photographs, towards our research archive.

Education

The Project has been, and will continue to be, an education to all those involved and, more importantly, we were able to play a part in making young people aware of the world conflicts and the part played by local men. We have already mentioned the involvement of young people at the launch event and the presentations that were given to school assemblies. We have maintained a close relationship with the school and, in particular, their Head of History. A few other examples would include: cross deliveries carried out on family vacations, with children and young adults taking part; Lord Williams's School Head Teacher, Head Boy and Head Girl delivering a cross to the grave of an ex-pupil in Watlington, Oxfordshire; a Lord Williams's School trip to Normandy in 2015 to deliver two Thame Remembers Crosses as part of their itinerary (see World War Two reports for R J Boiling and L Hodges); a nine year old pupil from a local primary school used Thame Remembers as the inspiration for a school project.

Tours

Our Battlefield Tour in October/November 2015 involved forty people from Thame travelling to France and Belgium for four nights. They visited the main memorials, The Menin Gate, Tyne Cot, Vimy Ridge, Thiepval as well as visits to the preserved trenches at Beaumont Hamel, Lochnagar Crater and a number of cemeteries where members of the party placed crosses at the graves of men from Thame. The BBC features provided excellent coverage of the tour. Another tour in May 2017 visited more locations including Loos Memorial, Hooge Cemetery and the Wellington Tunnels at Arras.

The Project Steering Group also undertook two separate reconnaissance tours in May 2014 and May 2015 in order to enhance our knowledge, explore destinations and generally ensure the smooth running of the Battlefield Tours, as well as delivering crosses to a few locations that would not be accessible by coach. Closer to home, we have taken members of the community on visits to the World War Two Command Bunker at Uxbridge, London the

Poppy Factory in Richmond, Surrey and, in June 2017, to the Portsmouth Naval Memorial, Hampshire.

A coach trip to the National Memorial Arboretum, Staffordshire in July 2018 was undertaken to lay the final crosses at appropriate memorials to the men we had not been able to honour due to the location of their resting place. It also gave the opportunity for all present to reflect and contemplate the ultimate sacrifice given by the men from Thame, and millions more, that we may live in a free and better world.

Throughout the Thame Remembers Project our funding has helped towards the travel costs to the many cemeteries and memorials but people covered their hotel, subsistence and other expenses from their own pockets.

Community Engagement and Volunteering

Community engagement is evident throughout this book, on our website and through our newsletters. Therefore no further comment is needed except to record our own appreciation for the many ways in which the local community, both as individuals and groups, have supported this Project and responded to the challenge. We never doubted that they would! The Project has been a huge task for the people steering it to success. We have been rewarded beyond expectation, have ourselves grown with the experience and feel that it has been a more than worthy venture that continues to give.

Field of Thame Remembers Crosses laid at Thame War Memorial in November 2017
One cross for each casualty, the small section represents
those still to be delivered at that time

1914

War broke: and now the Winter of the world
With perishing great darkness closes in.
The foul tornado, centred at Berlin,
Is over all the width of Europe whirled,
Rending the sails of progress. Rent or furled
Are all Art's ensigns. Verse wails. Now begin
Famines of thought and feeling. Love's wine's thin.
The grain of human Autumn rots, down-hurled.

For after Spring had bloomed in early Greece,
And Summer blazed her glory out with Rome,
An Autumn softly fell, a harvest home,
A slow grand age, and rich with all increase.
But now, for us, wild Winter, and the need
Of sowings for new Spring, and blood for seed.

Wilfred Owen
(1893-1918)

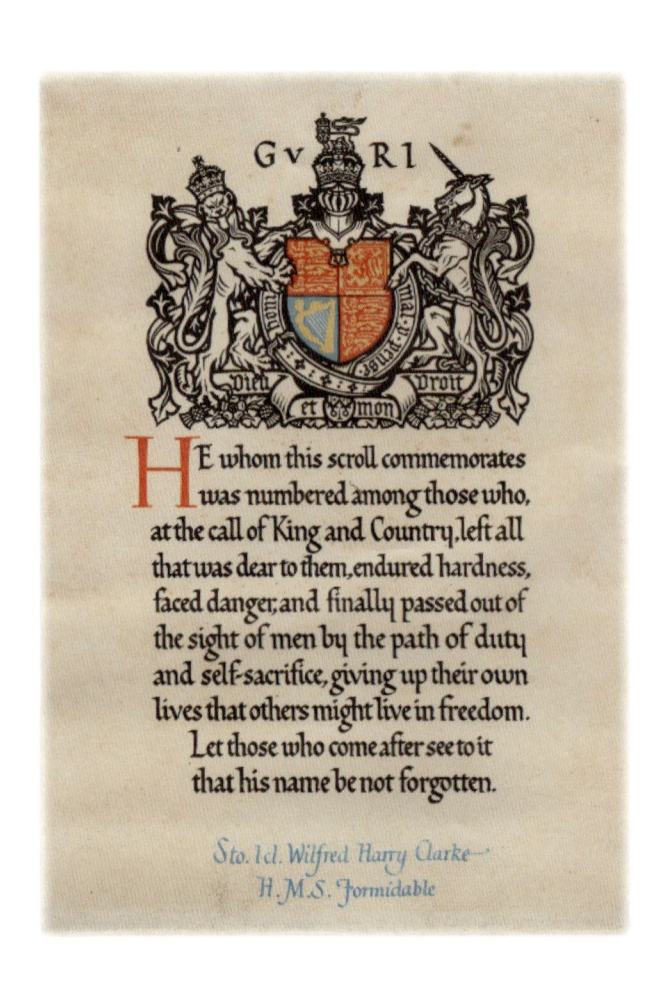

HE whom this scroll commemorates was numbered among those who, at the call of King and Country, left all that was dear to them, endured hardness, faced danger, and finally passed out of the sight of men by the path of duty and self-sacrifice, giving up their own lives that others might live in freedom. Let those who come after see to it that his name be not forgotten.

Sto. 1cl. Wilfred Harry Clarke —
H.M.S. Formidable

Thame War Memorials

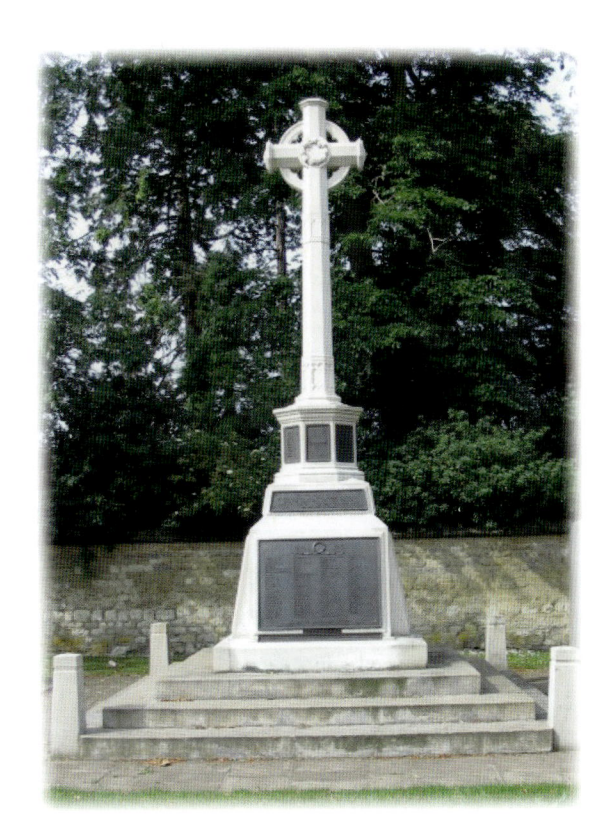

Thame War Memorial

Moreton War Memorial

When considering a local memorial to the war dead one may only think of the Thame War Memorial which of course is the most prominent and well-known monument in the town to honour those who have died in conflict, but there is also a War Memorial at Moreton and Memorial Boards were raised in the churches of St Mary's, All Saints', Christchurch and Moreton Chapel. Lord Williams's School also records former pupils and masters who perished in both World Wars. In addition there is a War Memorial Plaque in St Mary's Church commemorating five men from Thame who died in the Boer War.

The Thame War Memorial is built of Portland Stone and was financed by public subscription. Mr James T Robinson, architect and surveyor, prepared the plans for the Memorial and superintended the project, although the ground was prepared by Mr R G Holland and the Memorial was constructed by Mr Harris. It was unveiled by the Prime Minister, Mr David Lloyd George, on 30th July 1921.

The cataloguing of names for the Thame Remembers Project started with listing the 117 names on the Thame and Moreton War Memorials and then adding the names and information from the Church and School Memorial Boards. Surprisingly, there are two names on the St Mary's Church Memorial Board that do not appear on the War Memorial, perhaps because this Memorial Board was compiled at a later date.

The Moreton War Memorial and All Saints' Church Memorial Board provide details of the units in which the men served, although not entirely accurately but no additional names. One notes a ship that did not exist and another gives a Scottish regiment, when in fact he served with the Canadian Infantry.

Of the 62 names recorded on the School Memorial Boards only ten are also recorded on the War Memorial, which is not altogether surprising as many were pupils from local villages and boarders

16 | *Thame Remembers*

**Memorial Board in Christchurch
(Upper High Street)**

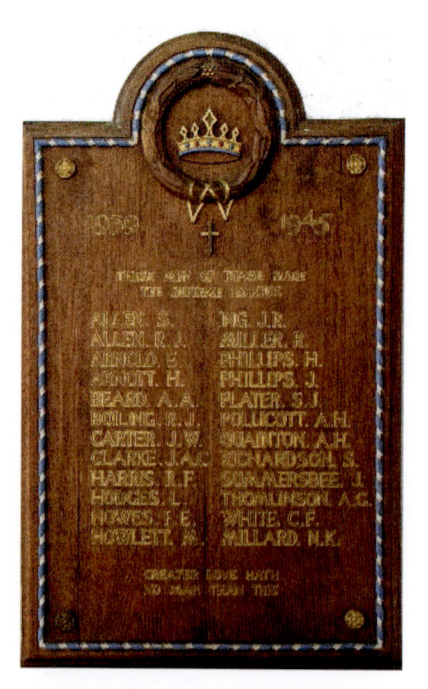

**World War Two Memorial
Board in St Mary's Church**

from further afield. A further 52 names were therefore added to the Thame Remembers list.

When studying the graves in St Mary's churchyard, the war graves being quite distinctive, it was noted that although there are ten recorded, only eight names are included on the War Memorial, adding a further two names to our list. There are also a number of graves where the family have recorded an inscription to a relative who died in conflict. Many of these names also appear on an existing memorial, but three are unique to the gravestones.

The methodology for the original listing of names to be placed on the memorials has not survived, but must have been based on local people putting forward the name of a loved one who had not returned from the war. Given the delicacy of the listing of the names it is likely that checking was not too robust and so it was almost inevitable that inaccuracies occurred. These inaccuracies were often just in the spelling of the surname or the use of a diminutive rather than a full name; (initial "B" for Bertie when his name was Hubert) or, as previously mentioned, in details of the military unit or ship.

The memorials and graves gave an initial target of 182 names for the Thame Remembers Project. However further research has discovered many men who were either born, lived, went to school or worked in Thame and are not included in that 182.

World War One Memorial Board in St Mary's Church

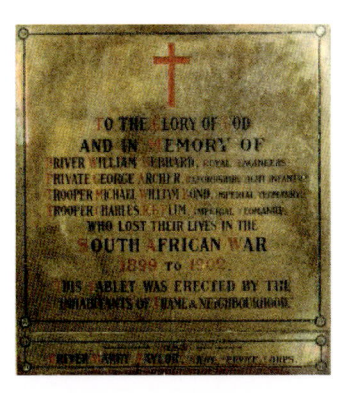

Boer War Plaque in St Mary's Church

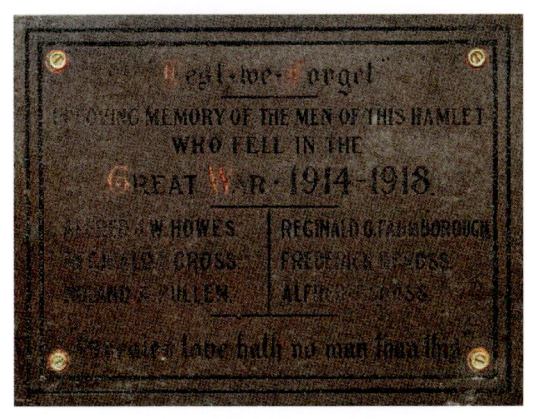

Moreton Chapel Memorial Plaque (now in Thame Museum)

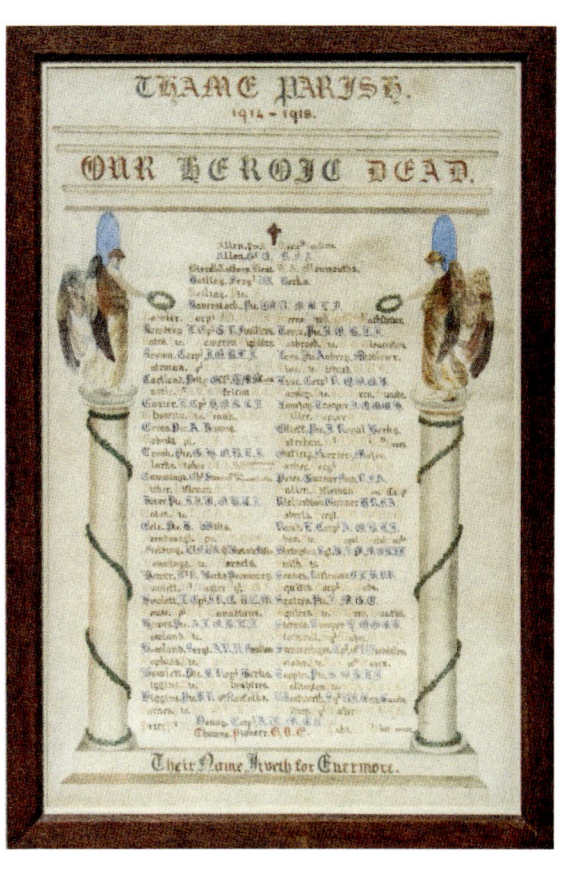

All Saints' Church Memorial Board (now in Thame Museum)

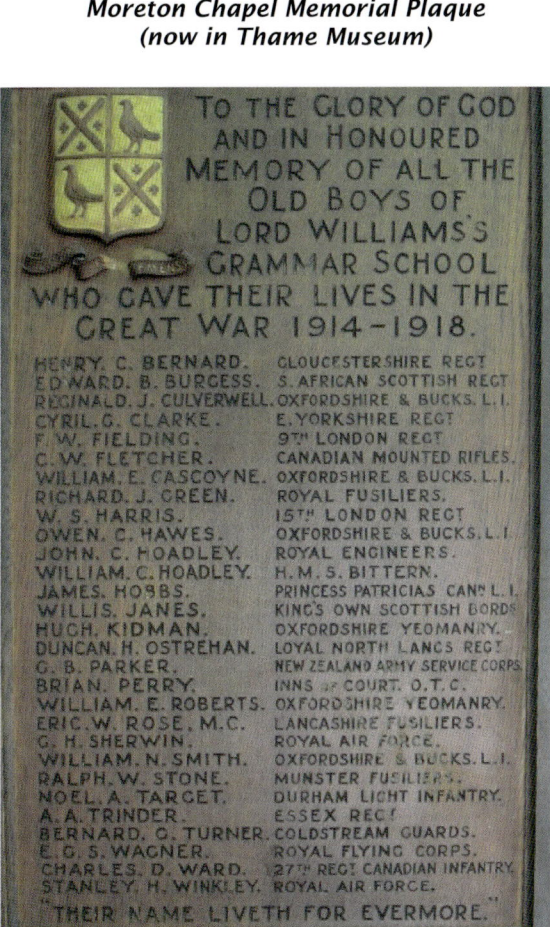

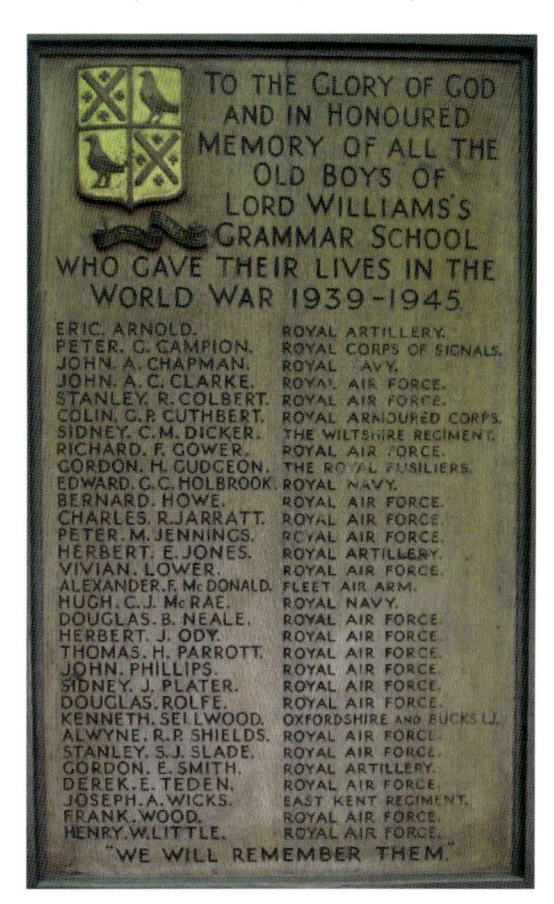

War Memorial Boards at Lord Williams's School

David Lloyd George's Speech

Speech by the Prime Minister, the Right Honourable David Lloyd George, at the unveiling of the War Memorial in Thame, Oxfordshire on 30th July 1921, as recorded by the Thame Gazette

The Prime Minister was greeted with rounds of applause as he stepped forward to respond to the vote of thanks. He said "Mr. Terrell, and if I may be allowed to do so address you; my neighbours. I despair of making my voice heard over the great multitude who have come together on this occasion, but permit me to thank you, Mr. Terrell, for the much too kind words you have used in respect of my services. I am only one out of millions who did their best for the old country in the hour of danger. (Applause) I claim no more. We have come here today to unveil a beautiful memorial to 87 men of Thame who laid down their young lives for freedom and fair play in the world. You have a record in this ancient town of which every inhabitant may well be proud. You have a population, I understand, of something just under 3,000. Out of that number 600 took part in the Great War, 600 volunteered, (Applause) 87 fell and 200 were wounded. It is a great record. It is a harrowing record, but a record of which you today ought to be proud. One which your children and your children's children, as long as they live one with another in Thame, will talk of in thrilling tones of pride. Seven years ago, on a Saturday, just before the Bank Holiday, these young men knew there were clouds in Europe, but they thought not that the thunderbolt would strike them down. Their minds were on the Monday that was coming, how to spend it for themselves and those with whom they were associated. In a few days they knew that freedom was in danger, that fair play was being trampled on; and there is no more sacred word in the English heart than fair play, (Applause) and they volunteered by the hundreds to fight in lands they had never seen and probably never dreamt of entering. And this Memorial erected here, and unveiled today will remind the men, women and children of Thame and the neighbourhood, maybe for centuries to come, of one of the noblest deeds in the history of our race.

Prime Minister David Lloyd George at the unveiling of Thame War Memorial

I was here fourteen years ago at a review of the Oxfordshire Yeomanry. I believe the present Lord Chancellor was one of the officers, but I see the Colonel here, and I am delighted to see him; an old friend, although we have been on opposite sides of the House. (Laughter). I have seen him walk into the wrong lobby many a time, but he always did it genially, and always had the respect and friendship of all men and parties in the House. (Applause) When they went to camp there were the Lord Chancellor, Mr. Winston Churchill and General Seely, and I met one or two officers there at the time. Although they were training for war, I wondered whether there was one of them who ever dreamt that, in seven years, they would be engaged in the greatest and most terrible war the world has ever seen, and they were.

The first territorial regiment to land in France. (Applause) You have got a great record, and there was your brave young Member *[Major Val Fleming MP for Henley]* who was with one of the Oxfordshire regiments and who fell. I had the honour of knowing him, a gallant and great memory added to the lustre of the House of Commons by his heroism. It is a fine story, and you may well be proud of it. It has altered the history of the world. The world goes in a different direction because these 87 men of Thame who gave their lives with many others. It has altered the great current of the human story, sent it in the right direction. Do you know what the British Empire raised for the war? The British Empire enrolled and called to the Colours from many lands and nations tens of millions of picked men of many races. They fought in three continents and on many oceans. It was the greatest army ever brought together. Ten million came from every clime, rallied to the same flag and for the same cause. They suffered heavily, 947,000 young men fell under the flag, the same flag I took in my hand just now, died under it to save its glory. Over two million were wounded and our total casualties over three million. In addition to this, the burdens which have been cast upon the shoulders of the citizens of this country as the result of this devastating war were enormous. These men, most of whom came to the flag voluntarily, fought not to repel the invader from their homes, but for fair play to other countries that were being trampled upon by a ruthless foe. That was an element in the sacrifice which ennobled it.

Great as our losses were, those of France were even greater. They were greater in the actual numbers of their dead and of their wounded; they were still greater in proportion to their population. And France, in addition to the heavy cost of the war, has also to repair her devastated provinces. It is inconceivable that the two countries which made such tremendous sacrifices for a common cause, and through their suffering won a common triumph for that cause, should quarrel over the interpretation of the Peace which they achieved at such cost. We have had some differences with France recently over the interpretations of the Treaty, and we have talked very plainly to each other. That is quite right. Plain speaking generally leads to good understanding. (Applause) Thoughts working in concealment are dangerous. It is much better to have it out, and we have both done so, with the most excellent results. We are I believe, today on the high road to an understanding. (Applause) The preliminary difficulties which were causing trouble have, I am glad to tell you, been accommodated, and it has been arranged that the Allies meet in a few days to settle this vexed question; and I hope finally. Britain only claims that she must have a voice in the interpretation of a peace she made such a sacrifice to win. She does not claim a predominant voice or a determining voice; that would be so arrogant a demand that no self-respecting ally could possibly tolerate it. We only ask for an equal voice. (Applause) We are not prepared to go beyond that. We recognize fully that the greater sacrifices of France give her a special claim for consideration; that her interests are more immediate in some of these questions; that the dangers are closer to her frontiers, more visible to her eyes; that historical causes, some of them recent and very fresh in her memory, make her apprehensions more vivid and poignant than ours. We are willing to allow for all that. I would only respectfully say that these considerations, although they give France a better right to a hearing for her case, are not of a character, which is apt to deflect calm judgment. The British have but one concern in all these questions; that the Peace so dearly won should be a real Peace, should be an immediate Peace. A deferred Peace is half a war. Let us have the Peace, which this noble blood was shed to purchase. They did not die that nations should continue to hurl hatred at each other and organize against each other even bloodier conflicts than those in which they fell. If Britain seems to be always restraining, always counselling patience, always urging moderation in the affairs of Europe, it is because this terrible war has taught us the value of peace.

Our sole anxiety is lest the Allies, by an unwise and harsh use of their undoubted power, should roll deeper and firmer into the soil those roots of future conflict, which were withering on the surface in the sunshine of the great victory. (Applause) If there is another war it will be terrible beyond thought. The machinery of destruction during the war was becoming more terrible year by year, month by month. Just before the bells of peace were set ringing we had ready more horrible machinery than the world had yet seen. I doubt not that similar devices were perfecting on the other side. The ingenious mind of man will go on developing those horrors. Were another war to fall upon the world, I will tell you from my own knowledge of what was going on, what developments are capable of being made, civilization would be destroyed. Europe might become as the north of France. We must be aware lest we bequeath to our children a legacy of concentrated hate which will one day explode shattering their happiness and leaving the world a wilderness and man a gaunt wanderer amongst the ruins of the civilization his folly has destroyed. That was not what the gallant young men of Thame died for. (Applause). Should this happen, those gallant young men will have died in vain! Millions more brave men on five continents will have sacrificed their lives to no good purpose. That is the reason why, as the whole might of the British Empire was, in August 1914, cast into the war, today the same power is thrown into the scales of peace." (Applause)

> "and this Memorial erected here, and unveiled today will remind the men, women and children of Thame and the neighbourhood, maybe for centuries to come, of one of the noblest deeds in the history of our race."

An Extract from Mr Lloyd George's Speech

The Research

War memorials provide basic information about an individual though often only a name. Where that name could be matched with the records of the Commonwealth War Graves Commission (CWGC), then the research that followed was straightforward. However, for many of the names these records showed a multitude of names that matched or closely matched the Thame War Memorial records and then, using other sources, each record had to be checked and eliminated until the correct person was identified.

A good source of information about individuals was found in the Thame Gazette with articles from men at the Front and from families recording the passing of their loved ones. These often included copies of the letters received from a man's Commanding Officer or NCO.

To make matters more difficult, the majority of British Army service records from the First World War were destroyed by a fire during bombing in the Second World War. So other data sources had to be relied on, such as census records and registers for births, baptisms and weddings. Thankfully Royal Navy and Royal Air Force records for World War One have survived, as do the records of the Commonwealth nations. These provided information for those men who served in these forces.

Research for casualties from World War Two has been more difficult as the service records are still held by the Services and not publicly available. The 1939 Register was released during our research but it excludes service personnel and redacts younger people. Our research, therefore, concentrated on family information, newspapers and unit diaries, where available.

We have endeavoured to research each name thoroughly and although we have followed a few false trails throughout the research, we now believe that we have correctly identified the majority of names on the War Memorials. If anyone should have additional information to that contained in this publication then we would be most grateful to learn of it. Contact can be made through the publisher or through a member of the Thame Remembers Steering Group at Thame Museum. After all our research had been completed there are still two names outstanding, J L Castle and H T Wilson. These are recorded later in the book with as much information as we have uncovered, in the hope that at some point in the future, information will come to light that will enable them to be identified in more detail.

Regimental/Service Numbers

Service numbers provide a vital piece of information to correctly identify a soldier, sailor or airman. However, to be able to follow many of the records correctly, it is important to have a brief understanding of the development of regimental numbers and their change to service numbers. A regimental number was issued to all servicemen and, prior to 1920, each regiment or corps had its own system of numbering, each starting at number one. Some numbers had a letter prefix which may indicate type of service, trade, period of joining or depot to which they belonged. This was particularly so with the Royal Navy. If a soldier transferred to a new regiment then he was allocated a new number. At this period a number was not unique to a particular person and there could be many men in different regiments with the same number. With the rapid enlargement of regiments during World War One many regiments, Oxford and Bucks Light Infantry being one, changed their numbering system, issuing all existing soldiers with a new number. It is worth noting that commissioned officers during World War One did not have regimental or service numbers.

A second system of numbering was introduced in 1920 under Army Order 388 when each regiment was allocated its own block of numbers. Number length was now standardised at seven digits and the same number was maintained throughout a soldier's career even if he was transferred to a different regiment or corps. Commissioned officers were allocated service numbers under the post 1920 system, however when promoted from the ranks they would be allocated a new/different number. During World War Two the blocks of numbers were allocated to central depots where soldiers were given a number prior to being posted to a regiment. This meant that it was no longer possible to trace a man's regiment from his service number.

Battleground Names.
The names given to strategic and tactical positions on a battlefield were often geographical, although with few such features on a fixed front of trenches it was generally the names given by the men themselves that were adopted into common usage. Some were evocative, with Hellfire Corner and Shrapnel Valley leaving little to the imagination. Many recalled familiar landmarks from their thoughts of home, examples being White City, Piccadilly and Lime Street. A large mine crater on the Somme is known as Lochnagar from the name given by a Scottish Regiment to the trench system from which the tunnel was dug to set the mine. Others reflected the Tommies' sense of humour in adversity. Sausage Valley may have described the shape of the observation balloon that the Germans flew over it, but it takes a different meaning when one notes that a neighbouring depression became known as Mash Valley. Place names, especially those difficult to pronounce were also frequently adapted, with the best known being Wipers as a euphemism for Ypres, other examples being Plug Street (Ploegsteert), Ocean Villas (Auchonvillers) and Mucky Farm (Mouquet Farm).

Army Structure
A few words of explanation may also be needed for the formations used in the organisation of a British Army. A rough guide to Infantry unit names and strength in 1914 was:

Name	Commander	Composition	Nominal Strength
Army Group	General	2-4 Corps	100,000-200,000
Corps	Lieutenant General	2+ Divisions	50,000
Division	Major General	3 Brigades	12,000-18,000*
Brigade	Brigadier	4 Battalions	4,000
Battalion	Lieutenant Colonel	4 Companies	1,000 (inc HQ)
Company	Captain	4 Platoons	227
Platoon	Lieutenant	-	50 men

In addition to these units there would be Headquarters for each Brigade, Division, Corps and Army Group. These are nominal strength figures and battalions during World War One were rarely at full strength more often down to 70% or even less.

* There would also be units of specialised Corps such as Royal Artillery and Army Supply Corps attached at Division level.

The term regiment is not used here, as the fighting units of a regiment were deployed as battalions and may be in different theatres of war at the same time. Each regiment has its own geographical base and headquarters and indeed organisational structure.

For instance the Oxford and Buckinghamshire Light Infantry prior to World War One had four Battalions. The 1st and 2nd Battalions were Regular Army based in India and at home respectively. The 3rd Battalion was the HQ and Training Battalion and the 4th was the Territorials or locally recruited part-time soldiers. As war progressed an additional Territorial Battalion (the 2/4th) was formed and Kitchener's recruits and conscripts created additional service battalions numbered from the 5th onwards.

The naming of battalions was also fairly irregular. Many of the "Pals Battalions" that were raised from a particular area or occupation took on names describing their connection to the area or occupation and were then allocated to an existing Regiment. For example the battalion raised in London as the Artists Rifles became the 28th (1st Artists Rifles) Battalion of the London Regiment and the Accrington Pals were in fact the 11th Battalion (Accrington) of the East Lancashire Regiment.

Monetary Values
In many of the reports in this book reference is made to the value of items such as a gratuity or a will. The amount may appear small by today's standards but its value at the time would have been quite significant. For instance a will valued at £280 in 1918 would be worth over £15,000 now and a gratuity of £24 in 1918 would have a value in 2018 of £1,300. Private soldiers in the British forces during World War One were paid one shilling a day all found, which equates to £5.50 today.

World War One

"I held a Council at 10.45 to declare war with Germany. It is a terrible catastrophe but it is not our fault. An enormous crowd collected outside the Palace; we went on to the balcony both before and after dinner. When they heard that war had been declared, the excitement increased and May and I with David, went on to the balcony; the cheering was terrific. Please God it may soon be over and that he will protect dear Bertie's life.
Bed at 12.00"

George V,
Diary, 4 August 1914

Note. He is referring to his two sons; David is the Prince of Wales and Bertie is the future George VI, who was serving with the Royal Navy.

Thame

St Mary's churchyard in Thame is the only cemetery in the town and serves the people of all religions and none. In many local churchyards there are war graves that date from the days of the First World War. St Mary's churchyard in Thame is no different, in that there are five such graves with dates that cover the whole period of the war.

In addition, our Project discovered one Thame man, Charles Boiling, who is remembered on the War Memorial and who died in Thame as a result of his war injuries but had no grave marker in St Mary's churchyard. A local funeral director, on hearing of this problem, kindly arranged for a suitable stone to be erected to mark his resting place. Also recognised was Lord Bertie of Thame who had been British Ambassador in Paris throughout the war and who was buried in Thame, although his only Memorial is a Plaque on the wall of the church choir.

All the war graves were honoured with the delivery of a cross on Sunday 3rd August 2014 to mark the beginning of the Thame Remembers Project. Crosses were also placed on graves where a serviceman who had died in conflict was commemorated with an inscription on a relative's grave.

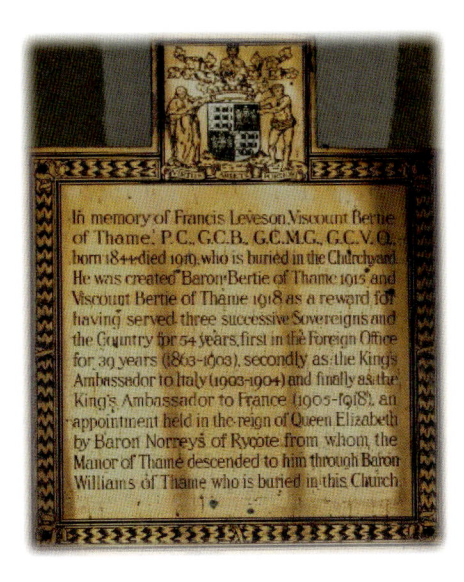

The Plaque for Lord Bertie in St Mary's Church

The new gravestone for Charles Boiling created by Surman and Horwood Funeral Directors

Those Remembered

28 January 1915

Henry Robert Higgins was born in early 1881 in Church Road, Thame to Robert Higgins and Anne (née Turner). His father Robert was injured in an accident and died in 1895. By 1901 the family had moved to 5 Southern Road, Thame. In 1911 Henry had left home and was working as a boiler man at Aylesbury Workhouse, Buckinghamshire. A year later, he married Elizabeth E Chappell in Aylesbury, but they do not appear to have had any children.

At the outbreak of war Henry was 32 years old and volunteered to serve with the Norfolk Regiment. He joined the 3rd Battalion which was a training and reserve battalion based at Felixstowe, Suffolk. Henry was taken ill and died at Felixstowe Cliff Military Hospital on 28th January 1915, age 34. He was buried in St Mary's churchyard on 1st February 1915. He is recorded as a Lance Corporal when he died but that may only have been a temporary promotion.

16651 Private Henry Robert Higgins, Norfolk Regiment, is remembered in Thame on the War Memorial and All Saints' Church Memorial Board.

The Thame Remembers Cross was placed at his grave on 3rd August 2014 by Councillor Ann Midwinter, Chair of South Oxfordshire District Council.

14 June 1915

Herbert Stevens was born in Thame in spring 1886, the second son of James Stevens and Caroline Louise (née Loosley). James was a butcher at 23 Upper High Street, Thame and Caroline was a schoolmistress.

By 1911 Herbert and his elder brother Fred were still living at home and were both butchers in the family business. The Thame Gazette reported that Herbert was a member of Thame Fire Brigade and played football for Thame for several seasons. He also played one or two seasons as a goalkeeper for Oxford City and occasionally for Reading.

Herbert had joined the Queen's Own Oxfordshire Hussars and went to France with them on 20th September 1914. On his return to England he was posted to the 2/1st Yeomanry, a reserve unit, which had moved to King's Lynn, Norfolk in April 1915. Herbert died at home of meningitis on 14th June 1915, age 29 years, and was buried in St Mary's churchyard on 18th June 1915.

1979 Trooper Herbert Stevens, Queen's Own Oxfordshire Hussars, is remembered in Thame on the War Memorial and on the Memorial Boards of St Mary's Church and All Saints' Church.

The Thame Remembers Cross was placed at his grave on 3rd August 2014 by Thame Town Councillor, Peter Lambert.

13 April 1916

William Honour was born in Moreton near Thame in late 1873 to William Honour and Sarah (née Dudley). In 1881 the family were living in a cottage by Lobbersdown Hill Farm, Moreton. William had left home by 1891 and was working in Thame as a grocer, but 10 years later he was boarding at a house in Bell Lane, Thame and described as a domestic groom. In 1911 he was working with his brother Joseph at a farm in Tetsworth, Oxfordshire again as a groom.

He married Emily Tyler at Great Haseley Church on 25th March 1913 and lived initially at a farm in Tetsworth. They had one son, Jim, who was born at Steeple Aston on 9th December 1913 and who died in 2004 without issue. William was a member of the local Wenman Lodge of Oddfellows. After William's death Emily moved to 55 High Street, Thame.

William, age 40, enlisted in the Army Service Corps at Chipping Norton, Oxfordshire on 21st October 1914 to serve in the Remount Depots where his skills as a groom would be fundamental. After only seven days training he was sent to France and served there from 28th October 1914 until he was kicked in the groin by a horse and invalided back to England on 17th February 1915.

After a period of Home Service he was admitted to the Red Cross Hospital in Thame in February 1916 and whilst there, being no longer fit for war service, was discharged from the army on 11th March 1916. He died at the hospital on 13th April, age 42, from an internal abscess and haemorrhage connected with his previous injuries. He was buried four days later in St Mary's churchyard. It was a large funeral involving many staff and wounded soldiers from the hospital plus twenty members of the Volunteer Training Corps in uniform, as well as many local dignitaries.

TS/3580 Private William Honour, Army Service Corps, is remembered in Thame on the War Memorial.

The Thame Remembers Cross was placed at his grave on 3rd August 2014 by Major Robert Bartlett of the Royal British Legion.

14 September 1916

Frederick Price was born in Thame in July 1886, the second of four sons born to George Price and Susan (née Newitt) living in Moorend Lane. Frederick at the age of 13, together with two of his brothers, was baptised at St Mary's Church on 26th February 1899. By 1901 the family had moved to 8 Church Road and at the age of 15 he was working alongside his brother as a farm labourer.

Frederick enlisted in London with the Royal Regiment of Artillery on 13th February 1911. He served as a driver with the 116th Battery, Royal Field Artillery (RFA) until February 1914 when he was transferred to the reserve list. A few months later, at the outbreak of the war, he was immediately remobilised and posted to the 29th Battery, 42nd Brigade, RFA, embarking with them to France on 18th August 1914. The Battery went on to see action at Mons and the Marne and, in 1915, at Bellewaarde and the Hooge. In September 1915, on returning to England, Frederick was posted to reserve brigades, before once again embarking for France in February 1916, this time with B Battery of the new 158th

(Accrington & Burnley) Brigade. The Brigade was known colloquially as "The Howitzers", although they had given up their howitzers the previous year and were then armed with quick-firing 18-pounder field guns. Fred was promoted to acting Bombardier (Corporal) on 26th February 1916. According to reports in the Accrington Gazette, *"the weather during the brigade's first few weeks in France was appalling, with much rain, snow and frost."* It was likely this, together with the stress of active service, caused a deterioration in Fred's health. On 15th June 1916 he was returned to England on medical grounds and was admitted to the 4th London General Hospital RAMC. He remained there until he was discharged as unfit for military service on 28th July 1916 with Potts Disease of the spine, a form of tuberculosis, which had led to paraplegia. He died on 14th September 1916, age 28, and was buried four days later in St Mary's churchyard.

64601 Bombardier Frederick Price, Royal Field Artillery, is remembered in Thame on the War Memorial and on All Saints' Church Memorial Board.

The Thame Remembers Cross was placed at his grave on 3rd August 2014 by John Howell, Member of Parliament for Thame.

23 February 1919

George Chowns was born in Thame in late 1878 when his parents, John Chowns and Mary (née Phillips) were living in North Street. He was baptised at St Mary's Church on 17th August 1882. The family moved to Moorend Lane, Thame in 1901 from where George was working as a driver for a butcher. George married Annie Phillips at Aylesbury Register Office, Buckinghamshire on 1st December 1906. By 1911 he was working as a carman and lived at 3 Church Row, Thame with his wife and three young sons, Fred 4, William 3 and Jack 10 months.

He was called up for service on 19th February 1917 when he was 38 years old, joining the 344th Road Construction Company, Royal Engineers as a Pioneer. He gave his home address as Ivydene Cottage, Aylesbury Road, Thame.

After training, he served in France from 12th May 1917 to 16th February 1919. During his demob leave, he contracted pneumonia and died at a Nursing Home in Thame on 23rd February 1919 age 41. He was buried in St Mary's churchyard on 27th February 1919.

He left a wife and six children living at 6 Hampden Avenue, Thame. The additional three children being; Kathleen born 1912, George born 1914 and Henry born 1916. His widow Annie was granted a pension of 42s 1d per week.

WR/26650 Pioneer George Chowns, Royal Engineers, is remembered in Thame on the War Memorial and on the Memorial Boards of St Mary's Church and All Saints' Church.

The Thame Remembers Cross was placed at his grave on 3rd August 2014 by Adam Buckland, former Mayor of Thame.

26 September 1919

Francis Leveson Bertie was born in London on 7th August 1844 to Montagu Bertie, 6th Earl of Abingdon and Elizabeth Lavinia Vernon-Harcourt and was educated at Eton College, Berkshire. He married Lady Feodorowna Cecilia Wellesley, daughter of Henry Richard Charles Wellesley, 1st Earl Cowley and the Honourable Olivia Cecilia FitzGerald-de Ros on 11th April 1874 at Draycott, Staffordshire. They had one son Vere Frederick Bertie, born 20th October 1878, who went on to become 2nd Viscount Bertie of Thame.

Francis was in the Foreign Office in 1863 and, between 1874 and 1880, held the office of Parliamentary Private Secretary to the Parliamentary Under-Secretary of State for Foreign Affairs. He was acting Assistant Clerk at the Foreign Office between 1880 and 1881, acting Senior Clerk at the Foreign Office between 1882 and 1885 and Senior Clerk at the Foreign Office between 1889 and 1894. He held the office of Assistant Under-Secretary of State for Foreign Affairs between 1894 and 1903. He was invested as a Knight Commander, Order of the Bath (KCB) in 1902 and as a Knight Grand Cross, Royal Victorian Order (GCVO) in 1903.

Bertie was invested as a Privy Councillor on 2nd March 1903 and was Ambassador to Italy between 1903 and 1905. He was invested as a Knight Grand Cross, Order of St Michael and St George in 1904 and was decorated with the Italian award of the Grand Cross, Order of Saints Maurice and Lazarus. He was British Ambassador to France between 1905 and 1918. He was invested as a Knight Grand Cross, Order of the Bath (GCB) in 1908 and was created 1st Baron Bertie of Thame on 28th June 1915. He was created 1st Viscount Bertie of Thame on 2nd September 1918.

Francis Leveson Bertie, 1st Viscount Bertie of Thame GCB, GCMG, GCVO, PC died in London on 26th September 1919, age 75. Four days later he was buried in St Mary's churchyard. His only memorial is a Plaque on the interior wall of the choir of St Mary's Church.

The Thame Remembers Cross was placed at his niece's grave on 3rd August 2014 by Councillor Anne Purse, Chairman of Oxfordshire County Council.

Lord Grey of Faldon wrote of Lord Bertie that:
> "his work and the position he made for himself as Ambassador in Paris were of the highest value to his country. Indeed his personality, in that very important and delicate post, had much to do with the maintenance of the entente between Britain and France during years that were very difficult and critical. He believed the entente with France not only to be practicable, but to be the policy which was best for his own country, for France, and for Europe generally."

24 December 1920

Charles Boiling was born in January 1896. He was the second of the eight children of Charles Boiling and Agnes (née Price) living at 11 Park Street, Thame and was baptised at St Mary's Church on 6th February 1896. In 1911, age 15, he was working as a farm labourer.

His service records survive, if a little singed round the edges. From them we learn that he joined the Oxford and Bucks Light Infantry on 14th December 1914 at Oxford. He served in England until 20th September 1915 when he was sent to France with the 7th Battalion and on 16th November 1915 the Battalion was sent to fight in Salonika. Records show that Charles (Charlie) was wounded in the right thigh and left leg on 18th August 1916 and medically evacuated back to England on 19th October 1916. At his Medical Discharge Board in December 1917, he wrote "*would like to learn a trade that did not entail walking*". He was finally discharged on 28th January 1918 and his Silver War Badge was issued on 31st January 1918. His character reference on discharge was excellent saying *"he was reliable, trustworthy and always willing and hardworking."* He returned to the family home, now at 5 Chinnor Road, Thame, where unfortunately his mother Agnes died at 46 years of age in November 1918. Charles, age 24, died in Oxford Infirmary on 24th December 1920 from tuberculosis (TB) and five days later was buried in St Mary's churchyard. The burial records do not give the location of his grave but we consider it reasonable to assume that he would have been buried with his mother.

16826 Private Charles Boiling, Oxford and Bucks Light Infantry, is remembered in Thame on the War Memorial and St Mary's Church Memorial Board. His grave is now marked with a modern stone similar to those used by the Commonwealth War Graves Commission.

The Thame Remembers Cross was placed at his gravestone on 3rd August 2014 by Rifleman Tom Bowen of The Rifles.

Britain

In Britain there are war graves in many church and civic cemeteries where uniformed casualties of the First World War are buried.

Most casualties who died were buried close to where they fell in battle, but many of the injured were evacuated back to hospitals in the British Isles. Those who then succumbed to their injuries were sometimes buried in a cemetery close to the hospital where they died, but more often their bodies were returned to their home town for burial.

Also, many soldiers were considered too old to serve overseas but yet had a valuable role to play on the Home Front where they may have died from accident or illness. Other men who are buried in Britain may have died during their training, either of illness or accident.

No matter how or where their death occurred all casualties would have been offered the familiar Commonwealth War Graves Commission gravestone, unless their relatives wished them to be buried in their family grave.

Those Remembered

15 June 1915

Algernon Evelyn Hemmings was born in Oxford on 12th August 1883 where his parents, James Hemmings and Fanny (née Stowe) lived in the St Ebbe's district. He was educated in Oxford, but was employed as a stoker at Gosport gas works in Hampshire when he married Ada Langridge in July 1907 at Alverstocke Church, Hampshire. By 1912 they had three children and were living in Gosport, where he joined the Dorsetshire Regiment as a territorial.

In 1914 Algernon was working at Thame gas works and living with his family at 5 Windmill Road. The youngest of their five children Gladys Blanch was born in Thame on 7th March 1914 and baptised at St Mary's Church on 16th December 1914. On 14th August 1914 Algernon went with the 1st Battalion as part of the British Expeditionary Force to France. In February 1915 he wrote. *"I might tell you that this campaign was very hard in the beginning, nothing else but shot and shell night and day but it is not quite so bad now. Our Battalion has been in some very tight places but thank God I have managed to pull through. We lost in one day 416 NCO's and men and 16 officers. This was some time ago…"*

He was wounded at the Battle for Hill 60, south east of Ypres, in April 1915 and evacuated to England where he died of his wounds at York hospital on 15th June 1915, age 31. By this time, his wife and five children had returned to live in Gosport and so it was there that he was buried a few days later.

7446 Private Algernon Evelyn Hemmings, Dorsetshire Regiment, is buried in Ann's Hill Cemetery, Gosport, Hampshire. He is remembered in Thame on the War Memorial and on the Memorial Boards of St Mary's Church and All Saints' Church.

The Thame Remembers Cross was placed at his grave on 15th December 2015 by Thame resident, Alex Pullen.

15 August 1915

George Alfred Edsell was born in Aberdovey, Wales on 18th January 1859 to James and Caroline Edsell, both teachers. He entered medical practice, receiving his training at St Bartholomew's Hospital and University College, London.

By 1887 he had moved to Thame and was in practice as a physician and surgeon with Herbert Grove Lee at 79 High Street. He married Annie Isabel Haines in Byfleet, Surrey on 14th July 1887 and they went on to have three daughters and three sons. All three sons were born in Thame and served in World War One and all survived. In 1889 he joined the Oxford and Bucks Light Infantry Territorials as a Surgeon Lieutenant, retiring in 1899 as a Surgeon Captain. He also served on Thame Urban District Council and was Chairman in 1897. He was an examiner and honorary life member of the St John Ambulance Association, surveyor to the medical department of the Admiralty and a member of the British Medical Association. He left Thame sometime after 1904, moving to Surbiton, Surrey where he became a local councillor and joined the 3rd Home Counties Field Ambulance RAMC as a Captain. He rose with promotion to Lieutenant Colonel and took command of the unit in 1911. When the Territorial Force was mobilised, and after a period of training, the 3rd Home Counties (83rd) Field Ambulance proceeded to France and then to Belgium, being deployed in the neighbourhood of Ypres. It was here that George contracted pleurisy. He was invalided home to Surbiton, where he died on 15th August 1915, age 56. His funeral took place on 18th August at Kingston upon Thames, Surrey where he was buried with full military honours.

Lieutenant Colonel George Alfred Edsell MD, Royal Army Medical Corps, is buried in Kingston upon Thames Cemetery, Kingston, Surrey. He is commemorated on Kingston upon Thames War Memorial and his name is to be added to Thame War Memorial.

The Thame Remembers Cross was placed at his grave on 25th February 2016 by Allan Hickman of Thame Remembers.

18 August 1915

Brian Perry was born in Enfield, Middlesex on 17th May 1897, the fourth son of Richard Henry and Rose Cross Perry and had six siblings. Richard, Brian's father, was a printer and advertising agent. The family moved to Berkhamsted, Hertfordshire sometime before 1911. Brian was educated at Berkhamsted School and then Lord Williams's Grammar School, Thame, where he won the School Championship Cup.

Brian followed his father into the printing business and, in 1911, was a printer's apprentice in Liscard, Birkenhead, Cheshire. He signed up after the outbreak of war and joined the Middlesex Regiment in September 1914. Records say he was a *"tall, well-developed young man,"* and he was soon accepted into the Inns of Court Officer Training Corps, arriving on 22nd October 1914. He received rapid promotion to Sergeant and *"showed promise of becoming a first class cavalry officer"*. The Inns of Court Officer Training

Corps was formed in London in August 1914 and moved to Berkhamsted on 26th September 1914, where they occupied tented accommodation in a field near the railway station until 1918. In June 1915 Brian contracted meningitis while away on a camp and became seriously ill. He died in the 3rd London General Hospital, Wandsworth, Surrey on 18th August 1915 at just 18 years old. Although he had not seen active service, he was given a full military funeral.

1937 Sergeant Brian Perry, Inns of Court Officer Training Corps, is buried in Rectory Lane Cemetery, Berkhamsted. He is remembered in Thame on Lord Williams's School Memorial Board.

The Thame Remembers Cross was placed at his grave on 21st October 2015 by Thame Mayor, Councillor Nichola Dixon.

18 March 1916

Albert Edward Outing was born in 1863 in Castle Hedingham, Essex. He lived in Cornard, Suffolk and went to the British School in Sudbury, Suffolk. On leaving school he became an apprentice blacksmith before enlisting with the 19th (Queen Alexandra's Own) Royal Hussars in December 1882. He was appointed Shoeing Smith in 1884 and by 1902 he had attained the rank of Farrier Quartermaster Sergeant.

He served in the Nile campaign in Egypt in 1884/5, being awarded the Egypt War Medal with Nile Clasp and the Khedives Star, then in the Boer War he earned the Queen's (South Africa) Medal and Clasps (including Defence of Ladysmith). In 1895 Albert married Bridget Bird (born in Dublin) at Trumulgherry, India, where the Regiment was based at the time.

He left the army in 1903 after service of 21 years, but went on to re-enlist at the start of World War One. He was not posted overseas with his Regiment, but was instead attached to the Army Veterinary Corps, serving at the base depot of the Household Cavalry. His wife had moved to Lashlake, Thame sometime after the start of the war. Albert died of pneumonia and cardiac failure in Fulham Military Hospital, London on 18th March 1916, age 52.

H/29395 Farrier Quartermaster Sergeant Albert Edward Outing, 19th Royal Hussars, is buried in Kensal Green Cemetery, Harrow Road, London. He is remembered in Thame on the War Memorial and on All Saints' Church Memorial Board.

The Thame Remembers Cross was placed at his grave on 14th July 2015 by Thame resident, Trudi Lambert.

7 June 1916

Charles Wood was born in Thame on 6th July 1876, the fifth child and third son of John Wood, a cordwainer, and Zilpah (née Moreton). They lived at 6 North Street and he was baptised at St Mary's Church on 29th December 1878. Charles enlisted in the Royal Marine Artillery (RMA) on 27th February 1896. In 1901 he was stationed as a gunner at the Headquarters of the RMA at Eastney near Portsmouth, Hampshire. He married Ellen Kate Wearne at Portsmouth on 29th August 1906. By 1911 he had been promoted to Corporal and was serving on HMS London (a pre-dreadnought battleship) in the Far East. At the start of the war he was serving on the battleship HMS Britannia until she ran aground in the Firth of Forth in January 1915. He was posted back to Portsmouth and spent time at HMS Victory, the Portsmouth Depot, before being posted in January 1916 to HMS Malaya, one of the new Queen Elizabeth-class battleships. During the Battle of Jutland on 31st May 1916 the ship was hit eight times sustaining major damage and heavy casualties. Charles was one of the 68 men wounded and was evacuated to hospital in Inverness, Scotland where he died of his wounds on 7th June 1916, age 39. His body was conveyed from Inverness to Eastney by rail and was accompanied to the station by an escort of naval and military men. The pipers of the Cameron Highlanders played a lament on the way.

RMA/6034 Sergeant Charles Wood, Royal Marine Artillery, is buried in the 'New Ground' of the Portsmouth (Highland Road) Cemetery, Hampshire. He is remembered in Thame on the War Memorial and on St Mary's Church Memorial Board.

The Thame Remembers Cross was placed at his grave on 15th December 2015 by Thame residents, Elizabeth Ramage and family.

18 February 1917

George Henry Sherwin was born on 10th September 1883 to Henry Hayles Sherwin and Emma (née Webb) of High Street, Waddesdon, Buckinghamshire and baptised in Aylesbury on 29th October. He had an elder sister, Agnes and three younger sisters, Eleanor, Kathleen and Nora. George attended Lord Williams's Grammar School in Thame, leaving in the late 1890s. When his father died in 1901, George, along with his mother and two of his sisters went to live in Leicester, (his mother's birthplace) where he was employed as a motor trade finisher. He married Evelyn G Webb in 1912 and set up home at 64 Queens Road, Leicester.

When the Military Service Act of 1916 extended conscription to include married men, George was called up, probably towards the end of 1916, and posted to the Royal Flying Corps. It is unlikely that George ever received a squadron posting as he died of pneumonia in Connaught Hospital, Aldershot, Hampshire on 18th February 1917, age 34.

56471 Air Mechanic 2nd Class George Henry Sherwin, Royal Flying Corps, is buried in Welford Road Cemetery, Leicester. He is remembered in Thame on Lord Williams's School Memorial Board and is also commemorated on Waddesdon War Memorial.

The Thame Remembers Cross was placed at his grave on 9th April 2017 by Thame residents, Ian and Jackie Welch.

17 February 1919

George Payne was born in North Street, Thame on 9th May 1866. His mother was Ann Payne, but no father was recorded on the birth certificate. He was baptised at St Mary's Church on 16th August 1888 when he was 22 years old.

George, who was a farm labourer, lived at Church Row, Thame with his mother and grandmother until 1888 when he married Rhoda Ann Brocklesby in Abingdon, Berkshire. Soon after their marriage they moved to Oxford where he worked as a coachsmith. They had two sons, Wilfred and Arthur and three daughters, Ellen, May and Phyllis.

George volunteered for service with the Royal Engineers and went to France on 10th August 1915 when he was age 49. Having survived the war he died, age 52, of influenza at Queen Alexandra's Military Hospital, Westminster on 17th February 1919.

97429 Sapper George Payne, Royal Engineers, is buried in Brookwood Military Cemetery, Woking, Surrey. His name is to be added to Thame War Memorial.

The Thame Remembers Cross was placed at his grave on 14th June 2015 by Thame resident, Margaret Bretherton.

9 October 1924

Donald Patrick Shaw was born on 29th March 1888 at Melcombe Regis, Dorset. He was the eldest son of Dr A E Shaw, headmaster of Lord Williams's Grammar School, Thame from 1899 to 1920. Donald was educated there from 1899 to 1907, being Head Boy for his last two years. He then went to Balliol College, Oxford, where he gained an Honours Degree in history. He taught at Weymouth College, Dorset and Westminster School, London before enlisting in 1914 in the Dorsetshire Regiment.

Donald was seriously wounded in the neck in 1915 while serving in France and nearly drowned when the hospital ship Anglia hit a mine in the Channel off Dover, Kent. He returned to France, promoted to Major and was awarded the DSO for gallantry following a raid by the Battalion near Beaumont Hamel in June 1918.

During 1918/19 he commanded the 6th Battalion of the Dorsetshire Regiment as Lieutenant Colonel and also led the Battalion in the Victory Parade in London. In 1919 he married Maud Vivian Stevens in Oxford and returned to Westminster School where he became a housemaster. He also took charge of the school's Officer Training Corps. He died of his war wounds at the Empire Nursing Home in Westminster on 9th October 1924. His funeral was held on 14th October 1924 and his coffin was borne on a six-horse gun carriage to Westminster Abbey and to his grave where the Last Post was sounded by soldiers of the Grenadier Guards.

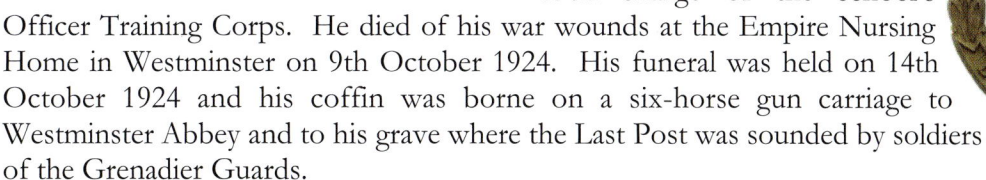

Lieutenant Colonel Donald Patrick Shaw DSO, Dorsetshire Regiment, is buried in West Norwood Cemetery, London. He is remembered in Thame on the War Memorial and on the Memorial Boards of St Mary's Church and Lord Williams's School.

The Thame Remembers Cross was placed at his grave on 23rd March 2015 by Thame resident, Derek Turner.

Recommendation for a medal by: Lieutenant Colonel E S Weldon, Commanding 6th Battalion, Dorsetshire Regiment

On the occasion of a Raid made by his battalion near Beaumont Hamel on June 8th 1918 this officer rendered me valuable assistance as second in command and I owe much to his loyal co-operation and energy. His keenness and enthusiasm inspired the men tremendously, both during training, at the Assembly, and afterwards, when he organised the collection of the wounded. When the enemy barrage prevented the wounded from being taken down to the Regimental Aid Post, he at once started to dress their wounds himself, and saw to the adjustment of their Box Respirators continuing his work under gas. He did valuable work in organising search parties and was untiring in his efforts to see that no part of the ground was overlooked. Both in the initial preparations and in the final assault he was of the greatest assistance to me and devoted his whole energy to minor tasks with the same enthusiasm with which he helped me in the greatest. He is in possession of no decoration either British or Foreign.

The Distinguished Service Order was awarded on 29th September 1918

In Flanders Fields

In Flanders fields the poppies blow
Between the crosses, row on row,
That mark our place; and in the sky
The larks, still bravely singing, fly
Scarce heard amid the guns below.

We are the Dead. Short days ago
We lived, felt dawn, saw sunset glow,
Loved and were loved, and now we lie
In Flanders fields.

Take up our quarrel with the foe:
To you from failing hands we throw
The torch; be yours to hold it high.
If ye break faith with us who die
We shall not sleep, though poppies grow
In Flanders fields.

Major John McCrae
(1872-1918)

We Shall Keep the Faith

Oh! you who sleep in Flanders Fields,
Sleep sweet - to rise anew!
We caught the torch you threw
And holding high, we keep the Faith
With All who died.

We cherish, too, the poppy red
That grows on fields where valour led;
It seems to signal to the skies
That blood of heroes never dies,
But lends a lustre to the red
Of the flower that blooms above the dead
In Flanders Fields.

And now the Torch and Poppy Red
We wear in honour of our dead.
Fear not that ye have died for naught;
We'll teach the lesson that ye wrought
In Flanders Fields.

Moina Michael
"The Poppy Lady"
(1869-1944)

Belgium

When World War One began, the German Schliffen plan required the invasion of neutral Belgium in an attempt to outflank the French armies, quickly capture Paris and knock France out of the conflict. On 2nd August 1914, the German government demanded that their armies be given free passage through Belgian territory. This was refused by the Belgian government and on 4th August German troops attacked. It was this action that technically caused the British to enter the war, as they were still bound by an Agreement to protect Belgium in the event of hostilities. In response to the German attack the British Expeditionary Force (BEF) was dispatched to Belgium's aid.

The BEF's first engaged the German Army in the Battle of Mons on 23rd August 1914. The massed rifle fire of the professional British soldiers inflicted heavy casualties on the Germans who attacked *en masse* over terrain devoid of cover. The British held up the German advance until the evening, when they began retiring to a second defensive line. In the retreat from Mons they were engaged by the Germans at the Battle of Le Cateau and although they, once more, inflicted heavy casualties they were overwhelmed and forced to pull back. The BEF continued their retreat covering some 200 miles in the next two weeks. It was a testament to their high level of training, fitness and morale that this retreat did not turn into a rout.

The Allies finally stopped the Germans at the River Marne where a stand was made to defend Paris. This led to the First Battle of the Marne, which was fought from 5th to 10th September 1914. This battle would prove to be a major turning point of the war as it denied the Germans an early victory.

From 13th September the First Battle of the Aisne took place, with the combatants starting to dig shallow trenches. Then, for a three-week period suicidal frontal assaults to break the deadlock saw horrendous casualties on both sides. As these failed, attempts were made to turn the other's flank, this period became known as the Race to the Sea.

The First Battle of Flanders followed, in which German, French and Belgian armies and the BEF fought from Arras in France to Nieuport on the Belgian coast. This took place from October to mid-November 1914. It included what became known as the First Battle of Ypres.

The Menin Gate Memorial to the Missing, is dedicated to 54,395 British and Commonwealth soldiers who were killed in the Ypres Salient during World War I and whose graves are unknown

By the end of the battle both sides had started to dig in and trench warfare replaced the manoeuvre warfare that had featured during the Race to the Sea. The continuous trench lines of the Western Front now stretched 400 miles from the North Sea to the Alps. The BEF initially held a small 20 mile portion of this line. However this area expanded steadily as the war progressed until by 1918 the British Armies held 100 miles of front from Ypres in the north to the River Somme in the south.

After the First Battle of Ypres static trench warfare became the norm. By early 1915, both sides had expended men, materiel and munitions at an unsustainable rate. They therefore began the process of re-arming and expanding their forces so that they could continue the fight. On the front line, deep trenches overwhelmingly favoured the defence, with their dugouts and strong points protected by belts of barbed wire, machine guns and artillery.

The Second Battle of Ypres was fought from 22nd April to 25th May 1915. The German intention was to seize this strategically important town after their failure the previous autumn to break the deadlock. It included the first use of poison gas on the Western Front. The release of chlorine from cylinders hidden in the German trenches surprised the Allies causing panic, mass casualties and leaving great gaps in the line. Urine soaked pads offered some protection and with great fortitude the German advance was stemmed. Both sides subsequently developed gas weapons and counter-measures, which changed the nature of warfare. By the end of the battle, the Ypres Salient was compressed and the town itself lay in ruins destroyed by artillery fire.

The front line around Ypres changed relatively little after the end of the Second Battle. The British held the town, while the Germans held the high ground of the Messines–Wytschaete ridge to the south, the lower ridges to the east and the flat ground to the north. The Ypres front was a salient bulging into German positions and was overlooked by their artillery on the higher ground. The result was a steady, but relentless attrition of the British forces defending the town.

Strategically, the British had always wanted to break out from Ypres and recapture Belgium to secure the northern Channel ports to deny their use to German U-boats. In 1916 the German assault at Verdun forced the British and French to attack on the Somme and it was not until mid-1917 that they were ready to initiate the Third Battle of Ypres also known as the Battle of Passchendaele. As a prelude to it, the British 2nd Army conducted an offensive to take the Messines Ridge. The tactical objective of the attack at Messines was to capture the German defences on the ridge which ran from Ploegsteert (Plugstreet) Wood in the south, through Messines and Wytschaete to Mont Sorrel in the north; the aim being to deprive the German 4th Army of the high ground south of Ypres. The ridge commanded a strategic position overlooking the British defences and logistic areas further north. It was from here that the BEF intended to conduct the attack on Passchendaele Ridge, before advancing up the Belgian coast to the Dutch frontier. The Messines Battle demonstrated that the British Army had embraced the lessons of the war so far. It began with the detonation of a series

Tyne Cot Cemetery with Ypres in the background. It is now the biggest Commonwealth War Graves Commission Cemetery containing the graves of 11,961 servicemen from the First World War

of mines beneath German trenches, which created 19 large craters and devastated much of the Front Line. It was followed by a co-ordinated combined arms assault. A massive creeping barrage covered the British troops as they secured the ridge, with support from tanks, cavalry patrols and aircraft. The effectiveness of the British bombardments was improved by centralised control of artillery and advances in survey, flash-spotting and sound ranging.

At the end of the Battle of Messines the much larger Third Battle of Ypres began on 11th July 1917 and lasted until November. The aim was to take control of the ridges south and east of Ypres in West Flanders. Passchendaele lay on the last ridge east of Ypres, 5 miles from a railway junction at Roulers, which was vital to the supply system of the German 4th Army. The next stage of the Allied plan was an advance to Thourout–Couckelaere, to close the German-controlled railway running through Roulers and Thourout. The stiff resistance of the German 4th Army, the unusually wet autumn and the early onset of winter, which had turned the battlefield into a quagmire, enabled the Germans to avoid a general withdrawal, which had seemed inevitable in early October. The campaign ended in November when, in the most atrocious conditions, the Canadian Corps captured Passchendaele.

The German spring offensive in 1918 included a major attack, through Flanders, with once again, the objective being the capture of Ypres and subsequently forcing the British back to the Channel ports. The Operation, known as *Georgette*, beginning on 9th April was to complement the larger *Operation Michael* on the Somme further south. Although the British were forced to retire they took a terrible toll on the advancing Germans and by the end of April, with their troops exhausted, the offensive was called off. The last Battle at Ypres in September forced the Germans to give up ground before their final capitulation in November 1918.

Ypres and the surrounding area is strewn with memorials and Commonwealth War Graves Commission Cemeteries. The most imposing, the Menin Gate Memorial to the Missing, is dedicated to over 54,000 British and Commonwealth soldiers whose graves are unknown and who were killed prior to 15th August 1917 in the Ypres Salient. After that date a further 34,997 names are recorded at the Tyne Cot Memorial in Tyne Cot Cemetery two kilometres from Ypres on the Passchendaele Ridge.

Tyne Cot Cemetery. *The Cross of Sacrifice that marks many Commonwealth War Graves Commission Cemeteries was built on top of a German pillbox in the centre of the cemetery, purportedly at the suggestion of King George V, who visited the cemetery in 1922 as it neared completion*

Those Remembered

8 May 1915

Henry Anthony Birrell-Anthony was the only child of Henry Anthony Birrell-Anthony and Mary Annette (née Reynolds). He was born in Maindy, Cardiff on 16th June 1887. In 1895 he went to Llandaff Cathedral School and was vice-captain of the cricket XI in 1899. He was also selected for the football XI and described as *"A promising full-back he kicks neatly and low with either foot, but is rather apt to leave his place"*. Henry moved to Stancliffe Hall Preparatory School, Derbyshire in 1899, when the headmaster of the Cathedral School, Ernest Owen opened a new school there. All of the Llandaff pupils, except for two, transferred with him.

Going on to Repton School also in Derbyshire in 1902, he represented Latham House at hockey and was selected for the cricket XI in 1904, becoming Captain in 1906. According to Wisden, his best season was his last, when he had a batting average of 13.61 and took nineteen wickets for 24.21 runs each. He was also good at long jump, taking the school record in 1906 with a jump of 21 feet and half an inch, the record having previously been set by C B Fry, a future world long jump record holder and England cricketer. After matriculating at the school in 1906 he went on to University College, Oxford and whilst there played cricket for the Freshmen's in 1907 and represented the University in Athletics, before going on to gain a BA in Jurisprudence in 1909.

Following his family's move to Thame to live at Glenthorne, High Street (his father being a solicitor) Henry took up a post as an articled clerk at the law firm of B L Reynolds in High Wycombe, Buckinghamshire. When war broke out in 1914, he enlisted with the Monmouthshire Regiment, being commissioned as a 2nd Lieutenant with the 1st Battalion on 9th September 1914.

The Battalion embarked for France on 13th February 1915, landing in Le Havre the following day and were immediately deployed to the Ypres Salient with the 84th Brigade. On 8th May 1915 Henry was killed when the Battalion suffered horrendous casualties during the valiant defence at Frezenberg Ridge, part of the Second Battle of Ypres. He was 27 years old. In the Battalion war diary the day after the battle, a total of 20 officers and 434 other ranks were listed as killed, wounded or missing. His father, who as a reservist commanded the second line 2/1 (Reserve) Battalion of the Monmouths throughout the war, erected a Memorial near St Julien to his son and all other officers and men of the 1st Monmouths who fell in the battle on that day.

Second Lieutenant Henry Anthony Birrell-Anthony, Monmouthshire Regiment, has no known grave and is commemorated on The Menin Gate Memorial, Ypres. He is remembered in Thame on the War Memorial and on the Memorial Boards of St Mary's Church and All Saints' Church.

The Thame Remembers Cross was placed at The Menin Gate Memorial on 31st October 2015 by Thame Museum Chairman, David Dodds and Jenny Dodds.

28 May 1915

William Edward Roberts was baptised in Thame on 16th April 1885, the son of William and Catherine Roberts. His father was a draper at 99-100 High Street and after his education at Lord Williams's Grammar School, William went into the family business.

In 1909 he joined the Henley Squadron of the Queen's Own Oxfordshire Hussars (QOOH), the local Oxfordshire Yeomanry, which at the time was commanded by Winston Churchill. In August 1914 the Regiment was one of the first territorial units to be mobilised, landing at Dunkirk on 20th September 1914. It also became one of the first territorial regiments to engage with the enemy on 31st October 1914 during the Battle of Messines, south of Ypres. William was Troop Sergeant serving in C (Henley) Squadron of the QOOH when he was killed on 28th May 1915 at Zouave Wood, near the Hooge, Ypres. He was 30 years old. According to letters from his colleagues and commanding officers he had been *"hit in the head by a sniper's bullet and died on the way to the casualty clearing station"*. He was buried at the nearby L'Ecole De Bienfalsance

British Cemetery before being reinterred in 1924. After his death his parents received a letter from his squadron commander Major Val Fleming MP (father of James Bond writer, Ian Fleming) and the following is an extract; "... *every one of us looked upon Sergt. Roberts not only as an excellent soldier, cool and plucky, hard working and reliable, - but as a friend. No-one who knew him could help liking him, no-one who had served with him could help respecting and admiring him; he was always so cheerful, so ready to turn his hand to anything, and in his new position as troop sergeant he was showing every day his sense of responsibility and his fitness to command. He died as you would have him die - painlessly, almost instantaneously, while doing his duty bravely, and as resolutely as he always did, ...*"

1498 Sergeant William Edward Roberts, QOOH, is buried in Bedford House Cemetery, Ypres. He is remembered in Thame on the War Memorial and on the Memorial Boards of Lord Williams's School, St Mary's Church and All Saints' Church.

The Thame Remembers Cross was placed at his grave on 21st May 2016 by Michael Hutson of Thame Remembers.

9 July 1915

Harry Price was the son of Susan Price living in Church Row, Thame. He was born in early 1875 and baptised at St Mary's Church on 30th May that year, together with his elder sister Lizzie. In 1877 his mother married Henry Phillips and both Lizzie and Harry assumed the surname Phillips. Henry and Susan went on to have a further five children.

In September 1893, reverting back to his birth name, Harry Price enlisted with the 3rd Battalion of the Oxfordshire Light Infantry as a militiaman. Then in February 1896 he transferred under a short service attestation to the Royal Engineers and served with them as a driver in the Boer War in South Africa from October 1899, returning to England in April 1900. He was awarded the Queen's (South Africa) Medal with Cape Colony Clasp, together with a war gratuity payment of £5. In 1901 he was based at Aldershot, Hampshire before being placed on the army reserve list in May 1902, on which he remained until 1912.

Harry Phillips married Margaret Annie Ward from Islip on 22nd February 1902 and they went on to have three sons and one daughter. In 1911 he was a general labourer living in Windmill Road, Thame with his wife and children. He served two short custodial jail sentences in 1912/13 and his wife was subsequently granted a separation order from him due to his non-payment of maintenance and violent behaviour.

At the start of the First World War, as a National Reservist, he enlisted in the Oxford and Bucks Light Infantry (Regt No 8935) but then transferred to the Hampshire Regiment. On 2nd June 1915 he arrived in France and entrained to Belgium as part of a reinforcing draft to the 1st Battalion which had incurred heavy casualties in the Second Battle of Ypres the previous month. On 6th July the Battalion was committed to an attack near Hulls Farm, west of the Yser Canal. Over the next few days, attacks being followed by German counter-attacks and heavy shelling, the Battalion once again suffered heavily and on 9th July Harry, age 40, was one of 13 men from the Battalion lost that day. Initially he was listed as missing and it was not until a year later in July 1916 that the authorities notified his family of his presumed death.

16303 Private Harry Price, Hampshire Regiment, has no known grave and is commemorated on The Menin Gate Memorial, Ypres. He is remembered in Thame on the War Memorial and on All Saints' Church Memorial Board.

The Thame Remembers Cross was placed at The Menin Gate Memorial on 31st October 2015 by Thame Museum Chairman, David Dodds and Jenny Dodds.

25 September 1915

The 42nd Infantry Brigade, including the 5th Battalion of the Oxford and Bucks Light Infantry, was ordered to attack Bellewaarde Farm east of Ypres at 04:20hrs on 25th September 1915, as a subsidiary attack in connection with the Battle of Loos. It was a disastrous day for the 5th Battalion, losing 13 out of 15 officers and 463 out of 767 men, killed, wounded or missing. Three men from Thame were to die that day, in the same action. By 18:00hrs the German front line had been gained and the attacking battalions withdrawn to be consolidated by fresh troops. The nine battalions of the 3rd Division lost more than 3,800 officers and men in an area no greater than a thousand yards square.

25 September 1915

Henry John Cozier was born in Thame in September 1879 and baptised at St Mary's Church on 2nd October. He was the fourth child of seven born to Richard and Phyllis Cozier living in North Street. He married Florence Wharton in Thame on 23rd May 1904 and went to live at 20 Wellington Street, from where, in 1911, he was working as a general labourer. They had five children but one of them, Elizabeth, died in infancy.

Henry would have had some military experience, most likely with the local Territorial Force or Special Reserve, before volunteering for enrolment on the National Reserve in Thame. His Reserve classification in the event of mobilisation was Class I which was for service with a combat unit at home or abroad.

When war broke out, he went with several other reservists from Thame to join the county's regiment, the Oxford and Bucks Light Infantry, 3rd (Reserve) Battalion and would have spent the next few months in Portsmouth involved with the training of new recruits before their posting to service battalions.

Eventually, in July 1915, Henry was posted to the Western Front as part of a reinforcing draft for the 5th (Service) Battalion. During the Battle of Bellewaarde Farm Henry, age 36, was posted missing, but it was not until the following year that his death was confirmed.

8867 Private Henry John Cozier, Oxford and Bucks Light Infantry, has no known grave and is commemorated on The Menin Gate Memorial, Ypres. He is remembered in Thame on the War Memorial and on the Memorial Boards of St Mary's Church, All Saints' Church and Christchurch.

The Thame Remembers Cross was placed at The Menin Gate Memorial on 31st October 2015 by Thame Museum Chairman, David Dodds and Jenny Dodds.

25 September 1915

Sidney Thomas Tappin was born in Watlington, Oxfordshire in 1890 where his father was a miller. He was one of five children born to John Tappin and Ann (née Keeley). His mother died in 1899 and Sidney, along with his younger brother, Roland, was living with his grandmother at College Farm in Cuxham in 1901.

By 1911 he was living at 22 High Street, Thame and working as a grocer's assistant for Messer & Co, with whom he was employed for over five years. He was a member of Thame Town Band and also played for the Thursday Football Club.

Sidney enlisted in the Oxford and Bucks Light Infantry in early September 1914 and was posted to serve with the 5th Battalion, which had been formed in Oxford in August as part of the new Kitchener's Army.

After several months of training, the Battalion landed in France on 20th May 1915 and immediately proceeded to the Front in Belgium. The Battalion was deployed in trenches south of Ypres and was involved in the Battle of the Hooge at the end of July, which saw the first flamethrower attack by the Germans. Sidney, age 25, was one of those lost in the Battle of Bellewaarde Farm and his body was never recovered or identified.

10648 Private Sidney Thomas Tappin, Oxford & Bucks Light Infantry, has no known grave and is commemorated on The Menin Gate Memorial, Ypres. He is remembered in Thame on the War Memorial and All Saints' Church Memorial Board.

The Thame Remembers Cross was placed at The Menin Gate Memorial on 31st October 2015 by Thame Museum Chairman, David Dodds and Jenny Dodds.

25 September 1915

Reginald Isaac Cross was the middle child of three of Thomas Cross and Zilpha Lewis (née Mott). He was born in Moreton, near Thame in early 1893, where his father was a cattleman on a local farm. His mother died in 1900 at Queen Charlotte's Maternity Hospital in Marylebone, London. Reginald and his sisters were bought up by their father in Vine Cottage, Moreton, from where by 1911 Reginald was working as a shop assistant.

He enlisted at Stow-on-the-Wold, Gloucestershire, with the Oxford and Bucks Light Infantry, his regimental number indicating this would most likely have been some time in 1914. At that time, he was living at Northend, Turville, near Henley-on-Thames, Oxfordshire where his father had remarried in 1915.

On 20th May 1915 Reginald, by now a Lance Corporal, embarked for France with the 5th (Service) Battalion and over the next few months would have spent a considerable amount of time in the trenches around the Ypres Salient, including seeing action at the Hooge at the end of July.

On 25th September Reginald, age 22, became one of the three men from Thame who lost their lives that day during the Battalion's part in the attack at Bellewaarde Farm.

16617 Lance Corporal Reginald Isaac Cross, Oxford and Bucks Light Infantry, has no known grave and is commemorated on The Menin Gate Memorial, Ypres. He is remembered in Thame on both Thame and Moreton War Memorials and on St Mary's Church Memorial Board.

The Thame Remembers Cross was placed at The Menin Gate Memorial on 31st October 2015 by Thame Museum Chairman, David Dodds and Jenny Dodds.

30 November 1915

Ernest Edward House was born on 21st July 1890 at Oakley, near Chinnor, Oxfordshire. He was one of the eight children of Henry House and Eleanor (née Croxford). By 1901 the family had moved to Thame, where his father continued his trade as a blacksmith. They lived in Chinnor Road and Ernest attended the Royal British School in Park Street. In 1911 he was working as a porter at Thame Workhouse. On 16th May 1912 Ernest resigned from his job at the Workhouse and he sailed on RMS Virginian to Montreal, Canada eight days later.

He was working as a decorator when war broke out and enlisted with the 17th Battalion (Nova Scotia Highlanders) of the Canadian Expeditionary Force (CEF).

On 28th September 1914 he signed his attestation papers at Camp Valcartier in Quebec, the main assembly and training base for the CEF prior to departure. Within a few days, the first contingent of the CEF left Quebec in 30 ships. The 17th Battalion sailed on the SS Ruthenia and landed at Plymouth on 14th October. The Battalion proceeded to encamp on Salisbury Plain and in January 1915 was redesignated as a Training/Reserve Battalion. Ernest, now with the rank of Corporal, was posted to the 14th Battalion (Royal Montreal Regiment), as part of a reinforcing draft in February 1915.

The 14th Battalion landed at St Nazaire, France on 15th February and over the next few months was deployed in the trenches of Belgium and northern France as part of the 3rd Infantry Brigade, 1st Canadian Division. The Battalion was in action in the Battle of St Julien, during the Second Battle of Ypres, and the Battle of Festubert, part of the Second Battle of Artois. In November 1915 Ernest was with the Battalion in trenches near Messines, Belgium. According to a letter written to his family by Sergeant W C Blackett, Ernest, age 25, was killed on 30th November when a German shell struck the dugout in which he was sleeping, causing it to collapse and killing him instantly. Sergeant Blackett went on to say *"Cpl House was undoubtedly one of the best soldiers that we had. Always cheerful and willing to do his share under any circumstances."*

47311 Corporal Ernest Edward House, Canadian Infantry, is buried at La Plus Douve Farm Cemetery, Hainaut. He is remembered in Thame on the War Memorial and on the Memorial Boards of St Mary's Church, All Saints' Church and Christchurch.

The Thame Remembers Cross was placed at his grave on 24th May 2015 by Thame residents, Nigel and Alison Champken-Woods.

25 January 1916

William Arthur Wallington was born in Lewknor, Oxfordshire in 1886 and baptised there on 19th September. He was the eldest of Arthur and Ruth Wallington's nine children. By 1901 the family had moved to Kingston Blount where William, like his father, was an agricultural labourer. On 11th May 1907 William married 17 year old Polly Mentor and went to live in North Street, Thame. They had four children all born and baptised in Thame. William Alfred in December 1907, Doris Freda Amelia in August 1909, Sidney John in December 1912 and Polly Elizabeth in August 1915.

In early 1915 William enlisted with the Oxford and Bucks Light Infantry as one of 'Kitchener's Volunteer Army' and was posted to one of the training battalions before joining the 5th Battalion on the Western Front in October 1915 as part of a reinforcing draft.

The Battalion was part of the 42nd Brigade, 14th Division and was deployed in trenches in the Ypres Salient. In January 1916 the Front around Ypres was generally quiet, but soldiers made sporadic raids on enemy trenches to keep them battle ready. William, age 29, was killed in action on 25th January 1916. He was the fourth man from Thame to lose his life with the 5th Battalion. His widow, with four children under nine years old, received £2 18s 11d in pay owed in March 1916 and a further £3 war gratuity in 1919.

18428 Private William Arthur Wallington, Oxford and Bucks Light Infantry, is buried at Talana Farm Cemetery, north of Ypres. He is remembered in Thame on the War Memorial and on the Memorial Boards of St Mary's Church and All Saints' Church.

The Thame Remembers Cross was placed at his grave on 20th May 2015 by Thame residents, Andrew and Joan Reid.

12 February 1916

Edward William James was born in Thame and baptised at St Mary's Church on 25th August 1895. He was one of the seven children of William James and Jane Elizabeth (née Hunt) living at 63 Lower High Street. By the age of 15, Edward was a gardener to a local florist.

Edward enlisted into the Oxford and Bucks Light Infantry early in the war. In September 1915 he embarked for France, part of a reinforcing draft to the 6th Battalion. Over the next few months the Battalion, part of the 60th Brigade, 20th Division, was regularly deployed in the trenches of northern France, before marching to Belgium in early February 1916. Although the Battalion during this time was not engaged in any major actions, nevertheless the number of casualties suffered continued to grow due to regular exposure in the front line trenches.

In the early hours of the morning of 12th February 1916, Edward, age 20, was one of three men from the Battalion killed when they came under shellfire whilst returning over open space from the trenches back to billets at Elverdinghe Chateau. The following is an extract from a letter received by his mother from his platoon commander Lieutenant Fagan "... *your son was killed this morning at about 2 o'clock by a shell. We had to cross an open space in coming back from the trenches when they suddenly opened fire upon us. He was not two yards away from me when he was hit and died instantaneously and without pain from a wound in the head. I am very sorry personally to lose him as he was a good soldier and always did his duty faithfully and ungrudgingly in the platoon.*"

17525 Private Edward William James, Oxford and Bucks Light Infantry is buried in Ferme-Olivier Cemetery, near Ypres. He is remembered in Thame on the War Memorial and on All Saints' Church Memorial Board.

The Thame Remembers Cross was placed at his grave on 20th May 2017 by former Thame resident, Gill Gillard.

4 April 1916

Albert Henry Green was born in Highgate, London on 20th March 1893. His father was Albert Lorenzo Green who worked in the building trade and his mother was Kate Tilley (née Beecher). He had a sister Winifred and a brother Robert. The family moved to Thame in the 1890s where Albert Lorenzo joined his father's ironmongery business at 3 High Street. Albert Henry's mother died in 1898 and his father went on to marry Florence Richmond of Thame the following year.

Albert Henry emigrated to Canada, sailing on The Virginian on 24th May 1912 and then finding employment as a packer. He also joined the local militia, the 15th Argyll Light Infantry. When Canada entered the war in August 1914, the Canadian Expeditionary Force was raised from the local militia regiments and Albert duly enlisted at Camp Valcartier, Quebec on 22nd September 1914 with the 1st Brigade, Canadian Field Artillery and was posted to the 2nd Field Battery. His attestation papers say that he *"stood at 5ft 7ins tall, of medium build, with fair hair"*. The Brigade's second-in-command was Major John McCrae who went on to write probably the most famous war poem "In Flanders Field".

On 3rd October 1914, the Brigade embarked for England on the SS Saxonia and on arrival set up camp near Amesbury, Wiltshire. In February 1915 they left England and disembarked at St Nazaire on 17th February immediately entraining to northern France. The Brigade faced its first real test in the defence of St Julien during the Second Battle of Ypres in April/May 1915. Other actions followed at Festubert and Givenchy, after which the Brigade moved to Ploegsteert where it remained for a long period of static warfare in the autumn/winter of 1915/16. On 4th April 1916, a section of the 2nd Battery was once again in action near Ypres and Albert, age 23, was one of three men killed.

40413 Driver Albert Henry Green, Canadian Artillery, is buried in Reningelst New Cemetery, south west of Ypres. He is remembered in Thame on the War Memorial and on All Saints' Church Memorial Board.

The Thame Remembers Cross was placed at his grave on 10th October 1917 by Mark Willis, a member of Thame Runners.

2 June 1916

Thomas Bates was born in 1888 and baptised at St Mary's Church Thame on 17th March 1889. He was the son of George Thomas Bates and his wife Jane. After his mother died in 1890, his father married Elizabeth Crowdy. Thomas continued to live with his father and stepmother, together with his four brothers and sisters and two step-siblings, in Bridge Terrace, Thame. By 1911, at the age of 23, he had moved to Waddesdon, Buckinghamshire to live with his sister Maud and her husband and was working as a farm labourer.

In January 1916 he enlisted with the 43rd Canadian Reserve Battalion (Cameron Highlanders of Canada) at Shorncliffe, Kent which was a major base for the Canadian Expeditionary Force. His enlistment papers record his birthplace as Inverness, Scotland, possibly to get around the Battalion's link with a Scottish regiment. After only five weeks training at East Sandling Camp, Kent he embarked to France in February 1916. At the end of May, following a short spell in a field hospital with myalgia, he was attached to the 177th Tunnelling Company, Royal Engineers who were based at Mount Sorrel, three kilometres east of Ypres. Two days later, on 2nd June, the Germans launched their attack against the Canadian 3rd Division at Mount Sorrel. Thomas, age 27, was posted missing on the first day of the Battle, but it was not until February 1917 that he was finally presumed dead, at which time his soldier's pay of $20 Canadian per month was stopped.

421123 Private Thomas Bates, Canadian Infantry, has no known grave and is commemorated on The Menin Gate Memorial, Ypres. He is remembered in Thame on the War Memorial and on the Memorial Boards of St Mary's Church and All Saints' Church.

The Thame Remembers Cross was placed at The Menin Gate Memorial on 31st October 2015 by Thame Museum Chairman, David Dodds and Jenny Dodds.

4 June 1916

James Hobbs was born at States Farm, Medmenham, Buckinghamshire on 19th September 1886. He was one of the four children of James Hobbs and Edith Ellen (née New). His father was a farmer and cattle dealer.

He attended Lord Williams's Grammar School in Thame as a boarder, where he was known as "Jimmie" Hobbs. He later served four years in the Imperial Yeomanry. In September 1911 he emigrated to Canada, sailing from Bristol on RMS Royal Edward arriving in Quebec on 14th September. He then travelled over 1,700 miles to settle in Regina, Saskatchewan, where he became a fireman.

On 30th July 1915 he enlisted at Regina as a Private in the 3rd University Company, one of the reinforcing companies being raised in Canada for the Princess Patricia's Canadian Light Infantry (PPCLI). The following day, 31st July, he married Ada Caulderwood living at 1232 Cameron Street, Regina.

James embarked on the SS Missanabie to England in early September 1915 and on 1st December was taken onto the strength of the PPCLI, joining the Regiment in the field on 21st January 1916 when it was in trenches at Kemmel, south west of Ypres. The Battalion was part of the 7th Brigade with the 3rd Canadian Division that remained in the Ypres Salient throughout the winter and spring of 1916.

When the Germans launched their attack at Mount Sorrel on 2nd June 1916 the Regiment was in trenches at Sanctuary Wood. They suffered heavy casualties and lost parts of their Front Line from shelling and the infantry attacks that followed. James, age 29, was one of the casualties, being posted as missing sometime between 2nd and 4th June. It was not until a year later in May 1917 that he was presumed to have died, allowing his accrued pay and war gratuity to be released to his wife Ada, who subsequently went on to remarry after the war.

475881 Private James Hobbs, Canadian Infantry, has no known grave and is commemorated on The Menin Gate Memorial, Ypres. He is remembered in Thame on Lord Williams's School Memorial Board. He is also commemorated in Canada on Regina War Memorial and the Honour Roll at St Peter's Anglican Church, Regina.

The Thame Remembers Cross was placed at The Menin Gate Memorial on 31st October 2015 by Thame Museum Chairman, David Dodds and Jenny Dodds.

31 July 1917

Lieutenant Duncan Haldane Ostrehan was the eldest son of John Elliot Duncan Ostrehan and Alice Rebecca (née Crouch). He was born on 11th March 1891 and baptised at St Peter & St Paul's Church, Worminghall, Buckinghamshire on 12th May 1891. By 1895 the family had moved to Bank House, Cornmarket, Thame where his father was the branch manager from 1895 to 1920. Duncan was educated at Lord Williams's Grammar School and in 1911 went on to study at the Agricultural College in Aspatria, Cumberland. In 1913 he was playing rugby for Vale of Lune RFU club in Lancaster. Duncan and his younger brother, Rodney Arthur, were both Privates in the 3rd County of London Yeomanry (Sharpshooters), a territorial regiment.

They both received commissions as Second Lieutenants on 23rd November 1914 with the 1/4th Battalion, Loyal North Lancashire Regiment, a territorial battalion which had been raised at Preston in August.

The Battalion landed in Boulogne in early May 1915, but Duncan and Rodney did not join them until after the Battalion's heavy losses in the action at Givenchy on 15th/16th June. In 1916 the Battalion took part in a number of actions during the Battle of the Somme.

On 31st July 1917 Duncan, by then a full Lieutenant, was posted as wounded and missing in action whilst in command of D Company during the Battle of Pilckem Ridge, the opening battle of the Third Battle of Ypres (commonly referred to as Passchendaele). His Colonel reported that *"he had been gallantly leading his Company all day but towards evening they had to fall back a little owing to the numerical strength of the enemy"*. Duncan, age 25, was one of nine officers and 44 other ranks of the Battalion killed that day with a further 267 posted as wounded or missing. Rodney Arthur Ostrehan survived the war and died in 1962.

Lieutenant Duncan Haldane Ostrehan, Loyal North Lancashire Regiment, has no known grave and is commemorated on The Menin Gate Memorial, Ypres. He is remembered in Thame on the War Memorial and on the Memorial Boards of All Saints' Church and Lord Williams's School.

The Thame Remembers Cross was placed at The Menin Gate Memorial on 31st October 2015 by Thame Museum Chairman, David Dodds and Jenny Dodds.

4 August 1917

Alfred Robert Howland was the eighth son of the nineteen children of William Howland and Alice (née Bateman). He was born in 1883, when the family were living in Pound Street, Thame (later Wellington Street).

In February 1901 at the age of 18, he enlisted at Hounslow, Middlesex with the Royal Fusiliers and went on to complete 12 years' service, during which time he served in South Africa, Burma and India. His early years with the Colours were a little chequered, as he served several periods in military prisons, including one period for striking an officer. However after 1904, when he signed on for a further eight years, his service record was relatively unblemished and he was discharged to the Reserves with the rank of Lance Corporal in February 1913. He married Harriet Elizabeth Loader at All Saints' Church, Birmingham in April 1914.

With the general mobilisation in August 1914, he was once again called to the Colours, joining the 1st Battalion of the Royal Fusiliers and embarked with the Battalion to France in early September 1914, part of the British Expeditionary Force. They were quickly engaged in actions in northern France, where Alfred received a wound to the thigh resulting in hospitalisation in Paignton, Devon. After his wound healed, he returned to his Battalion and was engaged over the next three years in actions at the Hooge in 1915, the Somme in 1916, Vimy Ridge and Messines in 1917. Alfred was conferred with the Montenegro Medal for Merit (Silver) on 31st October 1916 for distinguished service. On 31st July 1917 Alfred, age 34, was wounded at the Battle of Pilckem Ridge, near Ypres and died of his wounds at a casualty clearing station on 4th August.

L/8701 Sergeant Alfred Robert Howland, Royal Fusiliers, is buried in Brandhoek New Military Cemetery, near Ypres. He is remembered in Thame on the War Memorial and on the Memorial Boards of St Mary's Church, All Saints' Church and Christchurch.

The Thame Remembers Cross was placed at his grave on 10th February 2018 by Thame resident, Geoffrey Walker.

8 August 1917

Charles Hubert Howlett was born in 1890 in New Bradwell, Buckinghamshire where his father was a carpenter in the Railway Works. His parents were Alfred Howlett and Elizabeth (née Absolon). By 1899 Alfred had moved his family back to Thame to carry on the family coach building business and was also licensee of the Fighting Cocks at 1 High Street.

In 1908 Charles joined the Royal Garrison Artillery and in 1911 he was stationed in Gibraltar with No 6 Company. On his return to England he married Violet Hilda Hatton in Portsmouth in 1914. They lived in Southsea, Hampshire and had one child Violet G Howlett, born in 1916. In early 1915 Charles embarked for France with the 10th Siege Battery who were equipped with 9.2 inch howitzers. In December 1915 he was promoted to Sergeant and after some time at the siege battery training ranges at Lydd, Kent, he returned to the Front with the 16th Siege Battery. In March 1917 he was promoted to Battery Quartermaster Sergeant.

Charles went on to serve with the 85th Siege Battery. They had been equipped, probably in 1916, with the new 12 inch road howitzers, capable of firing 750 lb high explosive shells over 6 miles. The Battery was in action at the start of the Third Battle of Ypres and Charles received wounds causing him to be taken to one of the casualty clearing stations set up west of Ypres. He died there from his wounds on 8th August 1917, age 27.

28811 Battery Quartermaster Sergeant Charles Hubert Howlett, Royal Garrison Artillery, is buried in Brandhoek New Military Cemetery near Ypres. He is remembered in Thame on the War Memorial and on the Memorial Boards of St Mary's Church and All Saints' Church. He is also commemorated on Portsmouth War Memorial and on his brother Horace's grave in St Mary's churchyard.

The Thame Remembers Cross was placed at his grave on 31st March 2015 by Thame resident, Elizabeth Barker and family.

16 August 1917

Jack Archer Keene was born in Barnsley, Gloucestershire in early 1898. His parents Frank Keene and Sarah (née Archer) had married in Thame in November 1891. Jack had four sisters and six brothers all born in Thame. Two of his brothers served in the Royal Navy during the war. Percy survived, but Fred went down with HMS Pathfinder in 1914.

In 1911 Jack was a tinman's errand boy. He had joined the 4th Battalion (Territorials) of the Oxford and Bucks Light Infantry (Regt No 2071) early in the war. He had possibly lied about his age as he would have only been 16 at the time, the minimum age for service in the Territorials being 17 (18 for overseas service). Nonetheless, his young age still precluded him from going with the Battalion when they embarked for France in March 1915. Throughout the spring of 1916 the Battalion received regular reinforcing drafts in preparation for the Somme offensive and it is likely that Jack joined them in France during this time. The Battalion, part of the 145th Brigade in the 48th (South Midland) Division, served through the many phases of the Battle of the Somme.

At the end of July 1917, the Brigade entrained from northern France to the Ypres area of Belgium. Jack, serving with A Company, was killed on 16th August 1917 during the Battle of Langemark, the second allied general attack of the Third Battle of Ypres. He was 19 years old.

His outstanding pay of £5 17s 7d was paid to his father in 1917 and his war gratuity of £13 10s paid to his mother, who by 1919 had moved to live in Reading, Berkshire.

200330 Private Jack Archer Keene, Oxford and Bucks Light Infantry, has no known grave and is commemorated on Tyne Cot Memorial, Zonnebeke. He is remembered in Thame on the War Memorial and on All Saints' Church Memorial Board.

The Thame Remembers Cross was placed at Tyne Cot Memorial on 30th October 2015 by Thame resident, Richard Bowdery.

16 August 1917

John Olieff was born in Thame in 1891, the youngest of eight children of John Olieff and Elizabeth (née Shirley). By 1911, living at 5 Southern Road, he had followed into his father's occupation as a fellmonger, dealing with hides and skins. He was called up in 1916 to serve with the 2/4th Battalion of the Oxford and Bucks Light Infantry (Regt No 204116). Before being posted for active service, he was part of a contingent from the Oxford and Bucks Light Infantry that was transferred to the Royal Berkshire Regiment to reinforce their 2nd Battalion, arriving at the Front on 26th June 1917.

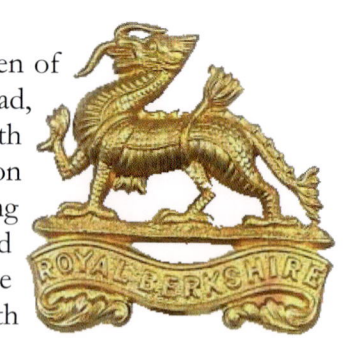

He was serving with the 2nd Battalion, Princess Charlotte of Wales's (Royal Berkshire Regiment), part of the 25th Infantry Brigade, 8th Division when they took part in the Battle of Langemark, the second allied general attack of the Third Battle of Ypres, or Passchendaele as it became more well known. After being used primarily as a reserve support Battalion at Pilckem Ridge at the beginning of August 1917, the Battalion formed part of the front assault waves when the attack to take the German "Green Line" east of Zonnebecke, began at 04:45hrs on 16th August. Early gains were made, but at a cost of 378 casualties, killed, wounded or missing. By the end of the day, enemy counter-attacks had forced the Battalion to retreat almost back to its starting line and they were reduced to an effective fighting strength of three officers and 115 men. John was 26 years old when he was killed in the action. In his will he left over £400, a substantial sum for the time.

220080 Private John Olieff, Royal Berkshire Regiment, has no known grave and is commemorated on Tyne Cot Memorial, Zonnebeke. He is remembered in Thame on the War Memorial and on All Saints' Church Memorial Board.

The Thame Remembers Cross was placed at Tyne Cot Memorial on 30th October 2015 by Thame resident, Richard Bowdery.

16 August 1917

George Squires was born in Thame in 1878, one of five children to Benjamin and Emma Squires of 36 Park Street, later of 71 Park Street. After serving an apprenticeship as a compositor with the Thame Gazette, he moved to Hemel Hempstead, Hertfordshire in 1901 to work as a print compositor for the John Dickinson Stationery Co (Lion and Basildon Bond) working at their plant at Apsley Mills. Along with a large number of the firm's employees he joined up in March 1916, enlisting with the Bedfordshire Regiment. He was sent to France with the 7th Battalion in July 1916 as part of a reinforcing draft due to the heavy losses sustained by the Battalion in the attack on the Pommiers Redoubt near Montauban on the first day of the Battle of the Somme. After further training and rest and recuperation, the reinforced Battalion saw further action on the Somme at Thiepval, Ancre Heights and the Ancre.

In 1917 after taking part in the Third Battle of the Scarpe at Arras, the Battalion moved to Belgium to prepare for the Third Battle of Ypres. They were first in action at Pilckem Ridge, followed by Langemark on 16th August. George, having been promoted to Corporal the previous May, was in B Company when they were ordered to attack a German strong point known locally as Inverness Copse. The British artillery barrage fell short and killed or wounded over 50% of the Company. George, age 39, was one of the casualties and buried in a battlefield grave, before being reinterred in 1920.

27854 Corporal George Squires, Bedfordshire Regiment, is buried in Tyne Cot Cemetery, Zonnebeke. He is remembered in Thame on the War Memorial and on the Memorial Boards of St Mary's Church and All Saints' Church.

The Thame Remembers Cross was placed at his grave on 30th October 2015 by Thame resident, Gill Read.

21 August 1917

Frederick Neil was born in Shabbington, Buckinghamshire on 13th February 1883, one of six children to Thomas and Ruth Neil. He married Hannah (Annie) Doran in Shabbington in 1910 and they had two daughters Rosina, who died shortly after birth, and Freda.

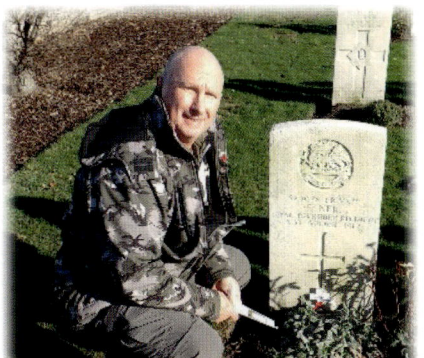

Like his father, Frederick was a farm labourer. As a married man he did not enlist at the start of the war. However, when conscription was introduced under the Military Service Act of 1916, it is likely he was called up towards the end of 1916. He was posted to the Oxford and Bucks Light Infantry (Regt No 204135) and undertook training with the Regiment's Training Reserve based at Wareham, Dorset. Before being posted for active service he was part of a contingent from the Oxford and Bucks Light Infantry that was transferred to the Royal Berkshire Regiment to reinforce their 2nd Battalion, arriving at the Front on 26th June 1917 as part of the 25th Infantry Brigade, 8th Division. On 16th August 1917 the Battalion fought in the Battle of Langemark, part of the Third Battle of Ypres and Frederick, age 34, was one of 120 men reported missing at the end of the day. Suffering from wounds to the head, he was captured by the Germans and taken to their field hospital (Feldlaz) at Iseghem, where he died of his wounds five days later on 21st August.

220078 Private Frederick Neil, Royal Berkshire Regiment, was originally buried in Iseghem Communal Cemetery German Extension, but in June 1924 he was reinterred at Harlebeke New British Cemetery in West Flanders. He is remembered in Thame on his wife Annie's grave in St Mary's churchyard and is also commemorated on Shabbington War Memorial, Buckinghamshire.

The Thame Remembers Cross was placed at his grave on 10th February 2018 by Thame resident, Stephen Boyson.

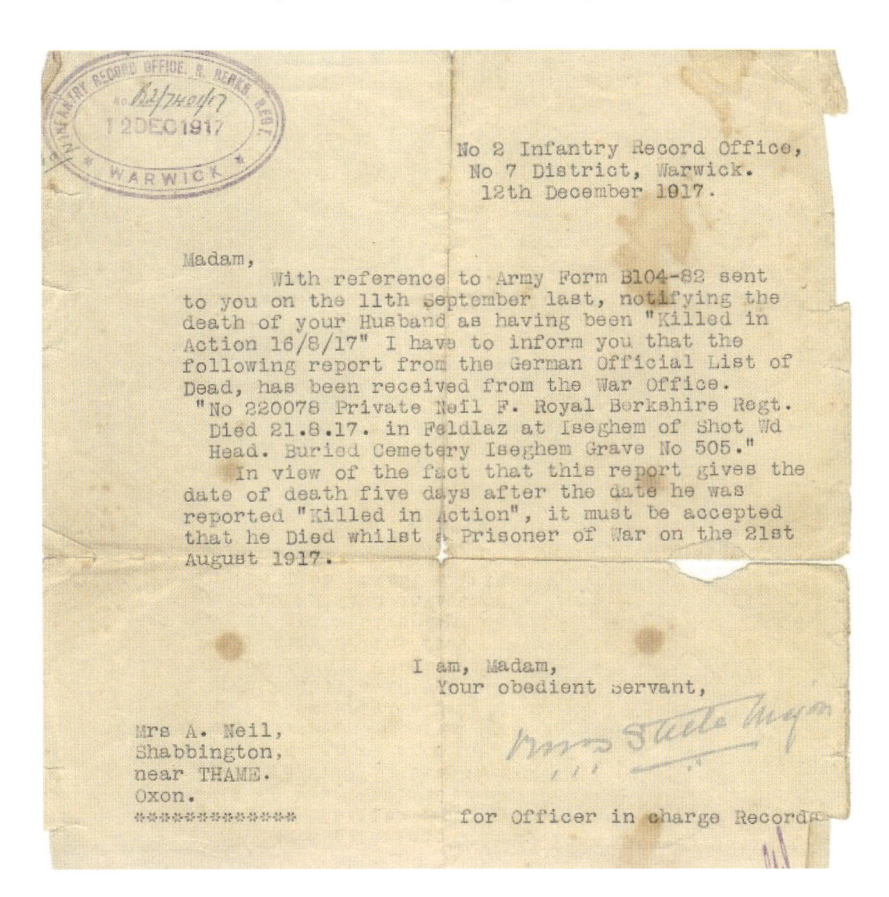

22 August 1917

William Elnahan Gascoyne was born in Whitechapel, London on 12th January 1895. He was one of the 14 children of Gilbert Gascoyne and Eliza Jane (née Shrimpton). By 1901 the family had moved to Long Crendon, Buckinghamshire the birthplace of his mother and where his father was manager of Horner's Works. William went to Long Crendon County School until he was granted a free place as a day scholar at Lord Williams's Grammar School in Thame. He spent five terms at the school from January 1909 until July 1910, when he left with an Oxford Local Junior Pass.

Just before the start of the war he enlisted with the 2nd (City of London Regiment) Royal Fusiliers, (Regt No 1698). The Battalion sailed for Malta in September 1914 and then to France at the beginning of 1915, landing in Marseilles on 6th January to join the 17th Brigade of the 6th Division. This was a regular army division and was at that time in the Front Line east of Armentières. The 2nd Londons remained there until June 1915 and then moved to the Ypres Salient, seeing action at the Hooge, Sanctuary Wood and Zillebeke. It was probably during this period at Ypres that William was wounded and invalided back to England for recovery and convalescence. He then applied for, and was selected for, officer training and was commissioned as a 2nd Lieutenant in March 1917 in the 2/4th Battalion of the Oxford and Bucks Light Infantry.

On 22nd August 1917 whilst engaged in an attack on Pond Farm during the Third Battle of Ypres, William, at the age of 22, was one of three officers killed by sniper or machine gun fire.

His widow Mary, who he had married just before his return to the Front, was living in Prospect Villa, Long Crendon and received his accrued pay and war gratuity of over £50.

Second Lieutenant William Elnahan Gascoyne, Royal Fusiliers, was initially buried in a battlefield cemetery, but his body was moved in 1919 to its final resting place in Tyne Cot Cemetery, Zonnebeke. He is remembered in Thame on Lord Williams's School Memorial Board and is also commemorated on Long Crendon War Memorial.

The Thame Remembers Cross was placed at his grave on 30th October 2015 by Thame residents, Mike and Jane Mitchell.

> "I now take the opportunity of writing to you regarding your son, who was killed in the attack of the 22nd, as I was his servant. I was with him within a few minutes of his death, and I am glad to be able to tell you that he died instantly, as he was shot through the head, so he did not suffer and he is buried about five yards in front of the line that he so nobly led his men up to capture and which we were able to hold. He was admired and respected by all who knew him and his men and fellow officers mourn his death nearly as much as I do who knew him all his life and who I am proud to say he was my friend although I was his servant, and I hope you will accept my sympathy with you over his death. But there is one thing to be proud of and that is, how I shall always think of him as I saw him on the morning of his death leading his men to the attack with a fearlessness that none can help but admire and he died doing his duty for his King and country and respected by all who knew him.
>
> Yours obediently, F Mortemore"

Letter written to William's parents by his batman Private F Mortemore, also from Long Crendon

8 September 1917

John William Bowler was born at Park Terrace, Thame in late 1894, the sixth of the seven children of Charles Bowler and Harriet (née Vincent). His father was a brickmaker at the local brickworks.

By 1901 the family had moved to Maidenhead, Berkshire and then to Reading where in 1911, John was employed as a butcher's assistant.

John enlisted with the Coldstream Guards at Caversham, Berkshire at the end of 1915. In 1916 he went to the Front and was most likely initially posted to the 7th (Guards) Entrenching Battalion before being posted to the 2nd Battalion as part of the reinforcing draft in September 1916. In 1917 the Battalion, as part of the Guards Division, took part in various actions in France, including the German retreat to the Hindenburg Line and the Battle of Arras, before marching on to Belgium at the end of June. On 8th September 1917, on the way back from a few days in trenches at Langemark to a rest area near Elverdingre, the Battalion came under German shell fire. John, age 23, was one of three soldiers killed.

17540 Private John William Bowler, Coldstream Guards, has no known grave and is commemorated on Tyne Cot Memorial, Zonnebeke. His name is to be added to Thame War Memorial.

The Thame Remembers Cross was placed at Tyne Cot Memorial on 30th October 2015 by Thame resident, Richard Bowdery.

19 September 1917

George Bowdery was one of twin boys born in Thame in 1891 to Benjamin Bowdery and Mary (née Chowns) and was baptised at St Mary's Church on 22nd February 1891. Following the death of his mother in 1892 his father married Thurza Cross, a widow, in 1897. George was then brought up in East Street and later Park Street with his seven brother and sisters. By 1911 he had left the family home and was living in Harrow, Middlesex where he was employed as a fishmonger.

In June 1915 George enlisted into the Royal Fusiliers. Initially this was with the 6th Battalion, a reserve and training battalion. He was then posted to the 32nd (East Ham) Battalion, which had been raised in October 1915, joining the 124th Brigade, 41st Division at Aldershot, Hampshire, before embarking for France in May 1916. During 1916 the Battalion was in action at the Battle of Flers-Courcelette and the Battle of the Transloy Ridges on the Somme. In 1917 they fought at the Battle of Messines and the Battle of Pilkem Ridge, the opening attacks in the Third Battle of Ypres (Passchendaele).

On 19th September 1917 George, age 26 and by then a Lance Corporal, was killed when the Battalion was preparing to attack "Tower Hamlets Spur" the following day. This was part of the Battle of the Menin Road Bridge which in itself was a component of the Third Battle of Ypres. Although initially reported missing, it was not until December that his death was confirmed.

17807 Lance Corporal George Bowdery, Royal Fusiliers, has no known grave and is commemorated on Tyne Cot Memorial, Zonnebeke. He is remembered in Thame on the War Memorial and on All Saints' Church Memorial Board.

The Thame Remembers Cross was placed at Tyne Cot Memorial on 30th October 2015 by his great nephew and Thame resident, Richard Bowdery.

20 September 1917

Sidney Stevens Edwards was born in Thame on 30th September 1893 and baptised at St Mary's Church on 10th October 1893. He was the youngest son of Frederick William Edwards and Harriet Hannah (née Mardlin). He had four elder sisters and two brothers. Sidney's father Frederick, who was landlord of the Birdcage in Cornmarket, Thame, died a few months before his son was born. Harriet went on to marry Frederick Gooding at Enfield, Middlesex in 1894. The family subsequently moved to Reading, Berkshire and in 1901 were living at the Black Horse in London Street, Reading. They then moved to London where Sidney went to the Oliver Goldsmith School in Peckham. In April 1911 he was boarding in Stoke Newington, London and employed as an assistant pawnbroker.

In March 1915 he joined the 5th (City of London) Battalion, London Regiment, which was known as the London Rifle Brigade (Regt No 1731). He served with them in France and Flanders from 3rd October 1916 until he was wounded at Beureraines, Arras on 26 March 1917. After his recovery, at the end of July, he was posted to the 2/5th Battalion. Sidney, age 23, was killed in action on 20th September 1917, the first day of the attack at the Menin Road Bridge during the Third Battle of Ypres. The Battalion sustained almost 250 casualties in the battle, of which over 60 were killed.

301071 Rifleman Sidney Stevens Edwards, London Rifle Brigade, was buried in a battlefield grave near where he fell. In March 1920 his body was reinterred at the New Irish Farm Cemetery, Flanders. His name is recorded on the London War Memorial website but he has no known Memorial in London. Sidney's name is to be added to Thame War Memorial.

The Thame Remembers Cross was placed at his grave on 31st August 2015 by Steve Perry and Verity Platek of Thame Remembers.

20 September 1917

Arthur Robert Howland was born in Thame in 1897. His parents, William Watts Howland and Annie Edden (née Orpen) had recently returned to live in Thame after several years in Wollongong, Australia. His father was a successful local builder and in 1911 they were living at 23 Queens Road. Arthur was the youngest of five brothers, Henry, William, Frederick and Leslie, all of whom served in the war and survived. Arthur joined the Oxford and Bucks Territorials in 1913 (Regt No 1859), and probably due to his age at the time being only 16 he was given the position of bugler. When war broke out, he was posted to the 2/4th Oxford and Bucks Light Infantry and embarked with them for France in May 1916.

In July the Battalion, with the 184th Brigade, 61st Division, was in the trenches and part of the force engaged in the diversionary attack at Fromelles during the Battle of the Somme. Arthur was wounded, one of the many casualties sustained by the Battalion during this unsuccessful attack.

When he recovered from his wounds he returned to the Front with the 6th (Service) Battalion of the Oxford and Bucks Light Infantry. Arthur, age 20, was killed on 20th September 1917. This was the first day of the Battle of Menin Road Bridge, during the Third Battle of Ypres, when 65,000 troops advanced on an eight mile front, screened by heavy mist and a stupefying bombardment. Although overall deemed to be a successful attack, it was not without heavy losses. The 6th Battalion suffering over 200 casualties killed, wounded or missing.

200228 Bugler Arthur Robert Howland, Oxford and Bucks Light Infantry, is buried in Bard Cottage Cemetery, Ypres. He is remembered in Thame on the War Memorial and on the Memorial Boards of All Saints' Church and St Mary's Church.

The Thame Remembers Cross was placed at his grave on 30th October 2015 by Thame residents, David and Cynthia Jackson.

4 October 1917

Harry Howland was born in 1875, the son of William Howland and Caroline Louisa (née Picketts) who lived in the High Street, Thame. He had ten brothers and sisters. His father William died in 1882 and by 1891 Harry lived at 12 Pound Street (later Wellington Street) with his mother and three of his brothers and sisters and was employed as an errand boy. By 1901 Harry had moved to Edmonton, Middlesex where he was employed as a butcher and in 1911 he had moved to Haywards Heath, Sussex and was working as an attendant at the Public Lunatic Asylum.

He married Emma Elizabeth Foreman on 9th October 1911 before moving to Hanwell, Middlesex where he took a job as a gardener.

Attesting for service under the Derby Scheme in November 1915 at the age of 40 years and 2 months, it was not until 1st August 1916 that Harry was enlisted into the Royal Garrison Artillery at No 1 Depot, Fort Burgoyne, Dover. He embarked for France on 10th March 1917 and after a spell with 183rd Siege Battery, followed by a short stay in hospital due to illness, he was posted to the 47th Siege Battery on 8th June. The Siege Battery was equipped with 4 x 8 inch howitzers, capable of sending large calibre high explosive shells in high trajectory, plunging fire.

The 47th Siege Battery war diary, reports that Gunner Harry Howland was killed and five other men wounded by hostile shell fire on 4th October 1917. He was 42 years old. The Battery was at Verbranden-Molen providing part of the artillery barrage for the infantry attack at the Battle of Broodseinde, part of the Third Battle of Ypres.

111402 Gunner Harry Howland, Royal Garrison Artillery, is buried in the Huts Cemetery on the road between Dickebusch and Brandhoek, an area which was used by field ambulances during the allied offensive on this front. His name is to be added to Thame War Memorial.

The Thame Remembers Cross was placed at his grave on 10th February 2018 by Michael Hutson of Thame Remembers.

26 October 1917

Harry William Oliver was born in Thame and baptised at St Mary's Church on 25th July 1889. His parents were Amos Oliver and Elizabeth (née Joiner) who had married at St Mary's Church in July 1888. They had four further children, Sydney Fred, Elise Maude, Albert James and Emily May. In 1911 the family were living at 12 Park Street, but Harry, age 21, was a fireman for the Hampstead Electric Light Company and lived with his uncle and aunt in West Hampstead, London.

He enlisted at Whitehall Recruiting Office with the 1st Battalion King Edward's Horse (Regt No 1934) on 14th May 1917. This was a Special Reserve cavalry regiment, originally set up with colonial volunteers resident in London - hence possibly why he put down his former occupation as a farmer in Queensland. However there is no record of him having travelled to Australia.

On completion of training on 8th September 1917 he was compulsorily transferred to the 6th Battalion Royal Fusiliers and then on 14th October transferred to the Queen's Own (Royal West Kent) Regiment. On 15th October 1917 he was posted to the Front, part of a reinforcing draft to the 1st Battalion who had sustained heavy casualties in the battles at Polygon Wood and Poelcapelle earlier in the month. The Battalion was once again in action on 26th October as part of the 5th Division, 13th Infantry Brigade, when at zero hour of 05:40hrs an attack was launched near Polderhoek and the Scherriabeek valley, the opening stage of the Second Battle of Passchendaele. By the end of the first day, Harry, age 28, was one of 211 men reported missing from the Battalion and later presumed dead. He had been at the Front for only nine days.

G/20154 Private Harry William Oliver, Royal West Kent Regiment, has no known grave and is commemorated on Tyne Cot Memorial, Zonnebeke. He is remembered in Thame on the War Memorial.

The Thame Remembers Cross was placed at Tyne Cot Memorial on 30th October 2015 by Thame resident, Richard Bowdery.

27 October 1917

Joseph Squires was born in the autumn of 1891. One of the eight children of Herbert Squires and Amelia (née Shurrock) living at 71 Park Street, Thame. In 1911 he was employed as a carter for a corn merchant and the following year married Susan Jane Munday of Long Crendon, Buckinghamshire. By 1916 they were living in Princes Risborough, Buckinghamshire and had three children, George William and Bertha Victoria, both born in Thame, and Benjamin Herbert born in Princes Risborough.

It is likely that Joseph was called up after conscription was extended to married men in late 1916 and he was initially posted with the 95th Training Reserve (TR) Battalion based at Chiseldon, Wiltshire, before being transferred to the 20th Battalion Machine Gun Corps. The Company was attached to the 20th Brigade of the 7th Division and served in many actions throughout 1917. It was during the Second Battle of Passchendaele, the last major action of the Third Battle of Ypres, that Joseph was wounded. At that time, the unit was situated along the Ypres-Menin Road, north west of Gheluvelt. The Battalion lost 33 men, either killed, wounded or missing, in the action that day.

Joseph, age 26, was evacuated back as far as the casualty clearing station at Lijssenthoek, south west of

Ypres, where he died of his wounds on 27th October 1917. Joseph had three other brothers who served in World War One. His younger brother Benjamin was killed in 1918 whilst serving in France serving with Grenadier Guards, but Albert and William survived.

13804 Private Joseph Squires, Machine Gun Corps, is buried in the Lijssenthoek Military Cemetery, Poperinge. He is remembered in Thame on the War Memorial and on the Memorial Boards of St Mary's Church, All Saints' Church and Christchurch. He is also commemorated on Longwick War Memorial and on the Church and the Market House Memorials in Princes Risborough.

The Thame Remembers Cross was placed at his grave on 31st March 2015 by Thame residents, Pieter-Paul Barker and family.

21 November 1917

Albert Victor Higgins was born in Moreton, near Thame in 1890, the youngest of the four children of Arthur and Elizabeth Higgins. In 1911 he was a gardener living in North Street, Thame, but when he enlisted at Oxford with the Army Service Corps in November 1915, he was in the employ of Mrs West of the Thame Motor Garage as a mail driver for the Thame, Wallingford and Didcot service. He was accepted into the Mechanical Transport (MT) section, (Regt No M2/138958). His attestation papers describe him as *"5 feet 8¾ inches tall, 135 lbs, with a girth of 37½ inches"*. After embarking for France on 2nd May 1916, he saw service as a driver for a number of ammunition supply companies. In June 1916 he was sentenced to two days field punishment for exceeding the 6mph speed limit in Bailleul in northern France.

In late September 1917 he received orders for a compulsory transfer to the 1/6th Cheshire Regiment. He was part of several reinforcing drafts necessary to replace the Battalion losses during earlier actions in the Third Battle of Ypres. Less than two months later on 21st November 1917 Albert, age 27, was killed at "Stirling Castle" which was alongside the Menin Road, north of Ypres.

51099 Private Albert Victor Higgins, Cheshire Regiment, has no known grave and is commemorated on Tyne Cot Memorial, Zonnebeke. He is remembered in Thame on the War Memorial and on the Memorial Boards of All Saints' Church and Christchurch.

The Thame Remembers Cross was placed at Tyne Cot Memorial on 30th October 2015 by Thame resident, Richard Bowdery.

16 March 1918

Edward Aubrey Lane was born in early 1892 in Stanton St John, Oxfordshire, one of seven children born to Richard Lane and Julie (née Wing). By 1901 the family had moved to Thame living in Rooks Place and then Lower High Street. By 1911 Edward had moved to Ealing where he was working as a compositor and it was here that he married Ellen Ada Turnbull at St Paul's Church, West Ealing, Middlesex in October 1915. They lived at 18 Salisbury Road, Northfield Avenue, Ealing and had a son, Aubrey Richard Matthew, born in April 1917.

Edward was attested for service in December 1915 under the Derby Scheme and was mobilised in April 1916 with the East Surrey Regiment (Regt

No 3969). He initially served with the 3/5th Reserve Battalion and then the 12th (Service) Battalion, embarking for France in October 1916. He was transferred to the 18th (1st Public Works Pioneers) Battalion of the Middlesex Regiment on 9th November and was appointed as one of the Battalion drummers. The Battalion came under the command of the 33rd Division with the Pioneers employed in works such as wire laying, trench construction and trench repair but at the same time were trained to fight as infantry. Throughout 1917 the Pioneers were kept busy on road and trench works in the Division's actions at such places as Arras and the Third Battle of Ypres. In March 1918 the Battalion was at Middlesex Camp, Passchendaele. On the night of 16th March at about 02:00hrs Edward, age 26, was one of three drummers killed when a German shell fell and exploded in the recreation hut.

41423 Private Edward Aubrey Lane, Middlesex Regiment, is buried in Potijze Chateau Grounds Cemetery, Ypres. He is remembered in Thame on the War Memorial and on the Memorial Board of All Saints' Church. He is commemorated on Ealing War Memorial.

The Thame Remembers Cross was placed at his grave on 30th October 2015 by Pauline Hawkett of Thame Museum.

16 September 1918

Frank Leslie Soanes was the youngest of eight children of James Soanes and Maria (née Hill). He was born on 6th October 1898 at 7 Wellington Street, Thame where his father was a hurdle maker and ran the Half Moon beerhouse. Frank was baptised at St Mary's Church on 17th November 1898. He was educated at the British School in Park Street and was a member of the Congregational Choir.

In February 1917 Frank joined the army. This was initially with the mechanical transport section of the Army Service Corps (Regt No M/297288). He was later transferred to the King's Royal Rifle Corps as a Rifleman and posted with the 18th (Arts and Crafts) Battalion, most likely in the summer of 1917 when the Battalion received various reinforcing drafts from the Army Service Corps in advance of the Third Battle of Ypres. In November 1917 Frank went to Italy with the Battalion, part of the British Army reinforcements to strengthen the Italian Front Line. The Battalion moved back to the Western Front in March 1918 at the start of the German spring offensive. They saw action at St Quentin, Bapaume, Arras and Estaires in France, before moving to the Ypres Salient in April. On 16th September 1918 the Battalion was at Vierstraat, near Ypres, when Frank, age 20, was killed. According to a letter to his parents from his platoon commander, "*he was on duty when an enemy trench mortar exploded and a portion of shell struck him in the back. He passed away after a few minutes suffering, dying as he was being carried to the rear.*"

R/38992 Rifleman Frank Leslie Soanes, King's Royal Rifle Corps, is buried in Groottebeek British Cemetery, Poperinge. He is remembered in Thame on the War Memorial and on the Memorial Boards of St Mary's Church, All Saints' Church and Christchurch. He is also commemorated on the gravestone of his parents in St Mary's churchyard.

The Thame Remembers Cross was placed at his grave on 20th May 2016 by Thame resident, Catherine Jones.

2 November 1918

Richard John Green was born on 9th April 1898 in Streatham, London where his father John Green was a tailor. Richard's mother Mary Jane (née Arnold) died shortly after his birth, possibly from complications during labour. Richard boarded at Lord Williams's Grammar School in Thame from September 1907 to July 1915 and was a member of both the cricket and football XIs.

After leaving school he went to live with his aunt Elizabeth, near Stratford upon Avon, Warwickshire to take up farming, but shortly after reaching his 18th birthday he enlisted with the Royal Sussex Regiment. Serving with the 4th Battalion, he travelled to Egypt and saw service in Palestine before the Battalion moved to France in May 1918. He returned from leave in England on 16th October 1918 to rejoin his unit on the Western Front. On 2nd November he was at a dressing station near Harlebeke attending to the wounded when he was killed by a German bomb dropped in an air raid over the British lines. He was 20 years old and this was just nine days before the Armistice. In his will he left over £900, a substantial sum at that time.

G/21442 Private Richard John Green, Royal Sussex Regiment, was initially buried in the local Harlebeke churchyard. It was not until May 1950, when along with several others, his remains were exhumed and reinterred at the Harlebeke New British Cemetery, West Flanders. He is remembered in Thame on Lord Williams's School Memorial Board, the last Old Tamensian to be killed.

The Thame Remembers Cross was placed at his grave on 23rd May 2015 by Thame residents, Joan and Andrew Reid.

10 November 1918

William Chowns was born on 24th January 1889 in Moreton, near Thame, the son of William Chowns and Emma (née Austin). He was the fifth child of a family of six boys and one girl. The family all emigrated to Canada between 1906 and 1911, except for Frank, who married and stayed in Thame. Frank was also killed in World War One serving in France.

William was working as a labourer in Humber Bay, Ontario, Canada when he was drafted on 20th February 1918, with no previous military experience, into the 19th Battalion Canadian Infantry (Central Ontario Regiment).

William was posted to the Western Front to join the Battalion with the 4th Infantry Brigade, 2nd Canadian Division. As the war neared its end, the Canadian Corps pressed on towards Germany. This phase of the war for the Canadians was known as the *Pursuit to Mons*. It was during these final thirty-two days of the war that the Canadians engaged the retreating Germans over about seventy kilometres in a series of running battles at **Denain** and **Valenciennes** in France and finally **Mons** in Belgium. It was just outside Mons on 10th November that William was killed instantly by a machine gun bullet through the head. He was 29 years old and this was one day before the Armistice. Some criticism was levelled at the Canadian Corps Commander for needlessly wasting lives to capture Mons once it was known that the cessation of hostilities was imminent. It was claimed that the soldiers who were killed and wounded in taking Mons were sacrificed for a symbolic rather than a strategic objective. Mons being the location where the war started for the British Expeditionary Force in 1914.

3107824 Private William Chowns, Canadian Infantry, was initially buried in Hyon Communal Cemetery, three quarters of a mile south of Mons, before being reinterred, in December 1920 in Mons (Bergen) Communal Cemetery, Mons. He is commemorated on Humber Bay Memorial in Ontario, Canada and his name is to be added to both Thame and Moreton War Memorials.

The Thame Remembers Cross was placed at his grave on 21st April 2018
by Thame resident, Brian West.

Attack

At dawn the ridge emerges massed and dun
In the wild purple of the glowering sun,
Smouldering through spouts of drifting smoke that shroud
The menacing scarred slope; and, one by one,

Tanks creep and topple forward to the wire.
The barrage roars and lifts. Then, clumsily bowed
With bombs and guns and shovels and battle-gear,
Men jostle and climb to meet the bristling fire.

Lines of grey, muttering faces, masked with fear,
They leave their trenches, going over the top,
While time ticks blank and busy on their wrists,
And hope, with furtive eyes and grappling fists,
Flounders in the mud. O Jesus, make it stop!

Seigfried Sassoon
(1886-1967)

France

By the end of November 1914 the British Expeditionary Force (BEF) had fought hard battles at Mons, Le Cateau, the Aisne and Ypres. Although originally composed of regular troops, the British Army had been substantially brought up to strength by reservists. The British army had been based at home in August and after moving to France and then Belgium suffered massive casualties in the fighting, losing most of its fighting strength. Small as it was, it had played a considerable role in stopping the German advance on Paris. After the so-called "Race to the Sea", both sides dug in and a continuous line of trenches ran from the Belgian coast to Switzerland.

The Army rapidly expanded to meet the needs of a continental war. Numbers were initially made up by the Territorial Force and the Reserve. From the spring of 1915, significant numbers of volunteers from Field Marshal Kitchener's New Army arrived. The British Force had also been quickly supplemented by troops coming from India and the Dominions (Australia, Canada, Newfoundland, New Zealand and South Africa).

The French, desperate to recover their lost territory and despite horrendous casualties, still believed in the spirit of the offensive and launched attacks in the Artois area in the spring and autumn of 1915. The British also attacked and broke through the German lines at Neuve Chapelle. Sadly, this initial success could not be exploited. It did prove, however, that with the right preparation and sufficient guns and men, that the British could take German Front Line trench systems. It also demonstrated the German expertise at mounting ferocious counter-attacks, a skill they maintained throughout the war. Neuve Chapelle also highlighted the desperate need for ammunition for the artillery and bigger guns. On the first day of the Battle, thirty percent of the artillery shells available to the First Army had been expended. This was equivalent, at the time, to seventeen days' production. The shell shortage also affected the British attack on Aubers Ridge in May and resulted in the "munitions scandal". The lack of ammunition, particularly high explosive shells, was blamed for the Army's failure.

As more troops arrived from Britain they relieved most French troops in Flanders, which meant that the BEF now held a continuous line from Givenchy-lès-la-Bassée in the south to just north of Ypres, as well as positions further south below Arras. Between 25th September and 13th October 1915, over twenty divisions took part in the Battle of Loos, which was notable for the first use of poison gas by the British. The gas proved no substitute for high explosive shells and, with the wire uncut in front of the German trenches, the infantry suffered heavy losses for minimal gains. Where they did succeed, violent German counter-attacks usually forced the British back close to their starting positions. The lesson learned by the German defenders in these 1915 autumn battles was the value of defence in depth, with second and third line positions established well behind the Front Line. The Germans also realised the need to increase the depth of dugouts to protect troops from heavy artillery fire. When the Battle drew to a close the British had suffered almost 60,000 casualties. The Loos Memorial commemorates over 20,000 British soldiers who fell in the Battle of Loos and who have no known grave.

Loos Memorial and Cemetery

The Chantilly Conference in December 1915 agreed upon a joint Anglo-French summer offensive on the Western Front. The French would take the lead with the British acting in support. This plan was thrown into disarray on 21st February 1916 when the Germans launched a massive attack at Verdun. The French were forced to commit more and more troops to its defence, which meant that they could no longer provide the bulk of the infantry for the joint offensive. For a variety of reasons it was decided that this offensive should take place where the two armies met, near the north bank of the River Somme.

Many of the attacking troops came from Kitchener's New Army. These volunteer troops were keen to get to grips with the 'Hun' but were very inexperienced, with hardly any of them having been engaged in a major battle before. Indeed, a few units only received their standard infantry rifles just two months before they attacked. The New Army included so-called 'Pals' battalions, which were locally recruited battalions, often, but not exclusively, from northern industrial towns. These consisted of friends and men from the same or similar trades, such as miners, who enlisted together on the understanding that they would be able to serve alongside their friends, neighbours and work colleagues.

In late June 1916 at the start of the battle a massive artillery barrage was laid down to try to ensure a successful attack. Over 400 guns would fire one and a half million shells, aiming to cut the wire in front of the German lines and destroy their trenches. The British infantry, it was thought, would only have to walk across No Man's Land and occupy the German positions. The length of the German front under attack stretched between the small village of Gommecourt in the north to Foucaucourt in the south. After seven days of artillery bombardment, the infantry went over the top at 07:30hrs on 1st July, the first day of the Battle of the Somme.

Thiepval Memorial and Cemetery

They soon discovered that the barrage had failed to cut the barbed wire and subdue the German defenders and they were mown down in droves. By the end of the first day the BEF had suffered some 58,000 casualties, of whom over 19,000 were killed. What success there was lay in the French sector and the southern part of the British attack, where most objectives were achieved. This was the largest loss of servicemen in action on a single day in the history of the British Army. As the casualty lists appeared in the newspapers at home over the following days it became clear it was a tragedy for many thousands of families in Britain. The Pals Battalions, whose casualties were often very high, could not recreate the same spirit afterwards and, of course, these losses impacted heavily on the communities from which they were drawn.

The Battle continued until 18th November, a period of four and a half months. In between the major operations, launched on 14th July and 15th September, the British fought continuous smaller battles to straighten the Line before these major attacks could take place. All the time the inexperienced British were developing their skills from gunnery to small-scale platoon tactics.

The names of these battles will live on forever in the Army's history. The locations, now marked by Commonwealth War Graves Commission cemeteries, are dotted along the route of the advance. They include: Albert (1-13 July); Bazentin Ridge (14-17 July); Pozières (23 July-3 September); Guillemont (3-6 September); Ginchy (9 September); Flers-Courcelette (15-22 September), which saw the first use of tanks; Morval (25-28 September); Thiepval (26-28 September); Le Transloy (1-18 October); Ancre Heights (1 October-11 November) and finally, marking the end of the Somme offensive, the Ancre (13-18 November). The late autumn rains had by then reduced the battlefield to a sea of mud and brought a halt to further operations. The BEF had suffered around

420,000 casualties and the French about 200,000. German casualty figures are controversial, but are thought to be about 465,000.

The awful slaughter on the Somme is now marked by a towering Memorial on dominating ground at Thiepval, which can be seen from miles around. It bears the names of more than 72,000 soldiers of the United Kingdom and South Africa who died in the Somme sector before 20th March 1918 and have no known grave. It also includes the sailors of the Royal Naval Division who fought as soldiers. Over 90% of those commemorated died between July and November 1916. The Memorial also serves as an Anglo-French Battle Memorial, recognising the joint nature of the 1916 offensive and this is further emphasised by a small cemetery containing equal numbers of BEF and French graves at the foot of the Memorial.

The first major event of 1917 was *Operation Alberich*, the German Army's withdrawal to the Hindenburg Line which ran from Artois (Arras) to the Aisne (Soissons) and took about five weeks to complete. This operation included the total destruction and devastation of the areas they evacuated. Buildings were blown up, trees cut down and wells fouled. Mines and booby traps were planted in the rubble.

The Canadian Memorial at Vimy

One key outcome of the Chantilly Conference in December 1915 was the commitment to ensure that all future offensive action between the Allies was closely co-ordinated. In 1917 this resulted in the BEF being instructed to support the French Nivelle Offensive planned for April 1917. The result was the Battle of Arras, fought in April and May.

The British effort was on a relatively broad front from Vimy in the north west to Bullecourt in the south east. After a huge bombardment, the Battle commenced at 05:30hrs on 9th April. In the north, and attacking alongside each other for the only time in the war, all four Canadian divisions and one British division took the northern part of Vimy Ridge after four days of hard fighting. Vimy became more than just an important battlefield victory as men from all regions of Canada were present at the Battle and after the war Brigadier General A E Ross declared "in those few minutes I witnessed the birth of a nation".

The British Third Army advanced along the Scarpe River making the deepest penetration since trench warfare began. A couple of days later, in the south, the Fifth Army attacked the Hindenburg Line but was frustrated by the depth of the German defences, making only minimal gains. The British armies then engaged in a series of smaller-scale operations to consolidate their new positions. Although these battles were generally successful in achieving their limited aims, they were costly and the 150,000 casualties of the Battle produced a considerably higher daily casualty rate than the Somme.

In 1922 the French government ceded to Canada, in perpetuity, a large area of Vimy Ridge, notably its highest point. On this ridge the Vimy Memorial, of gleaming white marble and embellished by haunting sculptures, was dedicated in 1936. It commemorates the 11,285 Canadian soldiers killed in France who have no known graves and is a Memorial to all those from Canada who served in the war. The British emphasis then moved back to the Ypres Salient and the Battles of Messines and Third Ypres.

A completely new approach was adopted at Cambrai in late November and December of 1917 with a radical artillery plan and the mass use of tanks, although the Germans responded to the substantial early success with a massive counter-offensive.

The Germans launched a series of offensives in the spring of 1918, bolstered by troops released from the Russian front after the October 1917 Revolution. There were four major offensives: *Michael* (the Somme); *Georgette* (the Lys and around Ypres); *Gneisenau* and *Blücher–Yorck* (which involved British divisions on the Aisne - as well as the French). For *Michael,* the Germans assembled a force of 74 divisions, 6,600 guns, 3,500 mortars and 326 fighter aircraft. This huge force was unleashed against the British, starting with a devastating hurricane bombardment and followed immediately by teams of specially trained troops who used infiltration tactics to get behind the British lines. The British defenders on the Somme, which at that time was the most weakly held part of the line held by the BEF were initially overwhelmed and fell back some forty miles, surrendering ground for which they had fought so bitterly in 1916. However, the BEF stopped the attack around Arras. The casualties on both sides were huge, but this offensive marked a return to open warfare. British resistance stiffened and the Germans failed to make a strategic and decisive breakthrough. With manpower and resources running low, the German offensives finally petered out in July 1918.

On 8th August 1918 the BEF launched the biggest and most successful series of offensives in its history: the 'Advance to Victory' or 'The Hundred Days'. In a series of battles, in coordination with the French and the Americans, the Germans were forced back many miles. With the British naval blockade causing desperate hardships for the Germans at home, the capitulation of their allies and thousands of American troops entering the fray, it was clear that Germany had lost the war. At the Eleventh hour of the Eleventh day in the Eleventh month the guns fell silent and peace returned to Europe although be it temporarily.

WE DON'T WANT WORDS, WE WANT DEEDS.

Those Remembered

14 September 1914

William Robert Loosley was born in Towersey, Buckinghamshire in 1888 and was the sixth of eight children of George Loosley and Sarah Ann (née Chowns). By 1901 William, age 13, was a live-in errand boy with grocer George Bailey at 107 High Street, Thame. In 1911 his widowed mother and family were living at 2 Bridge Terrace, Thame.

William joined the Grenadier Guards on 29th August 1906 at the age of 18. He departed for France on 13th August 1914 with the 2nd Battalion, part of the 4th (Guards) Brigade, 2nd Division. After the British Expeditionary Force's retreat from Mons and the halting of the German advance at the Marne the Battalion took part in the advance towards the river Aisne. William, age 26, was killed during the action of 14/15th September 1914 near the village of Soupir.

12843 Private William Robert Loosley, Grenadier Guards, has no known grave and is commemorated on La Ferté-Sous-Jouarre Memorial, Seine-et-Marne. He is remembered in Thame on the War Memorial and All Saints' Church Memorial Board. He is also commemorated on Towersey Memorial Board.

The Thame Remembers Cross was placed at La Ferté-Sous-Jouarre Memorial on 7th July 2015 by Thame resident, Helen Turner.

22 October 1914

James Arthur Greenhalgh was born in Bolton, Lancashire on 5th May 1889 to Joseph Greenhalgh, a mill and foundry furnisher, and Hannah (née Haslam). He was educated at St George the Martyr's School and Bolton Church Institute. He entered Manchester University in 1907, prior to which he was a student teacher at St James' School, Gorton, Manchester. He gained a BA and his Teaching Certificate Class II in 1910 and an MA in Philology in 1912. He was a member of the Officer Training Corps from November 1908 to September 1911.

After leaving University James was a classics master for two years at Lord Williams's Grammar School, Thame and then took up an appointment at Ashton-in-Makerfield Grammar School, Lancashire. James was a prominent footballer playing for his school, the University and Sale AFC. He also secured his rugby colours for three different counties.

He was on the Reserve of Officers and was commissioned as a 2nd Lieutenant to the 1st Battalion Cheshire Regiment on 6th August 1914 and left for France with the Battalion on 7th September 1914. They saw action at the Battles of the Aisne, La Bassée and Festubert. On 19th October 1914 at Violannes, his Captain was wounded and James took charge, driving the Germans out of their position. However, unable to hold it, he and his men withdrew to their own trenches, collecting the wounded on the way. Three days later the Battalion war diary records an enemy attack that took their trenches at bayonet point and the Battalion suffered heavy casualties including the death of James, age 25.

Second Lieutenant James Arthur Greenhalgh, Cheshire Regiment, has no known grave and is commemorated on Le Touret Memorial, Pas de Calais. He is remembered in Thame on Lord Williams's School Memorial Board. He is also commemorated on the War Memorials at the University of Manchester, Bolton Church Institute School, Ashton-in-Makerfield Grammar School and Christchurch, Timperley, Cheshire.

The Thame Remembers Cross was placed at Le Touret Memorial on 22nd October 2015 by Thame resident, Brett Chowns.

25 December 1914

Lewis Rhymes was born in Chipping Norton, Oxfordshire on 31st March 1885, the eldest son of Edwin Rhymes and Eliza (née Thompson). He worked as a farm labourer before enlisting with the 2nd Battalion, The Gloucestershire Regiment in 1904. He was transferred to the 1st Battalion in 1910 and was based at Portsmouth in 1911 prior to his discharge to the reserves later that year. After a short employment with the Chipping Norton Gas company, he became a policeman with the Oxfordshire Constabulary in August 1911.

Following his training in Oxford, PC79 Rhymes was posted to the Bullingdon Division in September 1912 and stationed in Thame. He married Ellen Sale in June 1914 at Abingdon and moved to live in married quarters in Bicester.

He was recalled to his Regiment on 4th August 1914 and disembarked at Le Havre with the 1st Battalion a few days later on 13th August. He participated in the Battle of the Aisne and the First Battle of Ypres, before being severely wounded in action at Festubert, near Givenchy on 20th December 1914. He was evacuated to the rear and died of his wounds in the base hospital at Boulogne on Christmas Day 1914, age 29. In the spring of 1915 Ellen gave birth to Edwin L H Rhymes, a son his father never saw.

7657 Private Lewis Rhymes, Gloucestershire Regiment, is buried in Boulogne Eastern Cemetery. He is commemorated on Chipping Norton War Memorial and his name is to be added to Thame War Memorial.

The Thame Remembers Cross was placed at his grave on 23rd May 2016 by Allan Hickman of Thame Remembers.

9 May 1915

Frank Chowns was born in Moreton near Thame in 1883, the second of six sons and one daughter to William and Emma Chowns. Frank joined the King's Royal Rifle Corps in April 1902 and served with them in South Africa from 1902 to 1904, following the Boer War. He married Rose Squires at St Mary's Church on 16th September 1905 when he was living at 13 Bell Lane, Thame. They went to live with Rose's parents at 50 High Street, Thame and had three daughters, Kate Elizabeth, Ethel Maude and Margaret Rose. His father had died in 1904 and by 1908 his mother and brothers had emigrated to Canada, whilst Frank remained in Thame with his new wife. He had been transferred to the reserve in 1905 and it would appear that he was recalled at the beginning of World War One. He was sent to France as part of the reinforcing draft for the 2nd Battalion arriving at Hazebrouk on 3rd December 1914. The family story says that on receiving the news of his call-up his wife Rose took his kit bag down to the farm where he was working and from there he departed for his Regiment. Frank, age 32, was reported missing whilst fighting in the Battle of Aubers Ridge on 9th May 1915. The 2nd Battalion were in a support role at the southern end of the attack at Richebourg, close to Le Touret. The Battle was said to be an unmitigated disaster for the British army with no ground won or tactical advantage gained.

4443 Rifleman Frank Chowns, King's Royal Rifle Corps, has no known grave and is commemorated on Le Touret Memorial, Pas de Calais. He is remembered in Thame on the War Memorial and on the Memorial Boards of All Saints' Church and St Mary's Church. He is also commemorated on Rose's parents' gravestone in St Mary's churchyard.

The Thame Remembers Cross was placed at Le Touret Memorial on 12th May 2015 by Thame resident, Brett Chowns.

16 May 1915

Sidney Thomas Parker was born in 1888 in Culham, Oxfordshire where his father Joseph was a police constable. By 1901 Joseph, his wife Susan (née Faulkner) and their four children had moved to Tetsworth, Oxfordshire. Joseph was still at the Police Station there 10 years later. On retiring from the police it would seem that Joseph took on the Plough Inn at Priestend, Thame before finally settling in Long Crendon, Buckinghamshire.

Sidney joined the Oxford and Bucks Light Infantry in the summer of 1907 when he was 18. He was a member of the 2nd Battalion which formed part of the 5th Brigade, 2nd Division at Aldershot, Hampshire on 2nd August 1914 and landed at Boulogne on 14th August 1914. He was in the area of the Western Front that saw some of the heaviest fighting of the early years of the war, such as Mons, the Marne and First Ypres. The Battalion entered the trenches near Richebourg l'Avoue on 10th May 1915 in preparation for their part in the Battle of Festubert (15th to 25th May 1915). Sidney, age 27, died in action at Richebourg l'Avoue on 16th May 1915.

8508 Acting Sergeant Sidney Thomas Parker, Oxford and Bucks Light Infantry, has no known grave and is commemorated on Le Touret Memorial, Pas de Calais. He is remembered in Thame on the War Memorial and on All Saints' Church Memorial Board. He is also commemorated on Tetsworth War Memorial.

The Thame Remembers Cross was placed at Le Touret Memorial on 12th May 2015 by Thame resident, Brett Chowns.

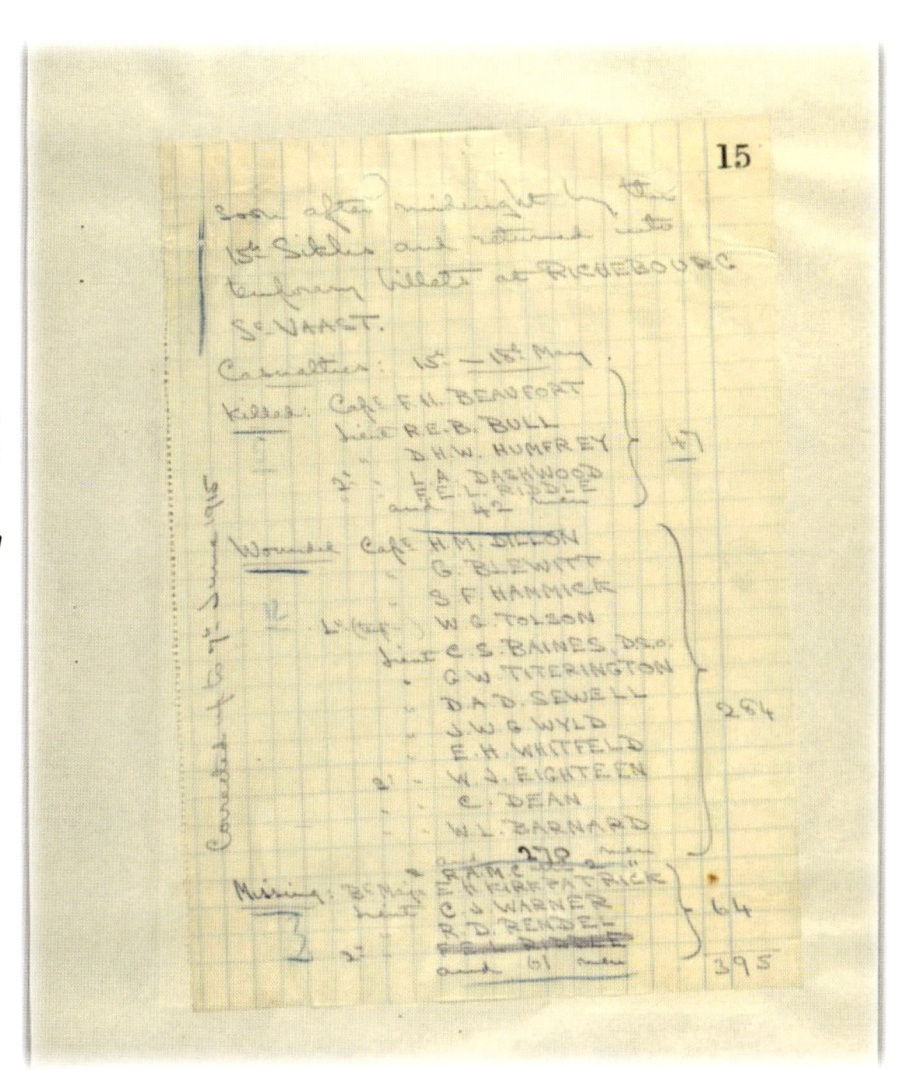

A page from the 2nd Battalion Oxford and Bucks Light Infantry war diary recording the casualties of 15th to 18th May 1915

17 August 1915

Reginald John Culverwell was born on 27th December 1893 in Long Crendon, Buckinghamshire where his father George was a farm labourer and later a coachman. His mother was Sarah Ann (née Kirk). John was a pupil at Lord Williams's Grammar School in Thame and in 1911 he was studying to be a teacher at the school.

He enlisted with the 4th Battalion Oxford and Bucks Light Infantry in late 1913/early 1914 which at that time was a territorial battalion, but in August 1914 it was fully mobilised as the 1/4th Battalion. He spent the next few months training with the Battalion near the village of Writtle in Essex, before embarking to France in March 1915 with the 145th (South Midland) Brigade.

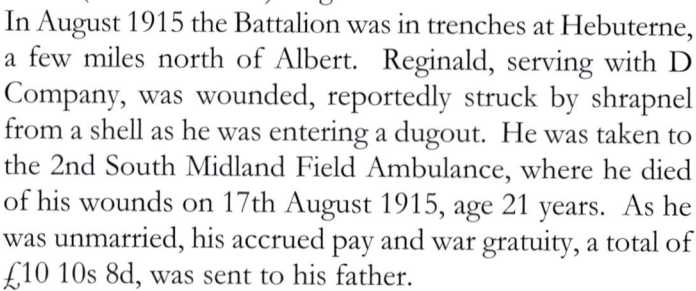

In August 1915 the Battalion was in trenches at Hebuterne, a few miles north of Albert. Reginald, serving with D Company, was wounded, reportedly struck by shrapnel from a shell as he was entering a dugout. He was taken to the 2nd South Midland Field Ambulance, where he died of his wounds on 17th August 1915, age 21 years. As he was unmarried, his accrued pay and war gratuity, a total of £10 10s 8d, was sent to his father.

1958 Private Reginald John Culverwell, Oxford and Bucks Light Infantry, is buried at the Louvencourt Military Cemetery, Somme. He is remembered in Thame on Lord Williams's School Memorial Board. He is also commemorated on the War Memorials at Nether Winchendon and Long Crendon both in Buckinghamshire.

The Thame Remembers Cross was placed at his grave on 18th April 2015
by Thame resident, Margaret Bretherton.

25 September 1915

William Spencer Drake was born in Thame early in 1885. He was the eldest of the eight children of William Drake, a carpenter, and Emily (née Wells) of 29 Park Street. By 1911 the family had moved to 165 High Street, Cheltenham, Gloucestershire where his father was a fruit merchant.

William enlisted in the Oxford and Bucks Light Infantry at Oxford early in 1901 giving his birth year as 1883. He was serving with the 2nd Battalion, yet when the Battalion went to France in August 1914 it appears that William stayed in Oxford. He rejoined the Battalion as part of a reinforcing draft in February 1915 and served with D Company. He was killed on 25th September in a battle at Givenchy, a subsidiary attack to the Battle of Loos. He was 30 years old.

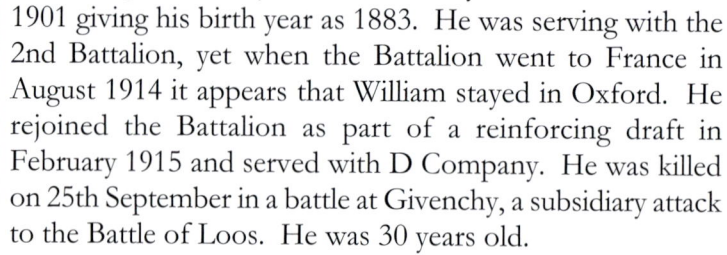

A report from a fellow Sergeant reads: "*Sergt W S Drake was killed in an attack on the German trenches about 06:30 on the morning of Sept 25th. He was very popular and highly respected by everyone who knew him in the Company and especially in his platoon - the men he led in the attack. I have no doubt you will be glad to know he did not suffer any length of time after being hit; he was not seen to move, so it is believed his death was instantaneous. We buried him on Sunday afternoon in the military cemetery at Cuinchy*".

6776 Sergeant William Spencer Drake, Oxford and Bucks Light Infantry, is buried in Guards Cemetery, Windy Corner, Cuinchy. He is remembered in Thame on the War Memorial and on St Mary's Church Memorial Board.

The Thame Remembers Cross was placed at his grave on 1st November 2015
by Thame Museum member, Brenda Mawdsley.

26 September 1915

Eric Leon Boiling was born in Thame in 1893 to 34 year old unmarried mother Jane Elizabeth Boiling. He was baptised at St Mary's Church on 25th March 1894. The family were living at the Red Cow, Aylesbury Road where Jane's mother, Jane Eliza Boiling, was the licensee. Jane married James Burnard in 1895 and they moved to 46 Park Street. By 1911 Eric was living with his uncle, Edward Boiling, in Wealdstone, Middlesex and working as a dental mechanic. Eric married Kathleen Kingshott in the St Martin's district of London in August 1915, just prior to leaving for the Front on 31st August. The G prefix of Eric's service number signifies that he joined for war general service in September 1914. He embarked for France with the 8th Battalion, East Kent (Buffs) Regiment on 1st September 1915. Three weeks later, on 26th September, the Battalion, as part of the 17th Brigade, 24th Division, joined the fight on the second day of the Battle of Loos. The inexperienced troops suffered heavily from machine gun fire when crossing open ground and then artillery fire in front of the uncut German wire. The Battalion almost ceased to exist, losing 24 officers and 610 other ranks killed, wounded or missing. Eric, age 22, was among them. His brother William Boiling served with the Royal Berks and died in April 1918.

G/2220 Private Eric Leon Boiling, East Kent Regiment, has no known grave and is commemorated on Loos Memorial, Pas de Calais. He is remembered in Thame on the War Memorial and on the Memorial Boards of St Mary's Church and All Saints' Church.

The Thame Remembers Cross was placed at Loos Memorial on 23rd May 2017 by Thame resident, Amanda Binnee.

26 September 1915

Cyril George Clarke was the only son of Freeman Clarke and Mary Ann (née Harris). He was born in Haddenham, Buckinghamshire in 1889 and had two younger sisters. His father was a baker at "Clementine" High Street, Haddenham. Cyril was educated at Lord Williams's Grammar School in Thame and went on to train as a teacher. By 1911 he was an elementary teacher assistant for Bucks County Education Committee. He received a commission as a Temporary 2nd Lieutenant on 23rd October 1914 and was posted to the 8th Battalion, East Yorkshire Regiment. The majority of 1915 was spent training at Halton Camp, Wendover, Buckinghamshire before leaving for France on 9th September 1915. Less than three weeks later, on 25th September 1915, the Battalion, part of the 62nd Brigade, 21st Division, took part in the main attack at Loos. They were fighting in the south east corner of Loos and the inexperienced troops suffered heavy casualties. Now a full Lieutenant, Cyril died of his wounds at No 6 Field Ambulance on 26th September 1915. He was 26 years old.

Lieutenant Cyril George Clarke, East Yorkshire Regiment, is buried in Noeux-les-Mines Communal Cemetery, near Bethune. He is remembered in Thame on Lord Williams's School Memorial Board and he is commemorated on the War Memorial in Haddenham.

The Thame Remembers Cross was placed at his grave on 5th May 2017 by Thame residents, Ian and Mary Cleare.

27 September 1915

Bernard George Turner was born on 28th November 1893 at The Gables, Bledlow Ridge, Buckinghamshire to John William Turner, an elementary school master, and his wife Emily (née Hainsworth). He attended High Wycombe Grammar School and also Lord Williams's Grammar School, Thame where he was a boarder. After leaving school, he gained a position with the London County Council and served as a clerk with the Fire Brigade.

Bernard joined the Coldstream Guards in September 1914 and served on the Western Front with the 1st Battalion in the Maxim Gun Section from January 1915. The Battalion took part in the Battle of Aubers Ridge in May 1915. Bernard, age 21, was shot through the heart and killed at Chalk Pit Wood near Hill 70 during the Battle of Loos on 27th September 1915.

11833 Private Bernard George Turner, Coldstream Guards, has no known grave and is commemorated on Loos Memorial, Pas de Calais. He is remembered in Thame on Lord Williams's School Memorial Board. He is also commemorated on Bledlow Ridge War Memorial and on High Wycombe Grammar School Memorial Board.

The Thame Remembers Cross was placed at Loos Memorial on 23rd May 2017
by Thame resident, Martin Binnee.

13 June 1916

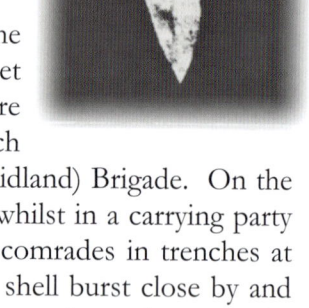

William Noel Smith was born in Basingstoke, Hampshire in 1892 to William Smith and Emma Elizabeth (née Tew), being the only son of six children. The family moved to Thame, firstly to Chinnor Road, then to Elmdene, Essex Road. He attended Lord Williams's Grammar School. Upon leaving school he joined his father in the family printing and stationery business in Upper High Street and in 1912, enlisted with the 4th Battalion (Territorial Force) of the Oxford and Bucks Light Infantry.

Upon the outbreak of war the Battalion was mobilised and set up camp in Writtle, Essex before embarking for France in March 1915 with the 145th (South Midland) Brigade. On the afternoon of 13th June 1916, whilst in a carrying party taking tea to his A Company comrades in trenches at Hebuterne, north of Albert, a shell burst close by and William was killed, age 24. His mother, who upon the death of his father in 1914 had moved back to Hampshire, was awarded his accrued pay and war gratuity of £9 15s.

1617 Private William Noel Smith, Oxford and Bucks Light Infantry, is buried in Hebuterne Military Cemetery, Somme. He is remembered in Thame on the War Memorial and on the Memorial Boards of Lord Williams's School, St Mary's Church and All Saints' Church. He is commemorated on Basingstoke War Memorial.

The Thame Remembers Cross was placed at his grave on 18th April 2015
by Thame resident, Cliff Baker.

WITH THE TERRITORIALS

We have received the following letter from Pte W N Smith, who is with the Thame Territorials at the Front.

British Expeditionary Force
Monday, June 13th

It must be almost two months since I last wrote, so perhaps a few more notes on the doings of the 4th Oxford's may be interesting. At that time we had just taken over trenches in a large dense wood, which we held till a week back; then we had a few days so called "rest" change of work would be a better description and three days ago came into a new line of trenches from which I am now writing. The writer of an article in a large 'daily' has pointed out that the wood we were holding played a leading part in the opening months of the war, changing hands several times before being finally taken by our troops. Many grim reminders of the severity of the fighting are to be seen: dotted singly and in groups all through the wood are large numbers of those little mounds which mark the resting place of gallant men. Thanks to the care bestowed by the troops who have held the woods most of the graves are well kept up, railed off and with a neat cross. We have ourselves whilst extending the trenches found poor fellows who had, no doubt been hastily covered over, and have done our best to mark where they lie. Caved in trenches and dugouts, ruins of houses and shell shattered trees all speak of those days. Times are pretty lively in the wood and one must accept as inevitable an ever increasing list of casualties which has risen from three to near fifty; among the fatalities was Lieut Herman Hodge (son of a former MP for our division), killed whilst sniping. Almost daily some part of the wood is shelled and a village on the edge of it has been much knocked about; the church and civic hospital are complete ruins and almost every house shows signs of bombardment. We have had several 'stack ups' and on the night when the battle for a now famous hill (it is no longer a hill) was raging, we were on for hours giving the 'Huns' rapid fire, whilst our artillery was also going strong; in retaliation, hails of bullets and grenades came back, and we quite expected to get the order to go over the parapet at daybreak. While the fight was on it was a continuous roar of thunder-like magnitude. Many nights we have been fetched to the parapet as signs of activity had been observed in the enemy trenches some 100 yards away. Two days before we left the wood we were shelled and I have two bits of shrapnel which came through our tent and fell close by my side; that morning our rear guard had a close shave when a shell fell within 2 yards of the sentry and failed to explode; of 40 shells which fell nearly all exploded but with this exception. Our time was divided between the firing line and the supports and we have had a pretty good dose of sand bagging and other fatigue work. Well shall I remember where a ration fatigue was going up to the firing trenches, a Maxim got on us; the opening shots whizzing over warned us to get prone and then a hail of bullets swept up and down our line striking the earth a few yards on our far-side and well, here we are. Two Thame lads have had bits of 'nerves'; whilst reading and leaning against a post a bullet nearly missed Billy Ladbrook and shattered the post over his head, and Pte R Eaton (Paddy) had a piece of cloth taken from his tunic's sleeve by a shrapnel bullet. After seven weeks in this wood we had four days doing drill etc. near a large town, where for the first time since I left England, had a wander round and had a chat to some of the folk. The three days we have been in these trenches nothing much has happened; this morning an attempt was made to blow up a portion of the trench to our right, but the enemy miscalculated the distance; the report and the explosion shook the trench and brought us quickly to the parapet ready for an emergency. The trenches are very massive as we are subject to a cross fire, bullets coming over from three directions. The weather has been most summer like, a while in the wood the mosquitoes were a great annoyance; now we are free from this pest and have dropped our 'Gott staffe mosquito' cry. All the Thame lads were extremely sorry to hear that Sergt W E Roberts had been killed in action, the Gazette with the news came last Friday.

With kindest regards Wm N Smith

Extract from the Thame Gazette 22nd June 1915

1 July 1916

Francis Willoughby Fielding was born in Towersey, Buckinghamshire on 8th October 1892 to Harry Fielding and Letitia Elizabeth (née Goodwin). Harry was an auctioneer and in 1911 the family were living at Essex House, Chinnor Road, Thame. They later moved to Stoneleigh in Kings Road, Thame. Francis attended Lord Williams's Grammar School and by 1911 had moved to Coventry to begin work in the fledgling motor industry as a draughtsman. He had volunteered for the Queen's Own Oxfordshire Hussars (QOOH formerly the Oxfordshire Yeomanry) during 1909 (Regt No 1522). They were mobilised at the outbreak of World War One and he travelled to France with the Regiment in September 1914, being the first Territorial unit to do so and the first to see action. The Regiment was involved in the doomed attempts to save Dunkirk and Antwerp from the German advance and then fell into the routine of trench warfare, holding the line at Messines. At some time during this early stage of the war Francis, by now a Corporal, was wounded by an exploding shell while carrying despatches and invalided back to England.

Commissioned with the rank of 2nd Lieutenant in April 1915, he returned to the Western Front with the 9th Battalion (Queen Victoria's Rifles) London Regiment. On 1st July 1916 the Battalion was one of the lead units in the attack at Gommecourt, a diversionary attack as part of the main Somme offensive. Unfortunately the Germans had too much warning and the Battalion suffered heavy losses, with Francis, age 23, being among them.

Second Lieutenant Francis Willoughby Fielding, London Regiment, is buried in Gommecourt British Cemetery No 2, Somme. He is remembered in Thame on the War Memorial and on the Memorial Boards of St Mary's Church, All Saints' Church and Lord Williams's School..

The Thame Remembers Cross was placed at his grave on 18th April 2015 by Michael Hutson of Thame Remembers.

14 July 1916

George Miller was born in Haddenham, Buckinghamshire in the summer of 1888, the second son of George and Lizzie Miller of Victoria Villas. Whilst his father was a shepherd and agricultural labourer, George became a threshing engine driver.

In January 1915 George enlisted in the Royal Engineers at the recruiting offices in Cockspur Street, London. His pre-war experience of driving engines enabled him to be given a 'skilled' classification and assigned to the 126th Field Company, with the 21st Division. The next few months were spent in camps, training in and around the Halton House estate near Wendover in Buckinghamshire.

On 5th September 1915 George married Beatrice Louisa Coxhill at St Mary's Church in Thame and on 11th September he was with the 126th Field Company when they left Milford Camp in Surrey for Southampton docks. There they embarked for France, landing at Le Havre the following day.

At the end of September, supporting the 64th Brigade, the Company was soon engaged in the Battle of Loos. They then spent the next few months in a relatively quiet part of the Front in northern France. In March 1916 they moved down to the Somme area, undertaking work to support fire trenches and front line trenches in preparation for the battle to come.

The war diary of the 126th Field Company indicates that they were in action from the first day of the Battle of the Somme, constructing strong points and consolidating positions gained by the infantry. On 14th July George, age 28, was one of five sappers posted missing in Bazentin Le-Petit Wood, where the 21st Division were heavily engaged in the Battle for Bazentin Ridge.

His body was never found and it was not until February 1917 that his wife Beatrice, who was living in Lashlake Villa, Aylesbury Road, Thame, received official notification of his presumed death and was awarded a pension of ten shillings per week. A month later Beatrice received a letter of sympathy from the King and Queen and in 1919 was awarded his war gratuity of £6.

65336 Sapper George Miller, Royal Engineers, has no known grave and is commemorated on Thiepval Memorial to the Missing of the Somme. He is remembered in Thame on the War Memorial and All Saints' Church Memorial Board. He is also commemorated on the War Memorial in Haddenham.

The Thame Remembers Cross was placed at Thiepval Memorial on 31st October 2015 by Thame residents, Linda Emery and Helena Fickling.

20 July 1916

John Boxell Shaw was born in Hammersmith, London in 1892 and was one of four children to Frederick Augustus Shaw and Susannah (née Moreton). Upon the death of his mother in 1897, he and his sister Florence were fostered by the postmistress in Cuddington, Buckinghamshire. Later he was living in Chinnor Road, Thame, his grandfather having been born in Thame.

He enlisted at Oxford with the Royal Welsh Fusiliers at the age of 17, his regimental number indicates that this would have been sometime in 1909. Initially posted with the 2nd Battalion, he would have served with them in Schwebo, Burma and Quetta, India (now Pakistan). The Battalion returned to England in early 1914, before embarking for France in August. He was awarded the 1914 Star and a 1915 Clasp. These were handed to his great nephew in 1982.

John was wounded during the Battle of Armentières in October 1914, in what is commonly known as the Race to the Sea and evacuated to England to the 2nd Northern General Hospital in Leeds, Yorkshire. After recovery and a spell at the infantry base depot, he was posted to the 10th (Service) Battalion. The Battalion mobilised for war and landed at Boulogne at the end of September 1915. While serving with the 76th Brigade of the 3rd Division, the Battalion was engaged in various actions in the Ypres Salient during 1915/16, before moving through northern France down to the Somme area in June 1916. Although not involved in the initial attacks in the Battle of the Somme, the Battalion took part in an ill-fated night attack on Delville Wood on 20th July 1916 in support of the South African Brigade. The Battalion won two Victoria Crosses but they suffered heavy casualties, including John, age 24, who was killed in action whilst serving with D Company.

9983 Private John Boxell Shaw, Royal Welsh Fusiliers, is buried in the Delville Wood Cemetery, Longueval. He is remembered in Thame on the War Memorial and on the Memorial Boards of St Mary's Church and All Saints' Church.

The Thame Remembers Cross was placed at his grave on 18th April 2015 by David Bretherton of Thame Remembers.

22 July 1916

Sidney Augustus Shrimpton was born in the parish of St Olave, Southwark, London on 16th January 1890. His mother was Emily Shrimpton from Long Crendon, Buckinghamshire but his father is not known. He returned with his mother to Long Crendon in 1891 where he was baptised on 24th March. They lived with her parents in the Post Office in the High Street, next to the Eight Bells public house. When his mother married John W Hinton in 1892, she moved a few doors away, leaving Sidney to be brought up with his grandparents.

In September 1910 it was announced in the London Gazette that Sidney had been appointed a postman in Thame. In 1911 he was boarding at 62 High Street, Thame with Lawrence Webster, also a town postman.

In early 1916 Sidney enlisted at Thame in the Royal Fusiliers (Regt No SPTS/4700). He initially joined the 30th (Reserve) Battalion who were at that time based at Oxford. This was a reserve battalion for the 23rd and 24th (Sportsmans) Battalions. However, Sidney was posted to the Western Front with the 9th Battalion. On 22nd July 1916 the Battalion was at Mailly-Maillet, near Beaumont-Hamel, Somme. Sidney, age 26, was one of several casualties sustained by the Battalion, due to shelling during the night

G/4700 Private Sidney Augustus Shrimpton, Royal Fusiliers, has no known grave and is commemorated on Thiepval Memorial to the Missing of the Somme. He is also commemorated on the War Memorial in Long Crendon.

The Thame Remembers Cross was placed at Thiepval Memorial on 31st October 2015 by Thame residents, Linda Emery and Helena Fickling.

24 July 1916

John Howlett was the son of John and Hannah Howlett of 15 Park Street, Thame. He was born in 1889, the youngest of seven children, he had three brothers and three sisters. After a short spell with the local Territorial Force, the Queen's Own Oxfordshire Hussars, he enlisted with the Royal Engineers in 1907. He obtained trade proficiency as a 'skilled', and then later, 'superior' painter and in 1910 he was transferred to the Reserve strength. His service records show that he was *"of very good character and very trustworthy and reliable."*

At the outbreak of war he was mobilised at Chatham, Kent and went to France with the British Expeditionary Force on 28th August with the 9th Field Company, Royal Engineers (RE). They were attached to the 4th Division and took part in various actions in northern France during the autumn of 1914. At the end of April 1915, the Company moved up into Belgium in support of the Division during the Second Battle of Ypres. They sustained a number of casualties in early May in Potizje Wood. John was one of the wounded, but as his wounds were only slight he was able to remain in the field with his unit. A few days later he was appointed Acting Lance Corporal. He was wounded in action for a second time in June, but again remained with his unit.

By the autumn of 1915, the 4th Division had returned to the Somme area of France. Over the next few months and throughout the spring of 1916 the 9th RE Field Company carried out various works associated with the construction and maintenance of the trench systems.

Although the Division was engaged on the Somme from the first day of the Battle and suffered heavy casualties, the 9th Company, working mainly in support repairing and constructing new trenches, incurred only a small number of casualties.

Unfortunately John, by then a full Corporal was one of them, receiving severe head and leg wounds on 16th July 1916. He was evacuated to No 6 General Hospital, Rouen, where he finally succumbed to his wounds, dying on 24th July, age 27 years.

As a result of his actions on 16th July he was awarded the Distinguished Conduct Medal. The citation, announced in the London Gazette on 22nd September 1916 reads, "*16774 L/Cpl (Acting Cpl) J Howlett, RE. For conspicuous gallantry and devotion to duty when in charge of a working party. A shell burst among them causing many casualties. Cpl Howlett's leg was broken and he received other very severe wounds he nevertheless continued to control his party*".

16774 Corporal John Howlett DCM, Royal Engineers, is buried in St Sever Cemetery, Rouen. He is remembered in Thame on the War Memorial and All Saints' Church Memorial Board.

The Thame Remembers Cross was placed at his grave on 5th May 2016 by Thame Museum member, Pauline Woods.

4 August 1916

Noel Alexander Target was born on 23rd November 1895 in London. He was the son of Felix Alexander Target MICE, Civil Engineer, Indian Public Works Department, who was living in Donnington, Pinner, Middlesex with his wife Nita (née Chilton.)

Noel was educated at Lord Williams's Grammar School, Thame between 1906 and 1909 and Haileybury College, Hertford. He played Rugby for Clifton Rugby Club in Bristol in the 1913/1914 season.

His career was originally aimed at the Indian Police but on the outbreak of World War One he joined the Army, being commissioned into the Durham Light Infantry as a Temporary 2nd Lieutenant on 22nd September 1914. He was promoted to Temporary Lieutenant in March 1915, although it was not until 25th November 1915 that he joined the 13th Battalion at Hallobeau in northern France. He received a regular commission as 2nd Lieutenant (Acting Lieutenant) in May 1916. On 3rd June 1916 the Battalion was deployed in trenches at Souchez, a few miles north of Arras. Noel, together with a fellow officer, led a raiding party on a German trench for which he was awarded the Military Cross. The citation published in the London Gazette reads *"For conspicuous gallantry. Lieuts Clark and Target led a successful raid on the enemy's trenches. At least twelve of the enemy were accounted for and five deep occupied dug-outs were bombed. Owing to the skill and rapidity of action there were only three slight casualties in their party."*

Towards the end of June, the Battalion, part of the 68th Infantry Brigade, with the 23rd Division, entrained for the Somme, to prepare for the battle to come. They were engaged for the first time on 8th July during the Battle of Albert, the Battalion war diaries once again note Lieutenant Target leading a patrol into the German trenches.

A few weeks later on the night of 4th/5th August, Noel, age 20 years, was killed in action during the Battle of Pozières. He was ordered to lead a bombing assault, with men from C Company, through Munster Alley to get around a German block in "Munster" trench. The attack failed and Noel and most of his men were killed by heavy machine gun fire.

The Brigadier-General later wrote *"I always regarded him as a promising officer and he proved his gallantry on many occasions; his loss will be felt very much in his Regiment, where he was admired by all ranks. In all the strenuous fighting in which we were engaged, he, by his cool daring, shone amongst the many brave men associated with him. He was buried in the trench he gave his life to hold."*

Second Lieutenant Noel Alexander Target MC, Durham Light Infantry, has no known grave and is commemorated on Thiepval Memorial to the Missing of the Somme. He is remembered in Thame on Lord Williams's School Memorial Board and is also commemorated on Clifton Rugby Club Roll of Honour, Bristol.

The Thame Remembers Cross was placed at Thiepval Memorial on 31st October 2015 by Thame residents, Linda Emery and Helena Fickling.

A framed Thame Remembers delivery report was presented to Clifton RFC on 21st November 2015 prior to the match at Thame between Chinnor RFC and Clifton RFC.

In accordance with 68th Brigade Operations Order No. 58, Lts D H Clarke and N A Target and a party of 23 men raided the enemy trench at M.32.D.O.2½. At 1 a.m. Divisional Artillery opened an intense bombardment on the enemy front line and the raiding party left our trench. At one minute past one the artillery lifted on the enemy supports and the raiding party climbed over the enemy parapet and into his trenches almost without being detected.

The attacking party consisting of Lts Clarke and Target, one bayonet man, and 3 bombers, then turned to the left and worked about 40 yards up the trench. On that time seven Germans were disposed of in the trench, three being bayoneted and two shot while the remaining two were pushed down dugouts and bombs thrown in after them. After working about 30 yards up the trench, the attacking party came to a sap on the left into which a bomb was thrown, whereupon a German rushed out, then apparently realising a raid was in progress, he turned back and got his rifle. He then rushed towards the attacking party and fired his rifle, but was at once shot. The party threw about 12 bombs into two deep dugouts.

By this time the first blocking party had worked about 40 yards up to the right of the point of entry and had attempted to erect a barricade. Two Germans were bayoneted in the trench in the act of coming out of dugouts. Four deep dugouts were successfully bombed with about 45 bombs by this party. After erecting the barricade this blocking party bombed the trench beyond. The second blocking party remained at the point of entry and ensured the safe withdrawal of the raiding party: the sergeant in charge shooting one German.

Owing to the wire having been cut so successfully by the 60lb trench [mortar] at 7.30 p.m., the wiring party of two men specially detailed to widen the breach in the enemy [wire] in order to facilitate the return of the raiding party had relatively little to do.

The time spent in the enemy trench was about 9½ minutes and the withdrawal was carried out without any trouble from machine guns or rifle fire, which was largely due to the excellent traversing of the enemy's parapet on our flanks by our Lewis guns.

Our total casualties were 3 O.R. wounded.

Our intense bombardment of one minute drove the enemy into their dugouts, thus facilitating a surprise. Enemy trenches were particularly good. All the dugouts were very deep, well constructed, and lit by electric light.

13th Battalion Durham Light Infantry War Diary entry for 3rd June 1916

24 August 1916

John Clare Hoadley was born in Port of Spain, Trinidad, West Indies in 1895 and was one of five children of John and Miriam Elizabeth Hoadley. He boarded at Lord Williams's Grammar School, Thame from 1906 to 1911. By this time his father had died and the family were living in Ealing, Middlesex. In June 1914 he was appointed as an examiner in the Exchequer and Audit Department office in London, with a salary of £100 per annum.

John joined the Royal Engineers in 1915. His regimental number was one of those allocated to the new Special Companies being set up for chemical warfare. He was posted to France on 13th July 1915 and this would likely have been to the Depot at Helfaut, where the first two companies, the 186th and 187th were being formed. In early 1916 the Special Companies were reorganised into the Special Brigade and John, with the rank of Chemical Corporal, was enrolled into the 1st Battalion which handled gas discharge from cylinders.

By the end of May the Battalion was allocated to the Fourth Army, the primary British Army for the Battle of the Somme. On 24th August 1916, in the northern sector of the battlefield, John and a colleague were going up the trenches to superintend some work when John was killed instantly on the bursting of a German shell. He was one of a number from the Battalion killed that day. All are buried, alongside each other, in Sailly-au-Bois Cemetery, Pas de Calais. He was 21 years old and in his will he left over £293. His sister Elsie Margaret Hoadley was named as the administrator.

106153 Chemical Corporal John Clare Hoadley, Royal Engineers, is commemorated on the Port of Spain Cenotaph, Trinidad and on the Memorial Board of the Exchequer and Audit Department in London. He is remembered in Thame on Lord Williams's School Memorial Board, alongside his younger brother William Cecil Hoadley, another former pupil of the school, killed in 1918 whilst serving in the Royal Navy.

The Thame Remembers Cross was placed at his grave on 12th May 2015 by Thame resident, Neil Davies.

30 August 1916

Harry John Shrimpton was one of four sons of Joshua and Mary Shrimpton living at East Street, Thame. He was born in 1882, but it was not until July 1909 that he was baptised in Lewknor, at the age of 27. This was probably in preparation for his marriage to Gladys Gwendoline Smith a few weeks later on 2nd August. They moved to 66 Park Street, Thame where they had three children, Constance Gwendoline, Douglas Henry and Edward.

As a former member of the local territorial Queen's Own Oxfordshire Hussars, retiring with the rank of Corporal, when the National Reserve was started in Thame, he became one of its first members and volunteered for general service. At the outbreak of the war, he went with several other Thame reservists and enlisted in the Oxford and Bucks Light Infantry, initially posted to the 3rd (Reserve) Battalion. On 7th July 1915 Harry, having recently been promoted to Corporal, entrained for the Front to join the 5th Battalion, part of the 14th Division, 42nd Brigade, who were operating in trenches near the Hooge in Belgium. In the autumn of 1915, it was reported that as a result of the Battalion's action at Bellewaarde Farm on 26th September, he was recommended for the Distinguished Conduct Medal, and received congratulations from Major-General V Couper, Commander of the 14th Division, on "*his gallant and meritorious conduct.*" No record has been found that this was formally ratified and awarded. It was this action that probably also contributed to Harry's promotion to Sergeant in October 1915.

Over the next few months the Battalion carried out various duties in trenches in northern France, interspersed with spells of rest and training, before moving down to the Somme in August 1916, where, on the 24th, they formed part of the attack on Delville Wood. Harry was one of the many casualties, receiving a gunshot wound to the chest. He was evacuated to hospital at Rouen where he died of his wound on 30th August 1916. He was 34 years old.

8862 Sergeant Harry John Shrimpton, Oxford and Bucks Light Infantry, is buried in St Sever Cemetery, Rouen. He is remembered in Thame on the War Memorial and on the Memorial Boards of St Mary's Church, All Saints' Church and Christchurch.

The Thame Remembers Cross was placed at his grave on 30th August 2016 by Thame residents, Nick and Hilly Carter.

Just over 100 years ago, Harry Shrimpton left our house in Park Street and boarded a troop ship for France. Having served with distinction for 15 months, he died of his wounds on 30th August 1916 after ferocious fighting at the Battle for Delville Wood. A century later, my wife Hilly and I left the same house and boarded the Dieppe ferry. And on the exact centenary of Harry's death, we were able to honour his memory in a simple ceremony at his grave in Rouen.

We are the current custodians of the Victorian terraced cottage in Thame where Harry, his wife Gladys and three young children lived before the Great War began. Nowadays, as we carry out our daily routines, it's easy to imagine our predecessors grouped around the fireplace or passing us on the stairs, or to glimpse a fleeting shadow through a doorway. And we can picture the scene as Harry gives his wife Gladys a farewell hug on the doorstep in Park Street, before he entrains with the Oxford and Bucks Light Infantry. Would he have had a last couple of pints on the previous evening at the Wenman Arms next door, or the Four Horseshoes opposite the house? Neither of these names exist now, but they would have been his local pubs back in the day.

It became important for Hilly and me to say our personal thanks to Harry for his selfless heroism and ultimate sacrifice. We made the commemorative trip accompanied by our dear friend Mike Dyer, one of the organisers of the unique Thame Remembers Project. This nationally recognised project is Mike's passion and he did a lot of research before our trip. He talked us through the Battle of Bellewaarde Farm, near Ypres, where Harry had been recommended for a medal. And in the manner of a war historian, Mike gave us a detailed account of the bloody struggle to take over Delville Wood, in which Harry, newly promoted to Sergeant, had been mortally wounded at the age of 34.

Despite the company of such an experienced visitor to France's war cemeteries, nothing really prepares the novice for the sight of 12,000 white headstones standing shoulder to shoulder as if in the serried ranks of a parade ground. Hilly and I stood open-mouthed as we took in the scene and contemplated our route through Rouen's beautiful St Sever cemetery to Harry's grave. In lovely late August weather, we were able to carry out our promise to the house where Harry and his family had once been happy. On the exact 100th anniversary of his death, we placed the Thame Remembers Cross in front of Harry's headstone, recited the 'Ode of Remembrance' in tribute and joined hands in heartfelt prayer. Thank you, Harry: for as long as our house stands and Thame exists, you will indeed be remembered.

Nick Carter

Nick's story of the delivery of a Thame Remembers Cross

31 August 1916

Harry Cooper Wilsdon was born in Thame in 1898 and baptised at St Mary's Church on 26th June 1898 at the same time as his brother George 9 and sisters, Elizabeth Mary 8, Nellie 6 and Elsie Harriet 3. They were all the children of Robert Thomas, a carpenter, and his wife Harriet. Robert had married Harriet Lemming at St Mary's Church, Thame on 25th September 1878 but by 1901 the family were living in Southall, Middlesex.

Harry enlisted at Hounslow with the Middlesex Regiment (Duke of Cambridge's Own) in early June of 1915, but must have lied about his age, as he had only just reached 17 years of age. However, this was not an uncommon occurrence at that stage of the war when the rate of volunteers was waning and the army was desperate for recruits. Harry was posted to the 14th Battalion, which was a reserve and training battalion. He then left for France on 6th October, joining the 13th Battalion as part of a reinforcing draft to make up for losses sustained by the Battalion in the Battle of Loos at the end of September.

The Battalion, part of the 76th Brigade, 24th Division, spent the autumn/winter months of 1915/16 in northern France and Belgium. At the end of April 1916 the they suffered heavy casualties from the German gas attack at Wulverghem, near Messines in West Flanders.

The Battalion entrained down to the Somme at the end of July and lost many men in attacks on trenches near Guillemont in the middle of August. On 31st August 1916 they had moved into trenches at Mametz when a German attack was launched. It was during this attack that Harry was killed at only 18 years old.

G/13020 Private Harry Cooper Wilsdon, Middlesex Regiment, has no known grave and is commemorated on Thiepval Memorial to the Missing of the Somme. He is also commemorated on St John's Church Memorial in Southall, Middlesex and his name is to be added to Thame War Memorial.

The Thame Remembers Cross was placed at Thiepval Memorial on 31st October 2015 by Thame residents, Linda Emery and Helena Fickling.

3 September 1916

Henry Claude Bernard was born on 31st October 1893 and was the eldest son of Dr Claude and Florrie Bernard who lived at 1 Spencer Terrace, Fishponds, Bristol. He was a great nephew of cricket legend W G Grace.

He was Head Boy at Lord Williams's Grammar School, Thame and went on to study mathematics at St John's College, Cambridge, where he was in the Officer Training Corps. He received a General List commission as a Temporary Second Lieutenant on 1st September 1914 and posted for duty with the 7th (Service) Battalion, Gloucestershire Regiment.

The Battalion, part of the 13th (Western) Division, left England for the Mediterranean area on 7th June 1915 and landed at Y Beach, Gallipoli, Turkey on 11th July. Henry was wounded by shrapnel in the right shoulder on 8th August when the Battalion was in an attacking line supporting the New Zealanders at the Battle of Chunuk Bair. The Battalion war diary says "... *Every officer and every CSM and CQM Sgts, were either killed or wounded and the Btn consisted of groups of men being commanded by junior NCO's or Privates*". He was evacuated to 19 General Hospital, Alexandria, Egypt and after a period of convalescence, he rejoined the Battalion in November. However, after only a few days, he was returned to hospital in Alexandria suffering from severe enteric. In early February 1916 he left Alexandria on HS Neuralia, landing in Southampton on 19th February. He was admitted to the 3rd Southern General Hospital in Oxford with paratyphoid which he had contracted whilst in Gallipoli. He reported back for duty with the 11th (Reserve) Battalion, Gloucestershire Regiment at South Camp, Seaford, East Sussex on 9th May, but was not pronounced fit for active service until 7th June. The 7th Glosters were by this time serving in Mesopatamia, [now mostly Iraq] so Henry, together with two other officers from the Glosters, was posted to France to be attached to the 3rd Battalion Worcestershire Regiment, serving in the 7th Infantry Brigade of the 25th Division.

This Battalion was heavily engaged in various actions during the Battle of the Somme and Henry, age 25, was killed on 3rd September 1916 in the attack on Thiepval Ridge in the Leipzig Salient. His two fellow officers from the Glosters also lost their lives in the same action. In his will he left an estate valued at almost £6800.

Second Lieutenant Henry Claude Bernard, Worcestershire Regiment, has no known grave and is commemorated on Thiepval Memorial to the Missing of the Somme. He is remembered in Thame on Lord Williams's School Memorial Board.

The Thame Remembers Cross was placed at Thiepval Memorial on 31st October 2015 by Thame residents, Linda Emery and Helena Fickling.

3 September 1916

Frederick James Goodman was one of eleven children of William and Esther Goodman of Back Lane, Chipping Norton, Oxfordshire. He was born about 1878 and in 1901 he was lodging in Thame where he worked as a rope maker for Messrs Putman and Sons in the Cornmarket. He married Ellen Carter White, a widow, at St Mary's Church, Thame on 20th September 1902 and their son Charles Frederick was born at 15 Southern Road, Thame on 14th September 1903. Prior to the war he was working as a tent maker and they were living in Summertown, Oxford with their two children, Charles and Ivy, and stepson Henry.

He enlisted in Oxford with the Oxford and Bucks Light Infantry in September 1914 and was posted to the newly formed 6th Battalion, part of Kitchener's New Army (K2). The Battalion moved to Aldershot, Hampshire to join the 60th Brigade of the 20th Division and then in March 1915 moved to Lark Hill Camp on Salisbury Plain, Wiltshire.

On 22nd July 1915 the Battalion crossed from Folkestone to Boulogne on the South Eastern and Chatham Railway packet steamer "Queen". After trench familiarisation and training, they spent a very miserable winter in wet and muddy trenches and then, in 1916, were engaged in various actions on the Western Front, including Mount Sorrel, near Ypres and Delville Wood on the Somme.

The 20th Division received orders to attack Guillemont on 3rd September. The 60th Brigade, originally intended to play a major role in the battle but was so depleted it was withdrawn and the 6th Oxford and Bucks, being the only Battalion of the Brigade left with any strength, was temporarily assigned to the 59th Brigade. By the end of the first day of the Battle, the Battalion had lost almost 300 officers and men, mostly from shell and machine gun fire. Frederick, fighting with D Company, was among the casualties. He was 38 years old.

15728 Private Frederick James Goodman, Oxford and Bucks Light Infantry, has no known grave and is commemorated on Thiepval Memorial to the Missing of the Somme. He is also commemorated on the War Memorial in Summertown, Oxford.

The Thame Remembers Cross was placed at Thiepval Memorial on 31st October 2015 by Thame residents, Linda Emery and Helena Fickling.

The Thame Remembers group at Thiepval Memorial which was shrouded in scaffolding for our visit.

3 September 1916

Roland Arthur Pullen was born in Long Crendon, Buckinghamshire in 1898 but by 1901 the family were living in Moreton near Thame. His parents were Charles Philip Pullen and Rose (née Hinton). Roland had three younger brothers, Harold, Charles and Herbert. In 1911 Roland, age 13, was working as a butcher's errand boy in Moreton.

Roland was living in Kilburn, London when he enlisted for service at St Pancras with the Rifle Brigade on 12th July 1915, giving his age as 19 years and trade as a butcher. After his training, Roland went to France on 15th April 1916 to join the 16th Battalion of the Rifle Brigade who had landed in France the previous month. The Battalion, serving with the 117th Brigade, 39th Division remained in trenches in northern France until mid-August when they moved down to the Somme area. On 3rd September the Battalion took part in an attack north of the River Ancre and sustained over 450 casualties with over 200 killed or missing. Roland was one of those killed and was buried in the Royal Naval Division Cemetery between Beaumont-Hamel and Hamel. He was 18 years old and his back pay of £8 10s and war gratuity of £4 was paid to his father Charles in Moreton. In October 1919 the cemetery was closed and his body, together with many of his comrades, was reinterred by the Commonwealth War Graves Commission.

P/1573 Rifleman Roland Arthur Pullen, Rifle Brigade, is buried in Ancre British Cemetery, Beaumont-Hamel, Somme. He is remembered in Thame on both Thame and Moreton War Memorials and on the Memorial Board of All Saints' Church.

The Thame Remembers Cross was placed at his grave on 31st October 2015 by Thame Museum member, Peter Gulland.

9 September 1916

Clifford Bert Bateman was born in Thame on 1st September 1893 and baptised at St Mary's Church on 5th October. He was one of the four children of Alfred Bateman and Eliza (née Chowns) living at 44 Wellington Street. In 1911 Clifford was a bill sticker, but in 1912 he enlisted with the Oxford and Bucks Light Infantry (Regt No 9632) and was posted to the 2nd Battalion.

The Battalion, as part of the 5th Infantry Brigade, 2nd Division, was one of the first divisions of the British Expeditionary Force to arrive in France in August 1914 and took part in the first British battle of the war at Mons and subsequent battles on the Marne and Ypres. This was followed in 1915 with action in the battles at Festubert and Loos.

In 1915 Clifford was in one of the Battalion machine gun sections, each consisting of four guns. On 1st January 1916 the machine gun sections of all four battalions of the 5th Brigade, were amalgamated and transferred to form the 5th Machine Gun Company. The Company was equipped with Vickers machine guns. Clifford was later transferred to the 48th Machine Gun Company and posted in April 1916 to serve with the 48th Brigade, 16th (Irish) Division. By then a Corporal, he would probably have been leading one of the gun detachments.

The 48th Machine Gun Corps were in trenches around Loos and Hulluch in northern France for most of the summer of 1916, moving down to the Somme at the end of August. On 9th September 1916, whilst taking part in the Battle of Ginchy, one of the battles of the Somme, Clifford was killed in action a few days after his 23rd birthday.

16008 Corporal Clifford Bert Bateman, Machine Gun Corps, has no known grave and is commemorated on Thiepval Memorial to the Missing of the Somme. He is remembered in Thame on the War Memorial and on the Memorial Boards of St Mary's Church and All Saints' Church.

The Thame Remembers Cross was placed at Thiepval Memorial on 31st October 2015 by Thame residents, Linda Emery and Helena Fickling.

9 September 1916

Oscar Tyrrell was born on 22nd May 1880 at 8 Rymer Street, Herne Hill, London to Abraham Oscar Tyrrell, a butcher, and Clementine Louisa (née Parrish). He had one sister Amy, who was two years older than him. In 1891 he was a pupil at Taplow Grammar School, Buckinghamshire and then went to Margate College, Kent. In 1911 he was was an unmarried auctioneer's clerk living at 35 Queens Street, Hammersmith, Middlesex. When Oscar joined up on 9th August 1915 he gave his address as 12 St Pauls Mansions, Hammersmith and his profession as a surveyor.

Oscar was granted a commission on 12th August as a Second Lieutenant and joined the 3/10th London Regiment, a training and reserve battalion based at Tadworth Camp, near Epsom, Surrey. He then joined the 1/10th Battalion in Egypt as a bomb instructor, where he was wounded in the premature explosion of a bomb and invalided back to England. After recovering, rather than being sent back to the 10th Battalion, now in Palestine, he was posted to the 1/12th Battalion which had lost a number of officers on the first day of the Battle of the Somme. He joined them at Sailly on 7th August 1916 and was posted "missing in action" on 9th September at the Battle of Ginchy, probably in an area known as the "Quadrilateral". He was 36 years old.

Second Lieutenant Oscar Tyrrell, London Regiment, has no known grave and is commemorated on Thiepval Memorial to the Missing of the Somme. He is remembered in Thame on his sister Amy's grave in St Mary's churchyard.

The Thame Remembers Cross was placed at Thiepval Memorial on 31st October 2015 by Thame residents, Linda Emery and Helena Fickling.

15 September 1916

Douglas Viney Lidington was born in Thame in 1879, the youngest of six children of William Lidington and Joanna (née Mather). At his baptism at St Mary's Church, Thame on 21st April 1879, his parents were described as licensed victuallers and in 1881 they were at the Spread Eagle Hotel in Thame, where his father was the hotel keeper. His brothers, Brighton Webster and William Richard also served in the First World War and survived.

Douglas listed himself as a butcher when he married Gertrude Emilie Adams at Warwick Parish Church on 6th March 1902. They later lived at 4 Adam Street, London.

He served with the 9th Battalion of the Norfolk Regiment. The Battalion was established in September 1914 part of Kitchener's New Army and eventually went to France in August 1915 serving with the 71st Brigade of the 6th Division. The Battalion spent the majority of 1916 in trenches in northern France and around the Ypres Salient, before moving down to the Somme in late summer.

The Battalion took part in the latter, 'successful', stages of the Battle of the Somme. Douglas, age 37, was killed on 15th September 1916 the first day of the Battle of Flers-Courcelette. The attack was launched at 07:30hrs from trenches in Trones Wood, the objective being the "Quadrilateral". Douglas was one of 450 casualties suffered by the Battalion that day, mostly cut down by machine gun fire. According to a letter received by his wife from his Platoon Commander, 2nd Lieutenant R A Jones, *"he was killed instantly by a bullet to his head."*

16335 Private Douglas Viney Lidington, Norfolk Regiment, has no known grave and is commemorated on Thiepval Memorial to the Missing of the Somme. He is remembered in Thame on the War Memorial and on the family gravestone in St Mary's churchyard.

The Thame Remembers Cross was placed at Thiepval Memorial on 31st October 2015 by Thame residents, Linda Emery and Helena Fickling.

LATE PTE. D. V LIDINGTON

We briefly referred last week to the death of Pte D V Lidington who was killed in action on September 15th, since then his wife has received the following letter from his commanding officer:

Dear Madam,--In reply to your enquiries of October 2nd, concerning your husband, I deeply regret to have to inform you that he was killed in action on the 15th September. I should have informed you before, but as I was the only officer left in the company when we came out of action, and as the battalion has had scarcely any rest since the 15th, you will understand that I have had little or no time for writing to the relatives of the many poor fellows who fell on that day. Of the actual circumstances of your husband's death I can give you little information, as I was not near him at the time, and unfortunately, the peculiar reticence which is a characteristic of the Norfolk man, does not enable me to glean any details. It may, however, console you in some small measure to know that his death, which was caused by a rifle bullet in the head, was painless and instantaneous. For many months your husband was in my platoon, and during that time I always found him a most willing and cheerful worker and a man in whom I could always place the utmost trust. His quiet, reserved manner, his marked ability and his gentlemanly character, singled him out as a man above the average. These qualities too gained for him alike the respect of his NCOs and of his fellow men. He always ungrudgingly bore his share of the hard toil of which life out here is made up, and when others grumbled he bore his discomfort like a man and a soldier. His platoon Sergt. would, I am sure, bear out all my remarks but he too, poor fellow, died of wounds received on the same day. By his death the battalion is left poorer by the loss of a good soldier who died as he would have wished, gallantly doing his duty. May I express my sincerest sympathy with you in the great loss you have sustained.—

I remain, dear Madam, yours very sincerely,
Robert A Jones, 2nd Lieutenant.-9th Norfolk,
B E F, Tuesday, October 10th, 1916.

Thame Gazette 28th October 1916

15 September 1916

Sidney Maskell Dicker was born in Brixton, London in October 1886. He and his sister May were brought up by their mother Louisa Dicker and uncle, Charles Maskell. Sidney married Dora Edith Jane Read, a Canadian from Halifax, Nova Scotia, at Lambeth Registry Office in October 1909. In 1911 they were living in Ballater Road, Brixton where Sidney was a stores dispatch clerk. They went to live in Grenfell Road, Mitcham, Surrey and had two children, Sidney Charles Maskell Dicker (b1910) and Muriel Ethel Dicker (b1914).

Sidney was only "*5ft 2ins tall* " when he enlisted into the 18th (Service) Battalion (Arts and Crafts), King's Royal Rifle Corps on 10th August 1915. The Battalion, under the orders of 122nd Brigade of the 41st Division, embarked for France on 2nd May 1916, landing at Le Havre. By the end of the month they were in trenches in the Ploegsteert Wood area of Flanders, part of the Ypres Salient, Belgium.

The Battalion entrained for the Somme at the end of August. On 15th September at 06:15hrs, they moved out of the trenches to attack the village of Flers, part of the Battle of Flers-Courcelette, which in itself was part of the Somme offensive. The Battalion suffered very heavy casualties on the first day of the battle losing over 350 men during the action. Sidney, age 29, was among them.

His wife and children moved to Thame shortly after his death, living at 46 Chinnor Road for a number of years. His son Sidney Charles Maskell Dicker went on to become a teacher, then a Captain in the Wiltshire Regiment. He was killed in Normandy in 1944.

C/6803 Rifleman Sidney Maskell Dicker, King's Royal Rifle Corps, is buried in Bulls Road Cemetery, Flers. He is remembered in Thame on the War Memorial and on the Memorial Boards of St Mary's Church and All Saints' Church.

The Thame Remembers Cross was placed at his grave on 18th April 2015
by Thame resident, Cliff Baker.

15 September 1916

Charles Dorsett Ward was the youngest of the six children of William Ward and Elizabeth (née Dorsett) and was born in Aylesbury, Buckinghamshire on 14th January 1891. His father was a hairdresser, but was later described as an accountant. Charles attended the National School in Aylesbury and in September 1902 moved to Lord Williams's Grammar School in Thame. In 1908, at only 17 years of age, he emigrated on the SS Kensington to Winnipeg, Canada where he went on to study law.

On 28th October 1914 he enlisted at Winnipeg with the Canadian Infantry and was posted to the newly formed 27th (City of Winnipeg) Battalion. Charles would have been with the Battalion, part of the 6th Infantry Brigade of the 2nd Canadian Division, when they left Quebec on 17th May 1915, sailing on the SS Carpathia landing in Plymouth on 29th May. (SS Carpathia was the ship that rescued survivors from the Titanic in 1912 and on 17th July 1918 was sunk by a torpedo from a U-boat), After several months spent training in Kent, the Battalion embarked for France, landing in Boulogne on 19th September and immediately entraining to Flanders in

Belgium. They remained in this area, spending long periods in the trenches, until early September 1916 when they entrained for the Somme.

On 14th September the Battalion moved into trenches in preparation for an attack the following day, the start of the Battle of Flers-Courcelette, in support of the Somme offensive. Attacking at zero hour of 06:20hrs, the Battalion went on to achieve most of its objectives and to take many prisoners. However, their losses were very high. By the time they were relieved on 17th September a total of 394 had been killed, wounded or were missing, including Charles, age 25, whose body was never recovered or identified.

71743 Corporal Charles Dorsett Ward, Canadian Infantry, has no known grave and is commemorated on Vimy Memorial near Arras. He is remembered in Thame on Lord Williams's School Memorial Board. He is also commemorated on a Memorial Plaque in the Methodist Church, Aylesbury.

The Thame Remembers Cross was placed at Vimy Memorial on 1st November 2015 by Thame resident, Alan Wylie.

30 September 1916

Christie West Fletcher was the seventh of nine children of Charles and Lucy Fletcher and was born in Kew, London on 12th December 1874 and baptised on 9th March 1876. His father was a member of the London Stock Exchange. He attended Lord Williams's Grammar School in Thame in 1891 as a sixth former and stayed for two years. Afterwards he travelled to India where he became an indigo planter for the Dholi Concern living at Mozufferpore, Tirhoot. While there he enlisted with the Bihar Light Horse (BLH), a volunteer cavalry regiment, based in northern India.

In the autumn of 1899, the Regiment volunteered half a squadron numbering 54 officers and men to join Lumsden's Horse, the name given to the Indian Mounted Infantry Corps. Christie was part of the squadron in A Company No 2 Section. They left Calcutta in February 1900 and took part in several actions against the Boers. The BLH contingent lost several men in an action at Karee Siding in Orange Free State, South Africa at the end of April.

On returning to India in January 1901 Christie received a commission with the Army Service Corps. His record with the Army Service Corps is unknown, but by 1908 Christie had returned to England where he married Louise Eveline Conway in Wandsworth, London in the summer of 1908. They had a daughter Lucy, born in January 1909. Later that year Christie, by now an electrical engineer, embarked on the SS Virginian to Canada, arriving in Quebec on 24th September, intending onward travel to Whonnock, British Columbia. His wife and daughter joined him in 1911 and they settled in Vancouver.

At the age of 40, he volunteered for the Canadian Expeditionary Force on 4th December 1914 and served as a Lance Corporal in the 2nd Battalion of the Canadian Mounted Rifles. The Battalion embarked for England on 12th June 1915. After a few months training at Shorncliffe in Kent, they disembarked in France on 22nd September 1915 as part of the 1st Canadian Mounted Rifles Brigade. The Battalion converted to infantry in January 1916, joining the 8th Infantry Brigade of the 3rd Canadian Division and fought in Belgium and France.

Christie, age 42, was killed on 30th September 1916, the day before the Battalion was due to attack the Ancre Heights on the Somme, a battle in which the Division would sustain almost 3,000 casualties.

107212 Lance Corporal Christie West Fletcher, Canadian Mounted Rifles, has no known grave and is commemorated on Vimy Memorial, Arras. He is remembered in Thame on Lord Williams's School Memorial Board.

The Thame Remembers Cross was placed at Vimy Memorial on 1st November 2015 by Thame resident, Alan Wylie.

25 October 1916

Albert Victor Young was born in Thame in 1883 to John Young and Caroline (née Newman) of the Four Horseshoes public house in Park Street. The youngest son of six children, Albert worked at the pub and was well known in the town. The family later moved to 5 Upper High Street, Thame.

In February 1902 Albert enlisted with the Royal Irish Rifles at Hounslow, Middlesex. According to his enlistment papers, he was at the time a serving member of the 7th Battalion Royal Fusiliers, a local militia in London. He was posted to India with the Royal Irish Rifles in November 1903, not returning until March 1910 when he was transferred to the Army Reserve.

As a National Reservist he re-enlisted, on the outbreak of hostilities, with the Oxford and Bucks Light Infantry (Regt No 10097). After a brief period of training he joined A Company, 2nd Battalion as part of a reinforcing draft at Dhuizel in northern France on 22nd September 1914. This was just in time to take part in the "Race to the Sea", followed by the First Battle of Ypres. On 27th November Albert was wounded in trenches near Bailleul and evacuated to a hospital in Lincoln.

After his recovery, just before Easter 1916, he was posted to the newly formed Machine Gun Corps (Infantry) and as part of a reinforcing draft, joined the 27th Machine Gun Company in France, serving with the 27th Brigade of the 9th (Scottish) Division.

In a letter home on 8th August, Albert describes the Company's involvement from 1st July on the Somme. Fighting in the southern sector with their Vickers machine guns, they were in regular engagement throughout the month, suffering heavy losses, but the Division steadily advanced as far as Delville Wood.

During October, the Battalion took part in the last major offensive on the Somme, the Battle of Le Transloy and on the morning of 25th October Albert, age 43, was killed by shellfire. It was reported at the time that he was buried with *"one of our own men who had fallen a few days before and with full respect and dignity"*, however, after the war his grave could not be identified.

30304 Lance Corporal Albert Victor Young, Machine Gun Corps, has no known grave and is commemorated on Thiepval Memorial to the Missing of the Somme. He is remembered in Thame on the War Memorial and on the Memorial Boards of St Mary's Church and All Saints' Church.

The Thame Remembers Cross was placed at Thiepval Memorial on 31st October 2015 by Thame residents, Linda Emery and Helena Fickling.

LETTER FROM THE FRONT.

We have received the following letter from Lance Corporal A V Young, of Thame, who is serving with a machine gun section in France: -

"Just a line to say I am all right and back once more from the ding-dong battle. We went into action on the 1st of July, and after seven days stiff fighting came back to the large guns for three days rest, went back again for another week, and then three days more rest and at it again for another week: so we had three weeks stiff fighting. We suffered heavily, but the Germans suffered double and more than us. Picked divisions were selected for this affair and our division was on the right and on the left of the French, so we had our hands full; and our division, which is composed of Scotch Regiments and South Africans, had a debt to pay for the battle of Loos last September, and well the Germans knew it when we got amongst them. This was the first experience for some of the South Africans in trench warfare, but they did themselves justice: they and the Gordon Highlanders at times fought themselves to a standstill. First you would see them chasing the Germans, and then the Germans chasing them; it was a ding-dong battle. I see fighting is going on at the same woods and village now, but we are gradually getting the upper hand of the Germans. There were times when the Colonels asked for relief, but the General said the position would have to be held at all costs, and bravely the division did it and repelled all counter-attacks until finally relieved by another division. I am not allowed to mention the names of regiments but I saw them all, and do not think any other Thameite would be in the advance in which I was in from July 1st to 27th. After two days march down we passed the Royal Fusiliers, in which Alf Howland is a Corporal; I did not see him, but I enquired and found his battalion was on the way up to the fighting. I also saw Arthur Rush "Brummy", in the 2nd Oxfords on their way in that direction; we passed them in a large town and just had five minutes chat with him. He was the only Thame man I have seen near the fighting. The Germans had some tremendous dug-outs built in the bank of a trench about 20 feet below ground and quite safe from shell-fire; they came in very handy for us as we advanced. We are out for a good rest and to get reinforced; we do not know for how long, or where we are for (perhaps the best). We had several machine-guns knocked out by shell-fire, so I had plenty of work keeping the teams going as I am armourer and artificer to this machine-gun company. The enemy are nearly all Bavarians and good fighters, and the ground is chalky, so you can tell how the trenches were when it rained, and the wood-work used for dug-outs were fir trees just cut down through the centre (no paring), so you see the strength; no wonder our shell fire would not pierce the dug-outs. I saw some great air fights, and to see the different artillery no wonder the poor Germans surrendered when they got our field artillery, horse artillery, garrison artillery, 9.2 siege artillery and 15in, in which I had great interest, being used by the Royal Marines Artillery; one could actually watch the shell travelling through the air. It was the first time I have seen a 15in gun in action, and they were shelling the German headquarters 12 miles away; goodness knows what the Germans thought - probably they thought they were dropping from the skies. We are having some grand weather now, and I hope it is improving the crops at home. The crops out here are looking well; I passed some bearded wheat in a field yesterday, and I measured it, some of it being six feet long, which I thought a good length. The women work hard on the land out here, and cows are milked by women. I think I must now close, wishing all your readers the best of luck."

Thame Gazette 8th August 1916

17 November 1916

Ralph Eaton was born in Thame in the summer of 1893. He was one of nine surviving children of Charles Eaton and Elizabeth (née Ward) living in 41 Park Street. In late 1913 he enlisted with the 4th (Territorial) Battalion of the Oxford and Bucks Light Infantry.

The Battalion, now re-designated the 1/4th, was part of the 145th Brigade in the 48th (South Midland) Division that landed at Boulogne on 30th March 1915. The Battalion was mainly in and out of trenches from then until the commencement of the Somme offensive, although, according to a letter from Private William Noel Smith also of Thame, Ralph had a very near miss in June 1915. "... *Pte R Eaton (Paddy) had a piece of cloth taken from his tunic's sleeve by a shrapnel bullet*".

On the Somme, the Battalion was mainly in support trenches until they took part in the Battle of Pozieres from 23rd July until the end of August, where they sustained heavy casualties. The Battalion war diary indicates that their remaining time on the Somme was interspersed between time in trenches and billets.

On 17th November 1916 Ralph was serving as a Battalion HQ orderly in support trenches near the village of Martinpuich. At about 15:00hrs shells fell approximately 15 yards outside and immediately opposite the entrance to the Battalion HQ killing Ralph, age 23, who was just outside. According to the letter sent to his parents from his former Platoon Commander he was buried in the nearest cemetery on the same day.

1893 Private Ralph Eaton, Oxford and Bucks Light Infantry, is buried in Martinpuich British Cemetery, Somme. He is remembered in Thame on the War Memorial.

The Thame Remembers Cross was placed at his grave on 7th July 2016 by Thame resident, Stuart Groves.

6 December 1916

Sam Howlett was born in Thame in 1890 and was one of seven children of William George Howlett and Mahala (née Perry). In 1901 he was living in Southern Road, Thame where his father was a beerhouse keeper and coachsmith at the Hole in the Wall beerhouse. By 1911 Sam had moved to Pangbourne, Berkshire and was employed as a grocer's assistant.

In September 1914 he enlisted with the Royal Berkshire (Princess Charlotte of Wales) Regiment. Sam was initially placed in the 9th (Reserve) Battalion based at Wool in Dorset. In late October 1915 he was posted to the 8th Battalion in France as part of a reinforcing draft for the losses incurred during the Battle of Loos earlier in the month. The Battalion was serving with the 1st Infantry Brigade of the 1st Division. Sam would have remained with the Battalion in northern France for the next few months, in and out of trenches and possibly taking part in some of the raiding parties. It was late April, when the Battalion was in the Maroc sector, that Sam was wounded for the first time. However, he returned to the Battalion in time for their move to the Somme in early July 1916, their first action in the battle being at Contalmaison. It was here that Sam was wounded again, this time in the knee. It is not known how serious this wound was and whether Sam recovered in time to serve in other actions that the Battalion took part in during the Somme offensive, such as at Mametz Wood, High Wood and Bazentin-Le-Grand, before being withdrawn from the Front Line at the end of September.

By the end of November, Sam had returned and was serving with B Company. At the beginning of December, they were in front line trenches around Warlencourt, a few kilometres south west of Bapaume. It was probably as a result of wounds received there, that he died at one of the casualty clearing stations in Dernancourt, near Albert on 6th December 1916. He was 26 years old.

18577 Private Sam Howlett, Royal Berkshire Regiment, is buried in the Dernancourt Communal Cemetery Extension, Somme. He is remembered in Thame on the War Memorial and on the Memorial Boards of St Mary's Church and All Saints' Church.

The Thame Remembers Cross was placed at his grave on 18th April 2015 by Patsy Baker of Thame Remembers.

7 January 1917

Ethelbert Godwin Stockwell Wagner was born on 12th March 1893 in Taiping, Perak, part of the Malay Federated States, where his father was a Deputy Commissioner of Police. Upon returning to England, he was admitted to Bedford Modern School in January 1900 and from 1904 he was one of three Wagner brothers who attended Lord Williams's Grammar School in Thame.

After leaving school he went to medical school at Birmingham University before joining the Royal Engineers and embarking for France on 22nd August 1914. He became a motorcycle despatch rider and attained the rank of Corporal before being discharged from the Engineers to take up a commission.

He became a Temporary Second Lieutenant with the 1st Battalion, Royal Warwickshire Regiment on 29th August 1915 and joined the Battalion in trenches in the Somme area of France on the same day. The Battalion war diary records him as leading a patrol to the German held area known as the "Quadrilateral" on 20th December. On 24th June 1916, just days before the start of the Battle of the Somme, he left the Battalion on detachment to the Royal Flying Corps.

After six days flying training in Maurice-Farman biplanes at No 5 Reserve Squadron, Castle Bromwich, Birmingham, he was awarded his flying ticket on 6th September 1916. He was posted for operational duties on 20th October with 32 Squadron who were based at Lealvillers in the Somme area of France.

Ethelbert was flying a DH2 aircraft when shot down and killed on 7th January 1917 in combat over Beugny in France. He was the ninth victim of Oblt Erwin Böhme of Jasta 2, who went on to become one of Germany's premier flying aces. Ethelbert, age 24, was buried initially in the German cemetery in Beugny, near Cambrai but was reinterred after the war.

Second Lieutenant Ethelbert Godwin Stockwell Wagner, Royal Flying Corps, is buried in the Achiet-le-Grand Communal Cemetery Extension, a few miles south of Arras. He is commemorated on the Ipoh War Memorial in Malaysia and is remembered in Thame on Lord Williams's School Memorial Board.

The Thame Remembers Cross was placed at his grave on 18th April 2015 by Michael Hutson of Thame Remembers.

22 January 1917

Willis Janes was the youngest of three sons of William Janes and Amelia (née Willis). He was born in Long Crendon, Buckinghamshire in 1889 and was baptised at St Peter-le-Bailey church in Oxford on 8th May 1889. Willis had two half-brothers and two half-sisters from his father's previous marriage. His father, who was a local police constable died in 1889. Willis was a pupil at Lord Williams's Grammar School, Thame and went on to become a schoolmaster at the Home for Little Boys in Farningham, Kent, a school for homeless and destitute boys from London.

Willis enlisted at the beginning of World War One with the 1/10th (Scottish) Battalion of the King's (Liverpool Regiment), Territorial Force (Regt No 3318). He went to France with the Battalion on 1st November 1914 and by the end of the month they were occupying trenches in Belgium. In 1915 he would most likely have been in the actions at Bellewaarde Farm and the Hooge. In October 1915 he was commissioned as a Temporary Second Lieutenant with the 6th Battalion, King's Own Scottish Borderers. He was wounded on 20th December when the Battalion was being relieved from trenches close to Dickebusch, near Ypres.

After a long period of recovery, Willis returned to the Battalion on 16th November 1916. Less than two months later, on 6th January 1917, when the Battalion was in trenches a few miles north of Arras, he was seriously wounded, reportedly from gunshots. He was evacuated to the British General Hospital in Le Tréport where he succumbed to his wounds on Monday, 22nd January 1917, age 27. His burial took place the following day, in the presence of his brother Lieutenant Ernest Janes, Royal Army Medical Corps and other officers. His accumulated war pay and gratuity of over £80 and was forwarded to his mother Amelia.

Second Lieutenant Willis Janes, King's Own Scottish Borderers, is buried in Le Tréport Military Cemetery, Seine-Maritime. He is remembered in Thame on Lord Williams's School Memorial Board and is commemorated on the War Memorial in Long Crendon.

The Thame Remembers Cross was placed at his grave on 19th June 2015
by Thame resident, Sue Motteram.

16 February 1917

George Edmund Ladbrook was born in Honington, a small hamlet near Shipston on Stour, Warwickshire in November 1884. He was the eldest child of the eight children born to George Ladbrook, a gardener, and Fanny (née Gee). After first moving to Dinton, Buckinghamshire, the family settled in Thame in the late 19th century, living in Bell Lane and later Park Terrace. In 1911 George Edmund was employed as a print compositor.

George was called up to the Gloucestershire Regiment, probably in the spring of 1916. He was posted to the 8th Battalion, serving with the 57th Infantry Brigade, joining them with one of the reinforcement drafts during the latter stages of the Battle of the Somme. On 11th January 1917 his name appeared on the daily wounded casualty list. This was most likely to have happened during the Battalion's last engagement on the Somme in the Battle of the Ancre in November 1916.

He returned to duty but died on 16th February 1917 whilst the Battalion was deployed in trenches opposite Serre in northern France, the scene of intense fighting the previous year during the Battle of the Somme. George, age 33, was buried in a battlefield cemetery nearby.

Two of his brothers also served during the war with the Oxford and Bucks Light Infantry and both survived.

27637 Private George Edmund Ladbrook, Gloucestershire Regiment, is buried in Courcelles-Au-Bois Communal Cemetery, Somme. He is remembered in Thame on the War Memorial and on All Saints' Church Memorial Board.

The Thame Remembers Cross was placed at his grave on 18th April 2015 by Mike Dyer of Thame Remembers.

7 April 1917

Cecil Amos Witney was the fifth eldest of eight sons of George Harry Witney and Charlotte Mary (née Pitcher). He was born in Stokenchurch, Oxfordshire, now Buckinghamshire, on 6th June 1882 and baptised there on 27th July. His father worked in the chair making industry.

After leaving school, Cecil started a career as a clerk at Messrs Hall & Co's store in Thame. He moved to the office of solicitor William Parker, and subsequently to solicitors Messrs Lightfoot and Lowndes. When Charles Simmons became clerk of Thame Urban & Rural District Council, Cecil took up the position as his assistant, where he remained until the outbreak of the war. He was permanent secretary of the Thame Goodfellows Society and a member of the Thame Football and Cricket Clubs, reportedly *"good at both"*.

In 1912 Cecil joined the Oxford and Bucks Light Infantry, 4th Battalion (Territorials) and quickly rose to the rank of Lance Corporal. When they were mobilised in August 1914, Cecil (Regt No 1865) joined them at Oxford and moved with them to Writtle, near Chelmsford, Essex. In December he was promoted to Corporal. By the time the Battalion, re-designated the 1/4th, embarked for France in March 1915 Cecil had been transferred to the 2/4th Battalion. The Battalion remained in England and Cecil was promoted to Company Sergeant Major of A Company in December. The following year the 2/4th Battalion went to France with the 184th

Brigade of the 61st Division, landing at Le Havre in May 1916. They remained in northern France for the next few months and took part in the attack at Fromelles, an unsuccessful diversionary tactic during the Battle of the Somme. It was not until mid-November, when the main battle had ended that they marched down to Albert and took up positions in the trenches on the Somme.

At midnight on Good Friday 1917, A Company was the lead attacking company in an advance towards St Quentin. The attack proved to be a failure, uncut wire forcing the attacking companies to withdraw. Cecil was one of ten men killed and over 40 wounded on 7th April. He was 35 years old and buried near the spot where he fell, but after the war his body was reinterred in a Commonwealth War Graves Cemetery nearby.

200230 Company Sergeant Major Cecil Amos Witney, Oxford and Bucks Light Infantry, is buried in Vadencourt British Cemetery, Maissemy, Aisne. He is remembered in Thame on the War Memorial and on the Memorial Boards of St Mary's Church and All Saints' Church.

The Thame Remembers Cross was placed at his grave on 10th September 2014 by Colin Evans on behalf of Cecil's nieces, Janice Tapping and Judith Sainsbury.

The following words are extracted from a letter sent by his Company Commander, Captain Kenneth R Brown to his mother:

".... what a tremendous amount of good he did in the company. I have never known him forget anything and I could always rely on him and trust him implicitly. He was undoubtedly a very fine soldier. Personally too, I had a great affection for your son and felt that I have lost in him a great friend. He did not know what fear was, and was on two occasions merited for his gallantry in action. I hope you will find that he is not forgotten in the next list of honours. His unselfishness is well shown by his last act. We were lying side by side against the German wire when a bomb burst behind us. His first thought was for me and he asked me if I was hit. I know that the Battalion is the poorer for the loss of a very brave and gallant soldier... "

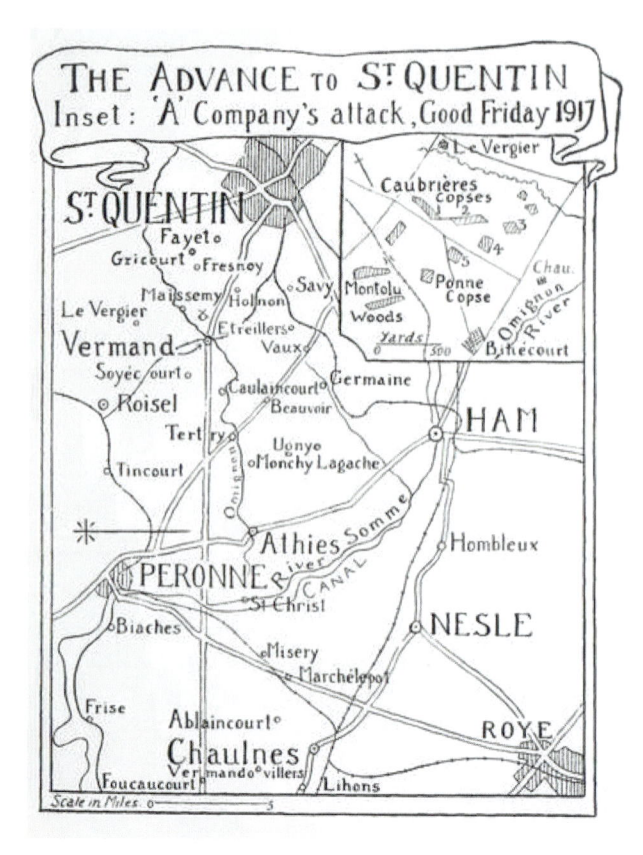

9 April 1917

William Newitt was born in Kingsey, Buckinghamshire in January 1888, the youngest of five children of Henry and Anne Newitt. At the age of 13 he was a ploughboy and agricultural labourer.

He was a member of both the village cricket club and the church choir. Later he took up employment with John Young, the landlord of the Four Horseshoes Hotel in Thame.

In March 1910 William emigrated to Canada on the Canadian Pacific ship SS Corsican and landed at Halifax, Nova Scotia on 1st April. He then travelled overland a further 2,200 miles to join his brother Frank, who had emigrated two years earlier and was working on a farm in Marquette, Manitoba.

In 1916 William was living in Saskatoon in the province of Saskatchewan where he enlisted with the Canadian Infantry on 3rd March. He was posted to the 13th Battalion, Royal Highlanders of Canada, arriving in England on 4th October 1916. The following month he joined the Battalion north of Arras, France, as part of the reinforcing drafts after the terrible losses that they had incurred in October attacking "Regina Trench", a heavily defended German trench network near Thiepval on the Somme.

For some months afterwards the Battalion endured the hard and ordinary work of the trenches but without any major action to relieve the monotony. That did not mean they did not sustain any casualties. There were the usual sniping incidents, trench raids, patrols and periods in which training was undertaken away from the Front Line. In April 1917 the Battalion, as part of the 3rd Infantry Brigade of the 1st Canadian Division, prepared for the attack on Vimy Ridge during the Battle of Arras. The attack began at zero hour of 05:30hrs on 9th April and by the end of the day Vimy Ridge was taken. The 13th Battalion was one of the support battalions and suffered relatively slight casualties, mainly from machine gun fire. William Newitt, age 29, was one of those lost and his body was never recovered or identified.

204367 Private William Newitt, Canadian Infantry, has no known grave and is commemorated on Vimy Memorial near Arras. He is also commemorated on the Memorial Board in St Nicholas Church, Kingsey, Buckinghamshire.

The Thame Remembers Cross was placed at Vimy Memorial on 1st November 2015 by Thame resident, Alan Wylie.

You Come from England

You come from England;
is she England still?
Yes, thanks to you
that died upon this hill.

John Maxwell Edmonds
(1875-1958)

9 April 1917

William James Lewis was born in Corsley, Wiltshire in 1886 to William Lewis and Isabella (née Thompson). By 1891 the family had moved to Kingsey, near Thame, where his father was employed as a gardener at Tythrop Park. William was educated at the Royal British School in Thame and from there he went on to become apprenticed to Mr F G Hawkins' clothing establishment in the Cornmarket. He later worked in Coventry and Nuneaton, before becoming manager of a clothier's business in Bognor, Sussex. He was also a member of the Bognor Red Cross Corps and worked for some time in Graylingwell Military Hospital, Chichester. In 1915 he married Clara Bowman in Bognor.

William was called up on 18th November 1916 and posted to the Household Battalion, an infantry battalion formed mainly from reserves of the Household Cavalry. It is likely he arrived at the Western Front as part of one of several reinforcing drafts that the Battalion received in March 1917.

On Easter Monday, 9th April 1917 in sleety weather, the Battalion, part of the 10th Brigade in the 4th Infantry Division, was allotted the task of advancing along the swampy banks of the Scarpe River near Arras to the ruined hamlet of Fampoux, which was under German occupation. William, age 21, was killed by shrapnel while dressing the wounds of one of his comrades. Although official records give his death as 11th April, the Battalion war diaries indicate that it occurred on 9th April.

1645 Trooper William James Lewis, Household Battalion, is buried in Mindel Trench Cemetery, St. Laurent-Blangy, Arras. He is commemorated on the Memorial Board in St Nicholas Church, Kingsey and his name is to be added to Thame War Memorial.

The Thame Remembers Cross was placed at his grave on 26th September 2016 by Thame resident, Mike Rains.

12 April 1917

Charles Alder Allen was born in 1892. He was the youngest of eleven children and the eighth son of Anne (née Alder) and Richard Allen, a corn factor's carman, of 45 High Street, Thame. He was baptised at St Mary's Church on 29th May 1892.

Charles enlisted in April 1915 with the Royal Artillery as a Gunner and used the alias "William Charles Alder" throughout his service. He was posted to the 156th Brigade, Royal Field Artillery, serving with the 33rd Divisional Artillery. "William" spent several months with the Brigade at Bulford Camp and Larkhill in Wiltshire, the home of the Royal Horse Artillery and Royal Field Artillery Training Schools, before he embarked for France on the troop transport SS Maidan, landing in Le Havre on 11th December.

"William" was serving with B Battery, armed with 18 pounder horse-drawn field guns. They spent the next few months in various actions in northern France on the Le Bassée front, moving down to the Somme in early July 1916. The Battery were quickly in action in places such as High Wood, Bazentin and Montabaun, laying down artillery barrages ahead of the advancing infantry.

In December 1916 "William's" name appeared on one of the wounded casualty lists, this is most likely to have happened when the Brigade was in action the previous month in the Maurepas-Bouchavesnes area, south of the Somme.

At the beginning of April 1917, the 156th Brigade started to lay down the barrage in advance of the attack on Vimy Ridge, the start of the Battle of Arras. "William" was wounded again and after evacuation through the casualty clearing system, died of his wounds at a base hospital in Wimereux on 12th April. He was 25 years old.

L/11878 Gunner Charles Alder Allen, Royal Artillery, is buried in Wimereux Communal Cemetery, Pas de Calais. He is remembered in Thame on the War Memorial and on the Memorial Boards of All Saints' Church and St Mary's Church.

The Thame Remembers Cross was placed at his grave on 19th June 2015 by Thame residents, Roy and Sue Motteram.

22 April 1917

Stephen James Roberts was born in Clerkenwell, London on 4th January 1889 to Charles William Roberts and Emma (née Francis). Charles was a commercial traveller and they lived at 6 Roberts Place, Clerkenwell. In late 1907 at Marylebone, age 18, Stephen married Maud Maria Crook of Long Crendon, Buckinghamshire. Their first son William Harry Charles was born the following year in early 1908. Stephen joined the Royal Regiment of Artillery in 1909 and by April 1911 he was serving with 90th Heavy Battery, Royal Garrison Artillery (RGA) in Multan, India (now in Punjab, Pakistan). His wife Maud was living at 8 Chinnor Road, Thame with her father, Harry Crook, a retired farmer from Long Crendon, their son William and another son, Donald George, who was born in May 1911.

In April 1915 the 90th Heavy Battery, with their 60 pounder (5 inch) horse-drawn guns, was withdrawn from India to support the 29th Division in the Dardanelles at Gallipoli, Turkey. Stephen served with them throughout the ill-fated campaign without injury. After the "successful" evacuation of the peninsular in January 1916 and a brief interlude in Egypt, the Battery was posted to the Western Front in March 1916. Stephen, now a Corporal, was transferred to the 60th Siege Battery, RGA, 7th Heavy Artillery Group. The Battery was in action virtually every day throughout the Somme offensive, sending over salvoes from their six inch guns, only being withdrawn to rest billets in the middle of November. The Battery remained in the Somme area throughout the winter of 1916/17. Unfortunately, on the night of 21st April 1917 at Philosophe, a German gas shell penetrated the cellar of the billet where Stephen was resting. He was heavily gassed and died the following morning. He was 28 years old.

29507 Corporal Stephen James Roberts, Royal Artillery, is buried in Philosophe British Military Cemetery, Mazingarbe, Pas de Calais. He is remembered in Thame on the War Memorial and on the Memorial Boards of St Mary's Church and All Saints' Church.

The Thame Remembers Cross was placed at his grave on 19th May 2015 by Thame resident, Sonja Francis.
His grandson, Ron Roberts placed a Thame Remembers Cross at his grave on 2nd November 2015.

30 April 1917

Arthur Rush was born in Thame in the autumn of 1880 to James Rush and Jane (née Howes) who lived in North Street, Thame. After the death of his father in 1895, his mother married William Eggleton and by 1911 the family had moved to Wellington Street.

In December 1897 Arthur joined the 4th Battalion (Territorial Force) of the Oxford and Bucks Light Infantry, his service record showing he was *"slight in stature being only 5ft 2ins tall and 7½ stone in weight"*. However, by 1899 he bought himself out of the Battalion by payment of £1.

He was working as a general labourer when at some stage before the war he re-enlisted with the Regiment. His service number suggests this was likely to have been with the "Special Reserve" 3rd Battalion which had been formed in 1908. On the outbreak of World War One, men in this Battalion formed the nucleus for reinforcements into the regular battalions. Arthur was posted to serve with the 2nd Battalion, part of the 5th Infantry Brigade of the 2nd Division, joining them in France as part of a reinforcing draft on 8th January 1915. He would have been in action with the Battalion in the Battles of Festubert and Loos in 1915 and on the Somme, at Guillemot and the Ancre, during 1916.

He had been promoted to Lance Corporal and was with the Battalion, when on 28th April 1917 they took part in the attack to capture the villages of Arleux and Oppy, part of the second phase of the Battle of Arras. Heavy casualties were sustained and Arthur was one of the wounded. He was evacuated to a casualty clearing station at Aubigny, a few miles west of Arras, where he died of his wounds on 30th April 1917, age 36.

8866 Lance Corporal Arthur Rush, Oxford and Bucks Light Infantry, is buried in Aubigny Communal Cemetery Extension, Pas de Calais. He is remembered in Thame on the War Memorial and on the Memorial Boards of St Mary's Church and All Saints' Church.

The Thame Remembers Cross was placed at his grave on 19th April 2015 by Michael Hutson of Thame Remembers.

Several members of the Thame National Reserve having volunteered for service at home or abroad left the town for Oxford on Friday morning. The following formed the contingent: Corporal H J Shrimpton, Lance Corporal H Cozier, Privates W Bowler, W Hampton, H Clarke, J Price, E Harbour, A Hastings, A Rush, W Higgins.

Thame Gazette 1st September 1914

3 May 1917

George Harry Thomas Crook was born in Long Crendon, Buckinghamshire in 1898. He was one of six children of Ellen and Harry Crook, a farmer and innkeeper at the Angel Inn. By 1911 the family, his father now being retired, had moved to Thame and were living at 8 Chinnor Road, Thame.

George enlisted with the Oxford and Bucks Light Infantry in November 1915, age 17. On reaching the age of 18, he became eligible for front line service and was posted to France with the 6th Battalion, where they were serving in trenches in the Ypres Salient. In late July the Battalion entrained for the Somme where George was wounded, probably in an attack during the Battle of Guillemont in early September when the Battalion incurred almost 300 casualties. He was evacuated to a hospital in Yorkshire, but once he had recovered, in January 1917, he returned to France, this time with the 5th Battalion, serving in the 42nd Infantry Brigade of the 14th Division.

George would have seen several actions with the Battalion during the battles around Arras, before being killed in action at the Scarpe River on 3rd May 1917. The 5th Battalion was one of the leading battalions on the first day of the Third Battle of the Scarpe, one of the phases of the Battle of Arras, and sustained 299 casualties out of a total strength of 533 officers and men who went into action. George was 19 years old.

20836 Private George Harry Thomas Crook, Oxford and Bucks Light Infantry, has no known grave and is commemorated on Arras Memorial, Pas de Calais. He is remembered in Thame on the War Memorial and on the Memorial Boards of St Mary's Church and All Saints' Church.

The Thame Remembers Cross was placed at Arras Memorial on 1st November 2015 by Thame Museum member, Ron Roberts.

3 May 1917

Stanley David Victor Dover was born in Moreton, near Thame on 28th February 1898, the third son of Charles Dover and Harriet (née Hall). He was baptised at St Mary's Church in Thame on 2nd April 1898. His father was the publican at the Bell Inn in Moreton. By 1911 the family had moved to the Rising Sun in the High Street, Thame and Stanley had become a telegraph messenger boy for the Post Office.

In 1916 when Stanley reached the age of 18 he was called up to join the Oxford and Bucks Light Infantry. He was drafted to serve with the 5th Battalion in France, most likely part of the 320 strong reinforcing draft the Battalion received in early September after their losses at Delville Wood.

The Battalion was soon in action again on the Somme, when the 14th Division, with whom they were serving, took part in the Battle of Flers-Courcelette with the loss over 4,500 men. The remainder of 1916 was relatively uneventful in the trenches in front of Arras. However, this was to be the lull before the storm. Stanley, and George Crook also from Thame (see above), would have been involved in actions from the start of the Battle of Arras in April 1917, but on 3rd May, during the first day of the Third Battle of the Scarpe, they were both posted missing and later presumed dead. Stanley was 19 years old.

27221 Private Stanley David Victor Dover, Oxford and Bucks Light Infantry, has no known grave and is commemorated on Arras Memorial, Pas de Calais. He is remembered in Thame on the War Memorial and on the Memorial Boards of St Mary's Church and All Saints' Church.

The Thame Remembers Cross was placed at the Arras Memorial on 1st November 2015 by Thame Museum member, Ron Roberts.

20 May 1917

Joseph Lovejoy was born in Thame in 1889 to William Lovejoy and Annie (née Johnson). He was baptised at St Mary's Church on 25th March 1894 and in 1911 he was a labourer living with his brother in Stokenchurch, Buckinghamshire. Joseph joined the local mounted territorials, the Queen's Own Oxfordshire Hussars (QOOH) in 1912. The Regiment was mobilised in August 1914, moving to Churn in Essex before embarking to the Front on 19th September. In doing so, the QOOH, became the first Territorial unit to see action in the war. They formed part of the 4th Cavalry Brigade in the 2nd Cavalry Division and were to spend frustrating periods waiting in readiness for the opportunity to push on through gaps in the enemy's line, which never materialised. They toiled in working parties bringing up supplies, digging defensive positions, suffering the discomforts of appalling conditions, frequently dismounting to fight fierce engagements on foot and in the trenches in Belgium and France.

Joseph, age 28, was killed on 20th May 1917 alongside his C Squadron Commander Major Val Fleming MP, the father of the writer Ian Fleming, and three others during an enemy bombardment on Guillemont Farm, a high point overlooking the German Hindenberg Line.

He was originally buried in St Emilie British Cemetery, Villers Faucon but when that cemetery was closed in 1930 his body was reinterred by the Commonwealth War Graves Commission.

1763/285091 Trooper Joseph Lovejoy, Queen's Own Oxfordshire Hussars, is buried in Templeux-Le-Guerard British Cemetery, Somme. He is remembered in Thame on the War Memorial and on All Saints' Church Memorial Board.

The Thame Remembers Cross was placed at his grave on 22nd May 2016 by Ian Jones MBE of Thame Remembers.

Mr and Mrs Lovejoy of North Street Thame have received news that their son Trooper J Lovejoy of the Queen's Own Oxfordshire Hussars was killed in action on Sunday week. The following letter was sent to them by his commanding officer.

Dear Mrs Lovejoy,
I am sorry to have to tell you that your son fell in action on Sunday morning, May 20th when my troop was holding an advanced position which the Germans attacked. He was killed instantaneously by a shell and I want you to know that he could not have suffered at all. He leaves a very good record of hard work done under already trying conditions and has now fallen with others of the command doing his duty to King and Country. He is buried with those who fell with him in a small cemetery at St Emilie. We lost our Squadron leader Major Val. Fleming in the same action and I am writing for his brother Captain Fleming as well as for myself, to express the very deepest sympathy in your sad loss.
Yours sincerely A C Rawlinson 3rd com QOOH B Exp

Thame Gazette 29th May 1917

8 June 1917

Reginald Phillips was born in Thame in 1893 and baptised at St Mary's Church on 10th May 1893. He was the youngest of the two sons and three daughters of William Phillips and Mary (née Goodenough). The family were living in Chinnor Road, Thame, but by 1901 had moved to South Newington, near Banbury, Oxfordshire. In 1911 Reginald was listed as a visitor on a farm in Tiddington and learning farming.

In 1914 he was working as a clerk for Aylesbury Dominion Dairy Ltd. He left them on 14th September to enlist with the Bucks Battalion in Aylesbury (Regt No 2626.) This was later 1/1st Buckinghamshire Battalion of the Oxford and Bucks Light Infantry. The unit was part of the South Midlands Brigade of the 48th Division, which landed at Boulogne on 30th March 1915 and by April were in position in the trenches, initially in Belgium, but by mid-July had moved to the Somme area of France. The Battalion took part in a number of the phases of the Battle of the Somme throughout July and August 1916 and then spent the latter part of 1916 and early 1917 in billets, or "relatively quiet" periods of ordinary trench holding. After the pursuit of the German retreat to the Hindenburg Line in March/April 1917, the Battalion took its fair share of deployments in the new Front Line trenches. Reginald, age 24, was one of the fatalities on 8th June 1917.

265866 Lance Corporal Reginald Phillips, Buckinghamshire Battalion, Oxford and Bucks Light Infantry, is buried in Hermies British Cemetery, Pas de Calais. He is commemorated on the Dominion Dairy Memorial Board now located in the Territorial Army Centre, Aylesbury and his name is to be added to Thame War Memorial.

The Thame Remembers Cross was placed at his grave on 31st October 2015 by Thame resident, Andrew Misseldine.

"Only one operation was undertaken by the Battalion during its tenure of these trenches. It had become apparent at the beginning of June that the enemy had established a night post amongst a cluster of bushes on our bank of the canal. The sniping from this post caused us considerable annoyance and some casualties to our working parties. It was therefore decided to capture it, and to dig a trench along the bank of the canal with a communicator running back to our present post. Two platoons of B Company were detailed to make the attack, forming up on a line parallel to the canal bank, each platoon being in two lines at fifteen yards' distance and on a frontage of fifty yards. Zero was fixed for midnight June 7/8, at which time a barrage from one section of field guns was placed on the enemy trenches. At zero plus five this barrage lifted, and the assaulting platoons charged with the bayonet. The enemy opened rifle fire before the assault, but was most effectually silenced by a Lewis gun posted on the right bank for the purpose of providing covering fire. After the assaulting platoons got in there ensued a bombing fight which lasted for a few minutes, but the enemy soon gave in. No attempt at a counter-attack was made, but rifle grenades were fired from the opposite bank at intervals throughout the remainder of the night. Bucks casualties were two killed and nine wounded. Eleven prisoners were taken and several of the enemy killed."

Extract from "The First Buckinghamshire Battalion 1914-1919" by P L Wright (1920)

4 July 1917

Charles Roy Munckton Morris was born in Thame on 9th October 1895 to Henry William George Morris and Anna (née Munckton) and baptised at St Mary's Church on 20th October 1895. His father was a pharmacist who had a chemist shop at 11 High Street, Thame. Over the next few years the family moved around Oxfordshire to Charlbury and Chipping Norton and, finally upon Henry's retirement in 1913, to Abingdon, (then Berkshire). Charles had an elder brother, Cyril George, who was also born in Thame and served in World War One as a Captain in the Royal Berkshire Regiment. He survived the war.

In early 1916, whilst he was working in the Godalming, Surrey branch of Capital and Counties Bank, now Lloyds, Charles enlisted in the Royal Fusiliers (City of London Regiment). He was initially posted to the 30th Battalion which was a reserve battalion for the 23rd and 24th Sportsman's Battalions, hence his service number starting SPTS, but by 1917 he was serving with the 9th Battalion, part of the 36th Brigade, 12th Division.

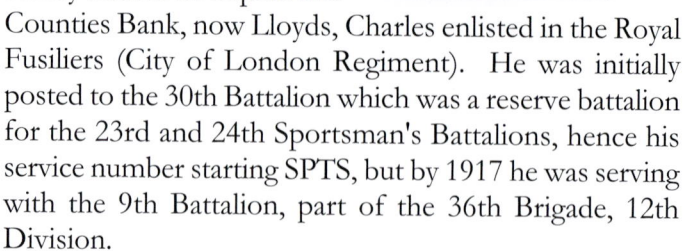

In early July 1917 the Battalion was in trenches at Monchy, near Arras. This was a relatively quiet period after the battles at Arras earlier in the year, the majority of the time being spent "cleaning up and improving trenches". Nevertheless, there was a good deal of shelling and it was probably during one of these attacks that Charles, age 22, was killed on 4th July 1917. In his will he left his estate of £164 12s to his father.

SPTS/4826 Private Charles Roy Munckton Morris, Royal Fusiliers, is buried in Monchy British Cemetery, Monchy le Preux, Pas de Calais. His name is to be added to Thame War Memorial.

The Thame Remembers Cross was placed at his grave on 19th April 2015 by Patsy Baker of Thame Remembers.

28 November 1917

William Henry Wentworth was born in Thame in 1890, one of three children to Henry Wentworth and Mary (née Mortimer). His father was a labourer and in 1891 the family were staying in lodgings in Kingston upon Hull, Yorkshire. By 1901 his father was suffering from paralysis and unable to work and the family had moved back to Thame living at 6 Church Road. Henry died in 1903 and William's mother Mary went on to marry Albert John Morgan the following year. In 1911 William was living with his mother and stepfather in Southern Road and was a cattleman on a farm.

Later in the year he enlisted with the Grenadier Guards. At the start of the war he was stationed at Wellington Barracks in London with the 3rd Battalion until they were mobilised with the 2nd Guards Brigade, Guards Division. They embarked at Southampton on the Clyde Steamboat Queen Alexandra, landing in Le Havre on 27th July 1915. The Battalion fought at the Hohenzollern Redoubt at the Battle of Loos in October and then there followed a few months in the trenches around Ypres. In late August 1916 the Battalion moved down to the Somme, where William was wounded most likely during the Battle of Flers-Courcelette in September. The remainder of 1916 and much of 1917 was occupied by various tours of duty in trenches around the Somme, moving back into Flanders in the summer of 1917. On 9th October the Battalion engaged in the Battle of Poelcapelle and William was subsequently awarded the Military Medal for bravery in the field. His family received notification of this award only a few days before the news of his death reached them. William, age 27, died of wounds at No 21 Casualty Clearing Station, Ytres, approximately 20 miles south east of Arras, on 28th November 1917. He had received his wounds the previous day when the 3rd Battalion attacked the village of Fontaine Notre Dame during the first Battle of Cambrai and all the officers and most NCOs of the Battalion became casualties.

15491 Sergeant William Henry Wentworth MM, Grenadier Guards, is buried in Rocquigny-Equancourt Road British Cemetery, Manancourt, Somme. He is remembered in Thame on the War Memorial and on All Saints' Church Memorial Board.

The Thame Remembers Cross was placed at his grave on 26th September 2016 by Thame resident, Sylvia Rains.

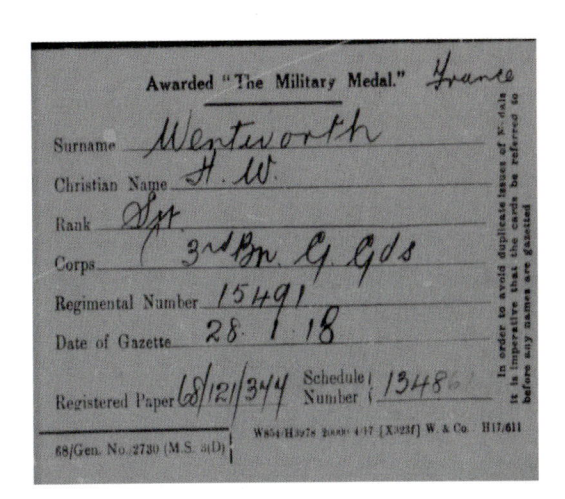

30 November 1917

Walter Sidney Harris was born in 1881 in Portswood, in the parish of South Stoneham, now part of Southampton. He was the eldest of the three children of Frances Martha (née Tame) and Walter Sidney Harris, a foreman and later Clerk of Works. In the 1890s the family were living in Shirburn, near Thame. Walter was a day boy at Lord Williams's Grammar School and was in the football team in 1897/8.

After leaving school he was employed as a clerk for the Post Office in London and it was here that he became friends with Edmund Le Messurier.

At the start of World War One, Walter was one of the early volunteers signing up with the 12th (Rangers) Battalion, London Regiment in September 1914. At the time this was a second line battalion stationed in England. It was not until April 1916 that Walter, having been transferred to 1/15th (Prince of Wales's Own Civil Service Rifles) Battalion in the previous January, left for France joining the Battalion near Vimy, where they were serving with the 140th Brigade of the 47th Division.

In the middle of September the Battalion fought their first action on the Somme during the Battle of Flers-Courcelette, followed by a costly attack on the Butte de Warlencourt during the Battle of Le Transloy. In 1917 most of the year was spent in the Ypres Salient, seeing action at Messines and the Third Battle of Ypres, but in September they returned to the trenches in northern France.

It was here that Walter, a member of the Lewis Gun section, was killed on 30th November during the German counter-attack at the Battle of Cambrai. He was 36 years old.

In his will Walter left almost £950, a substantial sum of money for those days, to be administered by Winifred Le Messurier, the wife and attorney of his friend, Edmund Le Messurier. Walter's brother Reginald, also a pupil at Lord Williams's Grammar School, served in the war as a Captain with the East Africa Rifles and survived.

532616 Private Walter Sidney Harris, London Regiment, has no known grave and is commemorated on Cambrai Memorial at Louverval, Nord. He is remembered in Thame on Lord Williams's School Memorial Board.

The Thame Remembers Cross was placed at Cambrai Memorial on 31st October 2015 by Thame resident, Joane Simpson.

6 January 1918

Edward Benoni Burgess was born in Transvaal, South Africa on 17th June 1892. His parents were Alfred Augustus Burgess, a gentleman, and Ada Eliza (née Jones). He was brought to England at a few months old and baptised at St John the Baptist Church, Bisley, Surrey on 28th August 1893.

Following his parents divorce in 1898, Edward and his elder brother Alfred, went to live with his maternal grandparents in Skittle Green, Haddenham, Buckinghamshire and both were educated at Lord Williams's Grammar School in Thame.

He returned to South Africa after leaving school and was employed as a *"pumpman"*. On 23rd August 1915 he enlisted in the 4th South African Scottish Regiment, joining B Company which was formed primarily from men of the Transvaal Scottish Regiment. The Regiment, as part of the 1st South African Infantry Brigade, embarked from Cape Town for England on 25th August 1915 where they spent two months training at Bordon in Hampshire. In January 1916 the Brigade sailed for Egypt to help quell a local uprising, before being transferred to the Western Front, landing in Marseilles in April 1916. The Regiment suffered heavy casualties throughout the war, particularly at Delville Wood on the Somme in July 1916. In December 1917 Edward, by now a Lance Corporal, was severely wounded in both legs and evacuated to hospital in Rouen where his right leg was amputated at the thigh. He died of his wounds on 6th January 1918, age 25 years.

5266 Lance Corporal Edward Benoni Burgess, South African Scottish Regiment, is buried in St Sever Cemetery Extension, Rouen. He is remembered in Thame on Lord Williams's School Memorial Board. He is commemorated on the War Memorial in Haddenham.

The Thame Remembers Cross was placed at his grave on 5th May 2016 by Thame resident, Gill Bellis.

21 March 1918

Frederick William Cross was born in Moreton near Thame in 1894. He was the middle child of nine surviving children of William George Cross of Moreton and Adelaide (née Higgins) of North Weston near Thame. In 1911 he was a 16 year old horseman living on a farm in Moreton with his parents and five siblings.

Frederick enlisted at Oxford in the Oxford and Bucks Light Infantry in October 1914. He was sent for training to the 3rd (Reserve) Battalion stationed at Portsmouth, Hampshire. At the end of September 1915 he was attached to the Royal Munster Fusiliers and sailed for Salonika, Greece to join the 6th Battalion which had recently been withdrawn from Gallipoli, Turkey. The Battalion took part in the Macedonian campaign with the 10th (Irish) Division. At some stage, Frederick was released back to the Oxford and Bucks Light Infantry and served, at various times, with the 5th and 2nd Battalions on the Western Front and finally with 2/4th Battalion serving with the 61st (South Midland) Division, part of Gough's 5th Army.

On 21st March 1918, the first day of the German spring offensive through the Somme, the Battalion almost ceased to exist as a fighting force, sustaining over 520 casualties whilst attempting to defend the Enghien Redoubt. Frederick, age 24, was one of the missing.

18915 Private Frederick William Cross, Oxford and Bucks Light Infantry, has no known grave and is commemorated on Pozières Memorial, Somme. He is remembered in Thame on both the Thame and Moreton War Memorials, St Mary's Church Memorial Board and the Moreton Chapel Memorial Plaque.

The Thame Remembers Cross was placed at Pozières Memorial on 29th October 2014 by Ian Jones MBE of Thame Remembers.

21 March 1918

George Asplin Pask was born in Thame in the spring of 1878 and baptised at St Mary's Church on 13th March 1879. He was the second child of George Pask and Jane (née Way) and was named Asplin for his grandmother's maiden name. Soon after his birth the family moved to Holywell Street, Oxford where his father was a college bedmaker. His parents were still living at the same address in 1921.

In May 1900 George married Alice May Harrison at St Albans, Hertfordshire where he was working as a print compositor. They had a son Charles, who was born and died in 1904, also a daughter Doris born in 1907 and died in 1919. By 1911 they were living in Tufnell Park, London where George went on to become an overseer compositor.

When the British Government passed the Military Service Act in 1916 and extended it to married men, George was registered and deemed to have enlisted on 24th June, but it was not until 21st February 1917 that he was called up, at the age of 38. He was initially posted to the 109th Training Regiment which, at the time, was based in Wimbledon, Surrey. At the end of November 1917 he was posted to the Middlesex Regiment, 20th Battalion and on 10th January 1918 transferred to 1/19th Battalion, London Regiment who were serving in the Somme area with the 141st Brigade of the 41st Division.

On 21st March 1918 the Germans launched their spring offensive. The 1/19th Londons were heavily attacked in their trenches near Marcoing, south west of Cambrai, the enemy using gas shells, followed up by infantry, forcing the Battalion to withdraw to rear defensive lines. George, age 40, was posted missing on the first day of the Battle, his presumed death being confirmed a year later.

G/52885 Private George Asplin Pask, London Regiment, has no known grave and is commemorated on Arras Memorial, Pas de Calais. He is also commemorated on Tufnell Park War Memorial in London and his name is to be added to Thame War Memorial.

The Thame Remembers Cross was placed at Arras Memorial on 1st November 2015 by Thame resident, Ron Roberts.

23 March 1918

Ralph Line was born in Hampstead, London on 24th June 1887 to Ruth (née House) and Richard Line, a butcher. The eldest of seven children, he was baptised in the Parish Church of Harmondsworth on 7th August 1887. After his father died in 1907 Ralph, together with his brothers and widowed mother, moved to Thame where they lived in Lower High Street. Ralph was employed in Thame as a warehouseman for the warehouse and distribution company, Pursers. He served for three years with the local territorial yeomanry, the Queen's Own Oxfordshire Hussars (Regt No 1947) and at the outbreak of war was one of the first to re-enlist. On 20th September 1914, he embarked with C (Henley) Squadron for France, disembarking at Dunkirk two days later. In October, in northern France, they were the first territorial unit to see action in the war, but thereafter spent much of the war with the 4th Cavalry Brigade in frustration, as no opportunities for a mounted cavalry breakthrough occurred. Therefore much of their time was spent in trenches, either as working parties or as mobile fighting infantry.

At the end of April 1915 Ralph was one of several members of the Regiment, including his future brother-in-law William Humphris, who were wounded by a bursting shell. He was invalided back to England and after a period for recovery he rejoined the Regiment in France. On 7th November 1917, whilst on leave, he married Sarah Jeannie Humphris of 24 Upper High Street at St Mary's Church, Thame. William Humphris survived the war but Ralph, age 30, was killed on 23rd March 1918 by machine gun fire during the Battle of St Quentin, part of the German spring offensive known as *Operation Michael*. His officer said *"he was such a gallant fellow, and one of the smartest NCOs in the regiment and will be much missed."* He was initially buried by the Germans in a local battlefield cemetery but was reinterred in 1919. His brother Richard was killed in Salonika in 1917.

285209 Corporal Ralph Line, Queen's Own Oxfordshire Hussars, is buried in the British Extension to Chauny Communal Cemetery, Aisne. He is remembered in Thame on the War Memorial and on All Saints' Church Memorial Board.

The Thame Remembers Cross was placed at his grave on 27th June 2018 by Thame resident, Adrian Dite.

28 March 1918

Sydney Allen was born in Thame and baptised at St Mary's Church on 25th March 1888. He was the son of Richard Allen and Anne (née Alder) and had nine siblings, including his brother Charles who also died during the war. The family lived at 45 High Street, Thame next to the Six Bells.

In 1911 Sydney was a printing compositor, living with his brother Edwin and his wife in Greenwich, London. Sydney married Laura Adelaide Fryatt in 1912 in Greenwich and went on to live in St Asaph Road in Brockley, South East London.

Sydney was called up in 1916 when the Military Service Act was extended to married men. He enlisted in Camberwell, London and posted to the Northumberland Fusiliers. Initially he was with 1/4th Battalion before being transferred to 1/5th Battalion, both battalions serving with the 149th Brigade of the 50th (Northumberland) Division. Sydney was wounded in November 1917 during the Second Battle of Passchendaele, the culminating attack during the Third Battle of Ypres, Belgium.

Having recovered from his wounds and returned to the Battalion, which was now in France, he was placed in V Platoon of C Company. Sydney was posted as missing in action on 28th March 1918, just after his 30th birthday, during the Battle of Rosières, part of the German spring offensive through the Somme area.

263029 Private Sydney Allen, Northumberland Fusiliers, has no known grave and is commemorated on Pozières War Memorial, Somme. He is remembered in Thame on the War Memorial and on the Memorial Boards of St Mary's Church and All Saints' Church.

The Thame Remembers Cross was placed at Pozières Memorial on 29th October 2014 by Ian Jones MBE of Thame Remembers.

28 March 1918

George Alfred Bateman was one of the seven children of James Bateman and Annie (née Pollicott). He was born in Gas Alley, Thame in 1878 and baptised at St Mary's Church on 29th February 1880. In 1891 George, age 13, was working as an agricultural labourer. By 1901 the family had moved to Four Ashes, Hughenden, near High Wycombe, Buckinghamshire where George was employed as a carter. Later that year he married Clara Bates and moved to High Wycombe, where they went on to have five children.

Shortly before the start of the war, George moved to Woking, Surrey and then enlisted in March 1915 with the Royal Engineers at Woolwich, London with the rank of Pioneer. He went to France in October 1915 and by 1918 was a Sapper, serving with the 144th Army Troops Company, attached to the Fifth Army. George, age 40, was killed on 28th March 1918 near Le Hamel in Picardy, where the Company was involved in the strengthening and defence of trenches during the German spring offensive. His widow, Clara, received £24 2s 10d in accrued pay and war gratuity.

89239 Sapper George Alfred Bateman, Royal Engineers, has no known grave and is commemorated on Arras Memorial, Pas de Calais. He is also commemorated on the War Memorial in Woking and his name is to be added to Thame War Memorial.

The Thame Remembers Cross was placed at Arras Memorial on 1st November 2015 by Thame Museum member, Ron Roberts.

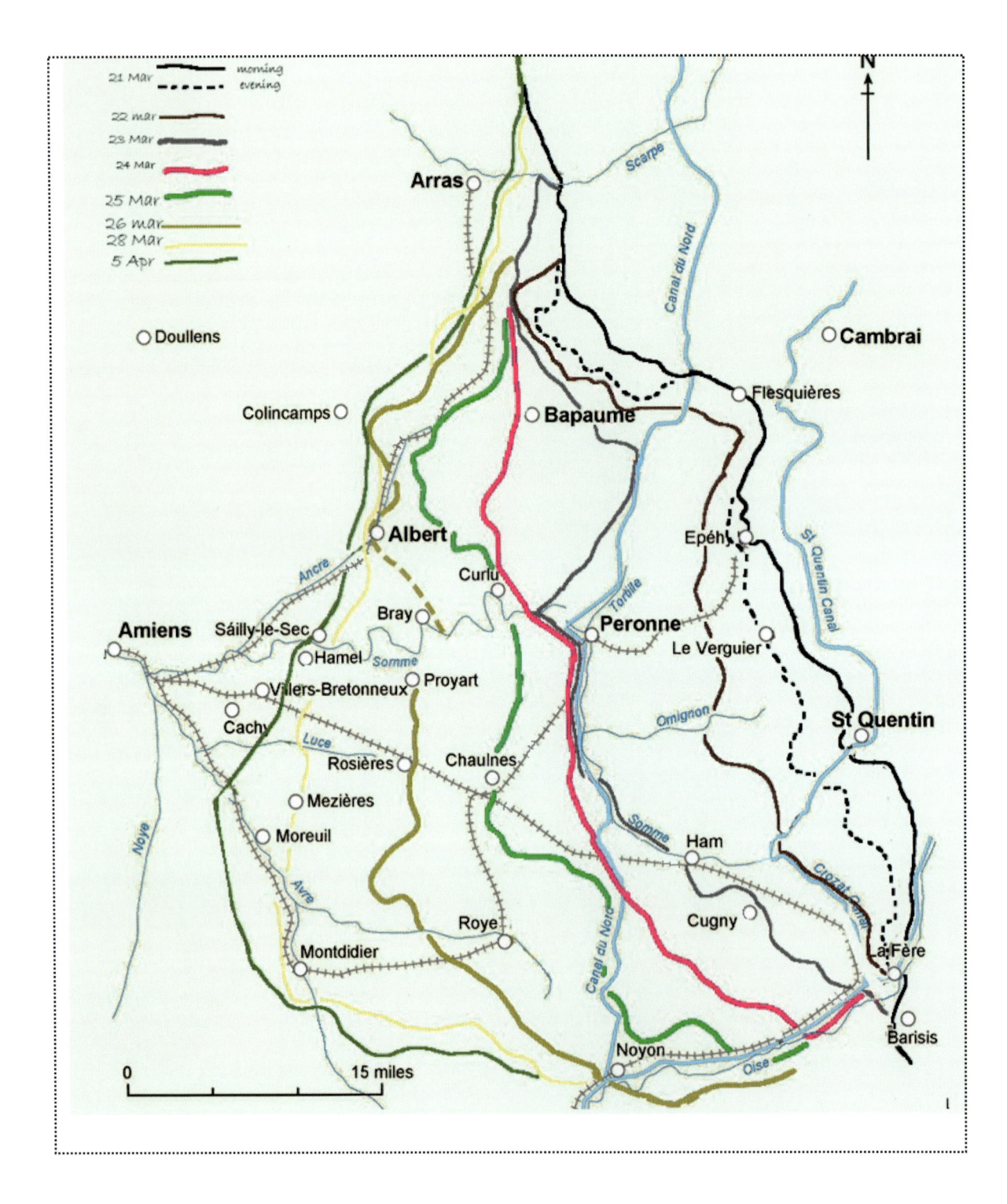

The evolution of the Front Line in the Somme area during the German offensive - Operation Michael in Spring 1918

28 March 1918

Benjamin Squires was born in Thame in 1897, one of the eight children of Herbert Squires and Amelia (née Shurrock) living at 71 Park Street, Thame. Three of his brothers also served in the war, Joseph was killed at Passchendaele in 1917 but both William and Albert survived.

In February 1915 Benjamin enlisted with the Grenadier Guards and, after training, embarked for France in October, joining the 4th Battalion. On 26th September 1916, serving in 3 Company, when taking part in an attack with the Guards Division at Lesboeufs, part of the Battle of the Somme, he received gunshot wounds to his left arm, chest and both legs. He was invalided home and spent almost twelve months in hospital. After recovery, he was drafted back to France returning to the Front in September 1917 to join the 2nd Battalion with the 1st Guards Brigade. On 28th March, during the 1918 First Battle of Arras, part of the German spring offensive known as *Operation Michael*, the Battalion trenches were heavily shelled and they had to repulse a number of German incursions which were supported by machine gun fire. Benjamin, age 21, was one of 22 men from the Battalion who were killed.

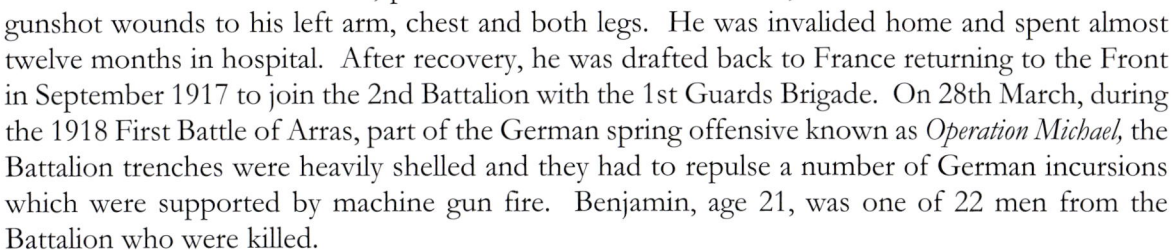

22664 Private Benjamin Squires, Grenadier Guards, has no known grave and is commemorated on Arras Memorial, Pas de Calais. He is remembered in Thame on the War Memorial, near to the name of his brother Joseph. He is also remembered on the Memorial Boards of St Mary's Church, All Saints' Church and Christchurch.

The Thame Remembers Cross was placed at Arras Memorial on 1st November 2015 by Thame Museum member, Ron Roberts.

30 March 1918

Hugh Kidman was one of four children of George Edward Kidman and Clara (née Newton). He was born in 1889 in East Adderbury, near Banbury, Oxfordshire where his parents were farmers and was baptised at the Church of St Mary the Virgin in Adderbury on 8th January 1890. By 1901 the family had taken over a farm in Waterstock, near Wheatley, Oxfordshire and Hugh went to Lord Williams's Grammar School in Thame. On leaving school he took up farming, working for his father.

In 1912 he enlisted with the local Territorials, the Queen's Own Oxfordshire Hussars (Regt No 1727). When the Regiment was mobilised at the start of World War One, the 1/1st Battalion embarked for France on 19th September 1914 and was the first territorial unit to see action in the war. It was part of the 4th Cavalry Brigade of the 2nd Cavalry Division, but spent much of the early war years until the spring of 1917 in defensive positions, waiting for the opportunity of a strategic breakthrough. It never came and they had to spend much of their time dismounted, either in trench working parties or as fighting infantry.

In March 1918 the Germans launched their spring offensive on the Somme and the 1/1st Battalion was heavily involved in the fighting south of St Quentin. On 23rd March Hugh was posted missing but it was subsequently revealed that he had been wounded and taken to a German hospital where he died of his wounds on 30th March. He was 29 years old.

285069 Sergeant Hugh Kidman, Queen's Own Oxfordshire Hussars, is buried in the Maubeuge-Centre Cemetery, Nord. He is remembered in Thame on Lord Williams's School Memorial Board.

The Thame Remembers Cross was placed at his grave on 21st April 2018 by Thame resident, Julie West.

1 April 1918

Herbert Arthur Stockwell was born on 2nd June 1891 in Balcombe Street, London. His mother was Harriet Stockwell of Tetsworth, Oxfordshire.

In 1901 Herbert (known as Bertie) was living with his grandfather Joseph in North Street, Thame. He worked for nine years at Joseph Putman's hardware shop in the Cornmarket. He was a member of the local Territorials of the Oxford and Bucks Light Infantry and was mobilised with them at the start of the war.

He was posted to the 5th Battalion, part of the 42nd Infantry Brigade, 14th Division and embarked with them to France on 20th May 1915 landing at Boulogne. By the end of the month they had moved into Belgium and were soon in action near the Hooge, just south of Ypres. Herbert was one of the many casualties sustained by the Battalion during this time, being reported as wounded in early August.

He saw regular action over the following years, including the Somme in 1916, followed by Arras and Passchendaele in 1917. Herbert rose through the ranks, being promoted to Company Sergeant Major in July 1917.

In November 1917 the Battalion was fighting at Passchendaele, Belgium, where Herbert was awarded the Military Cross.

The German spring offensive through the Somme in March 1918 saw the 5th Battalion, Oxford and Bucks Light Infantry heavily engaged in the Battle of Mont Saint-Quentin. Herbert, age 35, received a bullet wound to the head and was evacuated to one of the base hospitals in Rouen, where he died on 1st April 1918.

10951 Company Sergeant Major Herbert Arthur Stockwell MC, Oxford and Bucks Light Infantry, is buried in St Sever Cemetery Extension, Rouen. He is remembered in Thame on the War Memorial and on the Memorial Boards of St Mary's Church and All Saints' Church.

The Thame Remembers Cross was placed at his grave on 13th November 2014 by Thame resident, Charles Boundy.

Military Cross citation published in the London Gazette on 5th March 1918.

"For conspicuous gallantry and devotion to duty. His company had to pass through an intense barrage when going forward to re-inforce, and on reaching the position were subjected to five hours heavy bombardment. The success of the movement was largely due to his initiative and fearlessness. Though he was three time buried, he remained at duty, inspiring his men by his cheerfulness and gallant example. Later he again steadied the company under a heavy bombardment, and carried out a bombing attack on a party of the enemy who had penetrated the line".

Thursday 13th November 2014 – Normandy

St Sever cemetery and its extension lie near the middle of the section of southern, left bank Rouen, within one of the great sweeps of the River Seine. To the west the commercial and docklands centre spreads untidily back from the river; to the north spasmodic redevelopment continues towards the city centre, where the bright lights of the Christmas funfair on the left bank look across the bridges to the brooding spires of the cathedral. We are here to find the grave of one of Thame's war dead as part of its recognition of those who gave their lives in the First World War. Entering the cemetery we see traditional French family shrines and graves and then iron crosses for the French soldiers before the massed ranks of the Commonwealth war dead come fully into view. Sergeant Major Herbert Arthur Stockwell is commemorated by a headstone in section P, close to the walls of the new multi-sport ground and with a view back to the football stadium on the other flank. From the summary of his life I take it that he joined up at the start of the war, so had already survived nearly four years of camaraderie and hell, progressing to Sgt Major and being awarded the Military Cross for conspicuous bravery. He died on 1 April 1918, one of close to 100 we counted in that section to die on that day, and in turn one of the nearly 12,000 war dead buried in that cemetery. This was the time of the successive German offensives designed to break the stalemate, some months before the Allied push which finally brought victory. Though he died from wounds to the head Sgt Major Stockwell at least found peace in the relative safety of Rouen. His headstone is one of a pair, as with nearly all others, to suggest perhaps that we are not alone even in afterlife. They stand in rows, more ordered in death than ever in life, lit by a low sun, unruffled by the cool breeze. Roses grow in the soil; young acers with burnished late autumn colours stand like sentinels and the fronds of tall grasses rise between some lines like plumes on helmets. Although it is mid-November the mowing machines are still at work; theirs and the soft hum of traffic from surrounding roads are the only sounds. Hazel places the flowers by the headstone. I tuck the *Thame Remembers* cross into the ground and speak to Bertie for a while. We record the scene and sign the nearby visitors' book in the tiny space left available. We notice the diversity of those who died – from all parts of the country and Commonwealth. Even in the French section the names show how their colonies supported them. I note that in Bertie's case (was he still called that in the trenches I wonder?) his age at death is not mentioned on the headstone. That is one way to live on.

Charles Boundy

1 April 1918

Stanley Hugh Winkley was born in Stratford, Essex on 3rd June 1893 and was the third youngest son of Samuel Winkley, master butcher, and Deborah (née Taylor). Stanley was educated at Forest Gate School, Stratford from 1903 to 1906 and then boarded at Lord Williams's Grammar School, Thame until 1908.

He became a student at the Southend Technical Institute, Essex in January 1909 and took a two year course in electrical engineering. On the completion of his course he was awarded an Institute of Electrical Engineers Certificate in connection with the design of electrical machinery. He then entered the workshops of Messrs Childes Ltd of Willesden, Middlesex for practical training where he remained for nine months. In September 1911 he obtained employment with Submersible Motors Ltd in Southall, Middlesex as an assistant in the company's test department. In the spring of 1914 he joined the Lancashire Dynamo and Motor Company Ltd at Trafford Park, Manchester where he was employed on the technical staff in the test department, but relinquished his position with them in April 1915 in order to join the Army.

Stanley enlisted in the Inns of Court Officers' Training Corps in November 1915 and was sent for military training at Berkhamsted, Hertfordshire. Whilst awaiting his turn to go overseas, he made application to transfer to the Royal Flying Corps (RFC) and in March 1917 was attached to No 1 Officer Cadet Wing at Denham, Buckinghamshire, spending four weeks there, before being sent to No 2 School of Aeronautics at Oxford where he was taught to fly. He was given a commission as Temporary 2nd Lieutenant in the RFC in May 1917 and posted to No 3 Reserve Squadron, then stationed at Shoreham, Kent. A few weeks later he was posted to No 19 Training Squadron at Hounslow, Middlesex, where in August he obtained his "Wings" and was appointed a Flying Officer.

Stanley proceeded to France on 8th September for duty with No 18 Squadron, flying DH4 aircraft from Bellevue, on the Doullens-Arras railway, then in the Third Army area. From there he would have borne his share of the aerial fighting in the Albert Sector. After a spell back in England with 35 Training Squadron and 85 Squadron, he returned to France on 2nd February 1918 to 84 Squadron, flying SE5 aircraft with 22nd Wing, V Brigade, RFC. The Squadron was based at Flez, near the village of Quivières, 12 miles west of St Quentin and was heavily engaged in the aerial warfare then in progress, bringing down a number of enemy aircraft. The German spring offensive resulted in the Squadron being pulled back and at the end of March 1918 it was operating from an aerodrome in Bois de la Roche, north east of Abbeville. At 16:30hrs on 1st April 1918, by then having been promoted to Lieutenant, he left the aerodrome as pilot in charge of a bombing mission. It is believed he crashed in a wood near Mézières, but neither his body nor aircraft were ever found. He was 25 years old and one of 17 airmen lost on the first day of the official formation of the Royal Air Force.

Lieutenant Stanley Hugh Winkley, Royal Air Force, has no known grave and is commemorated on Arras Flying Services Memorial, Pas de Calais. He is remembered in Thame on Lord Williams's School Memorial Board.

The Thame Remembers Cross was placed at Arras Flying Services Memorial on 19th April 2015 by David Bretherton of Thame Remembers.

4 April 1918

Reginald George Farmbrough was born in Old Bradwell, Buckinghamshire on 26th July 1887. He was the youngest of seven children of Charles Griffes Farmbrough, a gentleman farmer, and Marian (née Clapham). He also had two half-siblings from his father's earlier marriage.

By 1911 he had left home and moved to Rycote, near Thame where he was assisting farmer Frank Chapman at Lobbersdown Hill Farm between Moreton and Tetsworth, Oxfordshire.

In 1914 he enlisted with the local territorials, the Queen's Own Oxfordshire Hussars (QOOH). The Regiment was mobilised at the start of World War One and embarked for France on 19th September 1914. They became the first territorial unit to see action in the war but as cavalry they spent much of the early years of the war, until the spring of 1917, in defensive positions.

In March 1918 the Germans launched their spring offensives on the Western Front. *Operation Michael* was the attack through the Somme and the dismounted QOOH, part of the 4th Cavalry Brigade with the 2nd Cavalry Division, was heavily involved in the fighting, suffering many casualties during the German advance. Reginald was wounded and evacuated to 12th General Hospital in Rouen. He died of his wounds on 4th April 1918. He was 33 year old and in his will he left over £280.

285173 Trooper Reginald George Farmbrough, Queen's Own Oxfordshire Hussars, is buried in St Sever Cemetery Extension, Rouen. He is remembered on both Thame and Moreton War Memorials and on the Memorial Boards of St Mary's Church and All Saints' Church.

The Thame Remembers Cross was placed at his grave on 13th November 2014 by Thame resident, David Laver.

5 April 1918

Eric William Rose was born in 1898. He was the eldest of three children of Alice Beatrice (née Farmer) and William Cox Rose, a dairy farmer of Moat Farm, Ford, near Aylesbury, Buckinghamshire. He was educated at Lord Williams's Grammar School in Thame, where he boarded from 1909 to 1914. It was reported that *"he showed great promise."*

On 11th December 1916, as soon as he was 18, Eric enlisted at Aylesbury with the Artists Rifles, which became the 28th (County of London) Battalion of the London Regiment. Like many other young men from public schools, he was placed in the Battalion's cadet school for officer training and was commissioned as a Second Lieutenant with the Lancashire Fusiliers on 28th August 1917. He was posted to 1/8th Battalion and joined them in France at the end of October. When the German Army launched their attacks through the Somme in March 1918, the 125th Infantry Brigade, of which 1/8th Lancashire Fusiliers were a part, was moved up to help defend the Line. On 25th March, having earlier in the day been captured and then escaped, Eric took over command of C Company during a counter-attack when his Company Commander, Captain R Alderson was killed. This was an action for which Eric was awarded the Military Cross for *"conspicuous gallantry and devotion to duty"*.

During the next few days the British Third Army was forced to retreat in front of the German advance. On 5th April, the final day of the German assault, the 1/8th Lancashire Fusiliers were in trenches near the village of Bucquoy. The day started with a heavy German artillery barrage, followed by fierce fighting, both flanks of the line being forced back. The last message received from Eric was that his much depleted Company was still holding their original position. The Battalion counter-attacked in the afternoon and regained some of the lost ground, but by then Eric had been killed. He was 20 years old and some confusion surrounds his burial place. Despite official reports that his body was never recovered from the battlefield, Rev T B Hardy VC wrote that he had found Eric's body in the ruins of Bucquoy and buried him there. The search for his grave continues by his descendants.

Second Lieutenant Eric William Rose MC, Lancashire Fusiliers, has no known grave and is commemorated on Arras Memorial, Pas de Calais. He is remembered in Thame on Lord Williams's School Memorial Board. He is also commemorated on the Artists Rifles War Memorial in the entrance portico of the Royal Academy in London and on the War Memorial in Ford, Buckinghamshire.

The Thame Remembers Cross was placed at Arras Memorial on 1st November 2015 by Thame Museum member, Ron Roberts.

The acting Commanding Officer of his Battalion, who was wounded in the same action, wrote the following letter from his hospital bed to Eric's father.

Dear Mr Rose,

Doubtless you will by now have received Col Macleod's letter and will realise that the news of your son's death is unfortunately true. I will endeavour to fill the gap between your son's last letter, (March 31st) and the last I heard of him.

On the evening of April 1st the Battalion took over a portion of the line. 'C' Company (which Eric had commanded since March 26th) was in the front line. For the next three days we had a quiet time, but not too comfortable, as we were in new trenches and the weather was very wet.

On the night of the 4th/5th April, I went round the line at about 3:30am and this was the last I saw of Eric. He was living in a sea of mud, and was very wet and tired, but cheerful. There was no sign that anything was going to happen then, but soon the enemy began shelling heavily.

This became a heavy barrage, and at about 9:30am we received word that an (enemy) Infantry attack had developed and had succeeded in getting a footing in (our) trenches. We at once counter-attacked with the few men available, but were held up by parties of the enemy with Machine Guns, which had got through our line.

It was now about 1pm and at 1:15pm. I received the only information we got from our original front line. This was a full and very clear message from Eric, timed at noon, to the effect that he was holding on, and endeavouring to cover more front.

This was the last I ever heard of what happened in front, for at 5pm when engaged in the ultimately successful counter-attack, I was wounded in the legs. Beyond this, I have since been told that Eric and 2nd Lieut. Clay - the other officer with 'C' Company - had both been found to have been killed. I am afraid I know no more.

Your boy came to my Company on joining the Battalion, and was one of the best officers I have had. He quickly became a great favourite with all. You would hardly credit it, that with his shy and retiring disposition, Eric was a fine fighter. In action, he was conspicuously gallant and coupled with it, a determination and coolheadedness which surprised even myself, who knew his efficiency out of the line. I am delighted that his Military Cross has come through. I was with him in the fighting for which he won it and can tell you that it was thoroughly well deserved.

Let me express to you and all members of the family, my most heartfelt sympathy with you in your loss, in which I share your sorrow. Your grief must be tinged with pride at having had such a son and in the manner of his death. I think that the resistance of 2nd Lieut E W Rose MC and his Company, when cut off from support and surrounded, will be one of the most treasured memories in the history of the Battalion.

I may add that 2nd Lieut Gibbons (a close friend) and Private Jamieson (Eric's assistant) were also wounded on April 5th.

I am Sincerely Yours
George W Sutton

Capt. 8th Lancashire Fusiliers.

16 April 1918

Joseph Brown was born in Thame in 1896, one of the four children of Ada Brown. In 1907 his mother married Arthur Bateman, who went on to adopt Joseph and his sister May. Elsie having left home and Dorothy having died in 1901.

In early 1914, whilst employed as a farm worker and living in North Street, Thame, Joseph enlisted with the local territorials, the 4th Battalion of the Oxford and Bucks Light Infantry (Regt No 2069).

Instead of being posted to the first line Battalion, 1/4th, Joseph was placed with the newly formed 2/4th Battalion, initially intended for home service. However, in the spring of 1915 it was decided that many of the second line battalions were to be prepared for overseas service. In May 1916 Joseph, with the Battalion, part of the 184th Infantry Brigade, 61st Division, embarked for France landing in Le Havre in the early hours of the morning of 25th May and immediately entrained for the Merville area of northern France. Although in regular action, including the disastrous Battle of Fromelles, it was perhaps fortunate that the Division was not called to take part in the Battle of the Somme, only moving down to the area after the main battle had finished.

However, Joseph would have been with the Battalion in various actions in both France and Belgium during 1917, including the Third Battle of Ypres (Passchendaele). By October they were back in northern France. In March 1918 the Battalion suffered heavy casualties during the last major German offensive of the war and almost ceased to exist as a viable fighting unit. Having received reinforcements, the Battalion was engaged in the Battle of the Lys in April, fighting around St Venant in northern France. Joseph, by now a Corporal, was killed by enemy shelling on 16th April 1918. He was 22 years old and his accrued army pay and war gratuity, of £27 2s 6d, was sent to his mother Ada, who was then living in Towersey Road, Thame.

200329 Corporal Joseph Brown, Oxford and Bucks Light Infantry, is buried in the St Venant-Robecq Road British Cemetery, Robecq, Pas de Calais. He is remembered in Thame on the War Memorial and on the Memorial Boards of St Mary's Church and All Saints' Church.

The Thame Remembers Cross was placed at his grave on 17th April 2015 by Thame resident, Catherine Jones.

19 April 1918

William Alfred Boiling was born in Thame on 6th March 1889 to Jane Elizabeth Boiling. They lived with his grandmother Eliza Boiling, innkeeper at the Red Cow beerhouse on Aylesbury Road. William had three siblings, Ethel, Eric and Agnes. It was not until he was nine years old that William was baptised at St Mary's Church, Thame on 28th July 1898. In 1895 his mother had married widower James Burnard, a GWR platelayer, and they were living at 46 Park Street, next door to the Four Horseshoes.

In April 1907 William joined the Royal Navy and was posted to HMS Acheron, an old hulk used for stoker training and anchored at the Nore in the Thames Estuary, However, the navy life was seemingly not for him, as in October 1907, although listed as *"of very good character,"* he discharged himself from HMS Cochrane, an armoured cruiser at Chatham, Kent.

In 1908 he enlisted with the Royal Berkshire (Princess Charlotte of Wales) Regiment and was posted to the 2nd Battalion who were serving in India. When war was declared, the Battalion was recalled to England, arriving on the troopship SS Dongala at Liverpool on 23rd October 1914.

After a brief stopover at Winchester where they joined the 25th Brigade, 8th Division, they left for France and arrived at Le Havre on 6th November.

It was probably in the spring of 1915 that William was transferred to 2/4th Battalion, where men with service experience were needed to assist with the training of these second line territorial battalions who had just been given orders to prepare for overseas service. The Battalion went to France with the 184th Brigade of the 61st Division in May 1916. Its first major action was in the Battle of Fromelles in July. This was intended as a diversionary attack for the Somme, but for the inexperienced 61st Division it turned out to be a disaster, giving them a bad reputation, perhaps unfairly, that they found very difficult to shake off for some considerable time. In March 1918 the 2/4th Royal Berks were in the Front Line near St Quentin sustaining heavy losses when the Germans started their spring offensive, *Operation Michael,* In early April the Battalion was moved north to take up a front line position near Robecq. It was there that William was wounded and died in the 54th Casualty Clearing Station at Aire on 19th April 1918. He was 29 years old and although no records have been found, it appears that William had married, his accrued pay and war gratuity being forwarded to his wife Margaret at Hinkley, Leicestershire. His brother Eric had been killed on 26th September 1915 during the Battle of Loos.

8911 Sergeant William Alfred Boiling, Royal Berkshire Regiment, is buried in Aire Communal Cemetery, Pas de Calais. He is remembered in Thame on the War Memorial and on the Memorial Boards of All Saints' Church and St Mary's Church.

The Thame Remembers Cross was placed at his grave on 19th May 2015
by Thame resident, Sonja Francis.

16 May 1918

Owen Charles Hawes was born into a farming family in Brill, Buckinghamshire on 17th February 1896. The eldest of the four children of Charles Hawes and Ellen (née Porten) known as Nellie. He was educated at Lord Williams's Grammar School in Thame where he became a member of both the football and cricket XIs.

At the outbreak of World War One Owen, age 18 and by then a teacher at Long Crendon County School, Buckinghamshire immediately enlisted with the 4th (Territorial) Battalion of the Oxford and Bucks Light Infantry and was posted to 2/4th Battalion. The Battalion, being a second line unit, was not called for overseas service until 1916, landing in France with the 184th Brigade, 61st Division on 26th May.

In the German offensive at St Quentin in March 1918 the Battalion was overrun and lost over 630 men, more than 450 of them being taken prisoner, including a number of the wounded. Owen, age 21, was one of the wounded and died in a German military hospital on 16th May 1918. He was buried by the Germans in a cemetery, 50 kilometres east of Cambrai. He left £501 in his will. However probate was not granted until 1943 when his mother proved his father's will.

200438 Private Owen Charles Hawes, Oxford and Bucks Light Infantry, is buried in Avesnes-Sur-Helpe Communal Cemetery, Nord. He is remembered in Thame on Lord Williams's School Memorial Board. He is commemorated on the War Memorial in Oakley, Buckinghamshire.

The Thame Remembers Cross was placed at his grave on 21st April 2018
by Thame resident, Brian West.

22 May 1918

Herbert Hiscock Richardson was born in Thame in 1884. The eldest of three sons of Mary Ann Hiscock and her employer John Richardson who lived in East Street, Thame.

After leaving school, Herbert took up his father's trade as a coach maker. In 1910 he married Nellie Bowler at Woburn, Bedfordshire and they went to live at Hampstead, London where he was employed as a wheelwright and bodymaker.

When the Military Service Act of 1916 extended conscription to married men, Herbert was called up and in April 1917 he was enlisted at St Pancras, London in the Royal Garrison Artillery. He was posted to the 126th Heavy Battery serving with the 22nd Heavy Artillery Brigade in France. The heavy batteries were equipped with four 60 pounder, 5 inch guns.

After a short spell in Ypres, Belgium, in the winter of 1917/18, the Battery returned to the Somme area of France in February 1918. They incurred heavy casualties in the German spring offensive and were pulled back to Englebelmer, north west of Albert. They continued to sustain casualties from German shelling and on 22nd May 1918 Herbert, age 34, was killed.

156617 Gunner Herbert Hiscock Richardson, Royal Artillery, is buried in Hedauville Communal Cemetery Extension, Somme. He is remembered in Thame on the War Memorial and on All Saints' Church Memorial Board. His name is commemorated on the memorial stone to Thomas Bowler, his wife's father, in St Michael's churchyard, Woburn Sands, Bedfordshire.

The Thame Remembers Cross was placed at his grave on 29th May 2016 by Thame residents, Marcus McEwan and family.

A Gun Unit of 126 Heavy Battery, Royal Garrison Artillery

6 June 1918

Alfred Thomas Cross was born in Moreton near Thame in 1899. One of nine surviving children of William Cross, an agricultural worker and Adelaide (née Higgins). Alfred was called up for service in May 1917 and received basic training with one of the Young Soldiers battalions of the Devonshire Regiment. He was then sent to the Front with the 2nd Battalion. On 27th May 1918 the 2nd Devonshires were part of the 8th Infantry Division, when they came under attack on what was the first day of the Third Battle of the Aisne, the last German offensive of the war. In a rearguard action at the Bois des Buttes the Battalion held the line alone, giving the remainder of their Division time to withdraw, but it was at the cost of over 550 men from the Battalion being killed or captured. Alfred was wounded and captured, probably when the Germans overran the local casualty clearing station at Mont Notre Dame. He died there of his wounds on 6th June 1918 at 19 years of age and was buried locally in the Mont Notre Dame Military cemetery. In March 1923 his body was reinterred by the Commonwealth War Graves Commission. His brother Frederick had been killed on 21st March 1918.

70422 Private Alfred Thomas Cross, Devonshire Regiment, is buried in Vailly British Cemetery, Aisne, France. He is remembered on both Thame and Moreton War Memorials and on the Memorial Boards of St Mary's Church, All Saints' Church and the Moreton Chapel Memorial Plaque.

The Thame Remembers Cross was placed at his grave on 27th June 2018 by Thame resident, Ann Dite.

The Monument to the 2nd Devonshires at Ville-aux-Bois-les-Pontavert. The inscription reads:

*2nd Battalion Devonshire Regiment
On the 27th May 1918 at a time when the British trenches were being subjected to fierce attacks, the 2nd Battalion Devonshire Regiment repelled successive enemy assaults with gallantry and determination and maintained an unbroken front till a late hour.
The staunchness of this Battalion permitted defences south of the Aisne to be reorganised and their occupation by reinforcements to be completed.
Inspired by the sangfroid of their gallant Commanding Officer Lt Col R H Anderson-Morshead DSO, in the face of an intense bombardment the few survivors of the Battalion, though isolated and without hope of assistance held on to their trenches north of the river and fought to the last with an unhesitating obedience to orders.
Thus the whole Battalion, Colonel, 28 Officers and 552 non-commissioned officers and men, responded with one accord and offered their lives in ungrudging sacrifice to the sacred cause of the allies.*

3 July 1918

Richard John Philip Hewetson, was the only son of the Reverend William Hewetson and Susan Kathleen (née Burgess). He was born on 14th August 1893 in Aston Pinxton, Warwickshire and moved to Thame in 1898 when his father was appointed vicar at St Mary's Church. They lived in the vicarage on Long Crendon Road until 1905 when they moved to Salhouse, Norfolk. Richard was educated at The Knoll, Woburn Sands, Bedfordshire and Dulwich Preparatory School, London afterwards at Repton School, Derbyshire and Oriel College, Oxford. While at school he won several cups for running, gained his football colours in 1911 and played in the freshers' match at Oxford in 1912. He was a school prefect and head of his house for two years. He belonged to the Repton Officer Training Corps (OTC) and gained Certificate A in 1911. Richard volunteered for service in August 1914, the day after his 21st birthday, joining the Loyal North Lancashire Regiment and was immediately offered his commission. He went to France to join the 1st Battalion in June 1915 and was wounded on 25th September at the Battle of Loos. He was hit early in the day and lay out in no man's land for nine hours. He was returned to England and, for some months, lost the use of his fingers. During his time at home he acted as assistant adjutant of the 3rd (Reserve) Battalion before going back to France in March 1917. He joined the 9th Battalion and was adjutant until the Battle of Messines, when he acted as liaison officer between a Canadian brigade and his own. After this, he became adjutant and quartermaster for the 2nd Corps Advanced Reinforcement Camp and later took part in engagements around Ypres and Westhoek, Belgium. He went back to England in October and was advised to accept home service, as his heart was overstrained. However, he requested to be passed fit for general service again and, although unfit, he was sent once more to France in April 1918. He rejoined the 9th Battalion, but was given command of a brigade instructional platoon because of his *"splendid work the year before in heartening up men"*. On 27th May his Division, the 25th, was sent with other tired divisions to rest on the Aisne which was over five miles away from their present location. They had been ordered to fill a gap which had occurred on the left flank three miles long. They had not been gone more than half an hour when they met with the enemy in large forces. They put up a fight which lasted nearly one hour, by which time they were practically surrounded and were eventually overwhelmed by the larger German force. Richard was taken prisoner with his leg smashed, but was not picked up by the German medics until the next day, by which time gas gangrene had set in. His leg was amputated by an English doctor who was also a prisoner, in a cellar converted into a field ambulance station. But, owing to dysentery and pneumonia, Richard died five weeks later on 3rd July 1918. He was 24 years of age and was buried by the Germans in Beaurieux French Military Cemetery. His body was reinterred in 1924 in a Commonwealth War Graves Cemetery.

Captain Richard John Philip Hewetson, Loyal North Lancashire Regiment, is buried in Vendresse British Cemetery, Aisne. He is commemorated on the War Memorials in Salhouse and Wroxham in Norfolk and his name is to be added to Thame War Memorial.

The Thame Remembers Cross was placed at his grave on 27th June 2018 by Thame resident, Adrian Dite.

8 August 1918

Albert Alexander Trinder was born towards the end of 1899 in Staines, Middlesex the youngest of the seven children of William Trinder and Annie (née Way). He was baptised at St Peter's Church, Staines on 11th January 1902. Shortly afterwards the family moved to Thame where his father was the manager of a boot and shoe shop at 126 High Street and where his mother died in 1903. Albert was educated at Lord Williams's Grammar School, Thame and on reaching the age of 18 he was called up for army service. Initially he was posted with 2/2nd London Regiment (Regt No 77137) and then transferred, probably in the spring of 1918, to the 10th Battalion, Essex Regiment. He was killed in action on 8th August 1918, the first day of the Battle of Amiens, the start of the summer offensive which ended the stalemate of trench warfare. He was only 18 years old and one of over 9,000 men who have no known grave and who fell in the period from 8th August 1918 to the Armistice whilst taking part in the Advance to Victory in the Artois region.

47527 Private Albert Alexander Trinder, Essex Regiment, is commemorated on Vis-en-Artois Memorial, near Arras. He is remembered in Thame on the War Memorial and the Memorial Boards of St Mary's Church, All Saints' Church, Christchurch and Lord Williams's School. He is also commemorated in St Mary's churchyard on the grave of his mother Annie.

The Thame Remembers Cross was placed at Vis-en-Artois Memorial on 19th April 2015 by Mike Dyer of Thame Remembers.

27 August 1918

John Alexander Summerhayes, known as Jack, was born at Dera Ghazi Khan, Punjab, India (now part of Pakistan) on 25th November 1898 and was baptised there on 29th January 1899. He was the third of eight children and the eldest son of Dr John Orlando Summerhayes, a medical director of the Church Missionary Society hospital and Lucy Alexa (née Currie), a missionary nurse. In 1907 they left India and in 1908 moved to Thame to live at Redholme in the High Street where Dr Summerhayes took up the post as town physician and surgeon.

Jack was educated at St Lawrence College, a boarding school in Ramsgate, Kent, where he attained school colours at cricket, football and hockey. He won the Open School Championship for boxing in 1917 and became captain of his house. When the school was evacuated to Chester in 1915, Jack joined the Officer Training Corps achieving the rank of Lance Sergeant. As soon as he reached the age of 18 he would have received his call up papers and was, according to information taken from his Medal Roll Index card, intended to join the 3rd (Reserve) Battalion of the Cheshire Regiment. However, it seems that his enlistment was deferred as he was still in education, not leaving school until 1917, and by which time he had gained a place to study medicine at Oxford University.

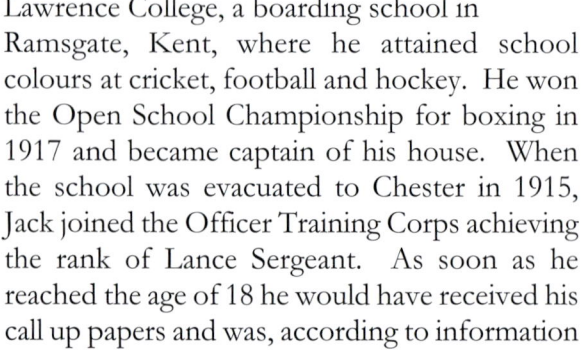

An extract from an Oxfordshire Paper which was quoted in the St Lawrence College Magazine of December 1918 states that very soon after entering Oxford *"the call to military service claimed him*

irresistibly and in spite of obstacles and disadvantages, attendant upon some eye injury sustained in childhood, he succeeded in entering a Labour Battalion, and went to the Front in February, subsequently attached to the 13th Battalion Inniskilling Fusiliers. His thoughtfulness and consideration towards his men won for him their respect and affection from the first and his quiet strength of character and soldierly ability resulted in his being given, by his Colonel, the exceptional promotion from 2nd Lieutenant to Captain commanding a Company."

On 27th August 1918 Jack, by now an acting Captain, and only 19 years old, was killed by a sniper during the Battalion advance under a creeping barrage from trenches at Vieux Berquin in northern France. His father had enlisted in the Royal Army Medical Corps at the start of the war and at the time of Jack's death was serving in Italy as a Lieutenant Colonel.

Captain John Alexander Summerhayes, Royal Inniskilling Fusiliers, is buried in the small military cemetery in Nieppe-Bois, Vieux-Berquin, Nord. He is remembered in Thame on the War Memorial and on the Memorial Boards of St Mary's Church and All Saints' Church.

The Thame Remembers Cross was placed at his grave on 16th February 2016 by Thame resident, Derek Turner.

27 August 1918

Mark Wells was born on 14th February 1892 in Rotherhithe, London. He was the third eldest of seven children of Louisa and Mark Wells, a police sergeant in the Metropolitan Police. By 1895 the family had moved to Hackney, where Mark attended Church Street School. His father retired from the police force and went on to become an innkeeper, firstly in Cholsey, Berkshire and then in 1915 the Greyhound in North Street, Thame. After leaving school, Mark, known as "Mickie", took up employment as a footman at Stoke Place, Stoke Poges, Buckinghamshire, the country estate of the Howard-Vyse family.

He was called up in 1916 under the Military Service Act, being enlisted at Watford in November 1916 and posted to the Queen's (Royal West Surrey) Regiment. After a few weeks training Mark joined the 6th Battalion in France, most likely in time for their participation in the Arras offensive of 1917 with the 37th Brigade, part of the 12th Division. The Battalion later that year took part in the Cambrai offensive and spent the spring of 1918 in heavy fighting during the German offensive through the Somme. Mark was one of two men from the Battalion killed on 27th August 1918, when the Battalion was engaged in the Battle of Amiens, pushing from Meaulte towards Mametz. He was originally buried in a small cemetery near where he fell, before being reinterred at his final resting place near Albert in October 1919.

T/265942 Private Mark Wells, Queen's (Royal West Surrey) Regiment, is buried in Quarry Cemetery, Montauban, Somme. He is remembered in Thame on the War Memorial and on St Mary's Church Memorial Board.

The Thame Remembers Cross was placed at his grave on 18th April 2015 by Ian Jones MBE of Thame Remembers.

Identity Disc for "Mickie" Wells

8 October 1918

Ralph Wentworth Stone was born in January 1890, the only son of Lieutenant Colonel Robert Warner Stone, former commander of the 2nd Battalion South Staffordshire Regiment, and Lucie Alleyne Stone. They lived in the Manor House in Long Crendon, Buckinghamshire. Ralph was baptised at St Mary's Church, Long Crendon on 12th February 1890. His father died when he was two years old. In 1901 Ralph was a boarding pupil at the Royal Naval School in Crofton, near Titchfield, Hampshire, a boys' preparatory school, before moving to Lord Williams's Grammar School in Thame.

At the age of 18 it would seem that Ralph wanted to seek his fortune as he left England in December 1907 on the SS Corinthic, bound for Wellington, New Zealand. He returned in January 1915 on the SS Mongolia, after spending time in the Malay States as a rubber planter.

Three months later, on 10th April 1915, Ralph embarked for East Africa with the 25th Battalion Royal Fusiliers, arriving in Mombasa on 4th May. The Battalion was part of the force defending British Colonies from attacks from the nearby German colonial territories. After suffering many casualties, due to both fighting and disease, the Battalion returned to England at the end of 1917. Ralph was subsequently posted to the 17th Battalion and then to the 4th Battalion, both of which were serving in France. They were engaged in the German spring offensive and then the big Allied counter-attack and breakout from the stalemate of trench warfare. Ralph was killed in action on 8th October 1918, during the Second Battle of Cambrai. He was 28 years old and was buried in La Targette British Cemetery, before being reinterred in 1923 when that cemetery was closed down.

G/15124 Private Ralph Wentworth Stone, Royal Fusiliers, is buried in Forenville Military Cemetery, Nord. He is remembered in Thame on Lord Williams's School Memorial Board. He is commemorated on the War Memorial in Long Crendon.

The Thame Remembers Cross was placed at his grave on 12th May 2015 by Thame resident, John Cook.

8 October 1918

Alfred Willis was born in Thame in 1886 to William Willis, a maltster and Harriett (née Grainger). He was one of six children and was baptised at St Mary's Church, Thame on 1st July 1886. By 1891 the family had moved to Bicester, Oxfordshire but in 1901 they were living in Brackley, Northamptonshire. Alfred married Elizabeth Viccars in Buckingham on 29th April 1908 and a son, William John, was born in 1910.

Alfred was employed as a gardener in Brackley when he was called up in November 1916. Initially he was posted to the Army Service Corps followed by various Training Reserve Battalions, until in August 1917 he was posted to 1/8th Battalion Durham Light Infantry, who were serving in France with the 151st Brigade of the 50th (Northumbrian) Division.

He was wounded in March 1918, receiving a gunshot wound to his right thigh during *Operation Michael,* the German spring offensive on the Somme. He was evacuated to England on the hospital ship HMHS Aberdonian, but by August 1918 was sufficiently recovered to be able to return to France, this time to the 18th Battalion. However, he was almost immediately posted to the 15th Battalion at Simencourt near Arras, arriving on 30th August.

Alfred was killed on 8th October 1918 in the attack at Angles Chateaux, Nord. He was 32 years old and one of 51 men from the Battalion who were killed during the Second Battle of Cambrai.

4155 Private Alfred Willis, Durham Light Infantry, is buried in Bois-des-Angles British Cemetery, Crèvecoeur-sur-L'Escaut, Nord. He is commemorated on the War Memorial in Brackley and his name is to be added to Thame War Memorial.

The Thame Remembers Cross was placed at his grave on 22nd May 2015
by Thame resident, Margaret Bretherton.

28 October 1918

Frederick Stopps, according to the 1911 census and his military record, was born in Thame around 1869, but exactly when and who his parents were is not recorded. Other census records indicate that he was born in Lambeth, London, although in 1881 he was shown as being at school and boarding with a local boot and shoe maker in Great Milton, near Thame. He married Ann Osborn at St Peter's Church, Walworth, London on 1st January 1891. They had eight children, all born in the Lambeth and Camberwell area, although only five survived infancy.

Frederick was a carman (a driver of horse-drawn transport for goods) and it was his work with horses that probably led to him enlisting with the 6th Dragoon Guards (Carabiniers) at Peckham, London in August 1914. The Regiment was part of the 2nd Cavalry Division (the same as the Queen's Own Oxfordshire Hussars in which many Thame men served) and took part in a large number of the main battles in France and Flanders during the war. It was during the final advance through Picardy that Frederick, age 47, died of heart failure on 28th October 1918.

Although records only give his rank as a Private, his wife Ann received his accrued back pay in 1919, which included a war gratuity of £24 10s which would seem to indicate that at some stage he had achieved the rank of Corporal.

D/10208 Private Frederick Stopps, Dragoon Guards, is buried in Estaires Communal Cemetery, Nord. He is commemorated on the London War Memorial Project.

The Thame Remembers Cross was placed at his grave on 1st November 2015
by Thame resident, Ann Barrington.

5 November 1918

William Bowler was born in Thame on 29th January 1886 to Harry Bowler and Mary (née Hollier). He was one of their fifteen children, although only ten were still alive in 1911. His father was a carpenter, but for a short time in the 1890s was also innkeeper at the Red Lion beerhouse in Park Street. William also took up the trade of a carpenter and in 1911 was living with his parents at 74 Park Street, although they later moved to 30 Park Street, the house previously occupied by Samuel Bowler, William's grandfather.

Before the start of the War, William had signed up with the Oxford and Bucks Light Infantry in 1908 and was subsequently placed on the National Reserve. In August 1914, along with several other Thame men, he was called to the Colours and left Thame to join the 3rd (Special Reserve) Battalion, initially at Cosham, Hampshire, before moving to barracks in Portsmouth. In September 1914 he was promoted to Lance Corporal and to full Corporal in May 1915.

The 3rd Battalion was primarily a training battalion for new recruits before they were posted to service battalions and William is most likely to have been one of the instructional team. However in October 1915 he was posted to France as part of a reinforcing draft to the 5th Battalion who the previous month had suffered very heavy casualties in the action at Bellewaarde Farm near the Hooge, Belgium.

Over the next two years, the Battalion was in action at many of the main battles of the Western Front, including the Somme in 1916, Passchendaele in 1917 and the German spring offensive in 1918. By the end of April 1918, the 5th Battalion was reduced to cadre strength only and many of the remaining men were dispersed to other battalions. The Battalion band, of which William Bowler was a member, joined 2/4th Battalion of the Regiment on 28th May 1918. On 5th November just six days before the Armistice William, age 32, died at a casualty clearing station in the village of Awoingt, northern France, as a result of a wound received to the abdomen from the accidental discharge of a captured German revolver that was being examined by one of his fellow musicians. In 1919 his mother, his father having died the previous year, received over £32 in accrued pay and war gratuity.

8875 Corporal William Bowler, Oxford and Bucks Light Infantry, is buried in Awoingt British Cemetery, Nord. He is remembered in Thame on the War Memorial and on the Memorial Boards of St Mary's Church and All Saints' Church.

The Thame Remembers Cross was placed at his grave on 24th March 2015 by Thame resident, Jill Gregory.

Hostilities will cease at 11:00hrs on November 11th.
Troops will stand fast on the line reached at that hour which will be maintained.
There will be no intercourse of any description with the enemy until receipt of instructions from GHQ.
Further instructions will follow.

Signal that was sent to all Units following the signing of the Armistice

Gallipoli

The eight month campaign in Gallipoli was fought by British, British Empire and French forces in an attempt to force Turkey out of the war and to relieve the deadlock of the Western Front in France and Belgium. It would also open a supply route to Russia through the Dardanelles and the Black Sea and maybe allow access to central Europe through the river Danube.

The Allies landed on the Peninsula on 25th/26th April 1915; the 29th Division at Cape Helles in the south and the Australian and New Zealand Corps north of Gaba Tepe on the west coast, an area soon to be known as Anzac Cove. On 6th August further landings were made at Suvla, just north of Anzac, and the climax of the campaign came in early August when simultaneous assaults were launched on all three fronts. However, the difficult terrain and stiff Turkish resistance soon led to the stalemate of trench warfare. From the end of August no further serious action was fought and the lines remained unchanged. With onset of winter and the prospect of low temperatures the Peninsula was successfully evacuated in December and early January 1916.

The Helles Memorial

The Helles Memorial serves the dual function of Commonwealth Battle Memorial for the whole Gallipoli campaign and a place of commemoration for those Commonwealth servicemen who died there and have no known grave, including those who died at sea. There are over 20,000 names commemorated on this Memorial.

Those Remembered

12 August 1915

Graham Chard Loader was born in Thame on 30th August 1891.
He was the youngest son of John Loader, a corn merchant and Martha Helen (née Chard) living at 18 Cornmarket. He was baptised at St Mary's Church on 26th October 1891.
The family moved to Newport, Isle of Wight where Graham went to the County School, before taking up a job as a bank clerk with the Capital and Counties Bank in Newport. In February 1909 he enlisted with the Hampshire Territorials and was commissioned with the 1/8th (Isle of Wight Rifles) Battalion in 1913. At the outbreak of war he volunteered for foreign service, being promoted to Captain on 19th June 1915.
The Battalion embarked for the Dardenelles on 29th July on the Cunard ship RMS Aquitania, then transferred by smaller boats to Suvla Bay where they disembarked on 9th August. On 12th August, hardly having time to acclimatise, the 1/8th were one of three battalions of the 163rd Brigade ordered to attack Turkish positions. Advancing over open ground, they came under heavy machine gun fire near Anafarta. Graham was hit by a bullet in the mouth, dying almost instantly. He was 24 years old and one of almost 300 casualties suffered by the Battalion on that day.

It was reported at the time that he was buried on the battlefield, but his grave could not be found when the cemeteries and memorial were being established after the war.

Captain Graham Chard Loader, Hampshire Regiment, has no known grave and is commemorated on Helles Memorial, Gallipoli Peninsula. He is remembered in Thame on the War Memorial and he is also commemorated on several memorials on the Isle of Wight.

The Thame Remembers Cross was placed at Helles Memorial on 21st June 2018 by Mike Dyer of Thame Remembers.

22 August 1915

William Ewen Hicks was born into a farming family in Cuxham, Oxfordshire in early 1898. He was the eldest of the six children of Edwin Hicks and Margaret Spence Hunter Hicks (née Ewen). By 1911 the family had moved to Clare Hill, Pyrton, near Watlington, Oxfordshire where William attended school.

In September 1914 William enlisted with the City of London (Rough Riders) Yeomanry, part of the London Mounted Brigade. He must have lied about his age, as he was only 16 years old at the time.

In April 1915 the Regiment embarked for the Mediterranean. Following a brief posting to the Suez Canal Defences, the Regiment was dismounted and landed at Suvla Bay, Gallipoli on the morning of 18th August moving into reserve positions at Karakol Dagh. They moved to C Beach, Lala Baba on 20th August and the next day advanced to Chocolate Hill under heavy fire. The Regiment took part in the attack on Scimitar Hill where they suffered heavy casualties. William, age 17, was wounded in the action and evacuated onto the hospital ship HMHS Nevasa where unfortunately he died of his wounds on 22nd August 1915 and was then buried at sea.

2411 Private William Ewen Hicks, City of London Yeomanry, has no known grave and is commemorated on Helles Memorial, Gallipoli Peninsula. He is remembered in Thame on the War Memorial and on St Mary's Church Memorial Board. He is also commemorated on the War Memorial in Pyrton.

The Thame Remembers Cross was placed at Helles Memorial on 21st June 2018 by David Bretherton of Thame Remembers.

Allan Hickman with the Thame Remembers Cross at Helles Memorial

24 September 1915

Sackville "George" Crick was born in Moreton, near Thame in the summer of 1861. He was the son of John Crick and Mary (née Mott) and had one full sister Mary Hannah, a half-brother Jonas Daniel, and half-sisters Jane and Rahab. The latter three children bore the name Mott as Mary was not married when they were born. Jonas was born in the workhouse in Thame where Mary and her children were resident in 1851. In 1881 Sackville was living at home in Moreton and working as a blacksmith.

He served for some years in the Royal Horse Artillery (RHA) before travelling to Toronto, Canada in 1886 where he first worked at the Royal Hotel and then he served for nine years in the Royal Canadian Mounted Police as a blacksmith. During his time in Canada he was known as "George Mott". He married Sarah Elizabeth Jackson in 1890 and they had three children Frederick, Violetta and Elsie all born in Canada. The family returned to England in 1897, using the name Crick, living firstly in Worksop and then Mansfield, both in Nottinghamshire, again Sackville worked as a blacksmith. A further daughter Elizabeth was born in 1899 in Worksop.

In September 1912 the family emigrated to Australia where Sackville Crick was employed at the Footscray Tannery, Yarraville, Melbourne. When he volunteered for the Australian Imperial Service on 30th October 1914 he said he was age 44 years and one month. He lied about his age as he was actually a few months over 53 years old. It may be to disguise his age that he enlisted as "George" Crick and did not mention his service in the RHA. He served as a farrier with the 12th Army Service Corps which embarked from Melbourne on 2nd February 1915 on HMAT Chilka. The 12th Army Service Corps was part of the 3rd Light Horse Brigade that saw action in Gallipoli and Egypt. "George", age 54, was taken ill and died of heart failure in Heliopolis, near Cairo on 24th September 1915. He was buried on 28th September in Cairo War Memorial Cemetery, Egypt.

His son Frederick was serving with the Grenadier Guards in Hampshire in 1911, but embarked with his young wife for Australia in May 1914. He must have been recalled, as he served with the Grenadier Guards throughout World War One receiving a Military Medal in 1916 and a bar to his Military Medal in 1919. He returned to Australia after the war and lived there until his death in 1964.

5046 Driver Sackville "George" Crick, Australian Army Service Corps, is buried in Cairo War Memorial Cemetery. His name is to be added to both Thame and Moreton War Memorials.

The Thame Remembers Cross was placed at his grave on 11th February 2017 by Thame resident, Wendy Townsend.

Cairo War Cemetery

Extract from George Crick's Australian Service Record showing the medals he was awarded

Greece

The Macedonian (Salonika) Front of World War One was created by the Allied Powers as an attempt to aid Serbia against the combined attack of Germany, Austria-Hungary and Bulgaria. The Expedition came too late and of insufficient force to prevent the fall of Serbia in 1915, but eventually a stable Front was established, from the Adriatic coast to the Struma River, pitting a multi-national Allied Force against the Bulgarian Army, which was bolstered at times with smaller units from the other Central Powers. The Macedonian Front remained quite stable, despite local actions, until the great Allied offensive in September 1918, which resulted in the capitulation of Bulgaria and the liberation of Serbia.

The Doiran Memorial

From October 1915 to the end of November 1918, the British Salonika Force suffered 8,400 casualties; 2,800 deaths in action, 1,400 from wounds and 4,200 from sickness. The campaign afforded few successes for the Allies and none of any importance until the last two months. The actions of the British and French force were hampered throughout by widespread and unavoidable sickness and by continual diplomatic and personal differences between neutral countries and Allies. On one front there was a wide malarial river valley and on the other difficult mountain ranges, which meant that many of the roads and railways that were required had to be specially constructed.

The Doiran Memorial stands roughly in the centre of the line occupied for two years by the Allied forces in Macedonia, who were fighting the Bulgarian forces. It marks the scene of the fierce fighting of 1917/18, which caused the majority of the battle casualties. The Memorial serves the dual purpose of Battle Memorial of the British Salonika Force (for which a large sum of money was subscribed by the officers and men of that Force) and a place of commemoration for more than 2,000 British servicemen who died in Macedonia and whose graves are unknown.

Those Remembered

24 April 1917

Francis Hopkins was born in Chinnor, Oxfordshire on 23rd December 1895 to John Hopkins and Mary Ann (née Loader). He was baptised at St Andrew's Church, Chinnor on 22nd January 1896. Francis was living with his widowed mother in Moorend Lane, Thame in 1901 and 1911. When he died, age 20, his mother was living at Lower High Street in Thame.

Richard Line was born in Hampstead, London on 1st December 1896 to Richard Line and Ruth (née House). In 1901 he was still living in Hampstead with his family but by 1911 his father Richard had died and left Ruth a widow with nine children. The two youngest were at home but the others were mainly in service in and around London. Richard was living in a children's home known as "The Houseboy Brigade" in Elizabeth Street, Pimlico. Sometime after 1911 the family moved to Thame to live in Lower High Street, including his brother Ralph who is also remembered on Thame War Memorial.

At Kitchener's calling Francis Hopkins (Regt No 13767) and Richard Line (Regt No 13765) both joined the Oxford and Bucks Light Infantry at Oxford. They were among a group of men transferred from the Oxford and Bucks to the Wiltshire Regiment, where they joined the 7th (Service) Battalion, which was also known as the Duke of Edinburgh's Regiment.

The 7th Battalion initially served in France but in November 1915 they sailed to Salonika.

In 1916 they were fighting near Kalinova having taken over from the French and by the end of 1916 they were in the area around Lake Doiran. The First Battle of Doiran took place between 22nd April and 8th May 1917. On the night of 24th April the 7th Battalion launched a night attack on the fortress of Grand Couronne, encountering devastating gun fire and unbreached wire. Fourteen out of the fifteen officers became casualties, together with about 300 other ranks, including Francis Hopkins, age 21, and Richard Line, age 20, of B Company, 7th Battalion.

14405 Private Francis Hopkins and 14432 Private Richard Line, Wiltshire Regiment, have no known graves and are commemorated on Doiran Memorial, Salonika. In Thame they are remembered on the War Memorial and the Memorial Boards of St Mary's church and All Saints' Church.

The Thame Remembers Cross was placed at Doiran Memorial on 5th October 2017 by Major Robert Bartlett, President of Thame British Legion.

> Mrs Line of Lower High Street has an official report that her son Pte Richard Line MGS Wilts Regt has been missing since the engagement of 24th April at Salonika and also the following letter dated May 11th from his officer.
>
> *Dear Mrs Line. I have been waiting to write to you in hope that I might be able to give you some news of your son. By now you will have heard that he has been reported missing after a fight we had on 24th April other than that we do not know, but there is a chance that he may be a prisoner in the Bulgars hands in which case he will be taken care of. The suspense and uncertainty will be very hard for you to bear and I can only offer you my deepest sympathy, written words can say so little but these come from my heart for he was one of the bravest soldiers and best Machine Gunners in the Regiment. I have known him since Sutton Verny days and had always taken special interest in him because he was (like me) a Londoner. You must be brave and hope and pray for the best and if those hopes are not realised you must be proud to remember that he died for his country as bravely and gallantly as any soldier could do, taking his gun into action across 50 yards of open country under heavy shell fire, to re-inforce another gun that had been knocked out. That he got into the Bulgars trenches we know. After that nothing is certain. His personal belongings will reach you in due course. If I get any further news I will write to you at once, if you have news or there is anything that I can do or help you I beg that you will let me know.*
> *Yours Truly*
> *Owen Rutter 2nd Lieutenant MG Section Wilts Regiment*
> *BEF Salonika*

Report from the Thame Gazette 5th June 1917

British Army in India

The term Army of India was instituted to refer to the overall command structure which directed the efforts of both the British Army in India and the Indian Army. The latter was made up of Indian soldiers in units mainly commanded by expatriate British officers. The Army of India included the Gurkhas, Sikhs and many other regiments who fought with great distinction in World War One.

The British Army in India was made up of regular formations posted from Britain for a tour of duty overseas. As the Army of India, they served on the Western Front, Gallipoli, East and West Africa, Mesopotamia and the North West Frontier. This explains how men from Thame were serving in India and fighting in these secondary theatres of war.

During the period 1914 to 1918 more than 31,000 officers and men from the Army of India died in combat or of disease. The latter often being the greatest cause of casualties.

Commonwealth War Graves Commission Kirkee Memorial at Poona, India

Those Remembered

5 May 1916

Alfred John Walter Howes was born in Moreton near Thame in 1885 and was the youngest of the ten children of Alfred Howes and Elizabeth (née Wyatt). He became an agricultural farm labourer in Moreton.

In 1907 Alfred joined the Oxford and Bucks Light Infantry, 1st Battalion and travelled to India, where the Battalion had been based since 1903. Serving with H Company, he was posted with the Battalion to Mesopotamia in November 1914, as part of the 17th (Ahmednagar) Brigade, 6th (Poona) Division. After a number of successful engagements against the Ottoman Turks, the Division was eventually defeated in a failed attempt to capture Baghdad and was forced to retreat to Kut-al-Amara in December 1915. They were under siege for several months without any relief and thus the Division, including 400 men of the 1st Battalion, surrendered to the Ottomans at the end of April 1916. Only 71 men of the Battalion survived captivity. Alfred, age 31, died at Shumran, Iraq on or about 5th May 1916.

8434 Private Alfred John Walter Howes, Oxford and Bucks Light Infantry, has no known grave and is commemorated on the Basra Memorial, Iraq. He is remembered in Thame on both Thame and Moreton War Memorials and on the Memorial Boards of St Mary's Church and All Saints' Church.

The Thame Remembers Cross was placed at the Basra Memorial Book, Commonwealth War Graves Commission Headquarters in Maidenhead, Berkshire on 9th May 2018 by Thame resident, Sue Hickman.

The Thame Remembers Cross at Basra War Memorial. Taken there by staff from the Commonwealth War Graves Commission

11 August 1916

William Thomas Baverstock was born in Chinnor, Oxfordshire in late 1888 to Frederick Baverstock and Amelia (née Larner). He was the eldest of six children and had four sisters, Ethel, Edith, May and Eva and a brother, Walter. By 1911 the family had moved to 72 Park Street, Thame. Walter also served with the Oxford and Bucks Light Infantry and survived the war.

In 1907 William enlisted in the Oxford and Bucks Light Infantry and was posted to India with the 1st Battalion. In the 1911 census he is listed as Overseas Military residing in Wellington, Nilgiris, Tamil Nadu, India.

The Battalion was under the command of 17th Indian Brigade of 6th (Poona) Division, Indian Army and was based at Trimulgherry Entrenchment, an artillery cantonment located in the area of Secunderabad in India.

In November 1914 the Battalion was posted to Mesopotamia where, in April 1916, it surrendered to the Ottomans after the siege at Kut-al-Amara. However, William had by that time returned to India where he died of sickness on 11th August 1916, age 27 and was buried in Sewri Cemetery in Bombay. In 1962, along with 628 others, his remains were reinterred in a mass grave at Kirkee 1914-1918 Memorial, Poona, India.

8423 Private William Thomas Baverstock, Oxford and Bucks Light Infantry, is commemorated on Kirkee 1914-1918 Memorial in Poona, India. He is remembered in Thame on the War Memorial and on the Memorial Boards of All Saints' Church and St Mary's Church. He is also commemorated on the Roll of Honour Board in Towersey, Oxfordshire..

The Thame Remembers Cross was placed at Kirkee Memorial on 10th December 2014 by Thame resident, Sarah Goss.

6 November 1918

Harry Eele was born in Thame in 1883, one of the nine children of William Eele and Emma (née Dorsett) living in Aylesbury Road. He became a fellmonger dealing in sheepskins and in 1904 he married Alice Clara Attwell in Thame. They lived in Wellington Street where they had six children.

It is likely that Harry was conscripted in 1916 when the Military Service Act included married men. Initially he was posted with the Wiltshire Regiment, probably to the 2/4th Battalion who were serving in India. He was then transferred to the 222nd Company of the Machine Gun Corps (Infantry) stationed on the North West Frontier area of what is now Pakistan. It was here, at Abbottabad, that Harry died from influenza on 6th November 1918. He was 35 years old and one of the millions of deaths due to the 1918 worldwide pandemic. Harry was originally buried in Abbottabad Cemetery, India but after the partition of India in 1947 the grave was neglected and subsequently lost.

164282 Private Harry Eele, Machine Gun Corps, is now commemorated on Karachi War Memorial, Pakistan. He is remembered in Thame on the War Memorial and on the Memorial Boards of St Mary's Church and All Saints' Church.

The Thame Remembers Cross was placed at the Wiltshire Regiment Memorial at the National Memorial Arboretum, Staffordshire on 22nd July 2018 by Allan Hickman, Thomas Shotliff and Lily Watford.

The Thame Remembers Cross at Karachi War Memorial. Taken there by staff from the Commonwealth War Graves Commission

Only a Volunteer

Why didn't you wait to be drafted
The answer is simple enough
You didn't need a brass band to lead you
You're made of the right kind of stuff
Your banquet will come when it's over
That's when you want to be cheered
And you will know you deserved it
Because you have volunteered

Anon

New Zealand

The countries of the British Empire played an important role in the Allied Armies. The strength of the British army at its peak is estimated at 8.5 million men of which approximately 100,000 were from New Zealand.

There were about half the above number in uniform in their own country providing support and training and, like in England, many of these men became casualties through accident and illness. Only one of them has a link with Thame.

Gravestones at Karori Cemetery

Those Remembered

5 April 1917

George Bertie Parker was born in Cowley, Oxford on 8th November 1866. He was the only son of George Parker, who was Clerk of the University Schools in Oxford and Sarah Ann (née Broadhurst). He was educated at New College School, Oxford and later became a boarder at Lord Williams's Grammar School, Thame. He matriculated as a Commoner (BA Queen's College) in 1885.

George joined the Horse Guards on 20th September 1888, but purchased his discharge 23 days later. He rejoined the Horse Guards on 30th May 1892, this time staying for nearly two years.

According to the 'Liber Vitae Reginensium' (Queen's College archives) he left university to enter the service of the British South Africa Company, becoming the Postmaster of Fort Tuli and was selected to lay the telegraph from there to Fort Victoria. Later he was sent by Mr Cecil Rhodes to Bulawayo to organise the Matabele Police.

G.B. PARKER

In 1896, at the age of 30, he was a Corporal in B Troop of the infamous "Jameson Raiders". He served in the Boer War, first as a Trooper with the Mounted Police of the South African Constabulary and then as a Sergeant in Loch's Horse joining on 10th February 1900. He was invalided back to England on SS Canada on 1st August 1900. In April 1909 he sailed from London on SS Ionic, arriving at Lyttleton, New Zealand in November.

He worked as a clerk for A J Gibbs in Forton, New Zealand until September 1915 when he enlisted with the New Zealand Expeditionary Force, taking five years off his age. He served on the Home Front at Featherstone Camp, Army Supply Corps and was promoted to Sergeant in April 1916. He died from throat cancer at the Victoria Military Hospital, Wellington on 5th April 1917, age 51 years.

18005 Sergeant George Bertie Parker, New Zealand Army Supply Corps, is buried at Karori Military Cemetery, Wellington. He is remembered in Thame on Lord Williams's School Memorial Board.

The Thame Remembers Cross was placed at his grave on 13th December 2014 by former Lord Williams's School Head Boy, George Bateman.

Greetings to our Soldier Boy from Maoriland

'Mid your dangers and your hardships
At this war-marred Christmas time,
Love sends you fondest wishes
From New Zealand's sunny clime.

R.J.P.

Palestine

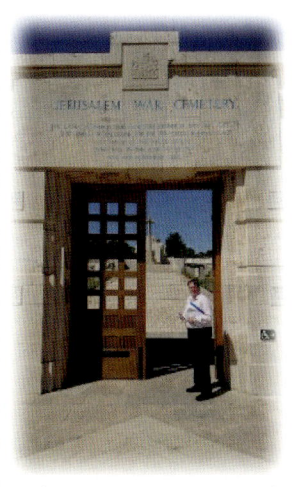

The Sinai and Palestine Campaign in the Middle Eastern theatre of World War One was fought between the British Empire and the Ottoman Empire, which had limited support from the Germans. Initially, in early 1915, the Ottomans attempted to seize the strategically important Suez Canal and, although this failed, the threat to it remained due to a lack of British resources in theatre. The complete withdrawal of troops from Gallipoli to Egypt concluded in January 1916, allowing the formation of the Egyptian Expeditionary Force. This, in conjunction with the Fourth Army, began an offensive to drive the Ottomans out of Palestine. In a series of battles they were ejected from Sinai and by December 1917 British troops, under the command of General Allenby, marched into Jerusalem. Subsequently, the British continued to push them back into Syria. The culmination of the campaign was in September 1918 when Damascus and Aleppo were captured and thousands of prisoners taken. The campaign came to an end when the Ottoman Empire agreed to the Armistice of Mudros on 30th October 1918.

The Entrance Gate of Jerusalem Cemetery

Those Remembered

21 November 1917

Richard Tuckey Hewer was born in Chilton Foliat, Berkshire (now Wiltshire) on 4th September 1887. He was one of three children born to John Tucker Hewer, a farmer, and Elizabeth Joan (née Tuckey) living at Manor Farm, Appleton, Abingdon, Berkshire. Richard attended Abingdon School from 1898 to 1904 and after leaving school he joined a firm of auctioneers with whom he worked as a clerk.

He joined the Abingdon Squadron of the Imperial Berkshire Yeomanry (Regt No 1040) sometime in 1906. When the Yeomanry was mobilised in 1914 he had risen to the rank of Sergeant and in April 1915 he went with the Regiment, part of the 2nd Mounted Division, to Egypt. Whilst there he was promoted to Squadron Sergeant Major. He then went with part of the Regiment (dismounted) to Gallipoli and took part in the storming of Burnt Hill. He later became ill with fever and jaundice and spent three months in hospital in England. On recovery he took a commission in the Regiment and rejoined them in Palestine as a 2nd Lieutenant. They took part in all the heavy fighting up to and just after the fall of Jaffa. Richard, age 30, was killed on 21st November 1917 while 'observing' for the artillery during the Battle of Nebi Samwil in front of Jerusalem.

Second Lieutenant Richard Tuckey Hewer, Berkshire Yeomanry, is buried in Jerusalem War Cemetery, Israel. He is remembered in Thame on the War Memorial and on the Memorial Boards of St Mary's Church and All Saints' Church.

The Thame Remembers Cross was placed at his grave on 7th July 2018 by John Howell, Member of Parliament for Thame.

Rendezvous

I have a rendezvous with Death
At some disputed barricade,
When Spring comes back with rustling shade
And apple blossom fill the air -
I have a rendezvous with Death

It may be he shall take my hand
And lead me into his dark land
And close my eyes and quench my breath -
It may be I shall pass him still
I have a rendezvous with Death
On some scarred slope of battered hill,
When Spring comes round again this year
And the first meadow flowers appear

God knows 'twere better to be deep
Pillowed in silk and scented down,
Where love throbs out in blissful sleep,
Pulse nigh to pulse, and breath to breath,
Where hushed awakening are dear ...
But I've a rendezvous with Death
At midnight in some flaming town,
When spring trips north again this year,
And I to my pledged word am true,
I shall not fail that rendezvous.

Alan Seeger
(1888 - 1916)

Tanzania

At the outbreak of World War One, Tanzania (then Tanganyika) was the core of German East Africa. From the invasion of April 1915, Allied Forces fought a protracted and difficult campaign against a relatively small but highly skilled German force under the command of General von Lettow-Vorbeck. When the Germans finally surrendered on 23rd November 1918, twelve days after the European Armistice, their numbers had been reduced to 155 European and 1,168 African troops.

Dodoma City lies some 300 miles inland from the Indian Ocean. It was occupied by South African troops on 29th July 1916 and a casualty clearing station was established there. Burials were made in Dodoma Civil Cemetery and following the Armistice the CWGC also reinterred bodies in this cemetery from Kilmatinde and Mpapua war cemeteries.

Dar es Salaam is the seat of national government and lies on the east coast of Africa. The War Cemetery contains 1,770 Commonwealth burials from the First World War, 67 of them unidentified, and 34 from the Second World War. Also 112 war graves that date from the First World War of other nationalities, the majority of them being Belgian and German.

Those Remembered

23 April 1917

David John Burbridge was born in Horsham, Sussex on 6th September 1886 to Joseph Henry Burbridge and Ellen Mary (née Brown). In 1901 the family were living in Lambeth, London. By 1911 he had moved to Thame where he was boarding at 32 Upper High Street with James West and family and was employed by him as an assistant motor engineer. In July 1911 he married James's daughter Ella Kate Stacey West at the Wesleyan Chapel. They had two children, Ivy Doreen born 14th September 1912 in York and Stanley David born 11th July 1914 in Thame (died 1917). They lived at Garfield, 34 Upper High Street, Thame. Ivy (also known as Joy) went on to marry the prominent violinist Alfredo Campoli. After they had moved to Belper, Derbyshire, David enlisted in the Army Service Corps at Coventry on 18th August 1915 and was accepted for machine gun service. In February 1916 he was posted to East Africa, embarking on the troopship HMT Huntsgreen, arriving in Mombasa, Kenya on 16th March 1916.

By 27th June 1916 he had been promoted to Acting Corporal and was attached to the 4th Light Armoured Battery at Dodoma, where he contracted malaria in January 1917. By 12th March 1917 David, age 20, was in hospital in Dar es Salaam suffering from dysentery, eventually dying from the disease on 23rd April 1917.

M2/117262 Acting Corporal David John Burbridge, Army Service Corps, is buried in Dar es Salaam War Cemetery. He is remembered in Thame on the War Memorial and on St Mary's Church Memorial Board.

The Thame Remembers Cross was placed at his grave on 14th November 2014 by Rev Hugh Prentice, former missionary in Dodoma, Tanzania.

19 June 1917

Arthur Henry Sutton was born in Thame in 1886. One of the eight children of William Robert Sutton and Ellen (née Hitchman) living at 113 High Street, Thame. He was baptised at St Mary's Church on 28th March 1886. His father was a grocer and innkeeper of the Bull public house at 1 Buttermarket, Thame. By 1901 both his parents had died and he was living with his sister Ellen in Hornsey, North London.

MiD Oak Leaf

Arthur joined the East Africa Transport Corps as a Private on 14th December 1915. He was 'Mentioned in Despatches' (MiD) in 1916 when he held the rank of Corporal. This was published in the London Gazette on 8th February 1917.

Arthur, age 31, died from blackwater fever on Tuesday 19th June 1917 and by this point he had been promoted to Head Conductor (Warrant Officer 1).

1762 Warrant Officer Arthur Henry Sutton, East Africa Transport Corps, is buried in Dodoma War Cemetery, Tanzania. He is remembered in Thame on the War Memorial and on St Mary's Church Memorial Board.

The Thame Remembers Cross was placed at his grave on 22nd October 2014 by Rev Hugh Prentice, former missionary in Dodoma, Tanzania.

Following an extended visit to Thame Rev Prentice was returning to his native Australia via Tanzania

At Sea

Royal Navy. British dominance of the high seas over previous centuries led the nation to expect that the Senior Service would play a major part in the First World War and that naval supremacy would be a key factor, as it had been at Trafalgar. As things turned out, the war was not characterised by monumental sea battles and the British Grand Fleet spent much of its time at anchor.

In 1914 the Royal Navy was by far the most powerful navy in the world. The Government took the view that Britain's very survival depended on ruling the waves and that the Royal Navy should possess a battle fleet larger than the world's next two largest navies put together. Germany also desired a navy in proportion to their military and economic strength and the early 20th century became a naval arms race between Britain and **Germany** to build dreadnought-class **battleships.**

At the beginning of World War One most of the Royal Navy's large ships were stationed at Scapa Flow in the Orkneys or Rosyth in Scotland in readiness to stop any large-scale breakout attempt by the Germans. Britain's cruisers, destroyers, submarines and light forces were clustered around the British coast and the Mediterranean Fleet, comprising of two battlecruisers and eight cruisers, was based in Gibraltar, Malta and Alexandria.

The British Navy suffered three early shocks. On 22nd September 1914 a single German U-boat (U-9) sank three cruisers with the loss of over 1,400 sailors. This was followed by HMS Audacious, a dreadnought battleship, sinking after hitting a mine off the northern coast of Ireland. Then in December 1914 the German First High Seas Fleet bombarded the coastal towns of Scarborough, Hartlepool and Whitby killing 18 civilians.

Naval actions took place off the coast of Chile and the Falkland Islands in 1914 and in the North Sea in 1915. The Royal Navy also provided crucial action during the Dardanelles Campaign in 1915, but the only major wartime confrontation between the Royal Navy and the German High Seas Fleet was the Battle of Jutland on 31st May 1916. Although the British lost more ships and more men, Jutland was seen as a victory by the British commanders because it reinforced the idea

Battle of Jutland Memorial in Denmark. Opened in 2016 to Commemorate the Centenary of the Battle

that Britain had command over the North Sea. Britain's larger fleet could maintain a blockade of Germany, cutting it off from overseas trade and resources, whilst Germany's fleet remained mostly in harbour behind a screen of mines.

After the Battle of Jutland the Royal Navy's main preoccupation was the battle against the German U-boats. While Germany was strangled by Britain's blockade, Britain, as an island nation, was heavily dependent on resources imported by sea. German submarines were of limited effectiveness against surface warships on their guard, but were very effective against merchant shipping. The U-boats sank hundreds of Allied merchant ships, resulting in many civilian deaths and causing shortages of food and other necessities. Defences against submarines were slow to be developed but they were eventually countered by grouping merchant ships into **defended convoys.** In early 1917 Germany declared unrestricted submarine warfare, including attacks without warning against all ships in the "war zone", including neutrals. This was a major factor in the US Declaration of War on Germany.

The Merchant Navy. Britain depended on civilian cargo ships to be the supply service of the Royal Navy; to transport troops and supplies to the armies; to transport raw materials to overseas munitions factories and munitions from those factories to where they were needed; to maintain, on a reduced scale, the ordinary import and export trade; to supply food to the home country and, in spite of greatly enlarged risks and responsibilities; to provide both personnel and ships to supplement the existing resources of the Royal Navy.

The year 1915 saw a dangerous escalation in the war at sea for the mercantile marine as Germany launched its first unrestricted submarine warfare campaign in February, in retaliation for the Allied naval blockade. All merchant ships in the seas around the British Isles were warned that they risked attack without warning. The Cunard flagship RMS Lusitania, torpedoed on 7th May, became one of the best known casualties.

U-boats were very effective against largely undefended merchant vessels and sank hundreds of Allied cargo ships, causing shortages of food and other supplies to the Home Front. The rate of attrition was greatly reduced with the introduction and gradual refinement of the convoy system whereby cargo ships travelled in large groups with a Royal Navy escort for protection.

By the end of the First World War, more than 3,000 British flagged merchant and fishing vessels had been sunk and nearly 15,000 merchant seamen had died, mostly as a result of German submarine attacks. They have no known grave other than the sea. British seamen, uncovenanted to the State, had never previously had to confront such an ordeal as that of 1914-18. The title 'Merchant Navy' was granted by King George V after the First World War to recognise the contribution made by merchant sailors.

Naval Memorials. Remembering those lost at sea is a very different proposition to those lost in land battles or in the air, as very few bodies were ever recovered to receive proper burial. To this day the wreck sites are protected as war graves but appropriate means had to be found to commemorate the men who had given their lives.

More than 50,000 men and women lost their lives while serving with the Royal Navy during the First World War and an Admiralty committee recommended that the three manning ports in Great Britain, namely Chatham, Plymouth and Portsmouth, should each have an identical memorial in the form of an obelisk. These were designed by Sir Robert Lorimer and constructed from Portland stone. They have the secondary function of providing markers for shipping.

The majority of the sailors of the Merchant Navy who died during wartime, with no known grave, are commemorated on Tower Hill Merchant Navy Memorial which stands on the south side of the garden of Trinity Square, London. Others may be remembered at their home port, for example, the Liverpool Naval Memorial.

Portsmouth Naval Memorial is located on Southsea Promenade, Hampshire and commemorates 9,633 sailors of the First World War

Plymouth Naval Memorial
is located on Plymouth Hoe,
Devon overlooking the Sound
and commemorates 7,232
sailors of the First World War

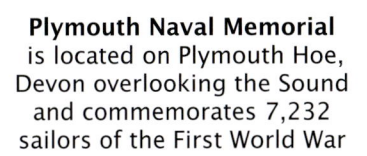

**Chatham Naval Memorial,
Kent**
is located on a hill and is
visible from miles around. It
commemorates 8,507 sailors
of the First World War

Tower Hill Merchant Navy Memorial
is located in Trinity Gardens, London.
It commemorates 11,919 sailors of the First World War

Those Remembered

5 September 1914

Fred Keene was the second of eleven children of Francis Keene and Sarah (née Archer). He was born in Park Street, Thame on 3rd April 1893. In 1901 the family were living at 53 Park Street and Fred's father was employed as a domestic coachman.

Fred was employed as a houseboy before enlisting with the Royal Navy as a boy servant on 22nd December 1910. He served initially on the shore establishment HMS Excellent, Whale Island, Portsmouth, Hampshire. He went on to serve as a Steward 1st Class on HMS Minerva and then HMS Amethyst before being posted to the scout cruiser HMS Pathfinder on 1st October 1913.

On 5th September 1914, Pathfinder was serving with the Rosyth based 8th Destroyer Flotilla out on patrol from the Firth of Forth when at 15:45hrs the cruiser was hit by a single torpedo fired from the German submarine U-21. The torpedo hit the forward magazine causing it to explode and Pathfinder sank in four minutes. There were only 18 survivors, 250 of the crew, including Fred, age 21, went down with ship. HMS Pathfinder was the first British warship sunk by a submarine in World War One and the wreck site is now designated as a war grave. Fred's younger brother Jack Keene died in Belgium in 1917 serving with the Oxford and Bucks Light Infantry.

HMS Pathfinder

L/2470 Steward 1st Class Fred Keene, Royal Navy, HMS Pathfinder, is commemorated on Portsmouth Naval Memorial, Hampshire. He is remembered in Thame on the War Memorial and the Memorial Boards of All Saints' Church and Christchurch.

The Thame Remembers Cross was placed at Portsmouth Naval Memorial on 14th June 2017 by Thame Mayor, Councillor Tom Wyse.

Thame Mayor, Councillor Tom Wyse, laying the Thame Remembers Cross at Portsmouth Naval Memorial

1 January 1915

On the night of 1st January 1915, in rough seas off Lyme Regis Bay in the English Channel, HMS Formidable took two direct torpedo hits and foundered quickly. Wilfred Clarke and Frederick North went down with the ship.

Wilfred Harry Clarke was born in Thame on 14th May 1895 and baptised at St Mary's Church on 16th July 1896. He was the son of Harry Clarke and Esther Sarah (née Guntrip) of 17 Chinnor Road, Thame. The eldest of four siblings, he was apprenticed to his father's cycle repair business. Wilfred enlisted in the Royal Navy on 30th September 1913, declaring his previous employment as a cycle repairer. He spent five months in training at HMS Pembroke II, Sheerness, Kent before joining the battleship HMS Formidable on 21st February 1914.

SS114908 Stoker 1st Class Wilfred Harry Clarke, Royal Navy HMS Formidable, is commemorated on Chatham Naval Memorial, Kent. He is remembered in Thame on the War Memorial and on the Memorial Boards at St Mary's Church, All Saints' Church and Christchurch.

Frederick James North was born in Thame on 29th December 1889. He was the son of James North and Annie (née Smith). Following his father's death in 1890, Fred lived with his widowed mother Annie and family, first at 37 High Street and later 11 Church Row, Thame. On leaving school, he worked as a weighbridge lad on the railway and then as a dairyman to Mr J K Elton of Thame.

On 26th August 1907 Fred, age 17, enlisted in the Royal Navy and like so many, he changed his birth year to appear a year older than he actually was.

Fred was posted to start stoker training aboard the ships HMS Acheron and HMS Minotaur and in between was posted to HMS Pembroke II, the shore establishment at Sheerness, Kent. As well as being a Naval Dockyard it also served as the Naval gunnery school.

He completed his Stoker G1 conduct badge training on 25th August 1910 and had a week's leave before being posted as a qualified Stoker 1st Class to HMS Pembroke II for 12 months. He was then posted to serve on HMS Formidable from 20th August 1911. On Christmas Day 1912, Fred married Frances Jane Cullip at Tempsford Church, Bedfordshire. The couple had two children who were brought up in Tempsford.

312071 Stoker 1st Class Frederick James North, Royal Navy HMS Formidable, is commemorated on Chatham Naval Memorial, Kent. He is remembered in Thame on the War Memorial and is also commemorated on the War Memorial in Tempsford.

The Thame Remembers Cross was placed at the Chatham Naval Memorial on 29th June 2015 by Thame residents, Sue Boyle and Margaret Skinner.

The Letter sent to Esther Clarke advising of her son's death on HMS Formidable

The Sinking of HMS Formidable 1st January 1915

In the early hours of 1st January 1915 *U-24* sank the pre-dreadnought battleship *HMS Formidable*, the largest ship yet to be sunk by a submarine

Formidable, along with the other seven pre-dreadnoughts of the 5th Battle Squadron of Vice Admiral Sir Lewis Bayly's Channel Fleet, left Sheerness at 10:00hrs on 30th December 1914 in order to carry out gunnery practice. They were escorted to Folkestone by six destroyers, but from there were accompanied by only two light cruisers, *HMS Diamond and HMS Topaze*. The destroyers on patrol in the Channel needed frequent maintenance because of weather damage. On the night of 28th December eight of the 24 based at Dover were under repair. Kapitänleutnant Rudolf Schneider's *U-24* spotted the battleships at 09:50hrs on 31st December. He was unable to get into a firing position and had to abandon the attempt at 13:30hrs in order to re-charge his batteries.

At 19:00hrs Bayly ordered his squadron to change course in accordance with a standing order that ships sailing at less than 14 knots in areas where U-boats might be operating should change course just after dark in case they were being followed by a U-boat. The squadron was making only 10 knots.

At 22:30hrs *U-24* got underway, with her batteries re-charged. She spotted three large warships at 01:08hrs on 1st January 1915. They were the lead ships of the 5th Battle Squadron. At 01:58hrs *U-24* fired a torpedo at *HMS Queen* from 750 yards at an acute angle. It missed, but neither it nor the U-boat were spotted by any of the British ships.

The other five battleships then appeared. *U-24* crossed their wake and at 02:25hrs fired two torpedoes at the last in the line, *HMS Formidable*. One of them struck her abreast the forward funnel. She lost steam and developed a 10 degree list to starboard. Boats were launched, but more than 500 men were left on board. They brought tables and other wooden items up in order to make makeshift life rafts. A well lit liner then appeared, and *Topaze*, which was picking up survivors, signalled her to help. She acknowledged, but continued on her way.

By 03:10hrs *U-24* had worked her way to *Formidable's* port side. She fired another torpedo, which hit the battleship amidships. This corrected the list, but caused *Formidable* to settle by the bows. Captain Noel Loxley of *Formidable* then ordered *Topaze* to leave the sinking battleship because of the risk that the U-boat posed to her. The light cruiser spotted *U-24*, but could not fire on her because of the positions of men in the water and *Diamond*. The U-boat then escaped.

The two light cruisers then attempted to rescue survivors, which was extremely difficult because of the wind and seas. *Formidable* sank at 04:39hrs. 547 men of *Formidable's* 780 strong crew were lost, including Captain Loxley.

The survivors included two Warrant Officers and 71 men who were rescued from their sinking launch in a gale by the Brixham trawler *Provident*, which carried only four hands: Captain William Pillar, First Hand William Carter, Second Hand John Clarke and Apprentice Daniel Taylor. All four were awarded the Sea Gallantry Medal.

3 February 1915

Bertram Wheeler Mason was born in Kurunegala, Ceylon on 29th April 1895, where his father was a District Judge in the Ceylon Civil Service. His parents were John Davenport Mason and Sophie (née Andrews). After retiring from Ceylon, John and his family lived in St Pauls Avenue, Cricklewood, London. Bertram initially attended Sunbury House School in Willesden Lane, Sunbury, Middlesex and then attended Lord Williams's Grammar School, Thame as a boarder from 1909 until 1911.

After leaving school, his initial intention was to train for the Civil Service but he joined Mr Philip E Farr FSAA as an articled clerk to begin his training to become an accountant. He joined the Society of Incorporated Accountants on 2nd February 1914.

In December 1914 he volunteered to join the crew of HMS Clan McNaughton as clerk to the ship's captain, Commander R Jeffreys RN. Bertram held the rank of 'Writer' in the Mercantile Marine Reserve. The Clan McNaughton was a 4,985 ton passenger cargo vessel, built in 1911 and requisitioned in November 1914 from the Clan Line Steamers Ltd, Glasgow, to become an armed merchant vessel and formally commissioned on 7th December 1914. She left Sheerness, Kent on 15th December and arrived in Liverpool on 17th January 1915. On the 23rd she sailed *"to the north"* but, according to Naval records, was back by the week ending 31st January. She set sail again and was last heard of at 06.00hrs on 3rd February when she was in the Atlantic north of Ireland and west of Scotland, where she made *"a wireless signal to HMS Hildebrand."* No distress signal was received and no wreckage or survivors were found by HMS Hildebrand despite searching until 5th February. HMS Clan McNaughton was therefore presumed sunk on 3rd February 1915 with the loss of all 281 crew. Some wreckage was found off Cape Wrath, north west Scotland later in February and it was presumed that the ship floundered in a storm.

Writer Bertram Wheeler Mason, Mercantile Marine Reserve, is commemorated on Plymouth Naval Memorial, Devon. He is remembered in Thame on Lord Williams's School Memorial Board.

The Thame Remembers Cross was placed at the Plymouth Naval Memorial on 19th August 2017 by Steve Perry and Verity Platek of Thame Remembers.

31 May 1916

Frederick George Beames Hake was born in Dorking, Surrey on 25th August 1888 the eldest son of Frederick Edward Hake and Sarah (née Beames). In 1891 the family were at the Fox Inn in Leafield, near Chipping Norton, Oxfordshire. His father Frederick died in Caterham, Surrey in 1896. In 1901 Sarah married Robert Rogers in Headington, Oxfordshire and the family went to live in Islip Road, Oxford.

Frederick was working as a telegraph messenger when he enlisted in the Royal Navy on his 18th birthday in 1906. He served as a seaman on the following ships: HMS Impregnable, St George, Royal Arthur, Cressy, Edgar, Powerful, Terrible, Excellent, Seahorse and Dreadnought before transferring to the Reserve on 4th January 1913.

HMS Black Prince

He purchased his discharge from the Royal Navy in order to join the Oxfordshire Police and was stationed at Thame as PC Hake until the start of World War One. On 2nd August 1914 he was recalled to the Navy and served on HMS Europa, a diadem-class cruiser, until May 1915. During a shore posting in mid-1915 he married Edith Elsie Stanley in Chipping Norton prior to his transfer to the cruiser HMS Black Prince.

HMS Black Prince was part of the Grand Fleet that took part in the Battle of Jutland. On the night of 31st May 1916 the ship disappeared without trace with the loss of all 857 crew. George, age 26, was among them.

230875 Able Seaman Frederick George Beames Hake, Royal Navy, HMS Black Prince, is commemorated on Portsmouth Naval Memorial, Hampshire. He is remembered in Thame on the War Memorial and on the Memorial Boards of St Mary's Church and All Saints' Church.

The Thame Remembers Cross was placed at Portsmouth Naval Memorial on 14th June 2017 by Thame Mayor, Councillor Tom Wyse.

12 March 1917

Francis Cartland was born in High Barnet, London on 3rd August 1893. The youngest of the seven children of George Cartland and Edith (née Hammond). George was a policeman but in 1899 took over as licensee of the Six Bells public house in Thame where he stayed until 1922. Both George and Edith are buried in St Mary's churchyard, Thame.

Francis joined the Royal Navy "Boy" service on 16th December 1907 when he was only 14 years of age, telling the Navy that he was born on 3rd August 1891. He served as a "Boy" on the training ships President, Ganges and Cressy and then, in 1910, as an Ordinary Seaman, age 17, on HMS Illustrious. He quickly gained promotion to Able Seaman and served on many ships including: Attentive, Excellent, Topaz, Minerva and Princess Royal. In January 1916 he was posted to HMS Dolphin at Gosport, Hampshire, which was the submarine base and training school, and then to the submarine depot ship HMS Lucia.

HM Submarine E48 (sister ship of E49)

He returned to Dolphin in December 1916 for training with HM Submarine E49. Also, in late 1916, he married Ada Elizabeth Rogers in Devonport, Plymouth, Devon.

On 12th March 1917 Francis, age 23, was on board HMSub E49, when it left Balta Sound in the Shetlands on patrol. The submarine hit a mine off Huney Island and sunk with the loss of all hands. The minefield had been laid in the channel between Balta and Huney Island off the Island of Unst by the German U-boat UC-76 two days before.

366403 Able Seaman Francis Cartland, Royal Navy HMS Lucia, is commemorated on Portsmouth Naval Memorial, Hampshire and on a monument on the Island of Unst. He is remembered in Thame on the War Memorial and on the Memorial Boards of St Mary's Church and All Saints' Church.

The Thame Remembers Cross was placed at Portsmouth Naval Memorial on 14th June 2017 by Thame Mayor, Councillor Tom Wyse.

The Thame Remembers Cross was also laid at a new Monument to HMSub E49 on the Island of Unst on 12th March 2017 by Unst resident, Harry Edwards on behalf of Thame Remembers.

The Ceremony and Monument at Unst commemorating the centenary of the sinking of E49

9 July 1917

Frank Tickner was born in Thame on 23rd September 1900 to Harry Henry Tickner and Edith Elizabeth (née Johnson) living at 42 North Street. He was baptised at St Mary's Church on 10th October 1900. His father was a builder's labourer moving where the work was and in 1911 the family were living in Barking, Essex where Frank, his brothers and sister went to school. Frank was a messenger boy in 1916 when he signed on with the Royal Navy two days after his 16th birthday, becoming "Boy 2nd Class" Frank Tickner. He was posted to the training ship HMS Impregnable at Devonport, Devon. On 31st May 1917, by now a "Boy 1st Class", he was given his first and only sea posting on the St Vincent-class dreadnought battleship HMS Vanguard.

HMS Vanguard

The ship being part of the Royal Navy's Grand Fleet, was based in the vast natural harbour of Scapa Flow in the Orkney Islands, Scotland. Just before midnight on 9th July 1917 the Vanguard suffered an explosion and sank almost instantly, killing an estimated 804 men. There were only two survivors and Frank, age 17, was not one of them. The explosion was probably caused by an unseen stokehold fire heating **cordite** stored against an adjacent bulkhead in one of the two **magazines** which served the amidships **gun turrets**. The wreck site is now a protected war grave and marked by a buoy in the centre of Scapa Flow.

J/59090 Boy 1st Class Frank Tickner, Royal Navy, HMS Vanguard, is commemorated on Portsmouth Naval Memorial, Hampshire. His name is to be added to Thame War Memorial.

The Thame Remembers Cross was placed at Portsmouth Naval Memorial on 14th June 2017 by Thame Mayor, Councillor Tom Wyse.

The Thame Remembers Cross was also laid at the buoy over the wreck of HMS Vanguard in Scapa Flow by a diver from the Joint Services Sub-aqua Club on 10th May 2015.

The Thame Remembers Cross in a floral wreath approaching the buoy marking the wreck of HMS Vanguard

26 February 1918

Albert Isaac Cumming was born in Torquay, Devon in 1869, the second youngest of eight children to carpenter John Cumming and Ann his wife. The family moved to London in the 1880s. Albert married Alma Elizabeth Hilton in Chelsea in June 1899. They went on to have two daughters, Alama Irene and Stella. The family relocated to Thame sometime after 1911, although Albert was often away at sea. His wife Alma remained in Thame until her death in 1941.

Albert was serving as Chief Steward on the hospital ship HMHS Glenart Castle when, at 04:00hrs on 26th February 1918, it was torpedoed by the German submarine UC-56, ten miles west of Lundy Island in the Bristol Channel. The ship had just departed from Newport, South Wales to collect wounded from the Western Front and had all her lights burning to identify herself as a hospital ship.

She sank in just seven minutes and Albert, age 49, was one of the 162 crew and medical staff who were killed, including all eight female nurses. There were just 32 survivors.

The incident caused widespread outrage as a war crime and there were reports that the U-boat surfaced and turned its guns on those in the water in an effort to cover up its mistake.

Chief Steward Albert Isaac Cumming, Merchant Navy HMHS Glenart Castle, has no known grave and is commemorated on the Merchant Navy Memorial at Tower Hill, London. He is remembered in Thame on the War Memorial and on the Memorial Boards of St Mary's Church and All Saints' Church.

The Thame Remembers Cross was placed at Tower Hill Merchant Navy Memorial on 26th September 2017 by Steve Lambell of Thame Players.

The Memorial Plaque to the crew of HMHS Glenart Castle at Hartland Point, Devon, close to Lundy Island

HMHS Glenart Castle

His Majesty's Hospital Ship *Glenart Castle* was a steamship originally built as *Galacian* in 1900 for the Union-Castle Line. She was renamed *Glenart Castle* in 1914 and was requisitioned for use as a British hospital ship during the First World War. She served as a hospital ship from 30th September 1914 until 26th February 1918, when she was hit and sunk by torpedoes from the German U-boat *UC-56*.

On that day *Glenart Castle* was leaving Newport, South Wales heading towards Brest, France. Fishermen in the Bristol Channel saw her clearly lit up as a hospital ship. John Hill, a fisherman on *Swansea Castle*, remembered "*I saw the Hospital Ship with green lights all around her - around the saloon. She had her red side lights showing and mast-head light, and also another red light which I suppose was the Red Cross light.*"

At about 04:00hrs two torpedoes slammed into the *Glenart Castle* on her starboard side, almost immediately all power was lost and all lights went out, the ship was plunged into darkness. They did not know, but the ship would be gone in seven minutes and in those few minutes there was no time for the orderly launch of the lifeboats to get all those onboard to safety. One boat had been destroyed by the explosions, others had much difficulty getting into the water, however seven boats were got away, but only one was ever found.

Most of the people on the ship were inside, probably sleeping and had little chance of getting off after the lights went out. A dark and rolling ship, sinking fast and listing hard makes moving about almost impossible. Add to that the adrenaline pulsing through their veins from fear, the panic from the thought of death and the sad fact is that only those who were awake, alert and on deck or close to an exit had any chance at all.

She sank stern first taking a number of her charges into the depths with her and leaving many others in the cold and churning waters. Heavy seas were running, rollers about 20 feet high were reported and this made searching for others almost impossible. Survivors could hear the cries of those in the water, but the voices soon faded as the cold took them one by one. Several hours after the sinking the first survivors were found by the French schooner *Faon*, the twenty-two cold souls were taken aboard and well treated by the Frenchmen. The ship remained in the area for two hours, but was unable to locate any other survivors so they made their way to Swansea arriving later that day.

The most dramatic rescue occurred at about 13:00hrs that afternoon when *USS Parker DD-48* arrived on the scene. They had received a signal about the sinking and Cdr Halsey Powell, USN made all haste toward the area. In all, nine survivors were pulled from the water by the men of the Parker. Several crewmen jumped into the cold water and pulled the survivors to the ship one by one.

Only 32 survivors were reported. 162 people were killed including Captain Bernard Burt, eight nurses including the matron Miss Kate Beaufoy, seven Royal Army Medical Corps medical officers and 47 medical orderlies.

Evidence was found suggesting that the submarine may have shot at initial survivors of the sinking in an effort to cover up the sinking of HMHS *Glenart Castle*. The body of a junior officer of *Glenart Castle* was recovered from the water close to the position of the sinking. It was marked with two gunshot wounds, one in the neck and the other in the thigh. The body also had a life vest indicating he was shot while in the water.

After the war, the Admiralty sought the captains of U-Boats who sank hospital ships, in order to charge them with war crimes. Kapitanleutnant Wilhelm Kiesewetter, the commander of *UC-56*, was arrested on his voyage back to Germany and interned in the Tower of London. He was released on the grounds that Britain had no right to hold a detainee following the Armistice.

4 April 1918

William Cecil Hoadley was born in Port of Spain, Trinidad on 14th November 1898 to Miriam and John Hoadley. His father John ran the long established Hoadley and Co business, the foremost gentlemen's tailors and military outfitters on Trinidad. William was educated at Lord Williams's Grammar School, Thame from 1908 to 1912 and Bishop Stortford School, Hertfordshire before he moved to the Mercantile Marine Service Association training school for merchant navy cadets at HMS Conway, Liverpool. He was there from 1914 to 1916 and he was classed as a *"good Cadet Captain."* On leaving he was nominated for Midshipman.

William joined the Royal Navy Volunteer Reserve in May 1916 and was posted to HMS Otway, an armed merchant ship, on 9th May 1916 as a Temporary Midshipman. He served on her as a junior officer until she was sunk by torpedoes on 23rd July 1917. He then joined HMS Bittern on 29th October 1917 and was assigned for gunnery duty.

The avon-class destroyer HMS Bittern was part of the Devonport Local Flotilla undertaking convoy escort and defensive patrols in and around the English Channel.

On 4th April 1918, she was involved in a collision with SS Kenilworth off the Isle of Portland, Dorset in thick fog. The Bittern was overwhelmed and sank quickly with the loss of all hands, including William, age 20.

HMS Bittern

A Court of Inquiry found negligence on the part of the master of SS Kenilworth. His instructions had been to hug the coast as closely as possible from Portland Bill, Dorset to Start Point, Devon. Instead he headed straight across the bay, showing no lights nor sounding for fog. At 03:15hrs the Kenilworth saw a red light and a ship *'small and low down'* at the moment of impact.

Midshipman William Cecil Hoadley, Royal Navy Volunteer Reserve, HMS Bittern, is commemorated on Plymouth Naval Memorial, Devon and Port of Spain Cenotaph in Trinidad. He is remembered in Thame on Lord Williams's School Memorial Board together with his brother John who died in 1916 serving with the Royal Engineers.

The Thame Remembers Cross was placed at Plymouth Naval Memorial on 19th August 2017 by Steve Perry and Verity Platek of Thame Remembers.

**Epitaph for those who died
at the Battle of Jutland**

Proud we went down,
and there content we lie
'Neath English sea
if not 'neath English sky.

Anon

Other Names

After all our research had been completed there are still two names outstanding and these are recorded here with as much information as we have uncovered. It is hoped that at some point in the future, information will come to light to enable them to be identified fully.

We have also recorded here the details of Joe Hinder whose name appears on Thame War Memorial but who did not die in the war. Thame is not unique in this, many War Memorials throughout the country contain the names of men who did not die in the war but, as they did not return to their home town, wrong assumptions were made.

Those Remembered

James Lawrence Castle

James Lawrence Castle was born in Thame in 1878 and baptised at St Mary's Church on 2nd September 1880. He was one of the ten children of veterinary surgeon James Lawrence Castle and his wife Adelaide Clara (née Lambourne) who lived in Priestend, Thame.

On 10th April 1900, at nearly 23 years of age, James joined the Imperial Yeomanry (Rough Riders) for service in South Africa. The records show him as a Private (Service No 16101) in the 20th Imperial Yeomanry gaining the Queen's South Africa Medal with Clasps for Cape Colony and Orange Free State. He returned to England in 1901 and in 1902 he signed up in Thame to join the South African Constabulary, a paramilitary force set up to police the new states. It was disbanded in 1908. James joined the South African Veterinary Corps with the rank of "Dresser" (Private) on 9th January 1915. His fate after that is not known. It is known that in 1911 James's brother Joseph Harry joined him in South Africa. Joseph was married with two children and died in 1916, age 24.

An extensive search of records in South Africa has not revealed any further information. The Thame Gazette 1918 list of those serving notes *"Driver J L Castle, South African VC, High Street"*. The Commonwealth War Graves Commission and other records do not show a James Lawrence Castle dying in World War One or in any conflict.

James Lawrence Castle, South African Veterinary Corps, is remembered in Thame on the War Memorial and St Mary's Church and All Saints' Church Memorial Boards.

The Thame Remembers Cross was placed at the Oxfordshire Yeomanry Memorial Tree, National Memorial Arboretum, Staffordshire on 22nd July 2018 by Thame residents Shelagh, Kira and Jessica Hutson.

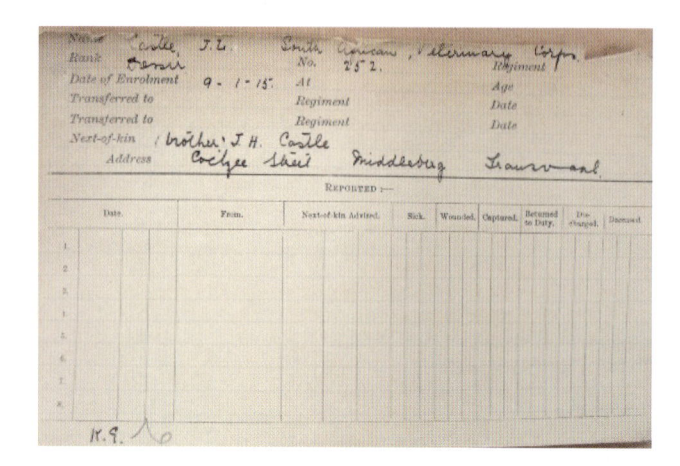

South African Veterinary Corps Record Card for James Lawrence Castle

H T Wilson

The name **H T Wilson** appears on both Thame War Memorial and St Mary's Church Memorial Board as dying during World War One, but no further details are provided. Whilst the name Wilson is a reasonably common name throughout the country there was only one Wilson family in Thame at this time. They lived in Church Row and there is no one in that family with the initials H T or even just H.

A search of the Commonwealth War Graves Commission records show four entries for servicemen named Wilson with the initials H T, but no connection with Thame can be established. Further searches of World War One records show five soldiers and one sailor named H T Wilson who served during World War One and survived, but again there is no apparent connection to Thame. It is possible that H T Wilson's links to Thame were through a relative and so it was worth extending the search to local villages where the name Wilson is more common. One possibility is Harry Wilson, Oxford and Bucks Light Infantry, who is commemorated on Haddenham War Memorial, but no second name is given and again no link to Thame has been established.

H T Wilson is remembered in Thame on the War Memorial and St Mary's Church Memorial Board.

The Thame Remembers Cross was placed at the Light Infantry Memorial, National Memorial Arboretum, Staffordshire on 22nd July 2018 by Thame resident, Roger Mackriell.

Thomas Joe Hinder

Thomas Joe Hinder was born at 12 Ewart Street, Brighton, Sussex on 5th December 1894. His parents were Thomas Hinder, a navvy, and Rachel (née Clark).

In 1910, and known as Joe, he was age 6 and living with Henry and Elizabeth Taylor at 62 Wellington Street, Thame, where he was described as their nephew. He was still there in 1911, age 16, and now described as their grandson and working in the lodging house business. Elizabeth Taylor died in Thame in 1914 and Henry in 1921.

Joe joined the Oxford and Bucks Light Infantry (Regt No 5759) probably in 1915 and was reported as wounded in the Thame Gazette of 21st November 1916. The Thame Gazette, in a list of soldiers serving in May 1918, states; *"Private T J Hinder OBLI, Wellington Street"*.

Towards the end of World War One he was transferred to the Labour Corp, part of the Army Service Corps (ASC), (Regt No 353506). In late 1918 the ASC became the Royal Army Service Corps (RASC).

Whilst still a soldier with the RASC Joe married Ellen Marie Evans in Cheltenham on 7th June 1919. After Ellen died on 6th December 1950 in Patchway, Gloucester, Joe married Florence Harriet Laird in the Sodbury area of Gloucester in late December 1950, although they had been together since before the General Register of 1939. Joe died on 18th October 1954, age 59, in Filton, Gloucester where he worked as a lorry driver. He had lived there since the 1930s, but there are no records of Joe having any children.

Although the name J Hinder is recorded on Thame War Memorial and on St Mary's Church Memorial Board it is clear that he did not die in conflict.

Signing of the Armistice 11th November 1918

World War Two

3rd September 1939

"This morning the British Ambassador in Berlin handed the German government a final note stating that unless we heard from them by eleven o'clock that they were prepared at once to withdraw their troops from Poland, a state of war would exist between us. I have to tell you now that no such undertaking has been received and that consequently this country is at war with Germany."

**Neville Chamberlain
Prime Minister**

Thame

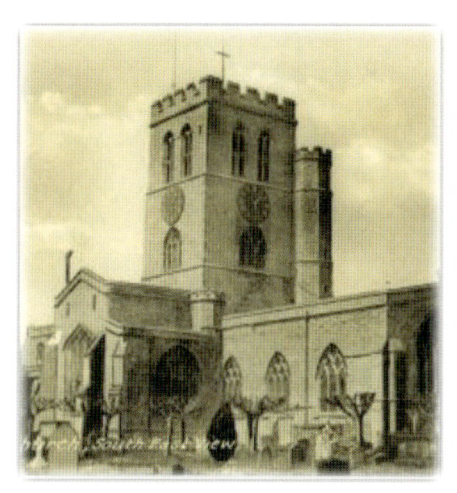

Whilst many men who died in the Second World War were buried close to where they fell, those who died in Britain were often returned to their home town or village for burial. Their death could have been because of enemy action and then being invalided home, but generally it was the result of an accident. These accidents would not have occurred if the man had not been on military service at the time, therefore their graves are usually marked by the familiar Portland stone headstones.

There are five graves for servicemen killed in the Second World War in St Mary's churchyard. Four are the traditional Commonwealth War Graves Commission style whilst the one for R J Allen is a family grave.

Those Remembered

4 November 1940

Ian Malcolm Keith Miller was born in Alton, Hampshire on 4th January 1915. He was the second son of Alfred Edward Miller and Elizabeth Florence (née Nott). Alfred was a pharmacist who worked in Ramsgate, Kent for much of his life. Ian attended Chatham House School in Ramsgate where he was captain of cricket and rugby and a senior prefect. On leaving school he joined the Surveyor's department of Broadstairs Council, Kent.

"Kim", as he was known, joined the Royal Air Force Volunteer Reserve (RAFVR), as a pilot, in January 1937 and became a promising flier. His first front line post was to fly Spitfires with 610 (County of Chester) Squadron based at RAF Acklington in Northumberland. It was during a training flight that his Spitfire Mk 1a L1049 was involved in a mid-air collision over Eglingham, Northumberland on 18th October 1940, forcing his aircraft to dive into the ground.

Kim, age 25, was badly injured and died in hospital on 4th November 1940. As his parents were quite elderly *"Kim's body was claimed"* by his brother Ronald Ivor Mason Miller, who was a master at Lord Williams's Grammar School, Thame. He was buried in Thame on 11th November 1940.

754480 Sergeant Ian Malcolm Keith Miller, Royal Air Force Volunteer Reserve, is buried in St Mary's churchyard. His name is to be added to Thame War Memorial.

The Thame Remembers Cross was placed at his grave on 4th August 2014 by Wing Commander Jenny Holmes of RAF Halton.

7 December 1940

Raymond John Allen was born on 21st May 1922, the only son of John Allen and Mabel Emma (née Wetherall) of 24 Chinnor Road, Thame. He was baptised at St Mary's Church on 9th July 1922. His father John was a postman and in 1939 the family were living at 44 Chinnor Road.

Raymond joined the Army at the start of World War Two as a Private in the Royal Army Ordnance Corps (RAOC) and served with the 2 AA Division Workshop in Leicester. On Saturday 7th December 1940, he was involved in an accident when the driver of the lorry in which he was travelling swerved to avoid a collision and Raymond and two others were thrown out. Raymond received injuries to his head from which he died at just 18 years of age.

7588611 Private Raymond John Allen, Royal Army Ordnance Corps, was buried in the family grave in St Mary's churchyard on 12th December 1940. He is remembered in Thame on the War Memorial and on St Mary's Church Memorial Board.

The Thame Remembers Cross was placed at his grave on 4th August 2014 by Major Ian Jones MBE of Thame Remembers.

24 September 1944

Anthony Austin Beard was born on 19th June 1923 in Cirencester, Gloucestershire to Oscar Beard and Ida Madeleine (née Barnes). The family moved to Thame in 1937 and lived at 17 Broadwaters Avenue. Anthony attended Great Haseley school and on leaving studied to become a toolmaker. As a toolmaker he was in a reserved occupation but insisted on his release to serve his country and so Anthony joined the Royal Air Force in 1942. Thanks to Captain FB Mitchell, he received able coaching in his preparation for joining the RAF and as an airman was showing every indication of a successful career, in that he made unusually rapid strides in the course of his service. He passed all his exams and enlisted as aircrew. After a period of training in England, he went to Canada for his flying training in Tiger Moths and soon gained his wings, following which he was granted a commission as a Pilot Officer. On returning to England, he was promoted again, this time to Flying Officer. Anthony had passed his flying training with distinction and rather than being posted to front line service he was sent to RAF Little Rissington in Gloucestershire as a flying instructor. On 24th September 1944 he was flying an Airspeed Oxford in bad weather when he suffered a flying accident and was killed, age just 21 years. In a communication from his Commanding Officer to his parents, it was said that he was *"an excellent instructor and a great asset to his comrades"*. He was buried with full military honours in Thame on 28th September 1944.

153415 Flying Officer Anthony Austin Beard, Royal Air Force Volunteer Reserve, is buried in St Mary's churchyard. He is remembered in Thame on the War Memorial and on St Mary's Church Memorial Board.

The Thame Remembers Cross was placed at his grave on 4th August 2014 by his younger brother and Thame resident, Peter Beard.

8 November 1944

Albert Horace Quainton was born on 26th March 1920 in North Weston near Thame. "Tiger", as he was known, was the youngest child of Sidney Cecil John Quainton and Edith Eliza (née Howes). He spent his childhood years in Moreton and went to school in Thame. On leaving school he went to work at the local brickworks and in 1937, with the family now living in Thame, he joined the Oxford and Bucks Light Infantry.

He was a motorcycle dispatch rider and was promoted to Lance Corporal in the 1st Battalion HQ Wing in August 1938. He went to France in November 1939 and would have been at the Dunkirk evacuation. He later served in Ireland and England before returning to France shortly after the D-Day landings of 6th June 1944.

On 24th July 1944 he was wounded while driving a jeep which had become pinned down under mortar fire at a crossroads just outside Caen, Normandy. Albert, age 24, was brought back to St Martin's hospital in Bath where he died from his wounds on 8th November 1944. Had he survived, his wounds would have left him paralysed, as his back and internal organs were badly damaged. His funeral was held at St Mary's Church on 13th November 1944.

5382931 Lance Corporal Albert Horace Quainton, Oxford and Bucks Light Infantry, is buried in St Mary's churchyard. He is remembered in Thame on both Thame and Moreton War Memorials and on the Memorial Board at St Mary's Church.

The Thame Remembers Cross was placed at his grave on 4th August 2014 by his niece and Thame resident, Rosalie Gibson.

9 February 1946

John Eric Jesse Phillips was born in Thame on 2nd February 1921 to John James Phillips and Emily May (née Eele) of 4 Bell Lane. His father's trade was a packer. Jesse married Ellen May Bowler in 1940 and they had three children: Eric, Charles (known as Roy) and David. The family lived at 16 Horton Avenue, Thame. Following his death Ellen married again and had a further seven children.

After leaving school in Thame Jesse joined the Royal Air Force Volunteer Reserve in November 1941 and progressed to Leading Aircraftman. He is listed in the Thame Welcome Home Fund of 1945, but was tragically killed on Saturday 9th February 1946, age 25, whilst still serving in the RAF. The motorcycle he was riding was involved in a collision with a car at the Bishopstone crossroads at Stone, Buckinghamshire and his death was recorded as "*misadventure*" at the subsequent inquest. His funeral was held at St Mary's Church on 13th February 1946.

1666457 Leading Aircraftsman John Eric Jesse Phillips, Royal Air Force Volunteer Reserve is buried in St Mary's churchyard. His name is to be added to Thame War Memorial.

The Thame Remembers Cross was placed at his grave on 4th August 2014 by Thame Town Clerk, Helen Stewart.

AIR RAID SHELTER

PERSONS MAY SHELTER HERE AT THEIR OWN RISK AFTER THE TAKE COVER NOTICE HAS BEEN GIVEN

Persons sheltering are not allowed to take Birds, Dogs, Cats and other Animals, as well as Mailcarts, on to the Company's premises.

BY ORDER.
Electric Railway House,
Broadway, Westminster.

Britain

After the fall of France, Britain stood alone against the Germans whose plans to invade and conquer hinged on gaining air supremacy over the RAF. When they were decisively defeated in the Battle of Britain, Hitler turned his attention to Russia. Britain became an island fortress and a secure base where the armed forces were expanded, trained and re-equipped. It then became the springboard from which offensive operations could be launched against the enemy culminating in the invasion of Normandy in 1944.

It is surprising how many servicemen are buried in the UK. These include those who were killed in training accidents and those wounded and returned to this country who then subsequently died. They are mainly buried in the community cemetery of their home town, although at Brookwood Cemetery in Surrey, which served the London metropolis for many years, there is a large military section.

The most significant memorial to those who have no known grave is the Air Forces Memorial at Runnymede, Surrey. Commemorated here are over 20,000 airmen who were lost in the Second World War during operations from bases in the United Kingdom and North and Western Europe. They served in Bomber, Fighter, Coastal, Transport, Flying Training and Maintenance Commands and came from all parts of the Commonwealth. Also some are from countries in continental Europe which had been overrun but whose airmen continued to fight in the ranks of the Royal Air Force.

The Air Forces Memorial at Runnymede, Surrey

Lockheed Hudson aircraft on patrol over the North Sea

Those Remembered

15 October 1940

Derek Edmund Teden was born on 19th July 1916 in Highgate, London to Frank Edmund Teden and Zilla (née Collingbridge). He was educated at Lord Williams's Grammar School in Thame and at Taunton School, Somerset. Derek played rugby for Richmond and represented England three times against Wales, Scotland and Ireland. In the 1939 electoral register he was living in Wood Green, London with his brother Frank.

He was granted a commission as an Acting Pilot Officer in the Royal Auxiliary Air Force with 604 (County of Middlesex) Squadron on 27th October 1938 and was mobilised in 1939 when war broke out, being confirmed as a full Pilot Officer on 1st December. On 15th October 1940 he was serving with 206 Squadron when he and his crew took off in a Lockheed Hudson to carry out a maritime patrol. This was essentially a reconnaissance mission over the North Sea to give early warning of any sea borne invasion. The operational plan was to be on station by 23:00hrs, fly two figure of eight pattern circuits and then return to their base. Derek, his aircraft and crew were never seen again, despite a concerted search the following day over their operational area. The circumstances of their fate is unknown and may have been due to mechanical failure rather than enemy action, but it was considered most likely that they encountered a German night fighter patrol and were shot down. Derek was just 24 years old.

90486 Pilot Officer Derek Edmund Teden, Royal Air Force, has no known grave and is commemorated on the Air Forces Memorial, Runnymede, Surrey. He is remembered in Thame on Lord Williams's School Memorial Board.

The Thame Remembers Cross was placed at the Air Forces Memorial, Runnymede on 14th December 2014 by Mike Dyer of Thame Remembers.

The Thame Remembers Cross and Wreath at Runnymede Memorial

Derek Teden's International Career

Derek played rugby for Taunton school old boys and was discovered by Richmond in a match between the two teams. A live wire prop Teden was invited to move his allegiance to the London club where his form soon began to move him through both the ranks of the Richmond club and those of English rugby. By 1937 Teden was playing for Middlesex and was further selected as a reserve for England's match against Ireland. He also came to the attention of the Barbarians' selectors and pulled on the famous black and white hoops for the first time in March 1937. Teden eventually made his breakthrough into the full England side on 21st January 1939 when he received the call from the selectors to take on Wales at Twickenham. Played in a sea of mud the treacherous conditions defeated the Welsh backs in a match that was to be decided by the opposing packs. The Welsh made a great battle of the game but were comprehensively outplayed up front. England had most of the play and it was generally accepted that in better conditions would have won by a far greater margin than the final three points to nil score line. For Teden it was to be a dream start to his international career, scoring the only try of the match and as The Times put it, *"what greater honour could have befallen a new front row man like D E Teden than to join in such a scrummaging triumph."*

After such a debut Teden's place in the England side was never in doubt and he was to play in both of the remaining matches of the season. Returning to Twickenham on 11th February England next took on the Irish. The Irish, with a better balanced team that was both agile and canny, outplayed an English side that was quite simply not good enough on the day. The English pack, generally regarded as the best out of the four home unions, had trouble holding its own, whilst their backs folded under the pressure that they faced. Teden himself had a good game tackling well and having another try disallowed, but in the final analysis Ireland were worthy of their five points to nil victory. England's final match of the 1939 campaign involved travelling to Murrayfield on 18th March, to take on Scotland, the previous season's champions. Rain before play was expected to favour the English, although few expected the complete ascendancy that their pack were to show as they overcame the debacle of the Ireland match. Such was their hold on the game that the Scottish backs were hardly to see the ball, although this was offset by the under performance of the opposing English back line. Despite their dominance throughout the match the English pack seemed content to pass the ball to their backs, who continually squandered their chances, rather than play it themselves and at the end of play England's nine point to six victory was thanks to a number of successful kicks rather than the tries that should have been scored. The following month Teden again joined the Barbarians, this time for their Easter tour to Wales, beating Cardiff by eleven points to six on 8th April and losing by twelve points to three two days later. Although he would finish the season with Richmond and turn out a few times for Rosslyn Park and in charity matches after the outbreak of war, Teden's all too short rugby career was now essentially over.

Report taken from The Rugby History Society website

11 February 1941

John Phillips was born in 1920 to Ernest James Phillips and Annie (née Eade) of Lower High Street, Thame. He was educated at Lord Williams's Grammar School and was then employed by Birch, Stockton and Fortescue solicitors in Thame. He later went to work in the offices of Oxfordshire County Council. John married Elizabeth Eunice Perman in December 1940 in the Ploughley Registration District (which included Thame).

John joined the Royal Air Force Volunteer Reserve and trained as a pilot. He was posted to 206 Squadron Coastal Command based at RAF Bircham Newton, Norfolk. On 11th February 1941 three aircraft from the Squadron were on "nomad" patrol over the North Sea. John, age 20, was one of two pilots in Lockheed Hudson Mk 1 T9289, VX-A. None of the aircraft returned. It was presumed that the aircraft ran out of fuel on the return leg and were abandoned over the sea. All the crew were lost.

742921 Sergeant John Phillips, Royal Air Force Volunteer Reserve, has no known grave and is commemorated on the Air Forces Memorial at Runnymede, Surrey. He is remembered in Thame on the War Memorial and on the Memorial Boards of St Mary's Church and Lord Williams's School.

The Thame Remembers Cross was placed at the Air Forces Memorial, Runnymede on 14th December 2014 by John's nephew and Thame resident, Dick Phillips.

20 April 1941

Bernard Howe was born in Melksham, Wiltshire on 10th April 1919 to Frank Howe and Ellen Matilda (née Woodman), His father was a career soldier with the Royal Army Medical Corps, being discharged in 1920 after 26 years of service. Bernard went to school at Shirburn, near Watlington, Oxfordshire where his mother was at one time a lady's maid for the Countess of Macclesfield. He won a scholarship to Lord Williams's Grammar School, Thame, where he was a pupil from 1930 to 1937. The picture is taken from the 1st XV rugby team photograph of 1935/36. In September 1937 he entered RAF College Cranwell, Lincolnshire as a Flight Cadet, receiving his commission in July 1939. He joined 25 Squadron at North Weald, Essex in August 1939 and served with the Squadron throughout the Battle of Britain, flying Blenheim Mark 1F night fighters. The Tamensian records him as a visitor to the school on 21st July 1940 *"B Howe who turned up (with J F Castle) on July 21 was very hush hush about his doings and revealed nothing more definite than he had always landed at his home base"*.

He was posted in January 1941 to 263 squadron at St Eval and then to Portreath, both in Cornwall, where he flew Westland Whirlwind Mk I fighters on convoy patrols. On 20th April 1941, on a visit to RAF Wittering, Cambridgeshire he was killed flying Whirlwind Mk I P6992 which dived into the ground after performing low level manoeuvres. He was 22 years old. The accident report at the time presumed this was due to a leading edge slat becoming detached.

33427 Flying Officer Bernard Howe, Royal Air Force, is buried in All Saints' churchyard, Wittering, Cambridgeshire. He is remembered in Thame on Lord Williams's School Memorial Board.

The Thame Remembers Cross was placed at his grave on 9th June 2016 by Thame residents, Alison and Nigel Champken-Woods.

4 April 1942

Charles Frederick Bristow was born in Sleaford, Lincolnshire on 10th October 1898, one of three children of Fred Bristow, a joiner, and his wife Rose (née Topps). After serving during World War One with the Army Service Corps (Regt No T290003) he married Elsie Lomas at St Mary's Church, Thame on 26th December 1924. She was the daughter of the manager of Thame gasworks. They then went to live in Cranwell, Lincolnshire where they had three children, Rita, Enid and Annie. At the start of the Second World War Charles was recalled to join the Pioneer Corps while Elsie and the children moved to live with Elsie's sister at 23 East Street, Thame.

Charles was one of the last to be evacuated from Dunkirk and thought to have died until he was spotted at Thame station by daughter, Rita. He was in a poor state not having washed or changed clothes for three weeks. Soon after, he transferred to 22 Bomb Disposal Company, Royal Engineers, where he was awarded the George Medal in recognition of his bomb disposal work during the winter of 1940/41. On 1st April 1942, with Lieutenant Walton, he attempted to defuse a British "Yellow Peril" balloon bomb on marshes near Great Wakering, Essex. The bomb exploded killing Lieutenant Walton instantly and severely wounding Charles in the abdomen. He died of his wounds on 4th April in St George's Hospital, London and was buried with full military honours. He was 43 years old.

13005511 Lance Sergeant Charles Frederick Bristow GM, Royal Engineers, is buried in St Andrew's churchyard, Cranwell, Lincolnshire. He is commemorated on the Church Memorial in Cranwell village and his name is to be added to Thame War Memorial.

The Thame Remembers Cross was placed at his grave on 9th July 2017 by Ian Jones MBE of Thame Remembers.

London Gazette 17th February 1942

The KING has been graciously pleased to approve the award of the George Medal, in recognition of conspicuous gallantry in carrying our hazardous work in a very brave manner to :-

No. 13005511 Corporal Charles Frederick BRISTOW, Corps of Royal Engineers, of Thame, Oxon. Awarded for work at the Gas Works, Romford and A13 road, Rainham, Essex. Cpl Bristow assisted Lt J P Walton on the 5th November 1940 in dealing with two 250kg bombs armed with both no 17 and 50 fuzes. These were in gasholders at the Romford Gas Works. The air conditions were so bad that work had to be stopped every twenty minutes. This work was completed in the shortest possible time, ensuring minimum damage and services to be re-started with the least disruption. Also this work was carried out whilst the air raid continued. Also on the 26th to 28th February 1941, Bristow assisted Walton in dealing with three remaining 250kg bombs of a stick of four straddling the A13 at Rainham, Essex. One of this stick exploded after 18 hours. Work commenced on these bombs after a safety period of four days, they were fuzed with both No 17 and 50 fuzes. The two when uncovered were found to be ticking, but immunized successfully.

(Note: Lt Walton had previously been awarded the George Medal in 1941)

Sgt Bristow's George Medal

The parachute attached to the bomblet that exploded. This was recovered from Charles's hospital locker by his wife

20 October 1942

John Austin Chapman, the son of plumber and glazier Hurrell George Chapman and teacher Margaret Lester (née Austin) was born in Wheatley, Oxfordshire in 1916. He attended Lord Williams's Grammar School in Thame between 1927 and 1932, leaving to become an apprentice at the Oxford Bus Company.

John enlisted in the Royal Navy in 1938 and was serving on the destroyer HMS Express as an Engine Room Artificer 4th Class (equivalent to Petty Officer) when she was one of the last to leave Dunkirk following the evacuation of the British Expeditionary Force (BEF) in May/June 1940. On 31st August 1940, she left Immingham, Lincolnshire to lay a minefield off the coast of the Netherlands. During the night of 1st September, HMS Express was damaged by a German mine and four officers and 55 men were killed. The destroyer HMS Ivanhoe was sunk in the action. John was 'Mentioned in Despatches' for his *"coolness and resource"* during the action.

HMS Express after the mine damage

John, age 26, was at home at Rosemary Cottage, Wheatley, when he died on 20th October 1942, leaving a wife, Hilda and young son, who was deaf and dumb. He was buried in Wheatley on 24th October 1942 and left £350 in his will.

P/MX 55979 Artificer 4th Class John Austin Chapman, Royal Navy, is buried in St Mary's churchyard, Wheatley. He is remembered in Thame on Lord Williams's School Memorial Board and is commemorated on the War Memorial in Wheatley.

The Thame Remembers Cross was placed at his grave on 31st August 2015 by Thame resident, Andrea Kachelleck.

6 December 1942

Norman Kenneth Millard was born in the Marylebone area of London in the summer of 1920 to Walter Douglas Millard and Lily Evlyn (née Jones). Following the start of the war Norman's family moved to Thame and lived at 92 High Street.

Norman joined the Royal Air Force Volunteer Reserve in August 1940 in London and trained as a Wireless Operator/Air Gunner. He was based at 28 Operational Training Unit, RAF Wymeswold, Leicestershire which flew Wellington bombers training aircrew. Norman was a member of the crew of Wellington 1C R1223 which took off on 6th December 1942 at 15:30hrs from Wymeswold for night flying practice. At 19:40hrs the bomber was seen on approach to the runway but before reaching the threshold it veered off the centre line and the throttles were advanced in order to go round again. While doing so, the Wellington crashed some three miles north east of Loughborough. Norman, age 22, was killed in the accident. Twenty-four hours after the crash the pupil pilot, Sgt Donald Lloyd, died from his injuries. The other crew members were Flt Sgt R M Williams and Sgt F R Page, who both survived.

1380773 Sergeant WOp/Air Gunner Norman Kenneth Millard, Royal Air Force Volunteer Reserve, is buried in Burton on the Wolds burial ground, Leicestershire, alongside Sergeant Lloyd. He is remembered in Thame on St Mary's Church Memorial Board and his name is to be added to Thame War Memorial.

The Thame Remembers Cross was placed at his grave on 9th April 2017
by Thame residents, Ian and Jackie Welsh.

"It is with the deepest regret that we learned of the death through a flying accident on Sunday week, of Sgt N K Millard, only son of Mr and Mrs W D Millard, of 92 High Street, Thame. We are sure the townspeople in general will sympathise with the bereaved parents in their sad loss. The funeral took place on Thursday at Burton on the Wolds with full honours."

Thame Gazette 15th December 1942

12 December 1942

Herbert Edward Jones was born in Henley, Oxfordshire in January 1917, the fifth of six children to Edward Jones, a railwayman, and Ann (née Kilvington), a dressmaker. His father was originally from Oswestry, Shropshire. The family moved firstly to Bristol and then to Watcombe Road, Watlington, Oxfordshire in 1916.

Herbert became a pupil at Lord Williams's Grammar School in Thame in September 1931. His school career appears to have been distinguished if not outstanding, becoming a House Prefect, member of the 1st XV rugby team and Vice Captain of the 1st XI cricket team. By December 1934 he is described as a *"student teacher"* before embarking on a two year teacher training course at Culham College, Oxfordshire qualifying in 1937 and taking up his first teaching post at a school in Wembley, London.

Herbert joined the territorials in 1938 and was mobilised at the outbreak of war. In April 1940 he started training to take up a commission but this had to be abandoned at his own request as he appeared to have lost confidence in himself. He was stationed with 363 Battery, 111th Light Anti-Aircraft Regiment, Royal Artillery at Cubbington, near Leamington Spa, Warwickshire. There was regular German bombing of the industrial heartland of Birmingham, Coventry and the Black Country in July and August 1942 so it is very likely that the unit saw a great deal of action during that period.

On the morning of Saturday 12th December 1942 Herbert, age 25, let himself into the Armoury, locked the door behind him and put a rifle to his head. The Coroner recorded a verdict of *"suicide while the balance of his mind was disturbed"*. His death was described by his Commanding Officer as *"a great loss to the service because of his ability."*

2050549 Bombardier Herbert Edward Jones, Royal Artillery, is buried in St Leonard's churchyard, Watlington, Oxfordshire. He is remembered in Thame on Lord Williams's School Memorial Board and he is commemorated on the War Memorial in Watlington.

The Thame Remembers Cross was placed at his grave on 19th March 2015
by representatives of Lord Williams's School
David Wybron (Head Teacher), Matthew Walker (Head Boy)
and Emily Keogh (Head Girl).

13 March 1943

Cyril Frank White was born on 25th October 1920 in Thame and baptised at St Mary's Church on 26th December. His parents were Frederick White and Hilda (née Bayliss) of 7 Tythrop Terrace, Thame. His father was a farm labourer who later went on to run the Abingdon Arms public house. Cyril enlisted in the Royal Air Force Volunteer Reserve in November 1940 at Oxford. He had completed his training as a Wireless Operator/Air Gunner by October 1942 and was at the Operational Training Unit at Finningley, Yorkshire from December 1942 to February 1943 before a posting to 199 Squadron at RAF Ingham, 15 miles north of Lincoln. His first operational sortie with 199 Squadron was on 4th March 1943 and his last, a bombing mission to Essen, Germany, was on 13th March 1943. The Wellington Mk X aircraft, L495, never returned and the aircraft with all five crew was presumed lost over the North Sea. Cyril was 22 years old.

1312741 Sergeant Cyril Frank White, Royal Air Force Volunteer Reserve, has no known grave and is commemorated on the Air Forces Memorial at Runnymede, Surrey. He is remembered in Thame on the War Memorial and on St Mary's Church Memorial Board.

The Thame Remembers Cross was placed at the Air Forces Memorial, Runnymede on 14th December 2014 by David Bretherton of Thame Remembers.

Extract from Sgt White's Flying Log Book showing his last flight over Essen in 1943

2 September 1943

Vivian Evelyn Lower was born in Edmonton, Middlesex on 6th May 1912 to Nynian Evelyn Walter Lower and Edith Grace (née Morley) of 289 The Cottage, Stoke Newington, Hackney, London. He attended Lord Williams's Grammar School in Thame from 1922 to 1929. By 1939 Vivian had followed his father into the banking profession and was living at Queens Lane, Stoke Newington,

A B24 Liberator aircraft

where he was also recorded as an ARP warden (Air Raid Precautions).

Vivian enlisted in the Royal Air Force Volunteer Reserve (Service No 1376898) after August 1940 as NCO aircrew and trained in the UK, then in Miami USA and finally in Canada becoming a navigator. Vivian was promoted from Flight Sergeant to Pilot Officer on 6th March 1943 whilst he was serving with 119 Squadron at Pembroke Dock, Wales.

He was part of the crew of a 119 Squadron Sunderland flying boat that crashed in the Bay of Biscay on 15th April 1943. All but three of the crew survived, but they were at sea in a dinghy for 15 hours before being rescued. On 17th April 1943, 119 Squadron disbanded and the crew were transferred as a whole to another Coastal Command unit, 224 Squadron based at St Eval, Cornwall, flying B24 Liberator aircraft but still on anti-submarine patrols.

On 2nd September 1943 aircraft "G for Golf" left St Eval on "PERC-A 58-2" patrol over the Bay of Biscay with nine crew on board. They took off at 04:11hrs and at 08:33hrs reported the presence of enemy aircraft. Nothing further was heard from the aircraft and all crew including Vivian, age 31, were presumed killed.

143871 Pilot Officer Vivian Evelyn Lower, Royal Air Force Volunteer Reserve, has no known grave and is commemorated on the Air Forces Memorial at Runnymede, Surrey. He is remembered in Thame on Lord Williams's School Memorial Board.

The Thame Remembers Cross was placed at the Air Forces Memorial, Runnymede on 14th December 2014 by Patsy Baker of Thame Remembers.

28 September 1943

Stanley John Slade was born in Henley, Oxfordshire in 1920 to Joseph Stanley Slade and Winifred Mary (née Walker). Stanley attended Lord Williams's Grammar School in Thame in the 1930s. In the Commonwealth War Graves records there is reference to his marriage to a Mary Theresa.

Stanley joined the Royal Air Force Volunteer Reserve in April 1941 as NCO aircrew (Service No 1443184) and was promoted from Flight Sergeant to Pilot Officer on 5th April 1943. He was serving with the Canadians in 405 (Vancouver) Squadron based at Gransden Lodge near Cambridge flying Lancaster Mk III bombers leading the bomber attacks as "pathfinders".

On 27th September 1943 six aircraft from 405 Squadron took part in a bombing mission to Hanover,

Germany. JB210, "D for Delta" took off at 19:45hrs with a full crew of seven including Stanley, age 23, and nothing was heard from them again. Four of the six 405 Squadron aircraft successfully returned, although a total of 49 aircraft were lost in the raid. As JB210 was lost without a trace, it was considered that the aircraft probably went down over the North Sea and the crew are all recorded as being killed on 28th September 1943.

143997 Pilot Officer Stanley John Slade, Royal Air Force Volunteer Reserve, has no known grave and is commemorated on the Air Forces Memorial at Runnymede, Surrey. He is remembered in Thame on Lord Williams's School Memorial Board.

The Thame Remembers Cross was placed at the Air Forces Memorial, Runnymede on 14th December 2014 by Margaret Bretherton of Thame Remembers.

20 February 1944

Peter Milton Jennings was born in Little Milton, Oxfordshire in late 1915 to John Thomas Jennings, a grocer in Little Milton, and Eva Hannah Milton (née Cooke). Peter attended Lord Williams's Grammar School in Thame from 1927 to 1932. He joined the Royal Air Force Volunteer Reserve as NCO Aircrew (Service No 905938) and served as a Sergeant pilot with 158 Squadron based at RAF Lissett in East Yorkshire where he flew Halifax bombers. He was commissioned from Flight Sergeant to Pilot Officer on 31st August 1943.

Peter was an experienced pilot who had already flown 23 operational sorties with 158 Squadron. At least 20 of those missions were with the same crew that took off in Halifax Mk III HX351 just after midnight on 20th February 1944 for a mission to bomb Leipzig, Germany. Nine minutes later the bomber crashed into a field just off a minor road connecting the villages of Atwick and Bewholme near the coast of east Yorkshire killing all the crew instantly.

The accident was investigated but the outcome was inconclusive. It appears that the pilot may have lost control after entering cloud as a result of which a tail plane failure occurred but this could not be proved beyond doubt. The crew were returned to their family homes for burial and Peter, age 28, was returned to Little Milton where he was buried on 26th February 1944.

157100 Pilot Officer Peter Milton Jennings, Royal Air Force Volunteer Reserve, is buried in St James's churchyard, Little Milton. He is remembered in Thame on Lord Williams's School Memorial Board. There is a Memorial to the crew at the crash site, put there by the brother of the navigator.

The Thame Remembers Cross was placed at his grave on 15th October 2015 by Thame resident, Sheila Wyse.

158 Squadron Handley Page Halifax bomber and crew

Northern Europe: Army

The casualties in this section fall into three distinct categories. Those who fell during the retreat to Dunkirk in 1940, those who died in the fighting in Normandy in the immediate aftermath of D-Day and those who lost their lives in the subsequent advance into Germany towards the end of the War.

France 1940

The first group were men who fought in the British Expeditionary Force (BEF) and were part of the dramatic campaign during which Germany conquered three countries in six weeks in the spring of 1940. To put things in perspective, the Germans brought 136 Divisions to the battle, the French 100 and the Belgium Army 22. The BEF had only 14 Divisions. Although too small to affect the eventual outcome, this force played a vital role in the northern phase of the campaign, holding a key position in the Allies' main front and defending it to the end. Its fighting withdrawal to the coast, whilst being attacked by two German armies from the east and west, was a notable military achievement. This small British force never lost its cohesion or ability to fight. When its final overthrow seemed certain most of the men were withdrawn to England, there to recover and to prepare to fight again.

Dunkirk Memorial

Normandy 1944

The successful Allied invasion of France on D-Day, 6th June 1944, saw the start of a bitter struggle for the Normandy countryside. The Germans were determined to stop a breakout from the beaches and threw some of their best battle-hardened and well equipped troops into the fight. They were assisted by the terrain (*bocage*) which favoured the defender. The result was that the fighting was vicious and often at close quarters. The Allied victory is often passed off as the result of superiority in firepower, air strength and supplies. This is a simplistic interpretation. Right from the start, success also hinged on the morale and capabilities of the frontline troops, especially the infantry, who would bear the burden of the fighting. Eventually the Anglo-American armies inflicted a major defeat on the German military machine. The British Army's role was pivotal, but victory came at a high price. Between D-Day and the end of August some 83,000 British, Canadian and Polish troops became casualties, of whom almost 16,000 were killed.

Germany 1945

After the German collapse in Normandy the Allies rapidly advanced through France, Belgium and into Holland. An attempt to shorten the war by encircling the Ruhr in *Operation Market Garden* failed and, partly due to the lack of supplies, the Allies were temporarily stalled. On 16th December 1944 the Germans launched a major attack through the Ardennes aimed at splitting the American and British Armies. This became known as the *"Battle of the Bulge"* and, although the Americans bore the brunt of the fighting, British units were involved on the northern side of the pocket and sustained many casualties. By 25th January 1945 it was clear that the German attack had failed and that they had expended a huge amount of irreplaceable men and equipment.

Despite it being obvious that they were going to lose the war the Germans continued to fight on all fronts to the bitter end. Sadly, this meant that servicemen were losing their lives right up to the end of the war.

Those Remembered

21 May 1940

Joseph Albert Wicks was born in Hayes, Middlesex in 1918 to William Wicks and Cecilia Martha (née Goddard). His father died in 1929 and Joseph became a boarder at Lord Williams's Grammar School in Thame from 1931 to 1934. His home address was given as Clock House, Cowfold, Sussex, which was a large country house belonging to the aristocratic Loder family. He also spent time with his cousin Albert H (Sam) Williams and aunt Mary who had a dairy farm in Headcorn, Kent and it was probably whilst there in 1939 that he joined the newly formed 5th (Territorial) Battalion of The Royal East Kent Regiment (The Buffs).

The Battalion, serving with the 16th Infantry Brigade of the 12th (Eastern) Division, left for France on 19th April 1940 and arrived in Le Havre the following day. They trained at a camp near Fleury Sur Andelle, Eure in Normandy and it was from there that the Battalion was taken in three-ton trucks to Doullens, near the Belgian border, to defend against the German advance. They were heavily outnumbered and, despite heroic defence, were overrun with many men killed or taken prisoner, only a few making it to the evacuation at Dunkirk.

However Joseph, age 22, did not see this action with the Battalion as he had either been taken ill or was injured at the training camp. He died there on 21st May 1940 and was buried at a nearby cemetery. In his will, which was proved on 10th September 1940, he left an estate of £3,435 to his spinster aunt, Mary Maud Goddard at Brookwood Farm, Headcorn, Kent.

6288045 Private Joseph Albert Wicks, Royal East Kent Regiment, is buried at Evreux Communal Cemetery, Eure, France. He is remembered in Thame on Lord Williams's School Memorial Board and is also commemorated on the War Memorial in Headcorn, Kent.

The Thame Remembers Cross was placed at his grave on 10th June 2015 by Thame residents, Meg and Graham Watson.

22 May 1940

Louis Herbert Plested was born in 1919 to Sidney William Plested and Gladys (née Honor) of Shabbington, Buckinghamshire. He had a sister Gladys born in 1928. He was very popular in the village and a good sportsman, cricket being his favourite game. Before the war he was employed by Messrs R G Holland and Son of Thame.

Louis was serving with the Territorial Battalion of the Oxford and Bucks Light Infantry at the outbreak of World War Two and was mobilised with the 4th Battalion in late 1939. The Battalion embarked from Southampton aboard TSS St Helier (a requisitioned Channel Island Ferry) on 18th January 1940. They disembarked at Le Havre the same day and travelled to northern France. Following the German invasion of the Low Countries the Battalion moved into Belgium, billeting in Alsemberg south of Brussels. On 17th May the retreat from Belgium began during which the British incurred numerous casualties and in the battle on the line of the river Scheldt (Escaut) on 22nd May 1940 Louis, age 21, was one of several men from the Battalion killed near the village of Bleharies, probably from artillery fire.

5387546 Private Louis Herbert Plested, Oxford and Bucks Light Infantry, is buried in Bruyelle War Cemetery, Hainaut, Belgium. He is commemorated on the War Memorial in Shabbington.

The Thame Remembers Cross was placed at his grave on 21st April 2018 by Thame resident, Julie West.

Bleharies on the River Scheldt

31 May 1940

Charles Stanley Kiddy was born in Risbridge, Suffolk in 1918, the eldest son of Charles Kiddy and Ethel (née Crissall). When the family moved to Thame, they lived in Thame Lodge, Thame Park, where his father was a gamekeeper. Charles went to Thame Church of England School, then under the headmastership of Mr FB Mitchell. Charles was *"very popular with his school fellows and was a valuable member of the first football XI"*. After leaving Thame he went to Surrey as an under-keeper, until 26th November 1936 when he joined the Grenadier Guards at Guildford. The Grenadier Guards formed part of the 1st Infantry Brigade which went to France in 1939 as part of the British Expeditionary Force (BEF). Charles was killed during the retreat of the BEF from Belgium towards Dunkirk in 1940. He was with the GHQ Company of the Grenadier Guards, serving as an officer's valet and died between 31st May and 1st June 1940, in or around the village of De Panne, where two battalions of the Regiment were helping cover the retreat. He was 22 years old and had been with the Regiment for 3 years and 7 months.

2615082 Guardsman Charles Stanley Kiddy, Grenadier Guards, is buried in De Panne Communal Cemetery, West-Vlaanderen, Belgium. He is commemorated on War Memorials at Brook and Mottistone on the Isle of Wight where his parents had moved to before the war. His name is to be added to Thame War Memorial.

The Thame Remembers Cross was placed at his grave on 8th June 2017 by Thame area residents, Piers Newth and Louise Allen.

20 July 1940

Albert George Thomlinson was born in Rhode Island, USA in 1914 to John William Thomlinson and Alice May (née Scott). He had two brothers John and Gordon and one sister Alice Evelyn Lloyd. The family moved to England, disembarking at Liverpool on 30th November 1921, and lived at Scotsgrove near Thame.

Albert enlisted with the Territorials on 30th April 1934 and when war broke out he was mobilised with the 4th Battalion, Oxford and Bucks Light Infantry. They formed part of the 145th Brigade 48th Division and left Southampton on 18th January 1940 aboard TSS St Hellier to join the British Expeditionary Force. The Battalion remained in France until 10th May when it moved to Belgium in response to the German invasion through the Low Countries. As part of the rearguard action of the retreat to Dunkirk, the 4th Battalion took part in the defence of Cassel, in northern France. However, the German forces had superior artillery capability and despite intense fighting the Battalion found themselves encircled and overwhelmed. Less than eighty men of the Battalion reached Dunkirk. Albert and many of his compatriots, including his two brothers, were captured and transported to Lamsdorf (Stalag VIIIB), a prisoner of war camp in eastern Germany. On 20th July 1940 Albert, age 26, as a prisoner of war, was taken ill and died in hospital in the nearby town of Neisse, East Germany (now Nysa, Poland). He was buried in the local cemetery and not the prison camp cemetery as would have been expected.

5381863 Private Albert George Thomlinson, Oxford and Bucks Light Infantry, is commemorated on Dunkirk Memorial, Nord, France. He is buried in the Old German Military Cemetery in Nysa, Poland, although the exact location is not known. He is remembered in Thame on the War Memorial and on the Memorial Boards of St Mary's Church and All Saints' Church.

The Thame Remembers Cross was placed at Dunkirk Memorial on 10th June 2015 by Thame residents, Iain and Alison Biddle.

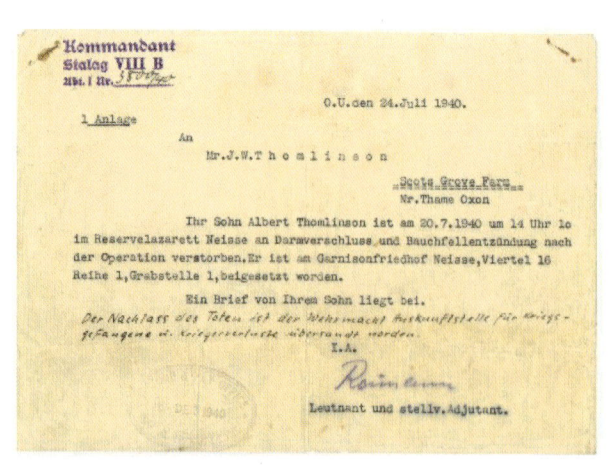

Letter from the Commandant of the Prisoner of War Camp informing the family of Albert's death

The Thame Remembers Cross was placed at the Old German Military Cemetery in Nysa, Poland by Iain and Alison Biddle on 22nd August 2018.

Thame Remembers Search for Albert's Grave

In 1940 the 4th Battalion of the Oxford and Bucks Light Infantry was part of the British army forming the rearguard action around Cassel in Northern France in support of the retreat to Dunkirk. Many of the soldiers were taken prisoner including three Thomlinson brothers from Thame. The boys, all from C Company, made it to a prisoner of war camp in eastern Germany where unfortunately Private Albert George Thomlinson is reported to have died.

Albert's name is commemorated on Dunkirk Memorial because the Commonwealth War Graves Commission (CWGC) have no record of where he is buried - until now.

Albert's family contacted the Thame Remembers Project as they have recently discovered papers sent from the Kommandant of the prisoner of war camp in 1940 giving details of Albert's death and burial.

We passed these on to the CWGC for them to investigate further and have since heard from them with a report from an investigator who visited the prisoner of war camp and the local town.

They were able to confirm that the brothers were among the first prisoners at Stalag VIIIB at Lamsdorf in 1940 and that Albert died in the nearby town of Neisse. Quite why he was in Neisse (modern Nysa, Poland) is not certain; maybe he was sent there when he became ill or maybe he was part of a working party and took the opportunity to report to the doctors. Either way he is recorded as dying in the hospital there, probably of appendicitis, and being buried in the nearby local cemetery.

Unfortunately the town of Neisse was obliterated in the Russian advance in 1945 and all hospital and civic records destroyed.

The cemetery does survive, although in a poor state with very few grave markers. Furthermore the details of the location of the grave sent to the family and the records at Stalag VIIIB do not agree, so, even though the CWGC investigator identified a probable area of the cemetery, the exact position of Albert's resting place cannot be determined.

Brothers John, Albert and Gordon Thomlinson OBLI

The Old German Cemetery, Nysa, Poland
The burial is probably within the mounds in the rear of the picture

8 July 1944

Leslie Hodges was born in Towersey, Buckinghamshire on 12th September 1918 to Charles Edward Hodges and Charlotte Elizabeth (née Stow) who were originally from Surrey but lived for a while at 53 Chinnor Road, Thame. He was the third youngest of twelve children. By 1939 his parents had moved to live in Banbury, Oxfordshire.

Leslie joined the 1st Battalion Oxford and Bucks Light Infantry when it was brought up to strength following the losses at Dunkirk and served initially in Northern Ireland. In 1942 they were brought back to England and in 1943 started to train for the forthcoming invasion of Europe. The 1st Battalion landed in Normandy on 24th June 1944 and the following day moved forward to take part in *"Operation Epsom"*, the intention of which was to take the city of Caen. It proved to be a formidable city to capture and the attack was unsuccessful. The 1st Battalion then moved to positions around the Odon bridgehead where it suffered from heavy German artillery fire. On the evening of 8th July 1944, a raid called *"Operation Sally"* was carried out by A Company led by Major Gordon "Tony" Jephson MC together with 25 infantry and the signallers and medics. The second-in-command was Lieutenant Henry Green and the purpose of the raid was to disrupt an expected counter-attack and to take prisoners for interrogation. The following is a first-hand account given by Private Percy Allen. *"I looked back to see Lieutenant Green and his section astride the railway line take the full force of the enemy attack with numerous bombs falling amongst his men. The section returned fire and did well to inflict about eight casualties upon the enemy which included a mortar detachment. However other German mortars and machine guns continued firing and Lieutenant Green was severely wounded by shrapnel, while Private Les Hodges, his batman, always close and loyal, tried to protect him, but was killed"*. Leslie was 25 year old and was buried next to Lieutenant Green. Allied troops entered the city of Caen the following day.

5382328 Private Leslie Hodges, Oxford and Bucks Light Infantry, is buried at Brouay War Cemetery, Calvados, France. He is remembered in Thame on the War Memorial and on St Mary's Church Memorial Board.

The Thame Remembers Cross was placed at his grave on 12th June 2015
by Lord Williams's School pupils.
(Thomas Higgins, Max Mordente, Jamie Wiles, Tom Hutt,
Owen Passingham-Hughes, John Williams and Kerry Shannon).

11 July 1944

Reginald Albert Miller was born in Thame on 23rd June 1920 to William Miller and Louisa Hannah (née Woodley) living at 78 Park Street. He was baptised at St Mary's Church on 22nd August 1920. His father William was a gardener and by 1939 they were living at 101 High Street. Reginald met Edna Linacre when she came to work in Thame in 1937 and they married in 1943 in Doncaster, Yorkshire whilst he was on leave. A son, Keith R Miller, who Reginald never saw, was born in Bentley, Doncaster in 1945. He enlisted in the Dorsetshire Regiment in 1937 and served as a signaller with the 1st Battalion 1st Dorsets during the siege of Malta. After resting in Alexandria his unit took part in the invasion of Sicily, returning to England in November 1943. Due to their invasion experience the Battalion was among the leading units for the assault on Normandy in the D-Day landings of 6th June 1944. They landed on Gold beach near St Hamel. The battle, by the British and Canadians armies, to break out from the beachhead towards Caen led to many lives being lost, including Reginald, age 23, who was killed on 11th July 1944.

5725766 Private Reginald Albert Miller, Dorsetshire Regiment, is buried in Bayeux War Cemetery, Calvados, France. He is remembered in Thame on the War Memorial and on St Mary's Church Memorial Board.

The Thame Remembers Cross was placed at his grave on 6th April 2015 by Steve Perry of Thame Remembers.

16 July 1944

John Robert Ing was born in Autumn 1917 to John Robert Ing and Dorothy (née Larner) of Long Crendon, Buckinghamshire. His father never saw his son, having died during World War One whilst serving in Portsmouth with the 3rd Battalion Oxford and Bucks Light Infantry. John excelled in all forms of sport at school and captained his school for two seasons when playing in the Anthony-Birrell Cup competition. Prior to the war he was an employee of Major Dyer of Lord Williams's Grammar School, Thame. He was familiarly known as "Jack" and married Doris Squires in 1938. They settled in her parents' family home at 44 Hampden Avenue, Thame where they had one son, John E, born in 1943. Doris continued to live in Hampden Avenue after World War Two. She married twice more and died in 1992.

John joined the 1st Battalion Oxford and Bucks Light Infantry when it was brought up to strength following the losses at Dunkirk and initially served in Northern Ireland. In 1942 they were brought back to England and in 1943 started to train for the forthcoming invasion of Europe.

The 1st Battalion landed in Normandy on 24th June 1944 and the following day moved forward to take part in *"Operation Epsom"*, the intention of which was to take the city of Caen. It proved to be a formidable city to capture and the attack was unsuccessful. The 1st Battalion then moved to positions around the Odon bridgehead where it suffered from heavy German artillery fire and were then held in reserve for a few days. On 14th July 1944 they were ordered to attack and take the village of Cahier. John, age 26, was one of the 35 men from the Battalion who were killed in the fighting on 16th July.

5388804 Private John Robert Ing, Oxford and Bucks Light Infantry, is buried in Brouay Cemetery, Calvados, France. He is remembered in Thame on the War Memorial and on St Mary's Church Memorial Board. He is commemorated on the War Memorial in Long Crendon.

The Thame Remembers Cross was placed at his grave on 5th June 2015 by Thame resident, David Gregory.

16 July 1944

Albert Henry Pollicott was born on 17th April 1915 to William Henry Pollicott and Florence Mary (née Holtham) of Moor End Lane, Thame. He was baptised at St Mary's Church on 25th July 1915. His father William was a butcher. In 1939 Albert married Ellen Caddo Bell in Aylesbury, Buckinghamshire and was employed by Messrs R G Howland & Sons, builders. A daughter Elizabeth was born in 1943.

Albert joined the 1st Battalion Oxford and Bucks Light Infantry when it was brought up to strength following the losses at Dunkirk. They served initially in Northern Ireland but in

1942 they were brought back to England and in 1943 started to train for the forthcoming invasion of Europe. The 1st Battalion landed in Normandy on 24th June 1944 and the following day moved forward to take part in *"Operation Epsom"*, the intention of which was to take the city of Caen. It proved to be a formidable city to capture and the attack was unsuccessful. The 1st Battalion then moved to positions around the Odon bridgehead where it suffered from heavy German artillery fire and was then held in reserve for a few days. On 14th July 1944 they were ordered to attack and take the village of Cahier. Albert, age 29, was killed in the fighting for Cahier on 16th July 1944.

5389298 Lance Corporal Albert Henry Pollicott, Oxford and Bucks Light Infantry, is buried in Brouay War Cemetery, Calvados, France. He is remembered in Thame on the War Memorial and on St Mary's Church Memorial Board.

The Thame Remembers Cross was placed at his grave on 6th April 2015
by Verity Platek of Thame Remembers.

24 July 1944

Sidney Charles Maskell-Dicker was born on 22nd July 1910 in Lambeth, London to Sidney Maskell Dicker and Dora (née Read). His father was killed in 1915 whilst serving with the King's Royal Rifle Corps. Sidney lived with his mother and sister Muriel in Chinnor Road, Thame and attended Lord Williams's Grammar School. He obtained a BSc in Education at Reading University going on to teach at The Royal Free School in Windsor, Berkshire and then the Central Boys School in Deal, Kent. He was a member of the Royal Society of Teachers and Fellow of the Royal Horticultural Society.

He enlisted at the outbreak of World War Two and was commissioned as a 2nd Lieutenant in the Wiltshire Regiment in November 1939. On the evening of 22nd July 1944 the 5th Battalion part of the 129th Brigade of the 43rd (Wessex) Division attacked the village of Maltot, west of Caen, which was captured the following day. D Company, with Sidney in charge, were dug in slit trenches on the outskirts of the village when the Germans counter-attacked. A shell from a German Tiger tank hit the trench killing Sidney instantly. He was 34 years of age and was buried near where he fell in the village of Eterville. His body was reinterred on 14th November 1945. He left over £440 in his will, to be administered by his "*beloved sister*" Mollie.

100923 Captain Sidney Charles Maskell-Dicker, Wiltshire Regiment, is buried at St Manvieu War Cemetery, Cheux, Calvados, France. He is remembered in Thame on Lord Williams's School Memorial Board and his name is to be added to Thame War Memorial.

The Thame Remembers Cross was placed at his grave on 15th September 2015
by Thame residents, David and Beryl Kew.

```
    I  DIE  REJOICING
FOR  MY  KING,  MY  COUNTRY
      AND  HER  LAWS
```

The Inscription on Sidney's Gravestone

10th Battalion Highland Light Infantry

The Highland Light Infantry (City of Glasgow Regiment) was a Scottish Regiment, although less than half of its ranks originated from Scotland. In the build-up to D-Day many men from other regiments including the Oxford and Bucks Light Infantry were transferred to the 10th Battalion. In the cemetery at St Charles de Percy there are 22 burials from the Battalion. Seven are from the Oxfordshire and Buckinghamshire area, five from the north of England, three from London, one from Somerset, one unknown and only five are from Scotland, with three of these being from Glasgow.

The Battalion was part of the 227th Brigade 15th (Scottish) Division which landed in Normandy a few days after D-Day and fought at the Second Battle at the Crossing of the Odon and across northern France.

"On Sunday, 6th August, the Gordons were to attack ESTRY and we were to pass through them and take LE THEIL. But ESTRY was too strong a point and the Battalion took over the attack after the Gordons had been pinned down. ESTRY and a dozen other similar little villages at the Western end of the German salient that was to become the "FALAISE POCKET" had all the weapons of defence; machine gun nests, dug-in tanks, mortars and 'call on' heavy artillery. Despite all this, by late evening of 6th August the forward companies had reached the area of the church where resistance was strongest. The village all that night, 6th/7th August and next day and night 7th/8th August, was a noisy, lively place; artillery exchanges, our own 3-in. mortars pounding the church area and the road itself covered by German Spandaus and the crossroads by the Maxim Machine Guns and 88mm gun of a dug-in Tiger Tank. The HLI were withdrawn in the early hours of the 8th August."

Extract from the History of the 10th Highland Light Infantry

6 August 1944

Kenneth Sellwood was born in late 1925 to William John Sellwood and Phoebe Elizabeth (née Sewell) of Tetsworth, Oxfordshire. He attended Lord Williams's Grammar School, Thame from 1937 to 1941.

Kenneth joined the Army General Service Corps in 1942 soon after leaving school and after training was posted to the Highland Light Infantry (City of Glasgow Regiment). He was a Lance Corporal in the 10th Battalion. Kenneth, just 18 years of age, was killed during fighting near the village of Estry in Normandy, France on 6th August 1944.

14499730 Lance Corporal Kenneth Sellwood, Highland Light Infantry, is buried in St Charles de Percy Cemetery, Calvados, France. He is remembered in Thame on Lord Williams's School Memorial Board and is commemorated on Tetsworth War Memorial.

The Thame Remembers Cross was placed at his grave on 25th May 2015 by Thame resident, Jenny Manger.

7 August 1944

Harry Arnott was born in Thame on 29th January 1917, but not baptised until the 26th August 1926 at the same time as his sister Clarice who was born in 1923. Harry was the son of Robert Arnott, bootmaker, and Mary Ann (née Loosley) of 103 High Street, Thame.

Harry took up his father's occupation as a bootmaker, but in 1940 he joined the Oxford and Bucks Light Infantry.

He was later transferred to the 10th Battalion of the Highland Light Infantry. Harry, age 27, was killed during fighting near the village of Estry in Normandy, France on 7th August 1944.

5388442 Private Harry Arnott, Highland Light Infantry, is buried in St Charles de Percy Cemetery, Calvados, France. He is remembered in Thame on the War Memorial and on St Mary's Church Memorial Board.

The Thame Remembers Cross was placed at his grave on 25th May 2015 by Thame resident, Kristian Winslade.

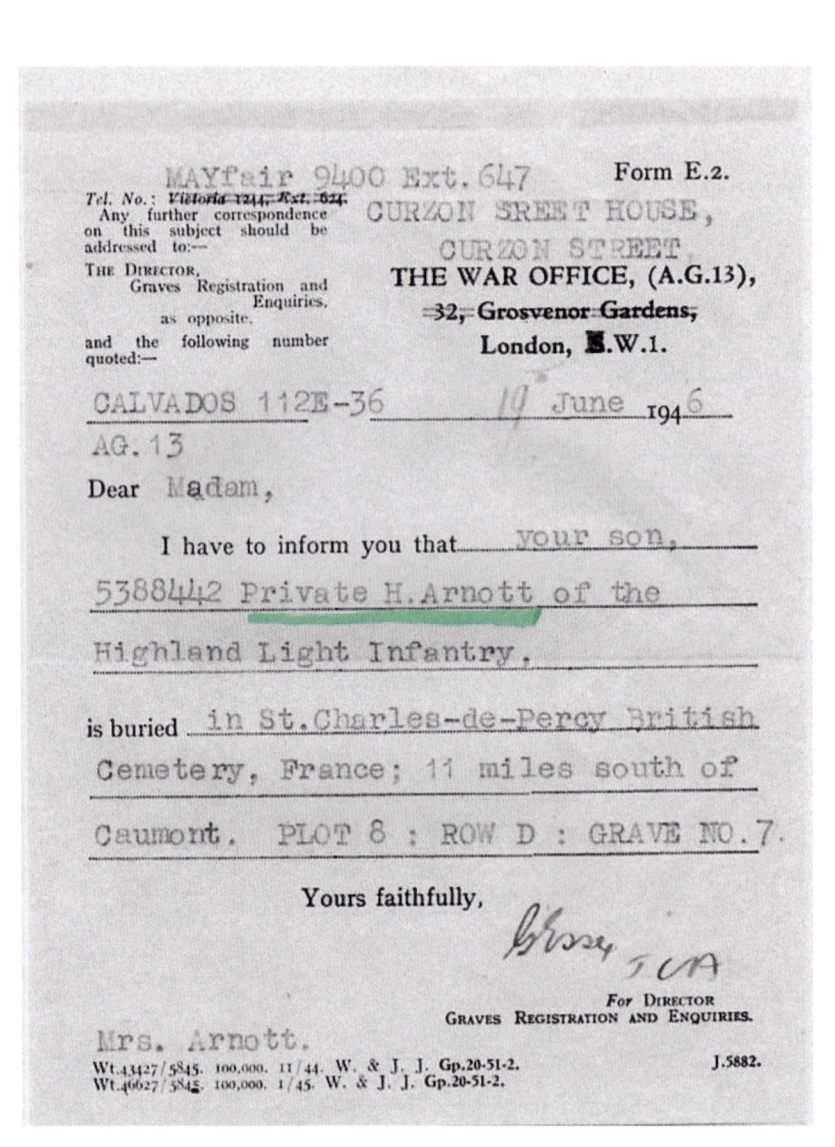

Letter to Mrs Arnott advising her of the burial of her son Harry

8 August 1944

Thomas John Tims was born in Bletchingley, Surrey on 20th June 1912 one of the six children of Walter Sidney Tims and Charlotte (née Love). By the start of World War One, the family had moved to Windsor, Berkshire and his father went on to serve as a Sergeant in the Middlesex and Bedfordshire Regiments.

Thomas married Blanche Mabel Emily Holmes at Uxbridge in 1939. They initially lived in Littlemore near Oxford but then moved to 31 North Street, Thame, from where they ran a fish and chip shop. His wife continued to run the fish and chip shop until her death in 1950. She remarried in 1947 and was then known as Emily Watson.

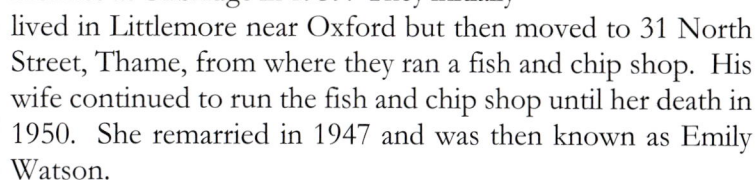

Thomas served as a Corporal with the 1st Battalion Oxford and Bucks Light Infantry. The Battalion had been brought up to strength following the losses at Dunkirk and served initially in Northern Ireland. In 1942 they were brought back to England and in 1943 started to train for the forthcoming invasion of Europe. The 1st Battalion landed in Normandy on 24th June 1944 and the following day took part in "*Operation Epsom*", which was intended to take the city of Caen.

The beginning of August found the Regiment in company positions at Gouvry receiving spasmodic attention from enemy artillery and mortars. On 8th August 1944 Thomas was in a carrier outpost on bridges at Le Locheur, south west of Caen, when a bomb from an RAF Typhoon fell in the area occupied by the carrier platoon. Thomas, age 32, and three of his comrades were killed by the bomb. They were buried locally at Colleville, France but their bodies were reinterred in September 1945 by the Commonwealth War Graves Commission.

5391039 Corporal Thomas John Tims, Oxford and Bucks Light Infantry, is buried in Brouay War Cemetery, Calvados, France. His name is to be added to Thame War Memorial.

The Thame Remembers Cross was placed at his grave on 12th June 2015
by Thame resident, John Francis.

The City of Caen in Ruins

13 August 1944

Ronald James Boiling was born in Thame on 20th January 1925 and baptised at St Mary's Church on 26th April 1925. He was the second son of Edward William Boiling and Florence Mary (née Rawlings) of 16 Wellington Street, although later they lived at 40 Wellington Street, Thame.

Ronald worked for Messrs W W Howland & Son, builders, prior to joining the Oxford and Bucks Light Infantry in March 1943 at 19 years of age. He was with the 1st Battalion that landed in France in late June 1944. They were part of *Operation Epsom* that was intended to take the city of Caen and later moved into the country east of Caen. Early on 13th August having crossed the River Orne on foot the Battalion at 04:00hrs moved through the village of Cesney-Bois-Halbout to take the crossroads at La Bijude. The attack met stiff resistance and was initially forced to withdraw but by 17:00hrs that day the crossroads had been taken. The Oxford and Bucks lost a number of men in the action including Ronald, age 20.

14556610 Lance Corporal Ronald James Boiling, Oxford and Bucks Light Infantry, is buried at Banneville-la-Campagne War Cemetery, Calvados, France. He is remembered in Thame on the War Memorial and on St Mary's Church Memorial Board.

*The Thame Remembers Cross was placed at his grave on 12th June 2015
by Lord Williams's School pupils.
(Thomas Higgins, Max Mordente, Jamie Wiles, Tom Hutt,
Owen Passingham-Hughes, John Williams and Kerry Shannon).*

8 January 1945

Frederick Ernest Howes was born in Headington, Oxfordshire on 29th February 1920. His parents were Frederick George Howes and Emily Amelia (née Merry) who had married in Headington the year before. By 1922 the family had moved to Thame, where his sister Freda and two brothers Leslie and Joseph were born, probably at the family home at 9 Horton Avenue. In 1939 Frederick was working as a farm labourer.

He joined the Oxford and Bucks Light Infantry at the start of World War Two and served with the 2nd Battalion, initially on Home Defence duties. In early 1942 they became the 2nd (Airborne) Battalion and trained as glider-borne infantry and as such they remained in England in readiness for the invasion of mainland Europe.

On D-Day they successfully took the Bridge on the Caen Canal between Caen and Ouistrehan, which became famous as *"Pegasus Bridge"*. Although it is not known if Frederick was with them.

At Christmas 1944 the Battalion was rushed to the Ardennes to assist with the defence against the German advance know as *"The Battle of the Bulge"*.

They took part in the battle for the town of Bure, losing several men, and in the following battles Frederick, age 24, was killed on 8th January 1945. He was buried at Resteigne (Belgium) Temporary Burial Ground before being reinterred in May 1947.

5389893 Private Frederick Ernest Howes, Oxford and Bucks Light Infantry, is buried in Hotton War Cemetery, Luxembourg Region, Belgium. He is remembered in Thame on both Thame and Moreton War Memorials and on St Mary's Church Memorial Board.

The Thame Remembers Cross was placed at his grave on 27th August 2015 by Thame Museum member, Ruth Pimm.

5 April 1945

Ronald Frank Harris was born at North Weston, near Thame on 4th September 1913 to Frank Harris and Kate (née Shorter). He was educated at Shabbington School, Buckinghamshire and on leaving school was employed as a counter-hand by Mr G Bailey a grocer in the Buttermarket, Thame. On 3rd August 1940 he married Mabel Gladys Newitt at St Mary's Church, Thame. They lived with her parents at 60 Wellington Street

Ronald joined the Oxford and Bucks Light Infantry at the start of World War Two and served with the 2nd Battalion, initially on Home Defence duties. In early 1942 they became the 2nd (Airborne) Battalion and trained as glider-borne infantry and as such they remained in England in readiness for the invasion of mainland Europe. Their mission on D-Day was to successfully take the bridge on the Caen Canal between Caen and Ouistrehan that became famous as *"Pegasus Bridge"*.

The Battalion returned to France in December 1944 as part of the defence against the German Ardennes offensive. After a short spell of leave, Ronald returned to the Battalion for the airborne assault in crossing the Rhine in late March 1945. They advanced into Germany, where Ronald, age 31, died on 5th April 1945 of wounds received during fighting in villages around the town of Petershagen, near Hanover, Germany. He was initially buried in Friedewalde Evangelist churchyard near Minden, Germany before being reinterred in July 1947.

5385941 Lance Corporal Ronald Frank Harris, Oxford and Bucks Light Infantry, is buried in Hanover War Cemetery, Germany. He is remembered in Thame on St Mary's Church Memorial Board and his name is to be added to Thame War Memorial.

The Thame Remembers Cross was placed at his grave on 5th April 2016 by Thame resident, Corporal Tim Jones (The Princess of Wales's Royal Regiment).

Frederick Howes and Ronald Harris were part of D Company of the 2nd (Airborne) Battalion Oxford and Bucks Light Infantry, although it is not thought that either were in the glider attack at Pegasus Bridge.

On 6th June 1944 the Battalion's involvement in the successful *"Coup de Main"* action at Pegasus Bridge, with D company and parts of B company, under the command of Major John Howard, proved to be one of the most remarkable British airborne actions during the Second World War.

The 2nd Battalion would continue to see airborne action, serving as part of the 6th Airborne deployment to the Ardennes and the Rhine Crossing in early spring 1945.

Pegasus Bridge a few days after the Battle with the Battalion's Gliders visible on the banks of the Canal

Cloth Shoulder Title as worn in World War Two

Northern Europe: RAF

The RAF bombing offensive against Nazi Germany was one of the longest, most expensive and controversial of the Allied campaigns during World War Two. Its aim was to severely weaken Germany's ability to fight, which was central to the Allies' strategy for winning the war.

During the battle for France and after the defeat of the Luftwaffe in the Battle of Britain it became clear that daylight raids by unescorted bombers would result in unsustainable losses. It was also clear that, at that time, the only practical method of taking the war to Germany was a strategic bombing offensive. The early night raids were largely ineffective and it took time for new aircraft to be designed and deployed, and also new tactics to be devised to make the raids more effective. On the night of 30th/31st May 1942, Bomber Command launched the first '1000 bomber raid' against Cologne. The Germans, who had already been strengthening their defences, were forced to take the threat much more seriously and from then on the anti-aircraft defences were continuously reinforced. The night fighters and additional anti-aircraft guns took a heavy toll on the bomber crews until the last few months of the war.

The result was that the losses among Bomber Command crews steadily climbed. By the end of the war, 55,573 had been killed out of a total of 125,000 aircrew (a 44.4 percent death rate). A further 8,403 were wounded in action and 9,838 became prisoners of war.

The Memorial to Bomber Command Crews unveiled in Green Park, London on 28th June 2012

The most well-known aircraft used in the bombing raids is the Avro Lancaster, but the RAF flew two other four-engine bombers namely the Handley Page Halifax and the Short Stirling. In the early stages of the war they also used the twin-engine Bristol Blenheim and Vickers Wellington aircraft as well as the Handley Page Hampden and Avro Manchester.

Avro Lancaster

Handley Page Halifax

Bristol Blenheim

Vickers Wellington

High Flight

Oh! I have slipped the surly bonds of earth,
And danced the skies on laughter-silvered wings;
Sunward I've climbed, and joined the tumbling mirth
Of sun-split clouds, – and done a hundred things
You have not dreamed of –
Wheeled and soared and swung
High in the sunlit silence. Hov'ring there
I've chased the shouting wind along, and flung
My eager craft through footless halls of air...
Up, up the long, delirious, burning blue
I've topped the wind-swept heights with easy grace
Where never lark or even eagle flew --
And, while with silent lifting mind I've trod
The high un-trespassed sanctity of space,
Put out my hand, and touched the face of God.

John Gillespie Magee, Jr
(1922-1941)

Those Remembered

12 May 1940

Thomas Hayward Parrott, known as Tim, was born on 26th November 1916 to Walter Lawrence Parrott, a member of the well-known family of solicitors in Aylesbury, Buckinghamshire, and his wife Katherine Mary (née Seaton). He was the second of three sons and was born in Kelerberrin, Western Australia. By the 1920s the family had returned to England and were living at Homefield, Oxford Road, Haddenham, Buckinghamshire.

In September 1929 Thomas went to Lord Williams's Grammar School as a boarding pupil and *"although of average academic ability, he was quite a good sportsman"*. In his last term in 1933, his housemaster wrote of him. *"He will probably leave in this term much to our regret. His modesty, good nature, skill and courage at games, particular Rugger, have made him deservedly popular."*

He was the first Old Tamensian reported killed in World War Two. Thomas served for a while with the Middlesex Yeomanry (part of the Royal Corps of Signals) and in June 1936 received his commission into the Royal Air Force. He trained as a pilot and was stationed with 77 Squadron at RAF Driffield in Yorkshire. In February 1940, having been promoted to Flying Officer, he was "Mentioned in Dispatches" following the RAF's longest war flight.

On the evening of 12th May 1940 he took off in Armstrong Whitworth Whitley Mark V N1366 on a bombing mission to Mönchengladbach, Germany. The aircraft crashed in the target area and Thomas, age 23, was killed together with three other members of his crew, one surviving to become a prisoner of war. This was the first bomber to crash inside Germany whilst carrying out a bombing operation on a mainland target. The crew were originally buried in Lohmannsheide Forest Cemetery, near Duisburg but were reinterred on 24th June 1947. His younger brother Peter Lawrence Parrot DFC served with distinction in the Royal Air Force during World War Two.

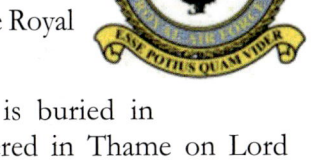

39112 Flying Officer Thomas Hayward Parrott, Royal Air Force, is buried in Reichswald Forest War Cemetery, Kleve, Germany. He is remembered in Thame on Lord Williams's School Memorial Board.

The Thame Remembers Cross was placed at his grave on 31st October 2015 by former Thame policewoman, Angela Tobin.

ON ACTIVE SERVICE
PARROTT. - Killed in action May 12th 1940,
Flying Officer Thomas Hayward Parrott
(Tim) second son of Mrs and the late Mr Walter Parrott,
of Haddenham, aged 23 years.
Buried at Lohmannsheide Cemetery, near
Moers, Dusseldorf, Germany, on May 14th.
"Our second little fellow, a loyal Boy Scout,
A Middlesex Yeoman, Per Ardua Ad Adstra."

Obituary from the Bucks Herald

11 August 1940

Richard Francis Gower was the son of Herbert Charles Alfred Gower and Ethel Marion (née Francis). He was born in Market Deeping, near Bourne, Lincolnshire in 1916, where his father was a pharmacist and optician.

By the 1920s, his father was running a pharmacy business at 95 High Street, Thame. Richard was admitted to Lord Williams's Grammar School as a day boy in September 1926 and was there for three years. He left in July 1929 and moved to Basingstoke Grammar School, Hampshire.

He was commissioned in the Royal Air Force in May 1938 and trained to be a pilot. In 1940 Richard was serving with 49 Squadron based at RAF Scampton, Lincolnshire. On the night of 11th August, he took off in a Handley Page Hampden Mk 1 bomber L4036 with a crew of four for an operation over Dortmund, Germany. It was reported the plane was brought down by flak and there were no survivors. He was 24 years old. The crew were all buried in a local cemetery at Waldfriedhof Loh, near Lüderscheid, Germany before being reinterred in 1947.

40693 Pilot Officer Richard Francis Gower, Royal Air Force, is buried in the War Cemetery at Reichswald Forest, Kleve, Germany. He is remembered in Thame on Lord Williams's School Memorial Board.

Handley Page Hampden

The Thame Remembers Cross was placed at his grave on 31st October 2015 by former Thame policeman, Kevin Tobin.

25 May 1941

Francis Wood was born on 14th December 1921. He was the youngest of the three sons of Henry and Anna Wood, of Aston Mullins Farm, Ford, Buckinghamshire. He attended Lord Williams's Grammar School, Thame from 1931 to 1939. Francis joined the Royal Air Force Volunteer Reserve after September 1939 and trained as a pilot. In 1941 he was serving with 18 Squadron at RAF Oulton based on the Blickling Hall Estate in Norfolk, where they flew Bristol Blenheim bombers. Francis, age 19, was flying Bristol Blenheim Mk IV L8864 on the day he died, 25th May 1941. On board with him were Sgt E G Baker and Sgt C N Harris. Three aircraft from the Squadron left the airfield at 05:50hrs on an anti-shipping mission. They carried out an attack on shore Battery Agger but their aircraft was hit by machine gun fire and crashed into the sea 30 metres off the coast of Thyborøn, Denmark at 08:10hrs. Frank's body was recovered from the sea, he had been hit in the head by a bullet. Sgt Baker's body washed ashore and was buried at Lemvig with Francis. Sgt Harris survived the crash and was subsequently captured and interned in a prisoner of war camp.

926082 Sergeant Francis Wood, Royal Air Force Volunteer Reserve, is buried in Lemvig Cemetery, West Jutland, Denmark. He is remembered in Thame on Lord Williams's School Memorial Board and is commemorated on Ford War Memorial.

The Thame Remembers Cross was placed at his grave on 17th July 2018 by Thame residents, Kristian Winslade and Tom Bowen.

5 May 1942

Herbert John Ody was born in Lydiard Tregoze near Cricklade, Wiltshire on 10th April 1915 to George William Ody, a farmer, and Mabel Annie (née Lewis). He attended Lord Williams's Grammar School in Thame from 1928 to 1931. Prior to the war, he was on the staff of Messrs Pursers Ltd, Thame as a general clerk and was living at Cranbrooke Road, Monk Risborough, Buckinghamshire. He was also a prominent member of Thame Hockey Club. Herbert, age 23, married Margaret Jessie Wilson in Watlington, Oxfordshire in early 1939. He joined the Royal Air Force Volunteer Reserve in late 1939 and his wife returned to live in High Street, Watlington. Herbert went on to train as a Wireless Operator/Air Gunner. By 1942 he was serving as a Sergeant with 12 Squadron, flying Wellington bombers from RAF Binbrook, Lincolnshire.

At 22:04hrs on 5th May 1942 he was one of the crew of Vickers Wellington Mk II, Z8495 that took off from RAF Binbrook. They were carrying a single 4000lb "cookie" bomb and were headed for Stuttgart, Germany. The aircraft crashed near Reuth, 8 km north east of Prüm, Germany presumably as a result of enemy action. There were no survivors. Herbert, age 27, left effects of £905 16s 7d to his widow. The crew were originally buried together in Olzheim cemetery, Buitburg-Prüm, Germany before being reinterred in 1948.

921915 Sergeant Herbert John Ody, Royal Air Force Volunteer Reserve, is buried in Rheinberg War Cemetery, Westphalia, Germany. He is remembered in Thame on Lord Williams's School Memorial Board and is also commemorated on Watlington War Memorial.

The Thame Remembers Cross was placed at his grave on 30th August 2015 by Thame town clerk, Graham Hunt.

9 January 1943

Stanley Riswin Colbert was born on 26th September 1921 in Sheffield, Yorkshire to George Cyril Colbert and Olive Bertha (née Haynes). The family later lived at Orchard House, Cuxham, Oxfordshire from where Stanley attended Lord Williams's Grammar School in Thame from 1934 to 1938.

In April 1940 Stanley enlisted in the Royal Air Force Volunteer Reserve and trained as a pilot. By 1943 he was serving with 97 Squadron based at RAF Woodhall Spa, near Lincoln. The Squadron initially flew Avro Manchester bombers before converting to fly Lancaster bombers.

On 9th January 1943 his aircraft R5738 took off at 17:07hrs on a mission to bomb Essen, Germany with a 4000lb "cookie" bomb. They were shot down by a night fighter at 19:10hrs, east of Eindhoven and crashed near Maasbree on the Dutch side of the Dutch/German border. Stanley, age 21, was buried in the Netherlands along with five of his crew. Air Gunner Sgt Dell (Royal Canadian Air Force) survived but subsequently died as a prisoner of war.

1165025 Flight Sergeant Stanley Riswin Colbert, Royal Air Force Volunteer Reserve, is buried in Jonkerbos War Cemetery, Nijmegen, Netherlands. He is remembered in Thame on Lord Williams's School Memorial Board and is also commemorated on Cuxham War Memorial.

The Thame Remembers Cross was placed at his grave on 1st October 2014 by Thame residents, Brian and Julie West.

15 April 1943

Gordon Wade was born in Plymouth, Devon on 22nd July 1919, one of the three children of Harry Wade and Florida (née Ashton).

In 1924 he went to Bombay, India to join his father who was a railway engineer, returning in 1926. He joined the Royal Air Force as an engineering apprentice in 1935, training at RAF Halton, Buckinghamshire. It is probable that it was during his time at RAF Halton that Gordon met his wife Mary Joan Abraham who was at that time living with her mother Florence and Florence's husband, Frederick Bush at Chestnuts, Upper High Street, Thame.

Gordon and Mary married in Cambridge in February 1942 and had one son, Marcus, who was born in Thame in 1942. On completing his apprenticeship, Gordon was posted to 7 Squadron as a flight engineer on Short Stirling bombers. The first Stirlings arrived at RAF Oakington, Cambridgeshire in October 1940. The Squadron being the first unit in the Royal Air Force to operate large four-engine bombers.

On 15th April 1943 Gordon, age 23, was in the crew of Stirling Mk III BK769 which left Oakington as part of a 462 bomber raid on Stuttgart, Germany. The aircraft was probably brought down by flak and crashed at Lembach, Germany killing all on board. The seven crew were buried together in Bavaria, Germany.

Gordon's wife Mary remarried and after the war continued to live at Chestnuts in Upper High Street, Thame.

568514 Sergeant Gordon Wade, Royal Air Force, is buried in Durnbach War Cemetery, Bad Tolz, Bayern, Germany. He is remembered in Thame the War Memorial.

The Thame Remembers Cross was placed at his grave on 3rd December 2017 by Thame resident, Iain Biddle.

A Short Stirling aircraft of 7 Squadron

20 October 1944

John Anthony Creemer Clarke was born in Amesbury, Wiltshire in early 1922 to John Creemer Clarke and Meta Lyons (née Thompson). John Anthony attended Lord Williams's Grammar School from 1936 to 1939. In September 1939 he was a bank clerk living in Maidenhead, Berkshire whilst his mother and father, a crop reporter with the Ministry of Agriculture, were living at 82 High Street, Thame.

John Anthony joined the Royal Air Force Volunteer Reserve after April 1940 (Service No 1167328) as NCO aircrew and trained as a navigator. He was commissioned as a Pilot Officer on 4th July 1944 when he was serving with 35 Squadron at RAF Graveley in Cambridgeshire.

The Squadron flew Avro Lancaster bombers and was designated as a "pathfinder" squadron. At 17:56hrs on 19th October 1944 Avro Lancaster ND755 departed on a bombing mission to Stuttgart, Germany. The aircraft was shot down by enemy aircraft and crashed north west of Wintzenbach, eastern France. It exploded on impact and all eight men on board were killed. The crew are all listed as killed in action on 20th October 1944. John was 22 years old and he had previously been awarded the DFC which was published in the London Gazette on 17th November 1944.

177263 Pilot Officer John Anthony Creemer Clarke DFC, Royal Air Force, is buried in Wintzenbach Protestant Churchyard, Bas-Rhin, France. He is remembered in Thame on the War Memorial and on the Memorial Boards of St Mary's Church and Lord Williams's School.

The Thame Remembers Cross was placed at his grave on 9th July 2017 by Thame resident, Iain Biddle.

The crew of ND755
E J Kiely (Air Gunner), R F J Bright (Bomb Aimer), C Johnson (Flight Engineer), F D T Phillips (Air Gunner), A Linton (Wireless Operator), R W Brown (Pilot), J A C Clarke (Navigator)

10 March 1945

Ernest George Thomas Harris (Ernie) was born in late 1923 in Shiplake, Oxfordshire to Ernest Edward Harris and Elizabeth Amy (née Marner). According to family information it is said that Ernest was *"a sickly child so their doctor recommended that the family move away from the damp atmosphere of Shiplake's proximity to the Thames."* The family subsequently moved to Binfield Heath, Oxfordshire where Ernest's sister Hilda was born in 1928, to whom he was very close. Without any firm plans for his future, Ernest's headmaster, suggested to his father that he might be interested in learning a trade at the newly opened Rycote School (Rycotewood) in Thame. As his father was only a driver for a local building company, a fully financed place at the school was a wonderful opportunity for Ernest. He was offered one of the first eight boarding places and started in 1938, initially at the old workhouse and then, when the workhouse was requisitioned for billets in 1939, at 30 Upper High Street. He stayed for four years learning the trade of cabinet making. There was talk about him going on to continue his studies at Loughborough College, Leicestershire but instead, in 1942, he joined the Royal Air Force Volunteer Reserve (Service No 1604508) enlisting at Oxford. By 1944 and now a Leading Aircraftman, he was selected for aircrew training. He trained at RAF Cranwell, Lincolnshire and then in Canada, receiving a commission as a Pilot Officer on 2nd June 1944.

Ernest was posted to 107 Squadron based at RAF Great Massingham in Norfolk where he was a navigator in de Havilland DH98 Mosquito Mk VI Fighter Bombers. He was promoted to Flying Officer on 2nd December 1944.

Ernest took off in Mosquito HR254 on a night intruder mission from an airbase at Cambrai-Epinoy, France on the evening of 10th March 1945. The aircraft crashed near Lüthorst, 18 km east of Holzminden in Germany, and Ernest, age 22, together with the Canadian pilot, Flying Officer Robert J O'Sullivan were killed. They were buried together in Lüthorst German Cemetery before both being reinterred in December 1946.

165387 Flying Officer Ernest George Thomas Harris, Royal Air Force Volunteer Reserve, is buried in the War Cemetery in Hanover, Germany. He is commemorated on Shiplake War Memorial and his name is to be added to Thame War Memorial.

The Thame Remembers Cross was placed at his grave on 1st July 2018
by Thame resident, Corporal Tim Jones (The Princess of Wales's Royal Regiment).

The Nazis entered this war under the rather childish delusion that they were going to bomb everyone else and nobody was going to bomb them. At Rotterdam, London and Warsaw, and half a hundred other places, they put their rather naïve theory into operation.
They sowed the wind, and now they are going to reap the whirlwind.

Sir Arthur (Bomber) Harris

Italy

After the successful invasion of Sicily, the Allies invaded mainland Italy on 3rd September 1943 when the British 8th Army landed on the toe of the peninsula. The date coincided with the signing of an armistice by the Italians.

On 9th September 1943, the American 5th Army landed at Salerno and after overcoming stiff resistance on the beaches established a second bridgehead. The two Armies then advanced swiftly up to the Gustav Line where they were held up over the winter. This line included the monastery at Monte Cassino which was the scene of bitter fighting considered by many to be on a par with the attritional battles of World War One. An attempt to outflank the Germans by a further landing at Anzio failed.

Cemetery and Monastery at Monte Cassino

Eventually the Gustav Line fell in May 1944, the Germans withdrew and Rome was taken by the Allies on 3rd June 1944. The Allies continued their advance up through Italy facing determined German resistance which produced some of the most fierce and costly fighting of the war, much of it in treacherous mountain terrain. After the D-Day landing in Normandy most of the news was about the advance through Western Europe and many of the soldiers fighting in Italy considered themselves to be a forgotten army.

At the end of the war the British and Commonwealth forces had lost over 89,000 men killed, wounded or missing fighting in Italy.

D-Day Dodgers

We're the D-Day Dodgers, way off in Italy
Always on the vino, always on the spree;
Eighth Army scroungers and their tanks,
We live in Rome, among the Yanks.
We are the D-Day Dodgers, way out in Italy.

We landed in Salerno, a holiday with pay,
The Jerries brought the bands out to greet us on the way.
Showed us the sights and gave us tea,
We all sang songs, the beer was free
To welcome D-Day Dodgers to sunny Italy.

Naples and Casino were taken in our stride,
We didn't go to fight there, we went just for the ride.
Anzio and Sangro were just names,
We only went to look for dames
The artful D-Day Dodgers, way out in Italy.

Dear Lady Astor, you think you're mighty hot,
Standing on the platform, talking tommyrot.
You're England's sweetheart and her pride
We think your mouth's too bleeding wide.
We are the D-Day Dodgers, in sunny Italy.

Look around the mountains, in the mud and rain,
You'll find the scattered crosses, some that have no name.
Heartbreak and toil and suffering gone,
The boys beneath them slumber on.
They are the D-Day Dodgers who stay in Italy.

Hamish Henderson
(1919-2002)

This poem attributed to Hamish Henderson was written in response to Lady Astor's comment in the House of Commons to the troops in Italy "Dodging D-Day" and was popular with the 8th Army

Those Remembered

12 November 1943

Stanley James Allen was born in 1912 to Thomas Charles Allen and Annie Caroline (née Waghorn) of High Street, Thame who later moved to 29 Horton Avenue. Stanley married Beryl Irene Jones in Cheltenham, Gloucestershire in 1939 and they lived in Little Shurdington, near Cheltenham.

Stanley joined the Oxford and Bucks Light Infantry and was posted to the 7th Battalion, when it was formed in 1940. He served with A Company throughout his service. The Battalion, part of the 167th Infantry Brigade, 56th London Division, sailed on RMS Almanzora in August 1942 to join the 8th Army in North Africa. Following the invasion of Italy and during the fighting in September 1943 west of Salerno in Italy, Stanley was awarded the Military Medal, *"for conspicuous gallantry and devotion to duty when in command of his platoon in a forward position west of Salerno. Sergeant Allen's platoon held the road through a defile on September 15th. A reconnaissance unit reported the approach of German tanks and infantry and he laid a mine trap across the road. The German tanks and infantry developed strong attacks against this vital position. Sergeant Allen, disregarding his own safety, handled his platoon with such skill and determination that all attacks were driven back and a large number of Germans killed. Sergeant Allen's dogged courage and personal example ensured that the road was barred to the enemy."*

Stanley, age 31, was killed during the Battle of Monte Camino, west of Salerno, on 12th November 1943.

5379224 Sergeant Stanley James Allen MM, Oxford and Bucks Light Infantry, is buried in Naples War Cemetery, Italy. He is remembered in Thame on the War Memorial and on St Mary's Church Memorial Board.

The Thame Remembers Cross was placed at his grave on 22nd August 2018 by John Ashfield, President of Chinnor RFC Thame.

7 June 1944

Gordon Halliday Gudgeon was born in Hendon, Middlesex in 1916 to Henry Halliday Gudgeon, LDS RCS and Daisy Caroline (née Morris), who lived in Holborn, Middlesex. Gordon attended Lord Williams's Grammar School from 1927 to 1932. He was a keen cricketer and rugby player and was in the Old Tamensian Rugby XV in 1936.

He enlisted in 1940 for officer training and was commissioned on 9th November 1940 as a 2nd Lieutenant in his local regiment, the Royal Fusiliers (City of London Regiment) which was based in Holborn, Middlesex. The Fusiliers formed part of the 8th Army, serving in North Africa and then Italy. Gordon, by now promoted to Lieutenant, was attached to the 1/6th Battalion of the East Surrey Regiment, part of the 10th Brigade, 4th Division, and fought at Monte Cassino in May 1944 before being killed on 7th June 1944 in the tough engagement at Lake Trasimene to take the Trasimene Line.

He was 28 years old and was initially buried in the Guidonia Cemetery before being reinterred in February 1945.

155650 Lieutenant Gordon Halliday Gudgeon, Royal Fusiliers, is buried in Rome War Cemetery, Italy. He is remembered in Thame on Lord Williams's School Memorial Board.

The Thame Remembers Cross was placed at his grave on 16th October 2014 by Thame resident, Peter Willis.

17 September 1944

Harry Phillips was born in Thame on 6th April 1908 to Harry Phillips and Eliza Jane (née North) and was baptized at St Mary's Church, Thame on 7th June. They lived at 36 North Street from where his father was an omnibus driver.

Harry worked as a carpenter for Howland Builders at Queen's Road, Thame. He was married at the age of 29 to Emma Hillsdon on 5th February 1938. They lived at 59 North Street, Thame and had three sons, Michael, Geoffrey and Anthony.

Harry was initially rejected for service as he had a trade but he finally joined the Royal Berkshire Regiment in Chichester, Hampshire He was taken ill whilst serving in Palestine and on recovery, his unit having moved on, was placed in the 8th Battalion, Manchester Regiment, which in 1943 was fighting with the 8th Army in North Africa. They continued the fighting into Italy and he was on duty on the front line when he was killed on 17th September 1944. A letter from the Battalion chaplain says *"Some shells came over and exploded near him. A splinter hit his head, killing him instantly"*. He was initially buried in a small military cemetery before his body was re-interred in 1945.

14570236 Private Harry Phillips, Manchester Regiment, is buried in Arezzo War Cemetery, Tuscany, Italy. He is remembered in Thame on the War Memorial and on St Mary's Church Memorial Board.

Report written by Gayna Gurdon (nee Phillips) his grand-daughter with help from his son, Geoffrey Phillips.

A Thame Remembers Cross was placed at his grave on 24th May 2015 by Thame Museum member, Yvonne Maxwell.

A Thame Remembers Cross was placed at his grave on 4th October 2017 by his son, Geoffrey Phillips and grand-daughter, Tracey Jane King.

Blood and Flowers at Monte Cassino

Hello dearest father and mother
Come sit by my grave for a rest
It's been a long journey from England
And I know you've been doing your best

Plant a few flowers at my graveside
In respect you came to this place
It's clear that you hated to come here
I can see from the look on your face

Everyone cheered when I left home
But I'll bet they're not cheering now
All these young lives just wasted for nothing
Now people just come here and bow

I'm sorry I never came home again
That was never my intention at all
I just climbed up the mountain, when ordered to
And perished on that Monastery wall

Thousands of us marched together
Knowing many were about to be lost
We were following orders… that's all we were told
Some orders !… just count up the cost

Look around at all of these gravestones
Four thousand, all ages and casts
None of them wanted to be here
Not one life was worth being lost

So what was this fighting all meant for
A few worthless acres of land
Our blood shed on Italy's dry soil
When we only came to give them a hand

But what did this venture teach us
Would we do it all over again
Will millions more still have to perish
For a fight so utterly insane

And now I much stay here forever
While you go and get on with your life
Take these memories home to my children
Say goodbye to my dear loving wife

Yes, my greatest regret is about her
That I'll never see her again
And the sight of my two lovely children
How can we ever explain

So now it is time for you going
Don't worry….I'm only here sleeping
Yet I still don't know why this all happened
But please, no more sadness or weeping

Jarlath Bancroft

(1950 -   )

© jarspoems.blogspot.com

Malta

Malta's position in the middle of the Mediterranean Sea made it a strategic British Naval base from the early 19th century.

The island was under siege from the air during much of the Second World War and was defended valiantly by aircraft of the Royal Air Force. Despite continual aerial attack the naval base operated throughout the war and the island was never taken.

The Air Forces Memorial, which stands at the entrance to Valletta town, commemorates 2,295 airmen who lost their lives during the Second World War whilst serving with the Commonwealth Air Forces, flying from bases in the Mediterranean area and who have no known grave. The Memorial was unveiled by The Queen on 3rd May 1954.

A Gloster Gladiator defending Valetta

Those Remembered

12 February 1942

Alexander Fahey McDonald, known to his friends as "Mac", was born in Port of Spain, Trinidad on 19th August 1920. His father Alexander Taylor McDonald was Scottish and his mother Mabel (née Fahey) of Irish descent. His father served in France in World War One as a 2nd Lieutenant with the British West Indies Regiment. Alexander was sent to England to be educated at Lord Williams's Grammar School, Thame from 1933 to 1937.

On leaving school he went to work for The Shipbuilding Conference in London, becoming assistant to the deputy chairman. It was there that he met his wife, Irene Roblou.

Having been accepted to train as an observer in the Fleet Air Arm, he was sent back to Trinidad for flight training at Royal Naval Air Station, HMS Goshawk. Returning to England in January 1942 he married Irene on 17th January and they honeymooned for a week in Torquay. Shortly afterwards he received his posting orders to HMS Grebe, a Fleet Air Arm shore base at Alexandria, Egypt. He sailed from the Clyde on the light cruiser HMS Cleopatra as part of a Malta convoy on 5th February 1942.

The ship came under attack on 11th February, near the entrance to Valletta Harbour and was hit by a 500lb bomb which passed through the forward structure. Nineteen crew died and Alec, age 21, was wounded, dying in hospital in Malta the following day.

Sub-Lieutenant Alexander Fahey McDonald, Royal Navy Volunteer Reserve, is buried in the Military Cemetery at Imtarfa, near Mdina, Malta. He is remembered in Thame on Lord Williams's School Memorial Board.

The Thame Remembers Cross was placed at his grave on 17th October 2014 by Allan Hickman of Thame Remembers.

The story of the romance leading to the purchase of a wedding dress in 1941 as recounted by the donor

We met at the Shipbuilding Conference, Grosvenor Place, in October 1939 when I joined the staff as a junior secretary. Alexander Fahey McDonald (Mac), a very grown up 19, 6' 3", sandy haired, athletic, was an assistant to the Deputy Chairman. His father had been an accountant from Aberdeen who went to work in Trinidad, married Mabel Fahey (of Irish descent) there, and had two sons. Mac was sent to school in England; tragically his father died suddenly a year or two later. Mac spent his school holidays with Scottish relatives or friends of his parents. When he finished school, it was decided he should train here. His brother remained in Trinidad for his schooling.

We went dancing, walked in the parks and over Parliament Hill Fields and Hampstead Heath, attended the odd cinema and concert, although Mac adored jazz as well. I discovered The Melodymaker and somebody named Jack Teagarden! We tried playing tennis but he was so good he knocked my racquet out of my hand. But we had fun in the open air swimming pool. He insisted I read all Somerset Maugham. Came Dunkerque and the Deputy Chairman offered to lend Mac his fare back to Trinidad, which he politely refused. He had sat his exams and was accepted to train as an Observer in the Fleet Air Arm. I thought I should join up but he said it was imperative I was home when he got leave. We were walking across Hyde Park when he began to describe where he would like to take me on our honeymoon in Trinidad, but that honeymoon would have to wait until the war was over. I said I couldn't go on my honeymoon without a proposal. He said "I'm not asking ya, I'm tellin ya." I said I wasn't going to be the only girl on honeymoon without a proposal. So he said "Will you marry me" and I said "Yes please." We were still 19. We were apprehensive about asking my parents if we could be officially engaged. Mac was a proud man and said he wasn't going to ask his mother's permission to get married, so we would have to wait until we were 21. The blitz started and there were near misses. Mac was called to Portsmouth and they took their turns fire watching on the roof at night, but they got on with their studies, and I loved waiting to meet the train when he got weekend leave. Mac was in Course 45, and believe it or not the flight training was to be in Trinidad. It was so very wonderful- he would see his family after so many years, and be away from the stress of bombing. In our early days he asked me my birthday and when I said "2nd August" he said "Are you sure?" which he often did. This time I said "If you ask me am I sure again, it is all off." It was because I was 17 days older--his birthday was the 19th! So it was while Mac was in Trinidad, and we had our 21st birthdays in August 1941, I was planning our wedding. My mother had always taken me to Bourne & Hollingsworth for my party dresses, and while I was at Camden School for Girls B&H took over the supply of school uniform, so to our favourite shop went my mother and I to buy my bridal gown. Family and friends chipped in to help with clothing coupons and ingredients for the cake. My two school friends, Dorothy and Ellen were to be bridesmaids, and a super dressmaker produced the dresses and little tricorn head pieces. Course 45 had a slow and tedious journey back but arrived safely in January 1942. Mac had grown a marvellous little beard but shaved it off while I was at the office--I had wanted everyone to see it! As a result of being with his brother, he announced that after the war he must come to England and stay with us to be trained. We were able to get organised within a few days, and the wedding was at Christ Church, Woburn Square, where I attended, on 17th January 1942. After the reception at the Berners Hotel, we went to a tea dance at Hatchetts in Piccadilly where Stephane Grappelli was playing, and caught the train to Torquay the next day for our English honeymoon! After our week, we went to Mac's relatives in Bournemouth, where he was able to play golf with his uncle. I had already been taught where to stand and be silent during play. Mac had been junior champion in Trinidad. Within a day or two my parents rang to say Mac had to go to Portsmouth for tropical gear, and while he was there his travel pass came for the night journey to Glasgow. He took passage on HMS Cleopatra. German dive bombers attacked in the Med and a near miss fatally injured Mac on 11th February and he died in Malta on 12th February 1942. He is buried in the war cemetery at Imtarfa. After the war was won, an office colleague Joyce borrowed my headdress for her wedding to her regular soldier who had decided to become a doctor while he was a prisoner of war. Another colleague Molly asked to borrow the gown and head dress for her wedding to Dennis Service.

http://www.iwm.org.uk/collections/item/object/30086941
One camisole, as worn by Irene Roblou, as part of her wedding trousseau

Irene Roblou's wedding dress camisole is held by the Imperial War Museum

3 April 1945

Charles Raymond Jarratt was born in Edmonton, Middlesex in 1921 to Charles William Jarratt and Amelia May (née Spicer) of Goring-by-Sea, Sussex and educated at Lord Williams's Grammar School, Thame from 1930 to 1939. In 1939 Charles William, a retired jeweller, was living with his family at Wynchmore, Hill Road, Watlington, Oxfordshire. Charles Raymond joined the Royal Air Force Volunteer Reserve after April 1940 and trained as an Air Observer. He served with 37 Squadron, which initially flew Wellington bombers and then later switched to fly Consolidated Liberator IV aircraft in a maritime reconnaissance role. From 2nd December 1943 to October 1945, 37 Squadron were based at Tottorella in Italy. Charles's aircraft went missing on patrol over the Mediterranean Sea on 3rd April 1945 and all on board were reported killed. He was 23 years of age.

1165202 Warrant Officer Charles Raymond Jarratt, Royal Air Force Volunteer Reserve, has no known grave and is commemorated on the Air Forces Memorial, Valletta. He is remembered in Thame on Lord Williams's School Memorial Board and is also commemorated on the War Memorial in Watlington.

The Thame Remembers Cross was placed at the Air Forces Memorial Valetta on 17th October 2014 by David and Margaret Bretherton of Thame Remembers.

Air Forces Memorial, Valletta, Malta

Consolidated Liberator Mk IV

Malta

The only peace and comfort,
Prayers by day and night,
Not for themselves, nor for their kin,
But England's sons who fight.
Their dampened spirits linger on,
As fire and hell prolong,
Their island homes are but a wreck,
And yet they live in song.

Straining, heedless of the storm,
Their daily task is done,
Simple, but inspired by all,
A job that's never won,
Their eyes are turned towards a land,
The mother of the free,
Where peace and comfort will be found,
To free a darkened memory.

Thus honour, praise and glory,
Bestowed upon the folk,
The gallant fear yet defy,
The tyrants of their 'yoke',
Lives and homes they sacrifice,
Their prayers for me and you,
To Malta, owes the Empire,
A debt to those silent few.

George Smith

Contributed to BBC WW2 Peoples War
by his daughter Janet Leake.
3rd June 2005

North Africa

El Alamein battlefield in Egypt was the site of a major victory by the British 8th Army during the Second World War, known as the Third Battle of El Alamein. Over three years the 8th Army and Axis (German and Italian) forces engaged in an ongoing conflict in the North African region. Initially, in 1940, the British forces pushed the Italians back as far as Tunisia but the German forces then rallied and the 8th Army was forced back towards Egypt, with Germany's commander, Rommel, intent on capturing Alexandria and the Suez Canal.

Entrance to El Alamein Cemetery

The siege at Tobruk hindered the German advance and gave the British time to recover. The First Battle of El Alamein saw the 8th Army stall the progress of Italian and German armies.

The Axis forces rallied and attacked again in the Second Battle of El Alamein. However, it was the Third Battle of El Alamein which changed the fortunes of the 8th Army, forcing the Axis out of Egypt and safeguarding the vital route of the Suez Canal. Prior to the Battle, the newly appointed leader of the 8th Army, Lieutenant-General Bernard Montgomery had spent months building up the British forces both with reinforcements and munitions. Finally, the British attacked on the night of 23rd October 1942 and by 5th November the Italian and German armies withdrew.

The victory at El Alamein was a vital turning point for the Allies, summarised succinctly by Winston Churchill, *"It may almost be said: Before Alamein we never had a victory. After Alamein we never had a defeat."*

Those Remembered

16 April 1941

Alfred Thomas Heley was born in early 1914 to Alfred Heley and Ethel (née Winstone) of Franklins Farm, Ickford Road, Shabbington, Buckinghamshire. Prior to joining the regular army, he was employed by Messrs Holland & Son, printers of Thame and was also a regular member of Thame Cricket Club 'A' team.

Alfred was serving in the regular army with the 3rd Battalion Coldstream Guards in Alexandria, Egypt when war broke out. This became part of the Western Desert Force fighting Rommel's Afrika Korps throughout North Africa. On 15th April 1941 the Battalion was ordered to attack a German "company" holding the ridge above Sollum (east of Tobruk). The German "company" turned out to be of battalion strength and the Guards could not take the ridge. They withdrew at 05:00hrs. Six men were killed, nineteen wounded and eleven missing. Alfred, age 25, was originally reported as wounded and missing before being confirmed as killed in the action on 16th April 1941.

2657231 Lance Sergeant Alfred Thomas Heley, Coldstream Guards, has no known grave and is commemorated on Alamein Memorial, Egypt. He is also commemorated on a Memorial at St Helen's Church, Albury, Oxfordshire.

The Thame Remembers Cross was placed at Alamein Memorial on 19th February 2018 by David Bretherton of Thame Remembers.

5 May 1941

Douglas Rolfe was born in Chinnor, Oxfordshire on 11th November 1919 to Frederick Adams Rolfe and Lizzie Maud (née Wilkinson). He attended Lord Williams's Grammar School in Thame from 1931 to 1937. The picture is taken from the 1st XV photograph of 1935/36. In 1939 he was living at home in Lower Road, Chinnor and working as a solicitor's clerk.

Douglas joined the Royal Air Force Volunteer Reserve after September 1939 and trained as a Wireless Operator/Air Gunner. He was posted to 38 Squadron flying Wellington Mk1A & 1C bombers. The Squadron was initially engaged in bombing mainland Europe but relocated to Egypt in November 1940. They operated from RAF Shallufa (Canal Zone) from December 1940 where they flew night bombing raids against ports in Libya, Italy and the Balkans.

In May 1941 the Squadron received a communication from Air Officer Commanding-in-Chief Middle East Sir Arthur Longmore, *"Please tell all personnel of your Squadron how deeply I admire the magnificent effort they have made during the last three weeks operations. We are passing through a critical phase of the war and it may well be that the blows struck by your Squadron may prove to have a vital effect on the course of the war."*

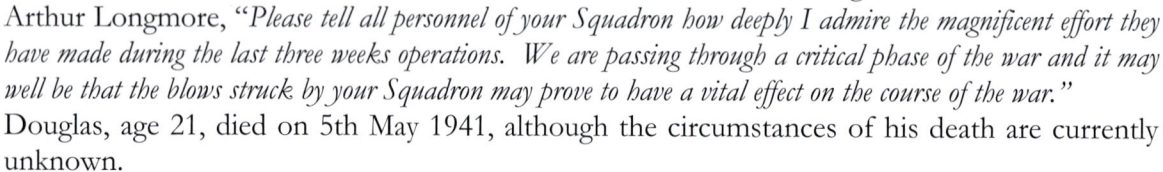

Douglas, age 21, died on 5th May 1941, although the circumstances of his death are currently unknown.

911408 Sergeant Douglas Rolfe, Royal Air Force Volunteer Reserve, is buried in El Alamein War Cemetery, Alexandria, Egypt. He is remembered in Thame on Lord Williams's School Memorial Board and commemorated on the War Memorial in Chinnor.

The Thame Remembers Cross was placed at his grave in El Alamein Cemetery on 19th February 2018 by Mike Dyer of Thame Remembers.

23 November 1941

Peter George Campion was born in the summer of 1916 to George Campion and Lily (née Moore) of West Ealing, Middlesex, where his father was a tailor. Peter attended Lord Williams's Grammar School in Thame as a boarder from 1927. On leaving in Easter of 1933 he returned to live with his parents at 24 Raymond Avenue, Ealing, Middlesex.

At the start of World War Two Peter enlisted with the Royal Corps of Signals and was posted to the Signals Troops stationed with the XIII Corps in North Africa. He was there from January 1940 and took part in the retreat from Benghazi after the German offensive in April 1941. He was in Tobruk during the siege which culminated in *Operation Crusader* in a failed attempt to relieve the garrison. This took place from 18th November to 31st December 1941 and it was during this operation that Peter, age 25, was killed on 23rd November. He left £521 in his will.

2576817 Signalman Peter George Campion, Royal Corps of Signals, is buried in Tobruk War Cemetery, Libya. He is remembered in Thame on Lord Williams's School Memorial Board and is commemorated on the War Memorial in Ealing.

The Thame Remembers Cross was placed at Alamein Memorial on 19th February 2018 by David Bretherton of Thame Remembers.
(The Memorial at Alamein serves all those who fell in Egypt and Libya.)

28 January 1942

Gordon Eric Smith was born in Cowley St John, Oxford in 1922. His father Cecil Benjamin Smith was a confectioner and his mother Lizzie Maria (née Wallin), a dressmaker. He was born into a large family, with at least ten brothers and sisters and attended Lord Williams's Grammar School in Thame between 1934 and 1938, by which time his family had moved to Wheatley, Oxfordshire.

During 1941 Gordon enlisted with the Royal Artillery and was posted to the 57th Light Anti-Aircraft Regiment based at Doncaster, Yorkshire before embarking for the Middle East in April 1941. The Regiment served in Syria and Palestine before moving to Egypt in October 1941. They were assigned to the 4th Indian Infantry during the *Operation Crusader* battles attempting to hold back the German Afrika Korps in Libya. Gordon was serving with the 171st Battery when he was captured and taken prisoner of war. Sometime between the 28th January 1942 and 20th May 1942, Gordon was on an Italian transport ship used for prisoner of war transfer to Europe. The ship was one of a number sunk by torpedoes from British submarines and Gordon, age 19, became one of over 800 prisoners of war who lost their lives at sea in the Mediterranean theatre. His brother Frederick served in the Royal Air Force and died on 30th October 1943.

1795499 Gunner Gordon Eric Smith, Royal Artillery, has no known grave and is commemorated on Alamein Memorial, Egypt. He is remembered in Thame on Lord Williams's School Memorial Board and is also commemorated on the War Memorial in Wheatley.

The Thame Remembers Cross was placed at Alamein Memorial on 19th February 2018 by David Bretherton of Thame Remembers.

13 June 1942

Maurice Horatio Howlett was born on 26th June 1916, the second eldest son and one of the six children of Frederick Howlett and Emily (née Wakelin) of Park Street, Thame, later of Priestend. In 1939 the family were living in Hampden Avenue. Prior to joining the army, Maurice was employed by Messrs Howland & Bush, coal merchants in Upper High Street, Thame. The Thame Gazette newspaper reported *"that he was a very good footballer"*.

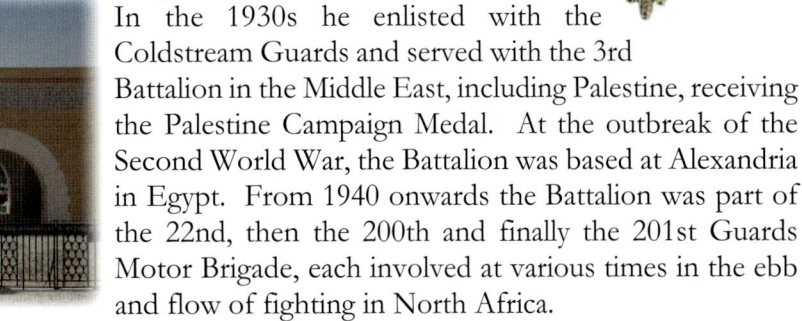

In the 1930s he enlisted with the Coldstream Guards and served with the 3rd Battalion in the Middle East, including Palestine, receiving the Palestine Campaign Medal. At the outbreak of the Second World War, the Battalion was based at Alexandria in Egypt. From 1940 onwards the Battalion was part of the 22nd, then the 200th and finally the 201st Guards Motor Brigade, each involved at various times in the ebb and flow of fighting in North Africa.

Maurice, age 25, was killed on 13th June 1942 on what became known in the North African campaign as "Black Saturday", when the Guards Brigade was forced, with heavy casualties, to abandon "Knightsbridge Box", a defensive position outside Tobruk during the Battle of Gazala.

2657295 Sergeant Maurice Horatio Howlett, Coldstream Guards, has no known grave and is commemorated on Alamein Memorial, Egypt. He is remembered in Thame on the War Memorial and on St Mary's Church Memorial Board.

The Thame Remembers Cross was placed at Alamein Memorial on 19th February 2018 by David Bretherton of Thame Remembers.

12 December 1942

Eric Arnold was born on 19th August 1919 in Thame to William John Arnold and Edith Harriet (née Castle) of 26 Nelson Street, where they were all still living at the time of the 1939 Register.

He was educated at Lord Williams's Grammar School, Thame and on leaving was employed in the service accounts department of Morris Motors Ltd at Cowley, Oxford. He was a member of the Morris Motors rugby club and played football on several occasions locally. At the outbreak of the war Eric was with the 80th Heavy Anti-Aircraft Regiment, a Territorial Unit of the Royal Artillery. They went to France in 1939 with the British Expeditionary Force and Eric was later evacuated at Dunkirk.

Eric served with 194 Battery during the Battle of Britain and the Blitz, before they were sent to North Africa. On 12th December 1942 the section in which he was serving was under shell fire from the enemy and given orders to disperse in order to avoid casualties. They subsequently received a further order to return to the gun position as the section was going out of action. Eric then started out, together with three of his detachment, to return to their guns. On the way one soldier was slightly wounded so Eric continued alone, leaving the wounded soldier in the care of the other. Although an extensive search was made at the time, he was not seen again and no further news was received concerning him. It was not until January 1944 that Eric, age 23, was declared dead, killed in action.

1446181 Sergeant Eric Arnold, Royal Artillery, has no known grave and is commemorated on Medjez-el-Bab Memorial, Tunisia. He is remembered in Thame on the War Memorial and on a memorial on his parents' grave in St Mary's churchyard.

The Thame Remembers Cross was placed at Medjez-el-Bab Memorial on 20th July 2018 by Catherine Jones of Thame Remembers.

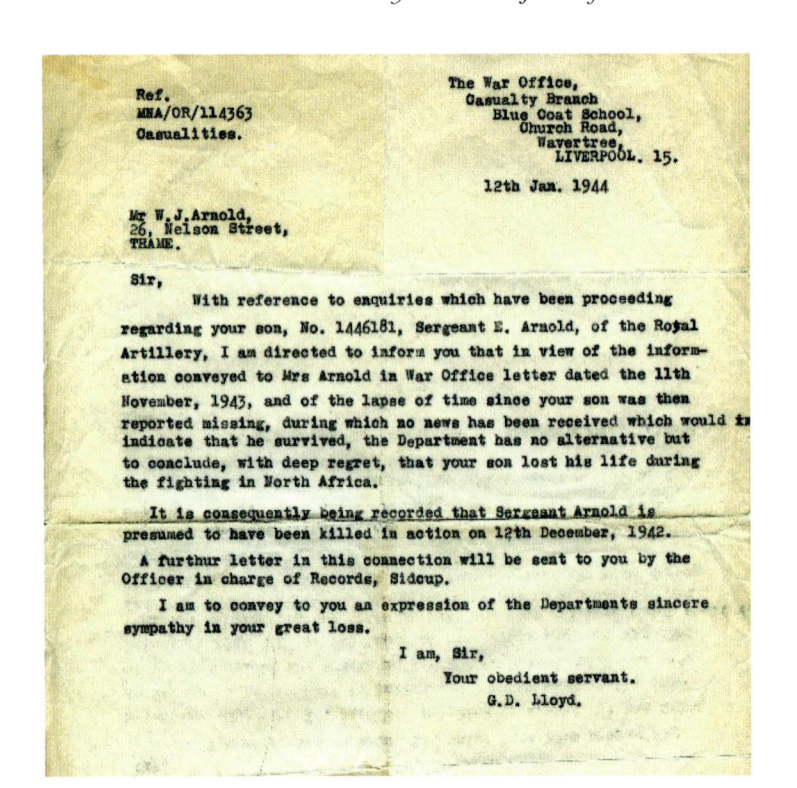

Letter received by Eric's parents in 1944

23 March 1943

Henry William Little was born in Oakley, Chinnor, Oxfordshire on 13th August 1913 to George Little, a farm labourer, and Emma (née Tolley). He entered Lord Williams's Grammar School in 1924 as a free place scholar and left in 1929 with a 3rd class honours school certificate.

In September 1939 Henry was living in Chapel en le Frith, Derbyshire and was employed in Local Government as an assistant finance officer. Soon afterwards he volunteered for service with the Royal Air Force. He married Margaret Isabel Patman at Dewsbury, Yorkshire in early 1941, before embarking on the armed merchant cruiser HMS Ranpura to Halifax, Nova Scotia, Canada in August 1941. He then travelled to the US Naval Air Station in Pensacola, Florida for aircrew training.

After returning to England he was posted to 70 Squadron at RAF Kabrit in Egypt. On the night of 22nd/23rd March 1943, Henry was navigator in Vickers Wellington Mk III (DF 698), being flown by Flying Officer Arthur Bebbington MM. The aircraft took off shortly after 21:00hrs and nothing further was heard of them. After six months the crew including Henry, age 29, were officially posted as missing, killed in action.

1027322 Sergeant Henry William Little, Royal Air Force Volunteer Reserve, has no known grave. He and the crew are commemorated on Alamein Memorial in Egypt. He is remembered in Thame on Lord Williams's School Memorial Board. He is also commemorated on the War Memorials at Chapel en le Frith, Derbyshire and Watlington, Oxfordshire.

The Thame Remembers Cross was placed at Alamein Memorial on 19th February 2018 by David Bretherton of Thame Remembers.

31 March 1943

William Freeman was born on 2nd December 1906 to Henry Freeman and Jane (née Hall) of 3 Chinnor Road, Thame and baptised at St Mary's Church on 27th January 1907. He was a grocer's assistant in January 1932 when he married Ethel Johnson at St Mary's Church, Thame. They went to live at 48 Bailey Road, Cowley, Oxfordshire where they had a son Alan. William was employed at Grimbly Hughes & Co Ltd, grocers in Oxford.

William served in the army in World War Two with the 6th Battalion, Queen's Own Royal West Kent Regiment. In November 1942 the Battalion was with the 36th Infantry Brigade, 78th Division when it landed near Algiers as part of *Operation Torch*. By March 1943 they were in action near Medjez-el-Bab, during the final push to Tunis, which is probably where William, age 36, was wounded. He died of his wounds on 31st March 1943.

5510504 Private William Freeman, Queen's Own Royal West Kent Regiment, is buried in Tabarka Ras Rajel War Cemetery, Tunisia. He is remembered on the grave of his parents in St Mary's churchyard, Thame. His name is to be added to Thame War Memorial.

The Thame Remembers Cross was placed at his grave on 20th July 2018 by Ian Jones MBE of Thame Remembers.

7 May 1943

Colin George Price Cuthbert was born in Brecknock, Wales in 1918. He was the younger of the two children of James Cuthbert and Edith Jane (née Davies). His parents were both school teachers and the family moved to Chinnor, Oxfordshire from where Colin attended Lord Williams's Grammar School, Thame from 1929 to 1936. He was awarded a closed exhibition (financial grant) to attend St Catherine's College in Oxford. Early in 1942 Colin married Dorothy Knowlson in Chinnor. His daughter Angela, who he never saw, was born in 1943.

At the beginning of World War Two he joined the 101 Royal Armoured Corps Officer Cadet Training Unit at Sandhurst, Berkshire and in August 1940 was given an emergency commission as 2nd Lieutenant with the Royal Tank Regiment.

By the end of 1942 his Battalion, the 51st Leeds Rifles, was fully trained and equipped with Churchill Mark IV tanks. The 51st Leeds Rifles was a long-standing Territorial Army unit which had converted to an armoured role in 1939. They embarked in January 1943 with the 25th Army Tank Brigade for North Africa. In May 1943 the Battalion was engaged in the Medjez sector in the final ground attack against the German forces in Tunisia. Colin, age 25, and by then a Captain, was killed on 7th May near Bou Arada, the day the British Army entered Tunis and six days before the final German surrender in North Africa. He was initially buried in Bou Arada Military Cemetery before his body was reinterred in July 1944.

145462 Captain Colin George Price Cuthbert, Royal Tank Regiment, is buried in Medjez-el-Bab Cemetery, Tunisia. He is remembered in Thame on Lord Williams's School Memorial Board. He is commemorated on the War Memorial in Chinnor and St Catherine's College Memorial Board in St Cross Church, Oxford.

The Thame Remembers Cross was placed at his grave on 20th July 2018
by Ian Jones MBE of Thame Remembers.

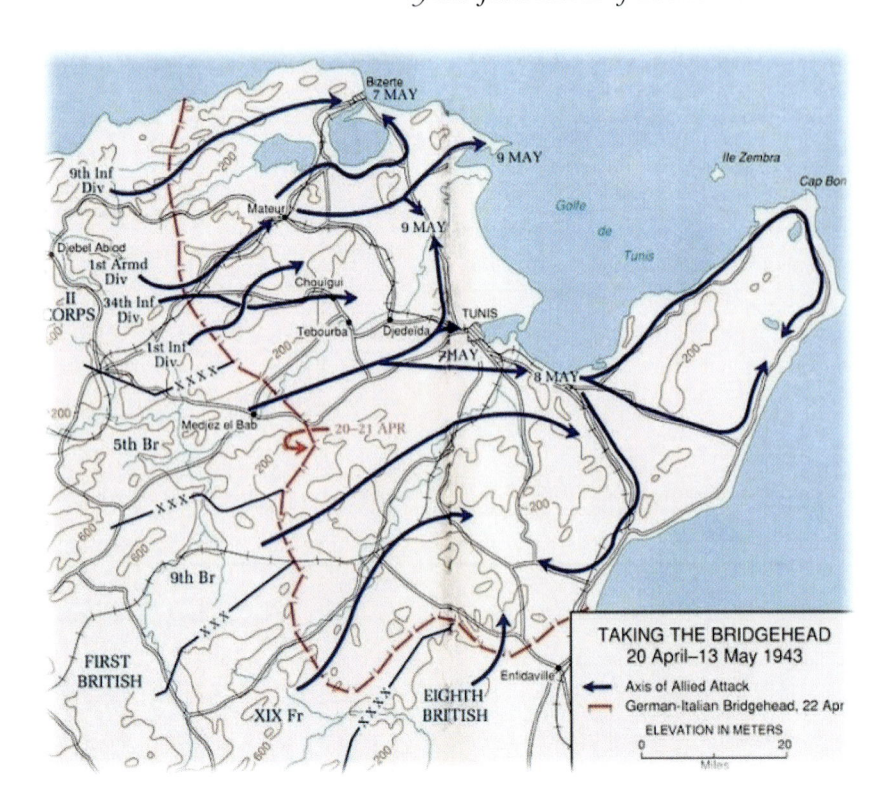

The Attack at Tunis May 1943

13 July 1943

Douglas Beaumont Neale was born in London in early 1919 to John Beaumont Neale and Eva Daisy (née Lewthwaite). Douglas's father had emigrated to Canada where he worked as an electrical engineer and served with the Canadian Expeditionary Force during World War One. When Douglas was only a few months old, he and his mother travelled to Canada. The family returned to England in June 1922 on the newly commissioned Cunard liner RMS Andania, eventually setting up home in Hillingdon, Middlesex. Douglas was a boarder at Lord Williams's Grammar School in Thame between 1932 and 1936.

He enlisted with the Royal Air Force after May 1940 (Service No 1267256) and was commissioned as a Pilot Officer in July 1941. He was promoted to Flying Officer in August 1942 and was then posted to Egypt as a flying instructor with No 5 Middle East Training School.

On 13th July 1943 at 00:35hrs Douglas, age 24, took off from RAF Shallufa (Canal Zone) on a torpedo training exercise in Wellington 1C, HX734, one of four planes on the exercise. According to reports the plane veered off track in a mist, crashing into a bank and catching fire. All five crew members were killed and they are buried together at Suez.

102132 Flying Officer Douglas Beaumont Neale, Royal Air Force, is buried in Suez War Memorial Cemetery, Egypt. He is remembered in Thame on Lord Williams's School Memorial Board.

The Thame Remembers Cross was placed at his grave on 21st February 2018 by Margaret Bretherton of Thame Remembers.

Three Vickers Wellington bombers from Shallufa over the Western Desert

Morning after the Barrage at El Alamein

There's a Devil in the dawn –
Horrific spawn of last night's hideous moon,
That hung above the gun's inferno
And smiled on men who died too soon.

There's a Devil in the dawn –
See him fawn on those who served him well,
Who, blinded, deafened, breathed the cordite reek,
Fed the ravening guns, and swore that it was hell.

The Devil will demand his pay
In blood to-day; but those who pass in sunlight will not see the Moon
Serenely light a desert hell for men who live
And smile on those who die too soon.

Bombardier F E Hughes

(dates not known)

Singapore

The war in the far east was fought from 8th December 1941 mainly against the Japanese who had invaded China, Burma and Malaya. Although victory over Japan (VJ Day) is celebrated on 15th August it was not until 12th September 1945 that the British returned to Singapore.

The RAF had about 50 Squadrons of aircraft in the Far East Air Force mostly based in India and Ceylon. They performed a variety of roles including ground attack and maritime patrol. Because of the nature of the land and sea missions very few bodies of RAF servicemen were ever recovered.

Kranji War Memorial, Singapore

Within Kranji War Cemetery in Singapore stands the War Memorial, bearing the names of over 24,000 casualties of the Commonwealth land and air forces who have no known grave.

The land forces commemorated on the memorial died during the campaigns in Malaya and Indonesia or in subsequent captivity, many of them during the construction of the Burma-Thailand railway, or at sea while being transported into imprisonment elsewhere. The Memorial also commemorates airmen who died during operations over the whole of southern and eastern Asia and the surrounding seas and oceans.

Those Remembered

18 July 1944

Alwyne Robert Peirce Shields was born in Umballa, India (now in Lahore, Pakistan) in 1922. His father Wallace John Shields from Stoke Newington, Essex was serving with the RAF and eventually reached the rank of Group Captain during World War Two. His mother was Constance Gladys (née Peirce) from Mile End in London.

His parents lived in Dinton, near Aylesbury, Buckinghamshire and Alwyne was a pupil at Lord Williams's Grammar School before enlisting with the Royal Air Force. He was posted to the Far East with 42 Squadron. After many operational sorties in 1943/44 flying Hawker Hurricane Mk IV ground attack aircraft, Alwyne took off from Tulihal airfield in the Imphal Valley in north east India at 16:35hrs on 18th July 1944 as part of a flight of six planes armed with 500lb bombs to attack Japanese positions in Myothit, Burma. His aircraft was last seen at about 8,000ft flying west, but it failed to return. Despite a number of searches for the missing pilot and aircraft, they were never found. He was 22 years old and left £309 14s 10d in his will.

124416 Flight Lieutenant Alwyne Robert Peirce Shields, Royal Air Force, has no known grave and is commemorated on Kranji War Memorial, Singapore. He is remembered in Thame on Lord Williams's School Memorial Board. He is also commemorated on the War Memorial in Ford, Buckinghamshire.

The Thame Remembers Cross was placed at Kranji War Memorial, Singapore on 18th December 2014 by Thame resident, Peter Lawrence.

22 April 1945

Sidney Jack Plater was born in Thame in 1915 to Harry Plater and Georgina Mary (née Soanes). He was a pupil at Lord Williams's Grammar School and went on to train in the pharmaceutical industry, becoming a member of the Pharmaceutical Society in 1939. He was also a Deacon of Christchurch in Thame for several years. While serving with the Royal Air Force, which he had joined in 1941, he married Bertha Maynard at St Andrew's Church, Enfield, Middlesex on 15th August 1943.

In 1944, with the rank of Flight Sergeant, he was sent to No 8 Operational Training Unit at RAF Dyce in Aberdeenshire to train as a photo-reconnaissance observer on the de Havilland Mosquito. His pilot was Flying Officer Thomas Bell, Royal Canadian Air Force, who he flew with throughout the remainder of his life.

He was posted to 684 Squadron at RAF Alipore, Bengal, India, where he carried out a number of photo-reconnaissance missions during 1945. On 22nd April Sidney and Thomas in Mosquito XVI NS675 took off at 07:05hrs from an airfield at Cox's Bazar, near Chittagong, India on a mission to Lankawi Island off the Malayan peninsula. The aircraft failed to return and, although wreckage and an upturned dinghy were seen in the sea the following day, there was no evidence of any survivors and the search was eventually abandoned. Sidney was 32 years old.

1386875 Warrant Officer Sidney Jack Plater, Royal Air Force, has no known grave and is commemorated on Kranji War Memorial, Singapore. He is remembered in Thame on the War Memorial and also on the Memorial Boards of Christchurch and Lord Williams's School.

The Thame Remembers Cross was placed at Kranji War Memorial, Singapore on 18th December 2014 by Thame resident, Peter Lawrence.

Peter Lawrence at Singapore Memorial, Kranji

At Sea

The Royal Navy

The Second World War involved the Royal Navy to a far greater extent than the 1914-18 war. While the British Expeditionary Force (BEF) in France experienced a 'phoney war' from September 1939 until May 1940, there was no 'phoney war' at sea. The Royal Navy's operations started on 3rd September 1939 and continued until the surrender of Japan in August 1945.

The Royal Navy was still the strongest navy in the world with the largest number of warships built and with naval bases across the globe. It played a central role in the evacuation of the retreating British army at Dunkirk and later orchestrated the sinking of Germany's mighty battleship and Hitler's pride, the Bismarck. Without the Royal Navy's defence of Britain's sea-borne trade, especially in the struggle against German U-boats in the Battle of the Atlantic, there would not have been food for the country, fuel for the RAF's operations or supplies to keep the army fighting in Europe, North Africa and the Far East.

In a war that started with Polish Cavalry and ended with the atomic bomb, technological advances were a key element in the continued domination of the high seas. Starting with a mixture of World War One and recently completed ships, the Fleet was reasonably well-equipped to fight conventional surface actions but the maritime war would soon revolve around the battle with the U-boat, the exercise of air power and eventually the ability to land large armies on hostile shores.

As the war progressed, the Royal and Dominion Navies expanded rapidly with large construction programmes, particularly escort carriers, destroyers, corvettes, frigates, submarines and landing craft. Vastly improved radar and anti-submarine weapons, and the tactics to use them effectively, were introduced. Aircraft carriers largely superseded battleships as the pride of the fleet. *Operation Ultra* against the German Enigma codes allowed the Allies to penetrate to the very heart of German and Axis planning and operations. The Royal Navy continually faced new threats and learned to deal with them technically, operationally and above all, successfully.

Naval supremacy was vital to amphibious operations such as the invasions of north west Africa, Sicily, Italy, and the Normandy D-Day landings. The suppression of the U-boat threat was an essential requirement for the invasion of northern Europe to ensure that the armies could be transported and resupplied.

By the end of the war the Royal Navy was dwarfed by its ally, the United States Navy, but provided support by sending a large task force to the Pacific. This largest ever foreign deployment of the Royal Navy attacked the oil refineries in Sumatra, to deny Japanese access to supplies, gave cover to the US landings on Okinawa and carried out air attacks and bombardment of the Japanese mainland.

The outstanding naval contribution to Britain's survival and eventual victory came at a heavy cost in terms of both ships and men. They had to face not just the violence of the enemy but also the violence of the sea and are commemorated at each of the Royal Navy Memorials on additional wall plaques. There are 14,954 names at Portsmouth, 10,097 names at Chatham and 15,937 names recorded at Plymouth.

Portsmouth World War Two Memorial Plaques

The Merchant Navy

Merchant seamen crewed the ships of the British **Merchant Navy** that kept the United Kingdom supplied with raw materials, arms, ammunition, fuel, food and all of the necessities of a nation at war, literally enabling the country to defend itself. Every possible type of vessel played a part, ranging from ocean liners serving as troopships between Australia and England, to small coastal vessels delivering coal from the north east of England to London's power stations. In doing this, they sustained a considerably greater casualty rate than almost every other branch of the armed services and suffered great hardship.

Britain's merchant fleet was the largest in the world during both World Wars. In 1939 a third of the world's merchant ships were British, crewed by some 200,000 sailors, with ages ranging from fourteen through to their late seventies and from all parts of the British Empire.

On 3rd September 1939, a few hours after war had been declared against Germany, the Montreal bound passenger ship SS Athenia was sunk by a U-boat west of Ireland with the loss of 112 passengers and crew. A convoy system, building on its success in World War One, was quickly introduced, providing groups of merchant ships with an escort of one or more warships for their journey to try to prevent attacks by German submarines.

Germany operated a policy of unrestricted submarine warfare, sinking merchant vessels on sight and 4,786 British-flagged ships were sunk and many merchant seamen died. The heaviest losses were suffered in the Atlantic, but convoys making their way to Russia around the North Cape and also those supplying Malta in the Mediterranean, were particularly vulnerable. More than a quarter of the sinkings were in home waters. For almost six years, barely a day went by without the loss of merchant shipping and their civilian crews. In one month alone, June 1941, U-boats accounted for the loss of over 500,000 tons of Allied shipping.

The Battle of the Atlantic was considered to be won by the Allies by mid-1943, when the tide finally turned with the provision of better training and equipment, air cover and special intelligence following the breaking of German Enigma Naval codes at Bletchley Park, Buckinghamshire, although U-boats continued to operate until the end of the war.

Although a figure of more than 36,000 has been stated, it is difficult to give the total number of merchant seamen who lost their lives during World War Two because the government of the time did not grant them the automatic right of commemoration by the **Commonwealth War Graves Commission.** Unlike the Armed Services in which every wartime death by whatever means was recorded and commemorated, the seamen of the Merchant Navy could only be commemorated if their death could be proved to be attributable to enemy action.

The Tower Hill Merchant Navy Memorial in London records the names of 23,886 merchant sailors who died in World War Two and have no known grave.

Those Remembered

10 April 1940

John Frederick Summersbee was born in Chipping Norton, Oxfordshire on 20th July 1911 to Stephen John Summersbee and Hilda (née Hall) who had married the previous year. Stephen was a blacksmith and they moved to 2 Rooks Lane, Thame where they were still living in 1939. On 1st January 1938 John married Alice Evelyn Thomlinson of Scotsgrove, near Thame and they went to live at 63 Chinnor Road.

Affectionately known to all his friends as 'Jack', he joined the Royal Navy as a boy sailor in 1926. For the last three years of his life he was in the submarine service. In July 1939 he joined HMSub Thistle N24 at Barrow-in-Furness, Lancashire on completion of her trials, and served as her Second Coxswain, soon to be promoted to Torpedo Coxswain.

At 16:04hrs on 9th April 1940 HMSub Thistle first spotted the German U-boat U-4 off the Norwegian coast and fired six torpedoes, none of which hit. At 02:13hrs on 10th April, U-4 surprised Thistle which was recharging her batteries on the surface near Skudenes, Norway and fired a spread of two torpedoes, sinking the submarine. All 53 hands on board were lost, including John, age 28.

P/JX 128645 Petty Officer John Frederick Summersbee, Royal Navy, HMSub Thistle, is commemorated on Portsmouth Naval Memorial, Hampshire. He is remembered in Thame on the War Memorial and on St Mary's Church Memorial Board.

The Thame Remembers Cross was placed at Portsmouth Naval Memorial on 14th June 2017 by Thame Mayor, Councillor Tom Wyse.

HM Submarine Thistle

14 December 1940

Hugh Charles James McRae was born on 29th November 1909, the only son of Sir Charles James Hugh McRea Kt JP and Lady Edith Sophia McRea (née Farnie). He had one sister Marjorie. When he was growing up the family home was in Hendon, Middlesex. Hugh went to Lord Williams's Grammar School, Thame in 1918 and then in 1926 joined the Royal Navy as an officer cadet at the training school HMS Worcester on the River Thames, where he won the King's Gold Medal, presented to him by the Duke of York. He is pictured with his medal. He was appointed a Midshipman in 1927 and went on to serve on a number of ships. He married Frances Mary Mason in Hendon in 1935 and they lived at Airandene, Wise Lane, Mill Hill, Middlesex. When Hugh was stationed in China in 1936, Frances moved there too, albeit having to sail on the commercial liner Perseus, which departed Liverpool in September 1936. A daughter Jean was born in Shanghai in 1937. After serving in China for two years, Hugh returned to the UK and joined the destroyer HMS Grafton in July 1938. The Grafton was assigned to the First Destroyer Flotilla in the Mediterranean Fleet and his wife and daughter set up home in Malta in January 1939. The Grafton was refitting in Malta when World War Two began. In June 1940, during the evacuation from Dunkirk and after successfully rescuing 1600 troops, the Grafton was struck by a torpedo from U-62. The captain and 14 others were killed. The ship was too badly damaged to be towed to safety and so once all the remaining crew had been rescued, she was sunk by gunfire from HMS Ivanhoe.

Wendy with the Captain and the Entertainment Officer of Queen Mary 2

Lieutenant McRea was subsequently Mentioned in Despatches and promoted to Lieutenant Commander and took command of the captured French torpedo boat Branlebas. The Branlebas which had a mixed French and British crew had been designed for Mediterranean operations. It was not suited to the operations in the English Channel and so it was no real surprise when the ship was lost in a storm on 14th December 1940, forty miles south west of Eddystone, Cornwall. Only three men from the complement of 104 were saved. Hugh, age 31, did not survive.

Lieutenant Commander Hugh Charles James McRae, Royal Navy, French Ship Branlebas, is commemorated on Portsmouth Naval Memorial, Hampshire. He is remembered in Thame on Lord Williams's School Memorial Board.

The Thame Remembers Cross was placed at the wreck site on 17th October 2016 from the rear deck of RMS Queen Mary 2 by Thame resident, Wendy Townsend.

The Thame Remembers Cross was placed at Portsmouth Naval Memorial on 14th June 2017 by Thame Mayor, Councillor Tom Wyse.

French Torpedo Boat Branlebas

1 November 1942

Sydney Alfred Richardson was born in Bicester, Oxfordshire on 2nd January 1911 to Edwin Richardson, a shoeing smith, and Florence (née Harris). Edwin was from Thame and by the start of World War One, the family had moved back to Thame and were living in Nelson Street. His father, Edwin, went on to serve with the Army Service Corps during the war.

In 1926, Sydney enlisted as a "Boy" in the Royal Navy and after training at HMS Ganges at Shotley, Suffolk, his first sea posting was on the battleship HMS Emperor of India. Then in 1927 he was posted to the newly commissioned battleship HMS Nelson.

By 1942 Sydney had completed his initial service of 12 years with the Royal Navy, but he was retained for war service and was assigned to HMS President III, the establishment for training DEMS (Defensively Equipped Merchant Ship) gunners and sailors.

On 1st November 1942 Sydney was a DEMS gunner on the troop transport ship SS Mendoza, which was a Ministry of War transport liner of 8,234 tons. The Glasgow registered Mendoza, an ex-Vichy French ship captured off Montevideo, was sailing under the Blue Funnel flag. Whilst sailing from Mombasa, East Africa, she was torpedoed and sunk by German submarine U-178 about 70 nautical miles east north east of its destination, Durban, South Africa.

She was carrying 153 crew and 250 passengers when it blew up taking the lives of 28 of her crew and 122 service personnel including Sydney, age 31. With her two propellers and rudder blown off, the ship settled by the stern. Ten lifeboats were launched and the survivors were attempting to reach land when the American ship SS Alava arrived and rescued them. Sydney left a wife, Ethel Florence.

P/JX 126446 Able Seaman Sydney Alfred Richardson, Royal Navy, SS Mendoza, is commemorated on Portsmouth Naval Memorial, Hampshire. He is remembered in Thame on the War Memorial.

The Thame Remembers Cross was placed at Portsmouth Naval Memorial on 14th June 2017 by Thame Mayor, Councillor Tom Wyse.

26 February 1943

Henry Bennett Cook was the son of Henry B Cook and Lily (née Hardern) and was born near Ashton, Lancashire in 1921. At the beginning of the Second World War Henry was with the County Courts branch of the Lord Chancellor's Department which had been evacuated from London and was based in Thame. He was a keen footballer and on the books of Arsenal FC as an amateur. Whilst in Thame he regularly assisted the town football and cricket clubs. When Thame football club was compelled to cease activities due to the war, he played for Oxford City until called up for service. He was also a popular member of the Thame Institute.

On 5th June 1942 Henry received a commission as a temporary Sub-Lieutenant in the Royal Navy Volunteer Reserve, with qualification for pilot duties in the Fleet Air Arm (FAA). On 26th February 1943, Henry was attached to 772 Squadron FAA, at HMS Landrail, the Royal Naval Air Station Machrihanish, Scotland and was killed whilst training for ship landing at the deck landing school. He was just 22 years old and his will was administered by his mother Lily, with effects to the value of £133.

Sub-Lieutenant Henry Bennett Cook, Royal Navy Volunteer Reserve, is commemorated on the Lee-on-Solent Naval Memorial, Gosport, Hampshire. His name is to be added to Thame War Memorial.

The Thame Remembers Cross was placed at Lee-on-Solent Naval Memorial on 8th July 2016 by Thame resident, Tim Green.

2 November 1943

Edward Greville Canning Holbrook was born in Dover in 1907, the only son of Charles Edward Holbrook and Kathleen Hay (née Canning). His father was a master mariner and Trinity House pilot and his mother a music teacher.

Edward went to Lord Williams's Grammar School, Thame in 1922, leaving in 1925. He then travelled to Canada with his mother, his father having died in 1921. He returned to England in 1930 and by 1938 he was an actor manager at Sadlers Wells in London. Edward married Leonora Paton in 1939 in London and they went to live in Cambridge.

He was commissioned as a Temporary Lieutenant (Special Branch), Royal Navy Volunteer Reserve, in August 1941 and became a specialist in mine clearing activities, for which he was (posthumously) Mentioned in Despatches *"for courage and skill in dangerous minesweeping operations during "Operation Antidote"* in the western Mediterranean in May 1943. Edward was based at the shore establishment HMS Cormorant, Gibraltar when on 2nd November 1943 he was killed, at the age of 36, with two other men, in an explosion off Naples, probably as a result of mine clearance. No bodies were recovered.

Lieutenant Edward Greville Canning Holbrook, Royal Navy Volunteer Reserve, is commemorated on Portsmouth Naval Memorial, Hampshire. He is remembered in Thame on Lord Williams's School Memorial Board.

The Thame Remembers Cross was placed at Portsmouth Naval Memorial on 14th June 2017 by Thame Mayor, Councillor Tom Wyse.

18 February 1944

James William Carter was born in Brentford, Middlesex on 28th May 1918, one of six children to James Carter and Eliza (née Wright). His mother died in 1923 after giving birth to triplets, none of them survived. James, together with his father and surviving brother and sister moved to Thame, probably in the 1930s, where James was employed at Messrs Pursers Ltd.

James served with the Royal Navy during World War Two and in 1944, as a Leading Seaman, was serving in the Mediterranean on HMS Penelope, an arethusa-class light cruiser.

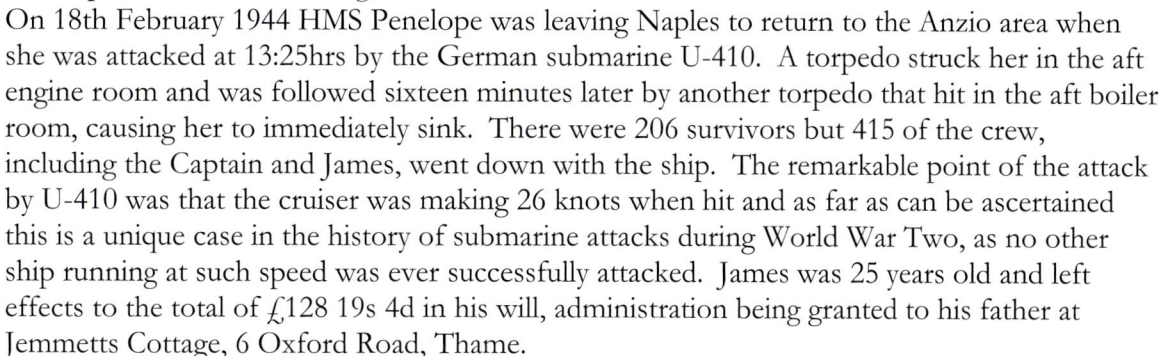

On 18th February 1944 HMS Penelope was leaving Naples to return to the Anzio area when she was attacked at 13:25hrs by the German submarine U-410. A torpedo struck her in the aft engine room and was followed sixteen minutes later by another torpedo that hit in the aft boiler room, causing her to immediately sink. There were 206 survivors but 415 of the crew, including the Captain and James, went down with the ship. The remarkable point of the attack by U-410 was that the cruiser was making 26 knots when hit and as far as can be ascertained this is a unique case in the history of submarine attacks during World War Two, as no other ship running at such speed was ever successfully attacked. James was 25 years old and left effects to the total of £128 19s 4d in his will, administration being granted to his father at Jemmetts Cottage, 6 Oxford Road, Thame.

P/JX 178841 Leading Seaman James William Carter, Royal Navy, HMS Penelope, is commemorated on Portsmouth Naval Memorial, Hampshire. He is remembered in Thame on the War Memorial and on St Mary's Church Memorial Board.

The Thame Remembers Cross was placed at Portsmouth Naval Memorial on 14th June 2017 by Thame Mayor, Councillor Tom Wyse.

HMS Penelope

News Reel of Embarkation

Where are you going to, laughing men?
For a holiday on the sea?
Laughing, smiling, wonderful men,
Why won't you wait for me?

God, how I love you, men of my race,
As you smile on your way to a war;
How can you do it, wonderful face
Do you not know what's before?

Laugh, laugh, you soldier sons
Joke on your way to the war
For your mothers won't laugh at the sound of the guns
And the tales of the filth and the gore.

Smile and joke young sailor Jack
For it's the self-same story:
There'll be no jokes when you come back
And bloody little glory.

Timothy Corsellis
(1921–1941)

Other Conflicts

Drummer Hodge

They throw in Drummer Hodge, to rest
Uncoffined -- just as found:
His landmark is a kopje-crest
That breaks the veldt around:
And foreign constellations west
Each night above his mound.

Young Hodge the drummer never knew --
Fresh from his Wessex home --
The meaning of the broad Karoo,
The Bush, the dusty loam,
And why uprose to nightly view
Strange stars amid the gloom.

Yet portion of that unknown plain
Will Hodge for ever be;
His homely Northern breast and brain
Grow to some Southern tree,
And strange-eyed constellations reign
His stars eternally.

Thomas Hardy
(1840-1928)

South African War

In October 1899 the South African Wars began between the British Empire and the Boers of the Transvaal and Orange Free State.

The Boers were the descendants of the original Dutch settlers of southern Africa. Britain took possession of the Dutch Cape Colony in 1806, sparking resistance from the Boers, who resented the anglicisation of South Africa and Britain's anti-slavery policies. In 1833 the Boers began an exodus into African tribal territory, where they founded the Republics of the Transvaal and the Orange Free State. The two new Republics lived peaceably with their British neighbours until 1867 when the discovery of diamonds and gold in the region made conflict between the Boer states and Britain inevitable.

Minor fighting with Britain began in the 1890s and in October 1899 full-scale war ensued. Initially the British Army was outnumbered until the mainly volunteer yeomanry and infantry units arrived. By the middle of 1900 British forces had captured most major Boer cities and formally annexed their territories. The Boers launched a guerrilla war that frustrated the British Army and so, beginning in 1901, the British began a strategy of systematically searching out and destroying these guerrilla units. By 1902 the British had crushed the Boer resistance and on 31st May the Peace Treaty of Vereeniging was signed, ending hostilities.

The Treaty recognized the British military administration over Transvaal and the Orange Free State and authorised a general amnesty for Boer forces. In 1910 the autonomous Union of South Africa was established which included Transvaal, the Orange Free State, the Cape of Good Hope and Natal, as provinces.

Those Remembered

8 May 1900

William Hubbard was born in early 1878. He was the second son of the nine children of Thomas Hubbard and Susannah (née Woodbridge). Although William was born in Haddenham, Buckinghamshire the family soon moved to Thame living in Moreton Lane and then Church Road. William attended the National School in Thame and worked as an errand boy for Mr F Cox of Priestend before joining the Royal Engineers on 7th April 1896. By early 1900 the 1st Division Telegraph Battalion was established in South Africa where William would have been employed driving horses and wagons in support of the essential telegraph communication lines.

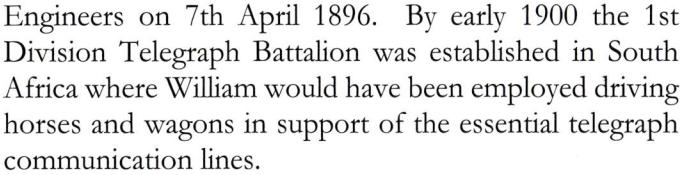

William, age 22, died of enteric fever (typhoid) on 8th May 1900 at Ladysmith and is buried in Bloemfontein,

322 Driver William Hubbard, Royal Engineers, is commemorated on the Royal Engineers Boer War Memorial at Brompton Barracks, Chatham, Kent. He is remembered in Thame on a Memorial Plaque in St Mary's Church.

The Thame Remembers Cross was placed at the Royal Engineers Memorial, Chatham on 26th April 2018 by Thame Museum members, Peter and Diana Gulland.

15 June 1900

George Archer was born in Thame in 1873 to parents John Archer and Mary (née Howlett) of Priestend, Thame and was baptised at St Mary's Church on 28th April 1873. His father John died later that year and his mother in 1884. By 1891 George, age 18, was working as a shoemaker and living in Priestend with his three brothers Robert, Philip and William, and two sisters Jane and Sarah. He joined the Oxfordshire Light Infantry during 1893. The 1st Battalion sailed for South Africa on 22nd December 1899 arriving in Cape Town on 13th January 1900. They were almost immediately in action at the Modder river and had a heavy engagement with the Boers at Paardeberg. At the beginning of June the Battalion moved up to Kroonstad and garrisoned various posts in that area. George, age 27, died of an unknown disease on 15th June 1900 at Bloemfontein where he is buried.

4610 Private George Archer, Oxfordshire Light Infantry, is commemorated on the Boer War Memorial at Edward Brooks Barracks, Abingdon, Oxfordshire. He is remembered in Thame on a Memorial Plaque in St Mary's Church.

The Thame Remembers Cross was placed at Abingdon Memorial on 17th May 2018 by Thame Market Trader, Chris Hurdman.

18 August 1900

Michael William Bond was born in Thame in 1873 to Frederick Bond a farmer and Sarah (née Bowers) of Moreton Field Farm, Moreton, near Thame and was baptised at St Mary's Church on 2nd July 1873. He attended Lord Williams's Grammar School as a day boy and then went on to assist his father on his 300 acre farm. Michael joined the Oxfordshire Yeomanry in 1893 and then the 59th Company (Oxfordshire) 15th Battalion of the Imperial Yeomanry when it was formed in 1899. They arrived in South Africa on 29th March 1900 and were soon in action succesfully beating the Boers at Boshof on 5th April 1900. Michael, age 26, died of enteric fever (typhoid) on 18th August 1900 at Kroonstad and is buried in Bloemfontein.

8051 Trooper Michael William Bond, Imperial Yeomanry, is commemorated on the Oxfordshire Imperial Yeomanry Boer War Memorial at Christchurch Cathedral, Oxford. He is remembered in Thame on a Memorial Plaque in St Mary's Church.

The Thame Remembers Cross was placed at the Imperial Yeomanry War Memorial, Christchurch Cathedral on 16th April 2018 by Thame residents, Elaine and Alan Kidd.

*Bucks Herald
1st September 1900*

THE TWO WARS.

"COMING HOME."

The name of Lieutenant C. E. Forrest, First Oxfordshire Light Infantry, appears in the list of sick and wounded officers who left Cape Town for England in the steamship Assaye on Aug. 22.

A THAME MAN TAKEN PRISONER, AND RELEASED BY "B. P."

Sergeant T. N. Birch, Kimberley Mounted Corps, of Thame, was taken prisoner with a number of his comrades on August 20, but was among the hundred prisoners released by Baden-Powell on the 22nd of this month.

DEATH OF TROOPER M. W. BOND.

We regret to have to record the untimely death, of enteric, in South Africa, of Trooper Michael William Bond, of the 59th Company Imperial Yeomanry, eldest son of Mr. and Mrs. F. Bond, of Moreton Field, Thame. The deceased first contracted the dreaded fever just over two months ago, and had consequently to go into hospital at Kroonstad. Here he apparently recovered; but, it is surmised, he subsequently had a relapse, passing away on Sunday week. Few in Thame were aware that he was even indisposed; nor did his parents entertain grave anxiety concerning his welfare. As a painful shock, then, came to Mr. and Mrs. Bond and family on Monday night the intimation from the War Office that their son had succumbed to the disease at Kroonstad on August 18. It was on the previous day (Sunday) that Mrs. Bond had received a letter from him from Kroonstad, dated July 25, in which he said: "No doubt you cannot make out not having heard from me for such a long time. I should have written before, but since the 9th of June we have been fighting every day, more or less, till the 19th, when I had to come down here and go into hospital with a slight attack of enteric fever, which, I am pleased to say, I have recovered from. It is very bad out here; in some places as many as twenty a day are dying. They treat you grandly whilst in hospital. The Sisters, all of them ladies, cannot do too much for you, and you are allowed whatever you want. I am now waiting for a train to bring me down to Cape Town, which will take four days from here. Then I expect I shall have to come home, as they won't allow anyone after having enteric to stay out here. I am sorry for that, as I shall miss a good job at £3:10 a week; so I expect I shall be home about the first week in September, if all's well, although I don't expect the Oxford Yeomanry will be home before Christmas, as they are still fighting somewhere up Pretoria way, where I wish I was with them. I cannot make out where your letters have all gone to. I have not had one yet, so I expect there must be a donkey-cart full somewhere. No doubt it is because we have been shifted about so, and the railway communications being cut off is the reason I have not had them, but I hope to get them before I have to come home."

The deceased, who was well-known in Thame and neighbourhood, was only 27 years of age. He was for some years a day-boy at Lord Williams' Grammar School, after which he assisted his father upon his farms, until the present Boer war had been in progress a few weeks. At the commencement of this year he volunteered his services when the country requisitioned the assistance of the Yeomanry in South Africa, and was accepted. On March 7, amidst a scene of enthusiasm, he left Oxford with the 59th Company, being accompanied by the following from Thame:—Quartermaster-Sergeant Lidington, Troopers C. Blood, H. Bailey, H. Barton, and C. Plim. From the time of his arrival at Cape Town he had written home with great regularity.

19 November 1901

Harry Taylor was born in 1879 in Derby, Derbyshire. By 1881 he was living with his grandparents Henry and Sarah Taylor in Thame at 55 Park Street. When he signed up to the army on 17th April 1896, Harry was working as a groom in Thame. He initially served with the 1st Battalion Oxfordshire Light Infantry (Regt No 4579) but after four months transferred as a driver to the Army Service Corps.

Harry, age 22, died of disease in Mafeking, South Africa on Tuesday 19th November 1901. His war gratuity went to his sister Phyllis Taylor in Thame.

In his Despatch of 2nd April 1901 Lord Roberts says: "*To do justice to the excellent work done by the Army Service Corps during the war, and to give lengthy details of the magnitude of the task assigned to this department, are beyond the limits of a paragraph in a despatch.*"

12683 Driver Harry Taylor, Army Service Corps, is commemorated on the Army Service Corps Boer War Memorial at The Cathedral Church of St Michael and St George, Aldershot, Hampshire. He is remembered in Thame on a Memorial Plaque in St Mary's Church.

The Thame Remembers Cross was placed at the Army Service Corps Memorial on 17th March 2018 by Thame residents, Barry and Carole Underwood.

28 April 1902

Charles Reginald B Plim was born in Thame in 1881 the only son of Charles Plim and Matilda (née Whiston) of 16 East Street. His father was a solicitor's clerk and County Court clerk. Charles was educated at Lord Williams's Grammar School. He joined the 59th (Oxfordshire) Company of the Imperial Yeomanry in December 1899 (Regt No 2251) but was invalided home in 1900 having contracted enteric fever (typhoid). He was working as a farmer when he re-enlisted in Thame on 1st October 1901 with 116th Company Imperial Yeomanry and embarked for South Africa on 3rd November. When he died he was serving with the Company that formed part of the flying column under Colonel Cooper, sent from Steinkopf to relieve the town of Ookiep, which was strongly held by the Boers. It was during this fight that the British casualties occurred, six being killed and eight wounded. Charles, age 20, was killed in action on 28th April 1902 and was buried at Klipfontein, Steinkopf.

8112 Trooper Charles Reginald B Plim, Imperial Yeomanry, is commemorated on the Oxfordshire Imperial Yeomanry Boer War Memorial at Christchurch Cathedral, Oxford. He is remembered in Thame on a Memorial Plaque in St Mary's Church.

The Thame Remembers Cross was placed at the Imperial Yeomanry War Memorial, Christchurch Cathedral on 16th April 2018 by Thame residents, Elaine and Alan Kidd.

Henry Reynolds

The Memorial Board at Lord Williams's School records the name of H Reynolds as dying during the Boer War. However this is incorrect, Henry Reynolds of Notley Abbey, Buckinghamshire was injured in the Boer War and survived. He married May Smart in 1904 and led a full life until he died in 1959 at the age of 87.

Korean War

On 25th June 1950 the North Korean army attacked the Republic of Korea (ROK) across the 38th Parallel. Two days later the United Nations (UN) urged member states to help the ROK repel the invading forces. In July the first American combat forces arrived and, at the beginning of August, the North Koreans were halted in an area which became known as the Pusan perimeter. On 29th August the first of the British contingent arrived when a force of 4,000 men landed in the south. Eventually, twenty-one UN member nations sent forces to Korea.

On 15th September the Americans, under General MacArthur, landed an amphibious force at Inchon and the North Koreans were forced to fall back in disarray. The Chinese Communist Forces intervened in October 1950 to prevent the collapse of their North Korean ally. This was followed in 1951 and 1952 by a series of offensives and counter-offensives which achieved little. In 1953 an armistice was signed between the UN and the Chinese North Korean Command.

In total over 90,000 British servicemen fought in Korea and they suffered a total of 1,078 killed in action, 2,674 wounded and 1,060 missing or taken prisoner. After the conflict a UN Central Cemetery was established at Busan (formerly Pusan). This is the only UN memorial cemetery and contains the graves of 2,300 men from 11 countries.

Those Remembered

27 October 1950

John Merrick Rudge was born in Dublin in 1920 where his father Captain Leonard Merrick Rudge MC MM was stationed with the 2nd Battalion Worcestershire Regiment. His mother was Lilian Maud (née King) who was born in Oxford. When his father left the army they settled near Manchester. His grandparents, James and Martha King lived in Thame.

After working as a commercial traveller and living in Stony Stratford, Buckinghamshire, John enlisted with the Royal Corps of Signals during World War Two and early in 1943 he married Patricia Mary Morris in Buckinghamshire.

In 1949 he was posted to Hong Kong with 30 Royal Signals, 27th Independent Infantry Brigade HQ, travelling on the troopship Halladale. At the end of August 1950 the Brigade was the first British army contingent to land in Korea.

John, age 30, was killed in Korea on 27th October 1950 serving with the 30 Royal Signals HQ, 27th Brigade. At that time the Brigade was engaged in the Battle of Chongju.

2273949 Corporal John Merrick Rudge, Royal Corps of Signals, is buried in Busan UN Cemetery in South Korea. He is remembered in Thame on his grandmother's gravestone in St Mary's churchyard.

The Thame Remembers Cross was placed at his grave on 22nd April 2015 by Thame resident and Korean War veteran, John Thompson.

John Thompson who placed the Thame Remembers Cross in Busan Cemetery was on a veterans' trip sponsored by the Korean Government

Fallen Heroes

Poppies lay on cenotaphs
for heroes that died in the wars,
they gave their lives for all of us
that's the reason, what they died for.

The fallen heroes lie
in every one of our hearts,
each year that passes by
we never let them part.

Not only the first and second world wars
but, in the Gulf and Afghanistan as well,
all of these fallen soldiers are remembered
went and are still going through a torturous hell.

The Korean War and Vietnam
can not be forgotten, at all,
those soldiers gave their lives
heroes died watching another fall.

Cynthia Jones
© 2007

Cyprus Emergency

The Cyprus Emergency (1955-1959) was a military action that took place on the island of Cyprus, primarily consisting of an insurgent campaign by the Greek Cypriot militant group, the National Organisation of Cypriot Fighters (EOKA), to remove the British from Cyprus so it could be unified with Greece. Both the British and EOKA were in turn opposed by the Turkish Cypriot group Turkish Resistance Organisation (TMT), who rejected union with Greece. It led to Cyprus being granted independence in 1960.

The insurgency began on 1st April 1955 with a series of explosions around government offices in Nicosia. After a series of follow-up incidents, a state of emergency was declared and troops deployed to suppress the uprising. The British encountered great difficulty obtaining effective intelligence on EOKA as, in general, the majority of the Greek Cypriot population supported and/or feared them. During the campaign violence erupted between the Greek and Turkish communities and these eventually split along ethnic lines. After three years of struggle it became clear that the only solution to the violence would be a political one.

In 1959, behind the scenes, diplomatic activity between the British, Greek and Turkish Governments eventually resulted in a compromise. Britain was to keep two large bases on the island, over both of which it would have sovereignty. Cyprus would be independent under the Presidency of Archbishop Makarios. The Government would be predominantly Greek, but with constitutional safeguards protecting the rights of the Turkish minority. There was to be an immediate ceasefire and an amnesty for political crimes committed during the Emergency.

From the British military perspective it was a vicious terrorist campaign and at its conclusion 371 servicemen had been killed and many more injured.

Those Remembered

9 September 1957

Joseph Arthur Castle was born in Thame on 13th December 1923 and baptised at St Mary's Church on 25th January 1924. He was the third eldest of five children born to Arthur John Castle and Constance Emily (née Filleul). The family lived at 104 High Street where his father was a printer and proprietor of the Thame Gazette newspaper. Joseph attended Lord Williams's Grammar School between 1934 and 1940.
He enlisted with the Territorial Army on 12th January 1942, shortly after his eighteenth birthday and served on Home Service with the Oxford and Bucks Light Infantry during World War Two. He transferred to the Royal Engineers on 29th May 1945, where he was promoted to Staff Sergeant. He served for six months with the British Army of the Rhine (BAOR) from December 1946 after which he re-enlisted as a regular soldier. Whilst serving with the 36 Army Engineer Regiment Joseph was awarded the British Empire Medal in the 1951 New Year's Honours list for *"exemplary work in constructing emergency camps during the Dock Strike and a bridge over the Thames for the Festival of Britain"*.

Joseph was promoted to Warrant Officer II on 8th November 1952 and served a tour of duty in Hong Kong with the Royal Engineers Works Services from December 1952 to November 1955. On his return he was promoted to Warrant Officer 1st class and posted to the BAOR. On 16th September 1956, during the Cyprus Emergency, he was posted to Royal Engineers Works Services, Episkopi, Cyprus, From there on 4th March 1957 he was temporarily detached to GE Bahrain with the Cameronians (Scottish Rifles). Joseph, age just 33 years, died in Bahrain of a heart attack on 9th September 1957 and was buried there with full military honours. He left over £2,000 in his will.

5392839 Warrant Officer Joseph Arthur Castle BEM, Royal Engineers, is buried in the Old Christian Cemetery in Manama, Bahrain. He is remembered in Thame on a Plaque in St Mary's Church. In 2009 his name was placed on the Cyprus Memorial in Kyrenia, Cyprus by the Cyprus Memorial Trust. His name is to be added to Thame War Memorial.

The Thame Remembers Cross was placed at his grave on 20th December 2015 by Thame residents, Ann and Adrian Dite.

Attending the ceremony in Bahrain were members of the Royal Navy as well as local dignitaries

The Memorial at the Old British Cemetery, Kyrenia, Cyprus

Afterword

The Steering Group

David Bretherton

David has used the skills gained in project management during his time as an engineer in the RAF to lead this Project from its conception. When appointed to train RAF apprentices at Halton he and his wife Margaret chose to move to Thame and can think of no better place to live. David has thoroughly enjoyed all aspects of the Project and especially all the cross deliveries that he has attended. There have been many highlights, including travel to Egypt and Turkey and the one aspect that he will always remember is the scale of Brookwood Cemetery in Surrey, but his main highlight was taking part in the nightly "Last Post" ceremony at Menin Gate, Ypres to read the exhortation.

Margaret Bretherton

Margaret has supported her husband from the inception of the Project and has been the mainstay behind purchasing and selling the marketing products especially the popular lapel badges. She has enjoyed the many trips to visit the battlefields of the Western Front and new experiences in Egypt and Gallipoli. She has appreciated experiencing the underground world of the World War One soldier and was especially impressed on the group visit to the Wellington Tunnels in Arras, France.

Mike Dyer

Mike encouraged David to launch Thame Remembers and has been engaged in making things happen from the outset. His business background helped to attract initial funding and to plan many of the events. He was largely responsible for establishing and nurturing our ongoing partnerships with BBC South and with Lord Williams's School. Mike has often remarked that this has been the most worthwhile and rewarding project he has ever undertaken, with many notable experiences and powerful memories. One lasting impression has been the contrast between the Commonwealth war cemeteries and German war cemeteries on the battlefields of World War One.

Allan Hickman

Allan has been a friend of David and Margaret for many years and it was as a direct result of a trip to the battlefields of France with David that led to the idea for the Project. Allan led the team of researchers at the start of the Project, but latterly taking on most of the detailed research himself, where the discipline of his work as an electrical design engineer came to the fore. Allan has enjoyed taking part in the Project visits to France and Belgium, but the highlight for him has been discovering the details of George Edsell MD and visiting his grave in Kingston upon Thames.

Ian Jones MBE

Ian joined the Project soon after it was proposed. He has a detailed knowledge of some World War One battlefields and used this information when planning trips to the area. He was also able, through the Durand Group, to get the Steering Group into World War One tunnels and a Souterrain, areas that are not normally open to the public. He also wrote the background introductions to the chapters in the Thame Remembers book. Ian has enjoyed visiting new battlefields in Europe, Gallipoli and Tunisia, but the highlight for him was laying a cross at the grave of Charles Bristow GM, who was killed on bomb disposal duties.

Catherine Jones

Being ex-military herself, Catherine was a fan of the Thame Remembers Project from the start and willingly accompanied her husband Ian on several of the battlefield tours. After she left the army she discovered a talent for the written word and took up writing professionally. She has twenty published books to her name – many about, or involving, soldiers and their families - so was delighted to be asked to contribute her skills by writing the dialogue for "Ten Tommies from Thame" to be staged at Thame Players Theatre at the end of the Project. Her most memorable moment of the Project was seeing Tyne Cot cemetery near Ypres, Belgium for the first time.

Patsy Baker

Patsy is Thame born and bred, has Thame in her blood and has devoted her time and energy to many good causes in the town. In 2012 she was selected to carry the Paralympic torch in recognition of her contribution to the community. She joined the Project in its early stages and soon realised its potential to involve the people of Thame of all ages and backgrounds in honouring the many local men and their families who made the ultimate sacrifice. Patsy is a pragmatic and energetic 'can-do' person who has brought her organisational skills to many aspects of the Project, especially the activities and events in Thame itself. She has taken part in the trips to France and Belgium and was particularly struck by the magnificence of the Canadian Memorial at Vimy Ridge but her fondest memory and proudest moment was laying a wreath at Thame War Memorial on Remembrance Day.

Steve Perry and Verity Platek

Steve and Verity have an interest in World War Two battlefields and joined the Project to lay Thame Remembers Crosses in France and Belgium. They took over the upkeep of the website and instigated the social media aspects, which have been important parts of the publicity for the Project. Their most memorable experience of the Project was laying a wreath at Plymouth Naval Memorial with their daughter Theia.

Kristian Winslade

Kristian has a keen interest in all aspects of World War Two, especially the D-Day landings and so was keen to help the Project. He has brought his design skills to the Project, working on most of the publicity material and especially the book cover. He has also delivered a number of crosses with his girlfriend Jenny. His most memorable moment was tracing troop movements through Normandy and heading south to the final resting place of two Thame soldiers.

Michael Hutson

Michael joined the Project at the request of his father-in-law David Bretherton. He organised the youth participation in the initial event at St Mary's churchyard and has been the group's driver on the recce trips to the Western Front. He has a keen interest in all things to do with World War One weaponry and has enjoyed experiencing the battlefields but his highlight was the privilege of visiting a private collection of rifles and other arms in Belgium.

Acknowledgements

The Project Steering Group is grateful to countless people for their help and contribution to the success of Thame Remembers. We have not named here all those who have delivered crosses as they are recorded against each delivery but there have been many others, both individuals and organisations, who have made notable contributions towards achieving our objectives.

Funding was vital from the outset and to sustain momentum for the whole four years. We are very grateful for the financial support received from the Heritage Lottery Fund, Oxfordshire County Council, Rewley Hodges Fund, Thame Town Council and South Oxfordshire District Council.

Thame Museum Trustees have provided overall governance and other organisations including the Commonwealth War Graves Commission, Oxford History Centre, Pentangle Internet, Royal British Legion and Surman and Horwood Funeral Services have given generous professional support. We also thank Carole Underwood for her help in the preparation of this book and Thame Digital Camera Club, Peter Lambert, and the late Nick White for their photographic contributions. Special thanks are due to the Cross Keys Pub, Project HQ, for sustaining us throughout.

We have held a great many events in telling our story and we acknowledge the considerable assistance from the Captain, Lt Cdr James Fickling, and crew of HMS Dauntless, K&A Scaffolding, Lord Williams's School, St Mary's Church, the Spread Eagle Hotel, Thame Cinema for All, Thame Cricket Club, Thame Food Festival, Thame Market Traders, Thame Show and The Last Post Association, Ypres. Thame Players have kindly hosted and co-produced our theatre productions, and thanks to those intrepid volunteers who have taken to the stage on our behalf.

Travel has been mainly down to the individuals when making Cross deliveries but our few organised excursions have been made easier with the help of: 3B Vehicle Hire, the British Embassy in Cairo, Heyfordian Travel, Leger Coaches, Ocean Villas and Spear Travels. We are also grateful to Alan Corbett who guided our first battlefield tour and to the Durand Group and Barry Bromley for opening up their facilities in France and Belgium. For their help in some of the more difficult areas, we must thank Cunard Line and the Captain of RMS Queen Mary 2, the Joint Services Sub-Aqua Diving Club and the Shetland Amenity Trust.

We formed a unique working partnership with BBC South (Andrew Douglas and Victoria Cook) which has spearheaded publicity throughout the Project, with further support from Radio Oxford, The Oxford Mail, Thamenews.net (Sonja Francis), Gulf Weekly and Family Tree Magazine. In addition we thank Ian & Dan Stark for their filming expertise and the Chinnor and Princes Risborough Railway, Thame Forge and Shaun Moore for the use of their locations. Thanks must also be given to Thame Town Council, its officers and successive Mayors for their ongoing support and assistance. Finally, we include special thanks to all the descendants and family members who have added to our research with photographs, medals, letters, documents and mementos and all the wonderful people of Thame who have delivered crosses and wreaths and supported our many events.

It is not possible to recall every aspect of every event or happening, so if we have inadvertently missed someone please accept our apologies.

The Thame Cross

The origins of the two-barred cross are steeped in ancient history. The association between Thame and a particular two-barred representation of the Holy Cross was born of conflict when in the early years of World War Two the people of Thame chose to make it their emblem, a symbol of their determination to do their bit for their country. The Thame two-barred cross was, more recently, adopted as the symbol for Thame Remembers.

The two-barred or double cross, often called the Patriarchal Cross, is a recognised representation of the Holy Cross and appears in religious art in a number of countries. In heraldry it denotes the rank of Bishop or Archbishop and, as the Bishop of Rome, St Peter is often depicted with a two-barred cross. As the Jerusalem (Patriarchal) Cross it was the origin of the two-barred cross emblem of the House of Anjou, later adopted by the Dukes of Lorraine. In World War Two the Cross of Lorraine was adopted by the Free French Forces led by General Charles de Gaulle, as a symbol of French resistance. The double traverse cross was a characteristic emblem in the centuries following the Crusades, which introduced Byzantine cross reliquaries with double cross traverses into Benedictine treasuries.

In 1940 a Thame man, Willocks MacKenzie, discovered a hoard of Mediaeval rings and coins in mud which had been recently dredged from the River Thame, close to the Prebendal, home to a number of wealthy and influential Churchmen during the Middle Ages. Among the treasures of the hoard was a magnificent reliquary ring, described as one of the finest in England, set with a two-barred cross carved from a single piece of amethyst. The last owner and place of origin of this ring is not known but it is thought that the hoard may have been lost or hidden around the time of the Reformation of the English Church in the 16th Century and it could possibly have belonged to the last Abbot of Thame, Robert King. The objects from the Thame Hoard, as it is known, are now in the Ashmolean Museum in Oxford.

In 1941 the people of Thame and local villages raised funds for a motor torpedo boat (MTB 219). A plaque was made to mark this contribution to the war effort and a representation of the amethyst two-barred cross on the ring was central to the design. The original plaque, which was fixed to the centre of the fore mess deck bulkhead of the vessel, is now on display in Thame Museum. This is the first known use of the two-barred cross to represent Thame and it has been part of the town's emblem or logo since then. It is central to Thame Town Council's official logo today, appears on the ceremonial chain worn by the Mayor and, when Thame Museum opened in 2007, its own logo was designed around the Thame Cross, as it has become known locally.

There are many variations to the two-barred cross. The two bars can be placed tight together (condensed) or far apart. They can be symmetrically spaced either around the middle or above or below the middle. One asymmetrical variation has one bar near the top and the other just below the middle. Finally the bars can be of equal length or with one shorter than the other.

The Soldier

If I should die, think only this of me;
That there's some corner of a foreign field
That is for ever England. There shall be
In that rich earth a richer dust concealed;
A dust whom England bore, shaped, made aware,
Gave, once, her flowers to love, her ways to roam,
A body of England's breathing English air,
Washed by the rivers, blest by suns of home.

And think, this heart, all evil shed away,
A pulse in the eternal mind, no less
Gives somewhere back the thoughts by England given;
Her sights and sounds; dreams happy as her day;
And laughter, learnt of friends; and gentleness,
In hearts at peace, under an English heaven.

Rupert Brooke
(1887–1915)

Addendum

Elegy in a Country Courtyard

The men that worked for England
They have their graves at home:
And birds and bees of England
About the cross can roam.

But they that fought for England,
Following a falling star,
Alas, alas for England
They have their graves afar.

And they that rule in England,
In stately conclave met,
Alas, alas for England
They have no graves as yet.

G K Chesterton
(1874-1936)

Those Remembered

Name	Page
A	
Charles Alder Allen	94
Raymond John Allen	160
Sydney Allen	105
Stanley James Allen	196
George Archer	224
Eric Arnold	206
Harry Arnott	182
B	
Clifford Bert Bateman	81
George Alfred Bateman	105
Thomas Bates	46
William Thomas Baverstock	130
Anthony Austin Beard	160
Henry Claude Bernard	79
Francis Leveson Bertie	29
Henry A Birrell-Anthony	40
Charles Boiling	30
Eric Leon Boiling	69
Ronald James Boiling	184
William Alfred Boiling	113
Michael William Bond	224
George Bowdery	53
John William Bowler	53
William Bowler	122
Charles Frederick Bristow	167
Joseph Brown	113
David John Burbridge	137
Edward Benoni Burgess	102
C	
Peter George Campion	204
James William Carter	219
Francis Cartland	147
James Lawrence Castle	154
Joseph Arthur Castle	229
John Austin Chapman	168
Frank Chowns	66
George Chowns	28
William Chowns	59
Cyril George Clarke	69
John Anthony Creemer Clarke	193
Wilfred Harry Clarke	143
Stanley Riswin Colbert	191
Henry Bennett Cook	218
Henry John Cozier	42
Sackville "George" Crick	125

Name	Page
George Harry Thomas Crook	97
Alfred Thomas Cross	116
Frederick William Cross	103
Reginald Isaac Cross	43
Reginald John Culverwell	68
Albert Isaac Cumming	150
Colin George Price Cuthbert	208
D	
Sidney Maskell Dicker	84
Stanley David Victor Dover	97
William Spencer Drake	68
E	
Ralph Eaton	88
George Alfred Edsell	32
Sidney Stevens Edwards	54
Harry Eele	131
F	
Reginald George Farmbrough	111
Francis Willoughby Fielding	72
Christie West Fletcher	85
William Freeman	207
G	
William Elhanan Gascoyne	52
Frederick James Goodman	80
Richard Francis Gower	190
Albert Henry Green	45
Richard John Green	59
James Arthur Greenhalgh	65
Gordon Halliday Gudgeon	196
H	
Frederick George Beames Hake	147
Ernest George Thomas Harris	194
Ronald Frank Harris	185
Walter Sidney Harris	101
Owen Charles Hawes	114
Alfred Thomas Heley	203
Algernon Evelyn Hemmings	31
Richard Tuckey Hewer	135
Richard John Philip Hewetson	117
William Ewen Hicks	124
Albert Victor Higgins	57
Henry Robert Higgins	26
Thomas Joe Hinder (survived)	155

Name	Page
John Clare Hoadley	77
William Cecil Hoadley	152
James Hobbs	46
Leslie Hodges	178
Edward Greville C Holbrook	218
William Honour	27
Francis Hopkins	127
Ernest Edward House	43
Bernard Howe	166
Alfred John Walter Howes	129
Frederick Ernest Howes	184
Alfred Robert Howland	48
Arthur Robert Howland	54
Harry Howland	55
Charles Hubert Howlett	48
John Howlett	74
Maurice Horatio Howlett	205
Sam Howlett	88
William Hubbard	223

I

Name	Page
John Robert Ing	179

J

Name	Page
Edward William James	45
Willis Janes	90
Charles Raymond Jarratt	201
Peter Milton Jennings	172
Herbert Edward Jones	169

K

Name	Page
Fred Keene	142
Jack Archer Keene	49
Charles Stanley Kiddy	175
Hugh Kidman	107

L

Name	Page
George Edmund Ladbrook	91
Edward Aubrey Lane	57
William James Lewis	94
Douglas Viney Lidington	82
Ralph Line	104
Richard Line	127
Henry William Little	207
Graham Chard Loader	123
William Robert Loosley	65
Joseph Lovejoy	98
Vivian Evelyn Lower	171

M

Name	Page
Sidney Charles Maskell-Dicker	180
Bertram Wheeler Mason	146
Alexander Fahey McDonald	199
Hugh Charles James McRea	216
Norman Kenneth Millard	168
George Miller	72
Ian Malcolm Keith Miller	159
Reginald Albert Miller	178
Charles Roy Munckton Morris	100

N

Name	Page
Douglas Beaumont Neale	209
Frederick Neil	51
William Newitt	93
Frederick James North	143

O

Name	Page
Herbert John Ody	191
John Olieff	50
Harry William Oliver	56
Duncan Haldane Ostrehan	47
Albert Edward Outing	33

P

Name	Page
George Bertie Parker	133
Sidney Thomas Parker	67
Thomas Hayward Parrott	189
George Asplin Pask	103
George Payne	34
Brian Perry	32
Harry Phillips	197
John Phillips	166
John Eric Jesse Phillips	161
Reginald Phillips	99
Sidney Jack Plater	212
Louis Herbert Plested	174
Charles R B Plim	226
Albert Henry Pollicott	179
Frederick Price	27
Harry Price	41
Roland Arthur Pullen	81

Q

Name	Page
Albert Horace Quainton	161

Name	Page
R	
Lewis Rhymes	66
Herbert Hiscock Richardson	115
Sidney Alfred Richardson	217
Stephen James Roberts	95
William Edward Roberts	40
Douglas Rolfe	204
Eric William Rose	111
John Merrick Rudge	227
Arthur Rush	96
S	
Kenneth Sellwood	181
Donald Patrick Shaw	35
John Boxell Shaw	73
George Henry Sherwin	34
Alwyne Robert Peirce Shields	211
Harry John Shrimpton	77
Sidney Augustus Shrimpton	74
Stanley John Slade	171
Gordon Eric Smith	205
William Noel Smith	70
Frank Leslie Soanes	58
Benjamin Squires	107
George Squires	50
Joseph Squires	56
Herbert Stevens	26
Herbert Arthur Stockwell	108
Ralph Wentworth Stone	120
Frederick Stopps	121
John Alexander Summerhayes	118
John Frederick Summersbee	215
Arthur Henry Sutton	138
T	
Sidney Thomas Tappin	42
Noel Alexander Target	75
Harry Taylor	226
Derek Edmund Teden	164
Albert George Thomlinson	176
Frank Tickner	149
Thomas John Tims	183
Albert Alexander Trinder	118
Bernard George Turner	70
Oscar Tyrrell	82

Name	Page
W	
Gordon Wade	192
Ethelbert Godwin S Wagner	89
William Arthur Wallington	44
Charles Dorsett Ward	84
Mark Wells	119
William Henry Wentworth	100
Cyril Frank White	170
Joseph Albert Wicks	174
Alfred Willis	120
Harry Cooper Wilsdon	79
H T Wilson	155
Stanley H Winkley	110
Cecil Amos Witney	91
Charles Wood	33
Francis Wood	190
Y	
Albert Victor Young	86

Names on the Memorials

The names are listed here as they appear on the memorials.

Thame War Memorial

World War One

Allen C A
Allen S
Bateman C B
Bates T
Baverstock W T
Birrell-Anthony H A
Boiling C
Boiling E
Boiling W
Bowdery G
Bowler W
Brown J
Cartland F
Castle J L
Chowns F
Chowns G
Clarke W
Cozier H
Crook G H
Cross A F
Cross F W
Cross R I
Cumming A
Dicker S
Dover S D V
Drake W
Eaton R
Eele H
Farnborough R G
Fielding F
Hake F G B
Hemmings A
Hewer R T
Higgins A
Higgins H R
Hinder J
Honour W
Hopkins F
House E E
Howes A J
Howland A R
Howland A R (Bob)
Howlett C H
Howlett J
Howlett S
James E W
Keene F
Keene J
Ladbrook G E
Lane A
Lidington D V
Line Ralph
Line R
Loader G C
Loosley W
Lovejoy J
Miller G
Olieff J
Oliver H W
Ostrehan D H
Outing G C
Parker S
Price F
Price H
Pullen R A
Richardson H
Roberts S J
Roberts W E
Rush C A
Shaw J B
Shrimpton H J
Smith W
Soanes F L
Squires B
Squires G
Squires J
Stevens H
Stockwell B
Summerhayes J A
Tappin S
Trinder A A
Wallington W A
Wells M
Wentworth W H
Wilson H T
Witney C A
Wood C
Young A V

World War One Additional Plaques

Burbridge D
Green A H
Hicks W E
North F J
Shaw D P
Sutton A H

World War Two

Allen R J
Allen S
Arnold E
Arnott H
Beard A A
Boiling R J
Carter J W
Clarke J A C
Hodges L
Howes F E
Howlett M
Ing J R
Miller R
Philips H
Phillips J
Plater S J
Pollicott A H
Quainton A H
Richardson S
Summersbee J
Thomlinson A G
Wade G
White C F

Moreton

War Memorial

World War One

Pte Alfred T Cross - Dev Regt
Pte Frederick W Cross - Ox & Bucks L I
L Cpl Reginald I Cross - Ox & Bucks L I
Trooper Reginald G Farnborough - Q O Ox Hussars
L Cpl Alfred J W Howes - Ox & Bucks L I
RFM Roland A Pullen - Rifle Brig

World War Two

Howes F E - Ox & Bucks L I - 8 Jan 45
Quainton A H - Ox & Bucks L I - 8 Nov 44

Moreton Chapel Plaque
(now in Thame Museum)

Alfred W Howes
Reginald I Cross
Roland A Pullen
Reginald G Farnborough
Frederick W Cross
Alfred T Cross

St Mary's Church War Memorial Boards

Great War 1914-1918

Allen C A
Allen S
Bateman C B
Bates T
Baverstock W T
Birrell-Anthony H A
Boiling C
Boiling E
Boiling W
Bowdery G
Bowler W
Brown J
Burbridge D
Cartland F
Castle J L
Chowns F
Chowns G
Clarke W H
Cozier H
Crook G H
Cross A F
Cross F W
Cross R I
Cumming A
Dicker S
Dover S D V
Drake W
Eaton R
Eele H
Farnborough R G
Fielding F W
Green A H
Hake F G B
Hemmings A
Hewer R T
Hicks W E
Higgins A V
Higgins H R
Hinder J
Honour W
Hopkins F
House E E
Howes A J
Howland A R
Howland A R (Bob)
Howlett C H
Howlett J
Howlett S
James E W
Keene F
Keene J
Ladbrook G E
Lane A
Lidington D V
Line R
Line Ralph
Loader G C
Loosley J
Lovejoy J
Miller G
North F J
Olieff J
Oliver H W
Ostrehan D H
Outing G C
Parker S
Price F
Price H
Pullen R A
Richardson H
Roberts S J
Roberts W E
Rush C A
Shaw J B
Shrimpton H J
Smith W
Soanes F L
Squires B
Squires G
Squires J
Stevens H
Stockwell B
Summerhayes J A
Sutton A H
Tappin S
Trinder A A
Wallington W A
Wells M
Wentworth W H
Wilson H T
Witney C A
Wood C
Young A V

World War 1939-1945

Allen R J
Allen S
Arnold E
Arnott H
Beard A A
Boiling R J
Carter J W
Clarke J A C
Harris R F
Hodges L
Howes F E
Howlett M
Ing J R
Millard N K
Miller R
Phillips H
Phillips J
Pollicott A H
Quainton A H
Richardson S
Summersbee J
Thomlinson A G
White C F

St Mary's Church Memorial Plaques

Boer War Memorial Plaque

Private George Archer - Oxfordshire Light Infantry
Trooper Michael William Bond - Imperial Yeomanry
Trooper Charles R B Plim - Imperial Yeomanry
Driver William Hubbard - Royal Engineers

Additional

Driver Harry Taylor - Army Service Corps

Brass Plaques

Joseph Arthur Castle RE
Warrant Officer died in Bahrain September 9 1957

Viscount Francis Leveson Bertie,
75 yrs buried 30 Sep 1919,
near this place.

Christchurch Memorial Board

World War One

W H Clarke
H T Cozier
R Eaton
A V Higgins
E E House
A R Howland
F Keen
H J Shrimpton
F L Soanes
B Squires
G Squires
J Squires
A A Trinder

World War Two

Sidney Jack Plater - a loyal deacon
of this church 1933-1945

All Saints Church Memorial Board 1914-1918 (now in Thame Museum)

Allen Pte S Northbld Fusiliers
Allen Gnr C RFA
Birrell-Anthony Lieut H A Monmouths
Boiling Sergt W Berks
Boiling Pte E
Baverstock Pte W T OBLI
Bowler Corpl W OBLI
Bowdrey L Cpl G R Fusiliers
Bates Pte T Cameron Highldrs
Brown Corpl J OBLI
Bateman Cpl C B OBLI
Cartland Petty Off F HMS Lucia
Castle Dr J L S African VC
Cozier L Cpl H OBLI
Chowns Pte Frank KRR
Cross Pte A Devons
Roberts Cpl S J RGA
Crook Pte G H OBLI
Clarke Stoker W H HMS Formidable
Cummings Chf Steward HMS Barnard Castle
Dicker Rifleman S KRR
Dover Pte S D V OBLI
Eaton Pte R OBLI
Eele Pte H Wilts
Farnbrough Tpr R G QOOH
Fielding Lt F W Q Victoria Rifles
Hemmings Pte A Dorsets
Hewer Lt R Berks Yeomanry
Howlett Qt Master Sgt RGA
Howlett L Cpl J RE DCM
House Cpl E E Canadians
Howes Pte A J OBLI
Howland Pte A R OBLI
Howland Sgt A R R Fusiliers
Hopkins Pte F Wilts
Howlett Pte S Royal Berks
Higgins Pte A V Cheshires
Higgins Pte H R 3rd Norfolks
James Pte W OBLI

Keene AS Fred HMS Pathfinder
Keene Pte J OBLI
Ladbrook Pte G E Gloucesters
Lane Pte Aubrey Middlesex
Line Pte Richard OBLI
Line Cpl Ralph QOOH
Loosley Pte W Gren Guards
Lovejoy Trooper J QOOH
Miller Sapper G RE
Olieff Pte J Royal Berks
Ostrehan Lt D V Ll Nth Lancs
Outing Farrier Major
Parker Sergt S OBLI
Price Gunner Fred RFA
Pullen Rifleman R Lon Rifle Bgde
Richardson Gunner H RFA
Roberts Sgt W QOOH
Rush L Corpl A OBLI
Shaw Pte J B Royal Welsh Fusls
Shrimpton Sgt H J MM OBLI
Smith Pte W OBLI
Soanes Rifleman F L HRR
Squires Cpl G Beds
Squires Pte J MGC
Squires Pte B Gren Guards
Stevens Trooper H QOOH
Stockwell Sgt Major OBLI
Summerhayes Cpt 13th Rl Inniskillens
Trinder Pte A A 10th Essex
Tappin Pte S OBLI
Wallington Pte W A OBLI
Wentworth Sgt W Gren Guards
Witney Sgt Major C OBLI
Price Pr H Berks
Young Corpl A W MGC
Chowns Pioneer G RE
Hake AS Rl Fleet Reserve

Lord Williams's School Memorial Boards

Great War 1914-1918

Henry C Bernard	Gloucestershire Regt
Edward B Burgess	S African Scottish Regt
Reginald J Culverwell	Oxfordshire and Bucks L I
Cyril G Clarke	E Yorkshire Regt
F W Fielding	9th London Regt
C W Fletcher	Canadian Mounted Rifles
William E Gascoyne	Oxfordshire & Bucks L I
Richard J Green	Royal Fusiliers
W S Harris	15th London Regt
Owen C Hawes	Oxfordshire & Bucks L I
John C Hoadley	Royal Engineers
William C Hoadley	H M S Bittern
James Hobbs	Princess Patricias Cann L I
Willis Janes	King's Own Scottish Bords
Hugh Kidman	Oxfordshire Yeomanry
Duncan H Ostrehan	Loyal North Lancs Regt
G B Parker	New Zealand Army Service Corps
Brian Perry	Inns of Court OTC
William E Roberts	Oxfordshire Yeomanry
Eric W Rose MC	Lancashire Fusiliers
G H Sherwin	Royal Air Force
William N Smith	Oxfordshire & Bucks L I
Ralph W Stone	Munster Fusiliers
Noel A Target	Durham Light Infantry
A A Trinder	Essex Regt
Bernard G Turner	Coldstream Guards
E G S Wagner	Royal Flying Corps
Charles D Ward	27th Regt Canadian Infantry
Stanley H Winkley	Royal Air Force

World War 1939-1945

Eric Arnold	Royal Artillery
Peter G Campion	Royal Corps of Signals
John A Chapman	Royal Navy
John A C Clarke	Royal Air Force
Stanley R Colbert	Royal Air Force
Colin G P Cuthbert	Royal Armoured Corps
Sidney C M Dicker	The Wiltshire Regiment
Richard F Gower	Royal Air Force
Gordon H Gudgeon	The Royal Fusiliers
Edward G C Holbrook	Royal Navy
Bernard Howe	Royal Air Force
Charles R Jarratt	Royal Air Force
Peter M Jennings	Royal Air Force
Herbert E Jones	Royal Artillery

Vivian Lower	Royal Air Force	Gordon E Smith	Royal Artillery
Alexander F McDonald	Fleet Air Arm	Derek E Teden	Royal Air Force
Hugh C J McRae	Royal Navy	Joseph A Wicks	East Kent Regiment
Douglas B Neale	Royal Air Force	Frank Wood	Royal Air Force
Herbert J Ody	Royal Air Force	Henry W Little	Royal Air Force
Thomas H Parrott	Royal Air Force		
John Philips	Royal Air Force		

Additional Names

Wtr Bertram Wheeler Mason	
James Arthur Greenhalgh	Cheshire Regt
Michael Bond	Imperial Yeomanry
C R B Plim	Imperial Yeomanry
Tpr H Reynolds	Imperial Yeomanry
H M S Wagner	(on memorial but survived)

Sidney J Plater	Royal Air Force
Douglas Rolfe	Royal Air Force
Kenneth Sellwood	Oxfordshire & Bucks L I
Alwyne R P Shields	Royal Air Force
Stanley S J Slade	Royal Air Force

St Mary's Churchyard

War Graves

Private Raymond J Allen
RAOC only son of J and M Allen accidentally
killed on active service 7 December 1940 age 18

Flying Officer Anthony Austin Beard
Pilot Royal Air Force 24 September 1944 age 21

WR26650 Pioneer George Chowns
Royal Engineers 23 Feb 1919 age 41 years

Private 16651 Henry Robert Higgins
Norfolk Reg 28 January 1915 age 34 years

TS3580 Private William Honour
Royal Army Service Corps 13 April 1916 age 42

754480 Sergeant Ian Malcolm Keith Miller
Pilot Royal Air Force 4 November 1940 age 25 years

1666457 Ldg Aircraftman John Eric Jesse Phillips
Royal Air Force 9 February 1946 age 25 years

64601 Bombardier Frederick Price
Royal Artillery 14 September 1916 age 30 years

5382931 L Cpl Albert Quainton
The Oxfordshire and Buckinghamshire Light Infantry
Died 8 November 1924 age 24

1979 Private Herbert Stevens
Q O Oxfordshire Hussars 14 June 1915

Memorials

Sidney Allen
28 March 1918 age 30 years.

Charles Alder Allen
12 April 1917 age 25 years

Eric Arnold 19 August 1919 to 12 December 1942
Killed in Action

Francis Leveson Viscount Bertie of Thame PPc GCB
GCMO born 1844 died 26 Sep 1919 who was buried in
the Churchyard 30 Sep 1919

16926 Private Charles Boiling (Charlie)
Oxford and Bucks Light Infantry
24 Dec 1920 Age 25. Buried near here

David Burbridge who died on active service in
East Africa April 1917 age 30 years.

Frank Chowns
died in France 9 May 1915

William Freeman
died of wounds in North Africa
March 31 1943 age 36

Algernon Hemmings Private 7446 1st Battalion 39th
Foot The Dorsetshire Regiment. 15 June 1915

Arthur Robert Howland age 21 years
killed in action in France 1917

Battery Quarter-Master Sergeant
Charles Hubert Howlett
killed in action in Belgium 8 August 1917 age 26 years

Douglas Viney Lidington
Pte 9th Norfolk Reg who fell in France
fighting for his country 15 September 1916 age 37 years

Frederick Neil
13 July 1888 to 21 August 1917 Killed in World War 1

John Olieff
Killed in France 16 August 1917 age 26 years

C R B Plim of the 116 Co Imperial Yy
fell in action Steinkop 28 April 1902 age 20 years
int. in Klipfontein South Africa

Sergeant W E Roberts QOOH
killed in action 27 May 1915 age 30 years

John Merrick Rudge
Royal Signals died of wounds in Korea
27 October 1950 age 30 years

Harry John Shrimpton
son of the above who was killed
in the Great War 30 August 1916

Frank Leslie Soanes
born 6 October 1898
killed in action 17 September 1918

Arthur Henry Sutton
died on active service at
Kambaghe East Africa 19 June 1917 age 31

Albert G Thomlinson 4th OBLI
died 1940 whilst a POW in Germany age 26 yrs

Albert Trinder
Killed in Action 3 August 1918

2nd Lieut Oscar Tyrrell
London Reg who fell in action
9 September 1916

Names to be Added

When the Thame Remembers Project was launched in the summer of 2014 research had identified the names of 182 men remembered in the town, principally on the War Memorials in Thame and Moreton but also on Memorial Boards in local churches, the Museum and at Lord Williams's School. Some names were duplicated in more than one place and a number of men are buried in St Mary's churchyard.

We had not anticipated that our research would lead us to finding other men from Thame who, for whatever reason, had not been commemorated on a memorial in Thame. Some of them had been born in Thame but moved away before war broke out or members of their family were no longer in Thame to represent them when the memorial was commissioned. Others may have only lived or worked in Thame for a few years before the war so had a more tenuous link and some were simply missed for no apparent reason.

It therefore seemed fitting and appropriate that these omissions should be remedied so that the men are suitably commemorated and remembered through future generations. Thame Remembers approached Thame Town Council, as the custodians of the Thame and Moreton War Memorials, to request that these names be added. The Council agreed unanimously that it would support the addition of further names to the Memorials, subject to suitable criteria and independent verification of the research findings.

There is no surviving record of any particular criteria used following either of the World Wars to determine who would qualify for inclusion, but research into the 182 names already remembered provided some clues that any obvious association with Thame had been deemed sufficient and that the default position was to include rather than to be judgemental. It also became apparent that other communities had encountered the same challenge and had been equally unable to trace any definitive guidance from previous practice.

The Thame Remembers Steering Group therefore undertook to prepare criteria that reflected the best interpretation of the original objective, which was to commemorate those people from the town who had given their lives in the service of their country. This was a delicate process which took months of work and many iterations and refinements before it was deemed fit for purpose. This criteria was then reviewed and accepted by the Council.

The next stage was to present the research findings, with supporting information, to a working group of Town Councillors to verify that the research was robust and that the extra names complied with the criteria. Most names were accepted whilst a few required further research and resubmission, resulting in a total of 30 additional names to be added to the War Memorial in due course.

Before the names can be added there are other considerations, both practical and financial, to be overcome but it is hoped that the names will be affixed in 2021 at a ceremony to mark the anniversary of the unveiling of Thame War Memorial by Mr David Lloyd George, Prime Minister, one hundred years earlier.

Addition of Names to a War Memorial in Thame

Criteria:

Names shall be eligible for inclusion on the Thame and/or Moreton War Memorial(s) if they meet the following criteria:

a) They served in HM Forces or Merchant Navy or other uniformed organisation in a theatre of conflict, or as part of any officially sanctioned international (UN/ NATO) deployment and died during the period of that conflict.

and

b) They were born in the parish of Thame, spent a significant part of their life in Thame, or their close family lived in the parish of Thame at the time of their death.

Notes: (These notes form part of the criteria)

1. HM Forces shall include all commonwealth or empire forces operating in support of a campaign or medal earning theatre of operation.
2. The period of the conflict shall normally be that declared by The Commonwealth War Graves Commission or the MOD. Deaths outside those dates may be considered where there are extenuating circumstances.
3. The parish of Thame is that pertaining at the time of the person's birth or death.
4. A significant part of their life is defined as normally more than three years or having carried out a public role within the town. Living or working in the town at the time of their enlistment would be considered significant.
5. Close family is defined as being: grandparent, parent, guardian, wife, husband, brother, sister or child.
6. No judgement should be made about their lifestyle or the circumstances of their death.

Process:

- Any person may put forward a name to be included on Thame or Moreton war memorial.
- A nomination should be made in the first instance to Thame Town Council, with full supporting evidence of eligibility.
- A panel of five councillors will be constituted, as the need arises, to consider the request and evaluate the evidence. If deemed necessary the panel may request further evidence or require independent verification of the evidence presented.
- The panel will make a recommendation to Council to either accept or reject the application.
- The final decision 'in principle' will be taken by the next Full Council in public session.
- How names may be added, how the additions should be funded and timing for implementation will be determined by the Council following approval and according to circumstances at the time.

Names put forward to be added to Thame War Memorial

Sapper George Alfred Bateman - Royal Engineers - d. 28 March 1918

Private John William Bowler - Coldstream Guards - d. 8 September 1917

Private William Chowns - Canadian Infantry - d. 10 November 1918

Driver Sackville "George" Crick - Australian Army Service Corps - d. 24 September 1915

Lieutenant Colonel George Alfred Edsell MD - Royal Army Medical Corps - d. 15 August 1915

Rifleman Sidney Stevens Edwards - London Regiment - d. 20 September 1917

Captain Richard John Philip Hewetson - Loyal North Lancashire Regiment - d. 3 July 1918

Gunner Harry Howland - Royal Garrison Artillery - d. 4 October 1917

Trooper William James Lewis- Household Battalion - d. 11 April 1917

Private Charles Roy Munckton Morris - Royal Fusiliers - d. 4 July 1917

Private William Newitt* - Canadian Infantry - d. 9 April 1917

Private George Asplin Pask - Middlesex Regiment - d. 21 March 1918

Sapper George Payne - Royal Engineers - d. 17 February 1919

Lance Corporal Reginald Phillips - Oxford and Bucks Light Infantry - d. 8 June 1917

Private Lewis Rhymes - Gloucestershire Regiment - d. 1 January 1915

Private Sidney Augustus Shrimpton* - Royal Fusiliers - d. 22 July 1916

Private Frederick Stopps* - Dragoon Guards - d. 28 October 1918

Boy 1st Class Frank Tickner - Royal Navy - d. 9 July 1917

Private Alfred Willis - Durham Light Infantry - d. 8 October 1918

Private Harry Cooper Wilsdon -Middlesex Regiment - d. 31 Aug 1916

Lance Sergeant Charles Frederick Bristow - Royal Engineers - d. 4 April 1942

Sub-Lieutenant Henry Bennett Cook - Royal Navy VR - d. 26 February 1943

Private William Freeman - Queen's Own Royal West Kent Regiment - d. 31 March 1943

Flying Officer Ernest George Thomas Harris - Royal Air Force - d. 10 March 1945

Private Ronald Frank Harris - Oxford and Bucks Light Infantry - d. 5 April 1945

Sergeant Alfred Thomas Heley* - Coldstream Guards - d. 16 April 1941

Guardsman Charles Stanley Kiddy - Grenadier Guards - d. 31 May 1940

Captain Sidney Charles Maskell-Dicker - Wiltshire Regiment - d. 24 July 1944

Sergeant Norman Kenneth Millard - Royal Air Force - d. 6 December 1942

Sergeant Ian Malcolm Keith Miller - Royal Air Force - d. 4 November 1940

Sergeant Herbert John Ody - Royal Air Force - d. 5 May 1942

Leading Aircraftman John Eric Jesse Phillips - Royal Air Force - d. 9 February 1946

Private Louis Herbert Plested* - Oxford and Bucks Light Infantry - d. 22 May 1940

Corporal Thomas John Tims - Oxford and Bucks Light Infantry - d. 8 July 1944

Warrant Officer Joseph Arthur Castle - Royal Engineers - d. 9 September 1957

*There was insufficient evidence against the criteria for the name to be added to the War Memorial, nevertheless they are still honoured with a Thame Remembers Cross.

Thame Servicemen of WW1

This list of names has been compiled mainly from the Absent Voters Register of October 1918. This was a Register of Electors who could not vote in their home town because they were away on active military service. The list is supplemented from names of "men in service" published in the Thame Gazette in May 1918 and from our own research. However, the Thame Gazette list was supplied by readers and therefore the details should be treated as very subjective.

The address given is the one which the man or his family have been most associated with and the unit is the one with which they served most or were with when they died.

The list contains 606 names, but if a person is not listed here then it does not mean that they did not serve, merely that the name is not recorded.

Private Albert John Adams; 22844, Royal Warwickshire Regiment 9th Btn; 3 Park Street	Survived
First Air Mechanic Arthur Adams; 235639, Royal Air Force; 21 North Street	Survived
Gunner William Charles Adams; 73260, Royal Garrison Artillery; Thame Park	Survived
Driver Ernest Edward Aldridge; 029815, Army Service Corps; 3 Queens Road	Survived
Private William Aldridge Jun; 53259, Royal Garrison Artillery; 3 Queens Road	Survived
Gunner Charles Alder Allen; 11878, Royal Artillery 156th Brigade; 45 High Street	Died of wounds
Private Sidney Allen; 263029, Northumberland Fusiliers 1st/5th Btn; 45 High Street	Killed in action
Gunner Thomas Allen; 135570, Royal Garrison Artillery; 10 Chinnor Road	Survived
Private Thomas Allen; 276232, Manchester Regiment; 49 Park Street	Survived
Lance Corporal Thomas Charles Allen; 574530, Grenadier Guards; 40 High Street	Survived
Driver William Allen; 75908, Royal Field Artillery; 10 Chinnor Road	Survived
Lance Corporal George Allnutt; Military Police; Moorend Lane	Survived
Private Horace Allnutt; 514699, London Regiment 1/14th Btn; Moorend Lane	Survived
Pioneer William John Arnold; 321749, Royal Engineers; Savernake 26 Nelson Street	Survived
Private Frederick Napoleon Attwell; 14980, Wiltshire Regiment 7th Btn; 9 Church Road	Survived
Private Thomas Charles Austin; 29117, Oxford & Bucks Light Infantry 7th Btn; 23 Park Street	Survived
Corporal Frank Edwin Bailey; 633347, London Regiment 20th Btn; 10 High Street	Survived
2nd Lieutenant Walter George Bailey DSO MC; 3rd Suffolk Regiment att. Norfolk Regt; 10 High Street	Survived
2nd Lieutenant William Charles Bailey MC; 4th Hussars; 10 High Street	Survived
Private Charles Baker; Army Service Corps; North Street	Survived
Sapper Walter Ernest Baldwin; 285629, Canadian Infantry 220th York Rangers; 82 Park Street	Survived
Private George Frederick Bance; 202320, Bedfordshire Regiment 2/5th Btn; Park Street	Survived
Corporal Arthur William Bateman; 9045, Army Veterinary Corps; 2 Towersey Road	Survived
Sapper George Alfred Bateman; 89239, Royal Engineers; 4 Prospect Place, 2 Towersey Road	Killed in action
Corporal Clifford Bert Bateman; 16008, Machine Gun Corps 48th Coy; 44 Wellington Street	Killed in action
Corporal George Henry Bates; S3/030272, Army Service Corps; 9 Chinnor Road	Survived
Corporal Leonard Bates; 153335, Royal Engineers Motor Cyclists; Park Grange Farm, Thame Park Road	Survived
Private Thomas Bates; 421123, Canadian Infantry 43rd Btn (Manitoba Regiment); 3 Bridge Terrace	Killed in action
Sapper Albert J Baverstock; 212859, Royal Engineers; Oatlands, Kings Road	Survived
Cadet Edgar William S Baverstock; Royal Air Force; Four Horse Shoes, 47 Park Street	Survived
Private Walter Reginald Baverstock; 200211, Oxford & Bucks Light Infantry; 26 Park Street	Survived
Private William Thomas Baverstock; 8423, Oxford & Bucks Light Infantry 1st Btn; 72 Park Street	Died of illness
Private Fred J Beamsley; 13973, Oxford & Bucks Light Infantry 7th Btn; Moreton	Survived
Driver William Joseph Beamsley; 7002, Royal Engineers; Moreton	Survived
Private Charles Benning; 6956, Army Veterinary Corps; 55 Park Street	Survived
Private Archibald Samuel Bird; S2746, Royal Navy Trg Reserve; 22 High Street	Survived
Colonel Henry Anthony Birrell-Anthony; Monmouthshire Regiment; Glenthorne, 28 High Street	Survived
2nd Lieutenant Henry Anthony Birrell-Anthony; Monmouthshire Regiment; 28 High Street	Killed in action
Sergeant Charles Blood; 13313, Royal Fusiliers; Bird Cage, 4 Cornmarket	Survived

Private Thomas Percival Blunt; 38476, Duke of Cornwall Light Infantry; 3 Upper High Street	Survived
Private Charles Boiling; 16826, Oxford & Bucks Light Infantry 7th Btn; 5 Chinnor Road	Died of illness
Private Edward William Boiling; 5609980, Devonshire Regiment 1st Btn; 5 Chinnor Road	Survived
Private Eric Leon Boiling; G/2220, East Kent Regiment 8th Btn; 46 Park Street	Killed in action
Sergeant William Boiling; 8911, Royal Berkshire Regiment 2/4th Btn; 40 Chinnor Road	Died of wounds
Gunner Christopher John Bowden; 64967, Royal Field Artillery; 9 Park Street	Survived
Seaman Fred Bowdery; L84, Royal Navy HMS Invincible; 37 Park Street	Survived
Lance Corporal George Bowdery; 17807, Royal Fusiliers 32nd Btn; 37 Park Street	Killed in action
Private Sidney William Bowdery; 21825, Oxford & Bucks Light Infantry 7th Btn; 37 Park Street	Survived
Driver Thomas John Bowdery; 20806, Royal Engineers; 37 Park Street	Survived
Sergeant George H Bowler; S2/018322, Army Service Corps; Park Street	Survived
Private John William Bowler; 17540, Coldstream Guards;	Killed in action
Corporal William Bowler; 8875, Oxford & Bucks Light Infantry 5th Btn; 30 Park Street	Died of wounds
Driver Albert Boyles; 199503, Royal Engineers; North Weston	Survived
Driver Charles Henry Bradbury; 65842, Royal Field Artillery; North Weston	Survived
Drummer Frederick George Bradbury; 33201, Essex Regiment 2nd Btn; North Weston	Survived
Private Harry Brandon; 523523, Oxford & Bucks Light Infantry; 62 Wellington Street	Survived
Driver Frederick Charles Brasher; 109497, Royal Field Artillery; 77 Park Street	Survived
Private Leonard Brazell; M2/138782, Army Service Corps; Bericote, Croft Road	Survived
Sergeant Arthur Jesse Briars; 200095, Oxford & Bucks Light Infantry 4th Btn; 69 Park Street	Survived
Air Mechanic Harold George White Briars; 6374, Royal Air Force; 69 Park Street	Survived
Corporal Hubert Alfred Briars; T/207962, Royal West Surrey Regiment; 69 Park Street	Survived
Trooper Algernon Sidney Briars; 285653, Queens Own Oxfordshire Hussars; 69 Park Street	Survived
Lance Corporal Sydney W Bristow; 24720, South Wales Borderers 4th Btn; Queens Road	Survived
Gunner Ernest Brown; 33720, Royal Garrison Artillery; Greyhound Inn, 44 North Street	Survived
Private Harold Brown; 72050, Northumberland Fusiliers; 83 Park Street	Survived
Corporal James Henry Brown; 285318, Royal Garrison Artillery; 83 Park Street	Survived
Corporal Joseph Brown; 200329, Oxford & Bucks Light Infantry 2nd/4th Btn; 2 Towersey Road	Killed in action
Lieutenant Reginald Loder Brown; Royal Naval Reserve HMS President; High Street	Survived
Private Sidney Sam Brown; 16656, Oxford & Bucks Light Infantry; 49 North Street	Survived
Private W S Brown; 3299, Royal Fusiliers 24th Btn; Towersey Road	Survived
2nd Lieutenant Frank Buckler; South Lancashire Regiment 2nd Btn; 74 Park Street	Survived
Corporal David John Burbridge; 4th Light Armoured Motor Brigade; 35 Upper High St	Died of illness
Private Stephen Burnard; 46134, Oxford & Bucks Light Infantry; Park Street	Survived
2nd Lieutenant Edward Coulston Bush; Manchester Regiment 1/8th Btn; 39 Upper High Street	Survived
Sergeant Frederick Howland Bush; 304900, Tank Corps; 39 Upper High Street	Survived
Driver Percy James Isaac Bush; 35637, Australian Field Artillery; 39 Upper High Street	Survived
Gunner Frederick Richard Cadwell; 821452, Royal Field Artillery; 4 Southern Road	Survived
Sergeant Henry Cadwell; S/2548, Royal Marines; Falcon 1 Thame Park Road	Survived
Private Richard Cadwell; 114778, Royal Army Medical Corps; 10 Southern Road	Survived
Private Edward Carter; 98506, Royal Berkshire Regiment 13th Btn; 43 Wellington Street	Survived
Able Seaman Francis Cartland; 366403, Royal Navy HMSub E49; Six Bells, 44 High Street	Died at sea
Gunner Victor Cartland; 31148, Royal Garrison Artillery; Six Bells, 44 High Street	Survived
Captain Arthur John Castle MM; Rifle Brigade; 131 High Street	Survived
Corporal Frederick Herbert Castle; 1641, Queens Own Oxfordshire Hussars.; 131 High Street	Survived
Driver James Lawrence Castle; South African VC; High Street	Reported to have died
Private Hubert H Cheeseman; 201995, Oxford & Bucks Light Infantry; Chinnor Road	Survived
Private Cuthbert F Cheney; 66447, Royal Army Medical Corps; Upper High Street	Survived
Gunner Edward V Cheney; 11690, Royal Field Artillery; Upper High Street	Survived
Corporal Henry J Cheney MM; 66448, Royal Army Medical Corps; Upper High Street	Survived
Private Jesse Thomas Cherry; 16862, Oxford & Bucks Light Infantry 7th Btn; Ashdene	Survived
Private William John Child; S2743, Royal Marines; 24 Park Street	Survived
Rifleman Frank Chowns; 4443, King's Royal Rifle Corps 2nd Btn; 50 High Street	Killed in action

Pioneer George Chowns; WR/26650, Royal Engineers; 6 Hampden Avenue	Died in an accident
Private William Chowns; 870, Oxford & Bucks Light Infantry; Wellington Street	Survived
Private William Chowns; 310782, Canadian Infantry 19 Btn; Moreton	Killed in action
Sergeant Alfred John Clarke; 625009, Royal Horse Artillery; 119 High Street	Survived
Sapper Archibald Percival Clarke; 153977, Royal Engineers; Nelson Street	Survived
Sergeant Harry Clarke; Oxford & Bucks Light Infantry; 17 Chinnor Road	Survived
Stoker John Clarke; S/111572, Royal Navy HMS Attentive; 37 Wellington Street	Survived
Sergeant Joseph C Clarke; 8/1015, Hampshire Regt Isle of Wight Rifles; High Street	Survived
Lieutenant Colonel Robert Joyce Clarke CMG DSO TD; Royal Berkshire Regiment; Croft Road	Survived
Stoker 1st Class Wilfred Harry Clarke; S/114908, Royal Navy HMS Formidable; 17 Chinnor Road	Died at sea
Private Francis George Clifton; M2/113433, Army Service Corps; 55 North Street	Survived
Private Albert Cobb; GS/24164, Royal Fusiliers; 21 Wellington Street	Survived
Shipwright Frederick Edwin Cook; Royal Navy HMS Galatea;	Survived
Driver William Edward Cook; 073116, Army Service Corps; 66 Park Street	Survived
Corporal Archibald Randolph Cooper; 08035, Army Ordnance Corps; 48 North Street	Survived
Private Sydney James Cope; 31057, Oxford & Bucks Light Infantry 3rd Btn; 87 Park Street	Survived
Private Alfred Ernest Cornish; 95521, Royal Berkshire Regiment; 6 Windmill Road	Survived
Private Frank Reginald Cornish; 34348, Northumberland Fusiliers 19th Btn; 6 Windmill Road	Survived
Trooper Frederick Cox; 285791, Queens Own Oxfordshire Hussars; Priestend	Survived
Private Frederick George Cox; 25622, Royal Warwickshire Regiment 5th Btn; 5 Park Terrace	Survived
Trooper William Cox; H/285253, Queens Own Oxfordshire Hussars; 5 Park Terrace	Survived
Private Percy Jack Cox; 437521, Canadian Infantry; Wellington Street	Survived
Private William John Cox; 67398, Worcestershire Regiment 6th Btn; Priest End Farm Priestend	Survived
Private Ernest Reginald Coxhill; 36835, Royal West Surrey Regiment; Lashlake 31 Aylesbury Road	Survived
Private Henry John Cozier; 8867, Oxford & Bucks Light Infantry 5th Btn; 5 North Street	Killed in action
Driver George Sackville Crick; 5046, Australian Army Service Corps 3rd Light Horse Bde; Moreton	Died of illness
Private Reginald Crisp; 2063, Oxford & Bucks Light Infantry; 12 Bell Lane	Survived
Private George Harry Thomas Crook; Oxford & Bucks Light Infantry 5th Btn; 8 Chinnor Road	Killed in action
Driver William Robert Crook; 680554, Royal Field Artillery; 8 Chinnor Road	Survived
Private Alfred Thomas Cross; 70422, Devonshire Regiment 2nd Btn; Moreton	Died of wounds
Private Frederick William Cross; 18915, Oxford & Bucks Light Infantry 2/4th Btn; Moreton	Killed in action
Lance Corporal Reginald Isaac Cross; 16617, Oxford & Bucks Light Infantry 5th Btn; Moreton	Killed in action
Private Sidney Cross; 270110, Royal East Kent Yeomanry 10th Btn; Moreton	Survived
Lance Corporal Ernest Cross; 18704, Oxford & Bucks Light Infantry 2/4th Btn; 5 Wellington Street	Survived
Driver Harry Cross; 65165, Royal Field Artillery; 17 Wellington Street	Survived
Private Wilfred Ernest Cubbage; 27787, Shropshire Light Infantry 7th Btn; 24 Queens Road	Survived
Lance Corporal Herbert Henry Cuell; 6228, Machine Gun Corps; 60 High Street	Survived
Chief Steward Albert Isaac Cumming; Merchant Navy HMHS Glenart Castle; 10 Wellington Street	Died at sea
Sergeant Charles Joseph Davis; 249752, Royal Engineers; Moreton	Survived
Gunner Reginald Dawe; 890726, Royal Field Artillery; 7 Queens Road	Survived
Private Sidney Dawe; 342354, Royal Engineers; 7 Queens Road	Survived
Corporal George Dawson; 17429, Oxford & Bucks Light Infantry 1st Btn; Thame Park	Survived
Rifleman Sidney Maskell Dicker; C/6803, King's Royal Rifle Corps 18th Btn; 46 Chinnor Road	Killed in action
Private William Diss; 111130, Royal Army Medical Corps; 29 Chinnor Road	Survived
Private Oliver William Dodwell; 9578, Army Veterinary Corps; 14 Cornmarket	Survived
Trooper Frederick William Dorsett; H/285244, Queens Own Oxfordshire Hussars; Priestend	Survived
Private Charles Owen Dover; 48563, Hampshire Regiment; Rising Sun 27 High Street	Survived
Gunner Horace Charles Dover; 73194, Royal Garrison Artillery; 1 Southern Road	Survived
Private Stanley David Victor Dover; 27221, Oxford & Bucks Light Infantry 5th Btn; 27 High Street	Killed in action
Air Mechanic William Ernest Dover; 123405, Royal Air Force; 41 Chinnor Road	Survived
Sergeant William Spencer Drake; 6776, Oxford & Bucks Light Infantry 2nd Btn; 28 Park Street	Killed in action
Private William Clint Duff; 2006, Royal Marines; Kings Road	Survived
Private Ernest Dunstall; 272381, Army Service Corps; 19 Wellington Street	Survived

Private Wallace Adrian Durston; M2/135647, Army Service Corps; Aylesbury Road	Survived
Private Herbert East; 236488, Royal Gloucester Hussars 1st Btn; Queens Villa 31 Chinnor Road	Survived
Private Cecil Walter Cherry Eaton; 34219, Oxford & Bucks Light Infantry 3/4th Btn; 73 High Street	Survived
Private Charles Eaton; 392163, Labour Corps; 41 Park Street	Survived
Private Herbert Edward Eaton; 178313, Royal Field Artillery; 73 High Street	Survived
Private Ralph Eaton; 1893, Oxford & Bucks Light Infantry 1st/4th Btn; 41 Park Street	Killed in action
Lance Corporal William Eaton; 13967, Oxford & Bucks Light Infantry 3rd Btn; 41 Park Street	Survived
Lieutenant Francis George Eckford; Royal Air Force; Gardens Thame Park	Survived
Captain Arthur Reginald Kepp Edsell; East Surrey Regiment; 78 High Street	Survived
Lieutenant Eric Valentine Edsell; East Surrey Regiment; 78 High Street	Survived
Lieutenant Colonel George Alfred Edsell MD; Royal Army Medical Corps; 78 High Street	Died of illness
Captain George Lynton Edsell; Hampshire Regiment; 78 High Street	Survived
Private Aubrey Reginald Edwards; 38857, Oxford & Bucks Light Infantry 7th Btn; 14 Chinnor Road	Survived
Rifleman Sidney Stevens Edwards; 301371, London Regiment 5th Btn; Bird Cage 4 Cornmarket	Killed in action
Air Mechanic Frank William Eele; 267621, Royal Air Force; The Bungalow Croft Road	Survived
Private Harry Eele; 164282, Machine Gun Corps Ex Wiltshire Regt 5th Btn; Moorend Lane	Died of illness
Private Henry George Eele; 18491, Royal Warwickshire Regiment 9th Btn; 2 Park Street	Survived
Private Jim Eele; 202341, Oxford & Bucks Light Infantry 2/4th Btn; 15 North Street	Survived
Private Robert Eele; 333016, Oxford & Bucks Light Infantry; 62 Wellington Street	Survived
Driver George William Eggleton jun; 59838, Royal Field Artillery; 11 Moorend Lane	Survived
Corporal Gilbert Victor Eggleton; 157155, Queens Royal West Surrey Regiment; 3 Moorend Lane	Survived
Private Sydney Charles Eggleton; 28186, Oxford & Bucks Light Infantry; 30 High Street	Survived
Sapper Cecil Charles Elbourn; 191679, Royal Engineers; 33 Chinnor Road	Survived
Private Frank Evans; 13768, Oxford & Bucks Light Infantry; Prospect Place 3 Towersey Road	Survived
Sapper Frederick John Evans; Royal Engineers; 3 Towersey Road	Survived
Private Frederick Richard Evans; 25199, Army Veterinary Corps; 4 Windmill Road	Survived
Lieutenant Stephen Ian Fairbairn; Royal Horse Guards; Thame Park House Thame Park	Survived
Lieutenant S G Fairbairn; Grenadier Guards; Thame Park House Thame Park	Survived
Lieutenant Evelyn Dalrymple Fanshaw; Royal Air Force; 13 Upper High Street	Survived
2nd Lieutenant George Hew Fanshaw; 19th Royal Hussars; 13 Upper High Street	Survived
Lieutenant General Hew Dalrymple Fanshaw KCB KCMG; 10th Division; 13 Upper High Street	Survived
Trooper Reginald George Farmbrough; Queens Own Oxfordshire Hsrs; Lobbersdown Farm	Died of wounds
Sergeant Benjamin Field; 3767, Army Veterinary Corps; 4 Chinnor Road	Survived
2nd Lieutenant Francis Willoughby Fielding; London Regiment 9th Btn; Stoneleigh, Kings Road	Killed in action
Private Albert Finch; 46550, Worcestershire Regiment 16th Btn; Kings Road	Survived
Private Francis Gale Fleet; 349470, Army Service Corps; 10 Upper High Street	Survived
Private William Fleming; M2/187211, Army Service Corps; 2 Bell Lane	Survived
Rifleman Harry Fothergill; 13257, Rifle Brigade; 9a Southern Road	Survived
Corporal Frank Fowler; DM2/189466, Army Service Corps; 20 Park Street	Survived
Private William Fowler; 200327, Oxford & Bucks Light Infantry; 20 Park Street	Survived
Private George Edwin Fuller; 52234, Labour Corps; 19 High Street	Survived
Lieutenant James Newlyn Gale; Royal Army Medical Corps; Greysmead, Thame Park Road	Survived
Corporal Wilfred Reginald George; 500268, Royal Engineers motor cyclist; 23 Cornmarket	Survived
Private Sidney Ginger; 7781, North Staffordshire Regiment 1st Btn; High Street	Survived
Private Dick Goodson; 27095, Oxford & Bucks Light Infantry; North Street	Survived
Private Herbert Grace; 52202, Worcestershire Regiment 1st Btn; 76 Park Street	Survived
Private Henry Albert Grace; 135005, Army Service Corps; Moreton	Survived
Sergeant Albert Green; 4/18A, New Zealand Contingent; 20 Chinnor Road	Survived
Driver Albert Henry Green; 40413, Canadian Artillery;	Killed in action
Sergeant Charles William Green; 12932, Oxford & Bucks Light Infantry 7th Btn; 14 Chinnor Road	Survived
Private George Greenwood; Royal Defence Corps; 75 High Street	Survived
Lieutenant Colonel Harman Grizewood; Sussex Regiment; Prebendal, Long Crendon Road	Survived
Gunner George Harry Guest; Royal Garrison Artillery; 12 Church Road	Survived

Sapper Joseph Robert Guntrip; 134629, Royal Engineers; 14 North Street	Survived
Bombardier William Stephen Guntrip; 67981, Royal Field Artillery; Sun Yard, 108 High Street	Survived
Able Seaman Frederick George Beames Hake; 230875, Royal Navy HMS Black Prince; Park Street	Died at sea
Private George Harber; 114090, Canadian Mounted Rifles 9th Regt; Priestend	Survived
Private Ernest Harbour; 13989, Royal Warwickshire Regiment 1st Btn; Priestend	Survived
Captain James Augustus Harmer; Army Veterinary Corps; Croft Road	Survived
Private Arthur James Harris; 3766, Army Veterinary Corps; 16 Park Street	Survived
Sergeant Frank Harris; 40415, Seaforth Highlanders; Police Station Chinnor Road	Survived
Able Seaman Thomas Henry Harris; J47615, Royal Navy HMS Mersey; Park Street	Survived
Sapper Walter Harwood; 89484, Royal Engineers; 4 Queens Road	Survived
Gunner Ernest Robert Hawes; 292687, Royal Field Artillery; 58 Wellington Street	Survived
Corporal Herbert James Hawes; 2744, Army Service Corps; 45 Wellington Street	Survived
Private Charles Hawkes; M2/073118, Army Service Corps; 16 Chinnor Road	Survived
Private Joseph Hawkes; 7430, Oxford & Bucks Light Infantry 2nd Btn; 79 Park Street	Survived
Sergeant Henry John Hawkins; Devonshire Regiment; 5 Bell Lane	Survived
Private Henry William Hawkins; 201915, Wiltshire Regiment 3rd Btn; 5 Bell Lane	Survived PoW
Private William Hawthorne; 31478, Oxford & Bucks Light Infantry; North Weston	Survived
Private Harry Hearne; 241734, Gloucestershire Regiment 9th Btn; 74 High Street	Survived
Sapper Albert C Hedges; 486440, Royal Engineers; 11 Chinnor Road	Survived
Driver Gordon R Hedges; Royal Engineers; 11 Chinnor Road	Survived
Private Algernon Evelyn Hemmings; 7446, Dorset Regiment 1st Btn; 5 Windmill Road	Died of wounds
Private Percy Giles Hester; 206156, Hampshire Regiment; 111 High Street	Survived
Private Raymond W Hester; 3854, London Regiment 18th Btn London Irish Rifles; 111 High Street	Survived
2nd Lieutenant Richard Tuckey Hewer; Berkshire Yeomanry 1st Btn; Park Street	Killed in action
Captain Richard John Philip Hewetson; Loyal N Lancs Regiment 3rd Btn; Vicarage, Crendon Rd	Died of wounds
Gunner H Hewitt; Royal Field Artillery; Park Street	Survived
Private Edwin Albert Hicks; Army Veterinary Corps; Croft Road	Survived
Private Albert Victor Higgins; 51099, Cheshire Regiment 1st/6th Btn; 51 North Street	Killed in action
Leading Signalman Charles Claude Higgins MM; J10417, Royal Navy HMS Attentive II; 51 North Street	Survived
Private William Higgins; 486106, Royal Horse Artillery; 51 North Street	Survived
Sergeant Aubrey Charles Higgins; 315262, Royal Hussars 13th Btn; Belle Vue, Moreton	Survived
Lance Corporal George Higgins; 7960, Oxford & Bucks Light Infantry 6th Btn; Moreton	Survived
Private Henry Robert Higgins; 16651, Norfolk Regiment 3rd Btn; 5 Southern Road	Died of illness
Corporal Charles Victor Hill; Queens Own Oxfordshire Hussars; Kings Road	Survived
Quarter Master Sergeant John Hill; 8780, Oxford & Bucks Light Infantry 8th Btn; Kings Road	Survived
Sapper Leo Hilliard; 291453, Royal Engineers; 81 Park Street	Survived
Private Thomas Joe Hinder; 5759, Oxford & Bucks Light Infantry; 62 Wellington Street	Survived
Private Leonard Hobbs; 14404, Wiltshire Regiment 7th Btn; Ivy Cottage North Street	Survived
Sergeant Charles Hodges; 240530, Middlesex Regiment 2/8th Btn; 33 Chinnor Road	Survived
Gunner Victor Vivian Hodges; 915925, Royal Field Artillery; Shirley, Kings Road	Survived
Private Sydney Holland; 15587, Army Veterinary Corps; 38 Upper High Street	Survived
Private William Holland; Army Service Corps; 38 Upper High Street	Survived
Private William Honour; TS/3580, Army Service Corps; 55 High Street	Died of illness
Private Francis Hopkins; 14405, Wiltshire Regiment; Wellington Street	Killed in action
Private Frederick W Hopkins; 17672, Royal Warwickshire Regiment; Wellington Street	Survived
Lance Corporal Frederick William Hopkins; 14728, Royal Army Medical Corps; Croft Villa, Queens Road	Survived
Corporal Ernest Edward House; 47311, Canadian Infantry; 14 Chinnor Road	Killed in action
Corporal William Frederick House; M2/080244, Army Service Corps; 3 Queens Villas, 1 Chinnor Road	Survived
Private Albert Victor Howes; 12136, Oxford & Bucks Light Infantry; Moreton	Survived
Private Alfred John Walter Howes; 8434, Oxford & Bucks Light Infantry 1st Btn; Moreton	Killed in action
Private Frank Howes; 85873, Machine Gun Corps 39th; Bates Leys Moreton	Survived
Private Frederick George Howes; 8537, Oxford & Bucks Light Infantry 6th Btn; Bates Leys, Moreton	Survived
Private Frederick Howes; 245295, Labour Corps; Moreton	Survived
Private Frederick George Howes; SS/2309, Labour Corps; Priestend	Survived

Private Harry Howes; 19902, Machine Gun Corps 4th; Priestend	Survived
Corporal Herbert Howes; 18284, Oxford & Bucks Light Infantry 1st Btn; 7 Priestend	Survived
Air Mechanic Horace James Howes; 232, Royal Air Force; Laburnam Cottages Moreton	Survived
Private Percy Howes; 445912, Royal Sussex Regimen; Moreton	Survived
Private Reginald Howes; 11354, Oxford & Bucks Light Infantry 6th Btn; Moreton	Survived
Private William Howes; 63034, Royal Warwickshire Regiment 51st Btn; Moreton	Survived
Lance Corporal William Howes; 200349, Oxford & Bucks Light Infantry 4th Btn; 7 Priestend	Survived
Lance Corporal Albert Victor Howland; 630074, London Regiment 2/20th Btn; 18 Wellington Street	Survived
Sergeant Alfred Robert Howland; 8701, Royal Fusiliers 1st Btn; 18 Wellington Street	Died of wounds
Private George E Howland; Royal Defence Corps; 18 Wellington Street	Survived
Private Harry Howland; 15604, Army Veterinary Corps; 18 Wellington Street	Survived
Private Percy Howland; 24984, Oxford & Bucks Light Infantry; 18 Wellington Street	Survived
Lance Corporal Robert Henry Howland; London Regiment; 18 Wellington Street	Survived
Gunner Thomas G Howland; 127166, Royal Field Artillery; 18 Wellington Street	Survived
Sergeant William Christopher Howland; 292667, Royal Garrison Artillery; 18 Wellington Street	Survived
Bugler Arthur Robert Howland; 200228, Oxford & Bucks Light Inf 6th Btn; 23 Queens Road	Killed in action
Sergeant Harry Howland; Machine Gun Corps; 23 Queens Road	Survived
Air Mechanic Leslie Herbert Howland; 210592, Royal Air Force; 23 Queens Road	Survived
Private William Howland; Canadian Infantry 63 Btn; 23 Queens Road	Survived
Lance Corporal Frederick Griffin Howland; Royal Berkshire Regiment 2/4th Btn; 37 Queens Road	Survived
Private Harry H Howland; 18903, Canadian Infantry 7th Btn; 37 Queens Road	Survived PoW
Private Sydney James Howland; A/211503, Australian Infantry; Hazlemere, 37 Queens Road	Survived
Private Thomas Howland; 2015386, Canadian Infantry; Hazlemere, 37 Queens Road	Survived
Private George Howland; 49260, Labour Corps; 10 Chinnor Road	Survived
Gunner Harry Howland; 111402, Royal Garrison Artillery; 50 High Street	Killed in action
Sergeant Harry Howland; 30566, Leicestershire Regiment; 58 Park Street	Survived
Quarter Master Sergeant Charles Hubert Howlett; 28811, Royal Garrison Artillery; 1 High Street	Killed in action
Driver Dan Howlett; M2/047360, Army Service Corps; North Street	Survived
Private Frederick Howlett; S/2696, Royal Marines 63rd Btn; 51 Park Street	Survived
Private George Howlett; 790, Royal Engineers; Park Street	Survived
Corporal John Howlett DCM; 16774, Royal Engineers 9th Field Coy; 15 Park Street	Died of wounds
Private Sam Howlett; 18577, Royal Berkshire Regiment 8th Btn; North Street	Died of wounds
Private William Howlett; 503443, Worcestershire Regiment; 3 Wellington Street	Survived
Private Mark Hudson; Army Service Corps; Towersey Road	Survived
Corporal William Charles Humphris; 3447, Queens Own Oxfordshire Hussars; 24 Upper High Street	Survived
Private Frederick Hunt; 260100, Royal Garrison Artillery; Queens Road	Survived
Private Herbert T Ibell; 72867, Royal Army Medical Corps; East Street	Survived
Sergeant Major George Jakeman DCM; 3327, Royal Field Artillery; 53 Park Street	Survived
Private Edward William James; 17525, Oxford & Bucks Light Infantry 6th Btn; 63 High Street	Killed in action
Private Edward Janes; 038600, Army Ordnance Corps; 8 Cornmarket	Survived
Private Francis William Jeffs; 204961, London Regiment 9th Btn; Lubbersdown Hill, North Weston	Survived
Private Harry Johnson; 258113, Oxford & Bucks Light Infantry; 44 North Street	Survived
Corporal Walter James Johnson; S/2694, Royal Marines; 39 Park Street	Survived
Private Arthur Charles Jones; 866, Army Service Corps; Moreton	Survived
Lieutenant Frank Gwyther Jones; Royal Air Force; Brook Cottage, Moreton	Survived
Lance Corporal Reginald Jones; 14021, Oxford & Bucks Light Infantry 7th Btn; 68 Park Street	Survived
Sergeant Arthur Thomas Jones MM; 12133, Oxford & Bucks Light Infantry; North Weston	Survived
Private John William Judge; Army Service Corps; Wellington Street	Survived
Private William Richard Judge; 342264, Labour Corps; 59 Wellington Street	Survived
Able Seaman Fred Keene; L/2470, Royal Navy HMS Pathfinder; 53 Park Street	Died at sea
Private Jack Archer Keene; 200330, Oxford & Bucks Light Infantry 1st/4th Btn; 53 Park Street	Killed in action
Leading Signaller Percy Frank Keene; J10915, Royal Navy HMS Mischief; 53 Park Street	Survived
Private Thomas James Kentish; 110550, Royal Army Medical Corps; Saracens Head, 118 Buttermarket	Survived

Lance Corporal Ralph Kilby; 6878, Royal Marines; Moorend Lane	Survived
Pioneer James Wheeler King; 119329, Royal Engineers; 13 East Street	Survived
Private William Kirtland; 206087, Oxford & Bucks Light Infantry; Chinnor Road	Survived PoW
Private Alfred Edward Ladbrook; 224032, 48th Div H Q Staff; 1 Park Terrace	Survived
Private Frederick William Ladbrook; 141829, Machine Gun Corps; 1 Park Terrace	Survived
Private George Edmund Ladbrook; 37367, Gloucestershire Regiment 8th Btn; 1 Park Terrace	Killed in action
Sapper John Ladbrook; WR272349, Royal Engineers; 1 Park Terrace	Survived
Private William Ladbrook; 92371, Tank Corps; 1 Park Terrace	Survived
Private Herbert Lammas; 15793, Royal Field Artillery; East Street	Survived
Private Cyril Leslie Henry Lane; S4/058834, Army Service Corps; 76 High Street	Survived
Gunner Reginald Sidney George Lane; 322968, Royal Garrison Artillery; 76 High Street	Survived
Private Edward Aubrey Lane; 41423, Middlesex Regiment 18th Btn; Rooks Place, High Street	Killed in action
Private Arthur Paxton Lawrence; 34478, Somerset Light Infantry 1st Btn; 21 Wellington Street	Survived
Captain Ronald Outram Lee; Royal Army Medical Corps; The Hollies 37 Upper High Street	Survived
Sergeant Alfred William Lemmings MM; 200229, Oxford & Bucks Light Infantry 4th Btn; 43 Park Street	Survived
Private George Ewart Lemmings; 200203, Oxford & Bucks Light Infantry 4th Btn; 43 Park Street	Survived
Private Henry Cooper Lemmings; 9987, Northamptonshire Regiment 5th Btn; 43 Park Street	Survived
Private Reginald Anthony Lemmings; 265595, Middlesex Regiment 1/9th Btn; 43 Park Street	Survived
Private Thomas Lemmings; 36211, Royal Berkshire Regiment 5th Btn; 13 East Street	Survived PoW
Private Fred Lester; Oxford & Bucks Light Infantry; 10 Church Road	Survived
Private George Lester; 135288, Canadian Infantry; 10 Church Road	Survived
Sapper James Lester; 270815, Royal Engineers; 49 Park Street	Survived
Private William John Lester; 67609, Royal Field Artillery; 10 Church Road	Survived
Major Brighton Webster Lidington TD; Royal Marines; Spread Eagle 16 Cornmarket	Survived
Private Douglas Viney Lidington; 16335, Norfolk Regiment 9th Btn; Spread Eagle 16 Cornmarket	Killed in action
Captain William Richard Lidington; Royal Marines; Spread Eagle 16 Cornmarket	Survived
Private Horace Jack Lindars; 23350, Essex Regiment; Gas Alley East Street	Survived
Private William Linden; PW/5269, Middlesex Regiment 26th Btn;	Survived
Corporal Ralph Line; 285209, Queens Own Oxfordshire Hussars; 24 Upper High Street	Killed in action
Private Richard Line; 14432, Wiltshire Regiment; High Street	Killed in action
Sergeant William Lines; 5758, Army Veterinary Corps; 84 High Street	Survived
Bombardier Frank Lines; 29736, Royal Garrison Artillery; 84 High Street	Survived
Private Frank Howard Loader; 82771, Royal Defence Corps; Malvern Chinnor Road	Survived
Captain Graham Chard Loader; Hampshire Regiment; 18 Cornmarket	Killed in action
Private Harry Loader; 123126, Machine Gun Corps; 2 North Street	Survived
Private Ernest Walter Lock; 43758, Royal Army Service Corps; 1 Church Road	Survived
Sergeant Albert Loosley; 8236, Oxford & Bucks Light Infantry; 2 Bridge Terrace	Survived
Private William Robert Loosley; 12843, Grenadier Guards 2nd Btn; 2 Bridge Terrace	Killed in action
Sapper Job Loosley; 139747, Royal Engineers; 7 Wellington Street	Survived
Trooper Joseph Lovejoy; 285091, Queens Own Oxfordshire Hussars 3rd Coy; 41 North Street	Killed in action
Sub Lieutenant William Henry Lowndes; Royal Navy HMS Crescent; 2 High Street	Survived
Private Charles G Mabbett; S4/070831, Army Service Corps; Chinnor Road	Survived
Private Frank Malin; 138743, Machine Gun Corps 8th; Moreton	Survived
Private Reginald Rupert Malin; 14440, Wiltshire Regiment 7th Btn; Moreton	Survived
Lance Corporal Richard Malin; 100462, Oxford & Bucks Lght Infantry; Moreton	Survived
Driver Thomas White Malin; 297366, Royal Garrison Artillery; Moreton	Survived
Sergeant Roderick Wallis Dolery Martin; 2017, Royal Air Force; 1 Cornmarket	Survived
Driver Aubery Ernest Matthews; 292688, Royal Garrison Artillery; 32 East Street	Survived
Private Harry Maunder; 940, Australian Army; 28 East Street	Survived
Cooks Mate Oswald May; M/21679, Royal Navy; 8 Park Street	Survived
Private Sidney May; 204384, Royal Garrison Artillery; 8 Park Street	Survived
Lieutenant John Arthur Mears; East Surrey Regiment; Oakleigh Kings Road	Survived
Lieutenant Sidney Tripp Mears; Devonshire Regiment 2nd Btn; Oakleigh Kings Road	Survived
Gunner Walter Charles Mellett; 179227, Royal Field Artillery; 2 Cornmarket	Survived
Private George A Mentor; 38155, Welsh Fusiliers 9th Btn; Windmill Road	Survived

Private Albert Merriman; 1787, Oxford & Bucks Light Infantry 8th Btn; 3 Chinnor Road	Survived
Private Alfred James Merriman; TS/4, Army Service Corps; 3 Chinnor Road	Survived
Private George Merriman; 457659, Labour Corps (ex Oxford & Bucks LI); 3 Chinnor Road	Survived
Lance Corporal Harry Merriman DCM; 200212, Oxford & Bucks Light Infantry 1st Bucks Btn; 3 Chinnor Rd	Survived
Private Fred John Messenger; 13971, Oxford & Bucks Light Infantry 7th Btn; 4 Park Terrace	Survived
Air Mechanic W Millard; 121064, Royal Air Force; 109 High Street	Survived
Private Cyril Edward Millard; 74193, Royal Army Medical Corps; 109 High Street	Survived
Private William Miller; 36608, West Somerset Yeomanry; Post Office High Street	Survived
Sapper George Miller; 65336, Royal Engineers 126th Field Coy; Lashlake Aylesbury Road	Killed in action
Rifleman Harry William Mitchell; 1933, London Regiment 8th Btn; 59 High Street	Survived PoW
2nd Lieutenant Frank Broadis Mitchell MC; Oxford & Bucks Light Infantry; 59 High Street	Survived
Private Harold Victor Henry Moreton; 353230, London Regiment 1/19th Btn; 127 High Street	Survived
Private H L Morgan; Welsh Guards; Thame Park	Survived
Stoker James Morgan; S111690, Royal Navy HMS Actaeon; 17 North Street	Survived
Second Lieutenant Cyril G M Morris; Royal Berkshire Regiment 9th Btn; High Street	Survived
Private Frederick Edwin Mott; 103299, Royal Army Medical Corps; Elmfield Moreton	Survived
Air Mechanic Edgar Ewart Mott; 13186, Royal Air Force; Elmfield Moreton	Survived
Private Charles Hubert Mott; 146374, Machine Gun Corps; Elmfield Moreton	Survived
Sapper Bertram Issac Mott; 64475, Royal Engineers; Elmfield Moreton	Survived
Sapper Arthur Edward Mott; 262945, Royal Engineers; Elmfield Moreton	Survived
Private Geoffrey Frank Mott; 331666, Canadian Field Artillery; 5 High Street	Survived
Private Wallace Raymond Mott; 696699, Canadian Infantry;	Survived
Private M Mumford; Grenadier Guards; Thame Park	Survived
Private A J Munday; 1616, Oxford & Bucks Light Infantry; High Street	Survived
Private Harry Walker Nelms; 37323, Royal Defence Corps; 14 Park Street	Survived
Lance Corporal Herbert Edward Newitt; 156625, Army Service Corps; 21 High Street	Survived
Driver Edward Newitt; T2/SR/02382, Army Service Corps; 29 High Street	Survived
Driver Henry Newitt; 85487, Royal Engineers; 9a North Street	Survived
Stoker Joseph Newitt; SS10546, Royal Navy HMS Mistletoe; 9a North Street	Survived
Sapper Jack Newitt; 58636, Royal Engineers; 9a North Street	Survived
Private Robert Newitt; 45120, Royal Inniskilling Fusiliers; 9a North Street	Survived
Private Charles Newitt; 14309, Army Veterinary Corps; 34 North Street	Survived
Private George Wilfrid Newitt; 17937, Royal Marines HMS Revenge; 34 North Street	Survived
Private Henry Charles Newitt; 51487, Machine Gun Corps; 34 North Street	Survived
Aircraftsman Harold Newman; 217494, Royal Air Force; Essex House 149 Chinnor Road	Survived
Aircraftsman Frank Newman; 217503, Royal Air Force; Essex House 149 Chinnor Road	Survived
Private Henry Thomas North; 452573, Canadian Infantry; Church Road	Survived
Private William John North ; 12125, Oxford & Bucks Light Infantry; Moreton Cottages Moreton	Survived
Private J North; London Territorials; Park Street	Survived
Stoker 1st Class Frederick James North; 312071, Royal Navy HMS Formidable; 11 Church Road	Died at sea
Private William North sen; Royal Defence Corps; Moreton	Survived
Private George Victor North; 18192, Oxford & Bucks Light Infantry; Moreton Cottages Moreton	Survived
Private John Olieff; 220080, Royal Berkshire Regiment 2nd Btn; 5 Southern Road	Killed in action
Private George Olieff; 122654, Royal Army Medical Corps; 5 Southern Road	Survived
Air Mechanic Percy Oliver; 211189, Royal Air Force; Tythrop Terrace 35 Wellington Street	Survived
Private Harry William Oliver; G/20154, Royal West Kent Regiment 1st Btn; 38 Park Street	Killed in action
Gunner Frederick Oliver; 261668, Royal Field Artillery; 50 Chinnor Road	Survived
Lance Corporal Sidney Fred Oliver; P5525, Military Mounted Police Regt; Park Street	Survived
Private Albert James Oliver; M2/119699, Army Service Corps; 38 Park Street	Survived
Corporal William H Osbourne; 1668, Royal Warwickshire Regiment; Queens Road	Survived
Lieutenant Rodney Arthur Ostrehan; Loyal N Lancashire Regiment 4th Btn; Bank House 13 Cornmarket	Survived
Lieutenant Duncan H Ostrehan; Loyal N Lancashire Regiment 4th Btn; Bank Hse 13 Cornmarket	Killed in action
Sergeant Albert Edward Outing; H/29395, 19th Hussars (Queen Alexandras Own); Aylesbury Road	Died of illness

Private J A Page; High Street	Survived
Driver A B Page; Royal Engineers; High Street	Survived
Private C Painter; 1568, Oxford & Bucks Light Infantry; East Street	Survived
Sergeant Sidney Thomas Parker; 8508, Oxford & Bucks Light Infantry 2nd Btn; Priestend	Killed in action
Driver Frederick John Parsler; 102008, Army Service Corps; Moorend Lane	Survived
Gunner Herbert Parsler; 495491, Royal Field Artillery; Moorend Lane	Survived
Pioneer James Parsler; 337267, Royal Engineers; 8 Southern Road	Survived
Sergeant John William Parsler; 01010, Army Ordnance Corps; 11 East Street	Survived
Private Charles Payne; 37920, Bedfordshire Regiment 3rd Btn; 4 Church Road	Survived
Private Henry Anthony Payne; 13771, Royal Marines; 58 High Street	Survived
Sapper George Payne; 97429, Royal Engineers; 14 Church Road	Died of illness
Private Walter James Payne; 2288535, Canadian Infantry; 4 Church Road	Survived
Gunner Frank Lewis Peach; 301108, Royal Garrison Artillery; 4 North Street	Survived
Trooper Eric C Pearce; 1571, Queens Own Oxfordshire Hussars; Laurels High Street	Survived
Gunner Reginald Pearce; 700280, Royal Garrison Artillery; 33 High Street	Survived
Private Ronald Pearce; 104121, Labour Corps; Highfield Oxford Road	Survived
Air Mechanic Walter Harold Pearce; 208516, Royal Air Force; 115 High Street	Survived
Private P Pearman; 14497, Oxford & Bucks Light Infantry; Park Street	Survived
Sapper George Stratford Randal Peddle; 152547, Royal Engineers; 132 High Street	Survived
Lance Corporal Charles William Phillips; 67831, Royal Field Artillery; 2 Park Terrace	Survived
Driver Christopher Phillips; 291286, Army Service Corps; 33 North Street	Survived
Private Ernest James Phillips; 202231, Bedfordshire Regiment 11th Btn; 46 High Street	Survived
Trooper Frederick Phillips; H/285256, Queens Own Oxfordshire Hussars; 12 Bell Lane	Survived
Private Harry Phillips; 3768, Army Veterinary Corps; 36 North Street	Survived
Driver John Phillips; 38173, Royal Field Artillery; 4 Bell Lane	Survived
Lance Corporal Reginald Phillips; 265866, Oxford & Bucks Light Infantry; 3 Park Terrace	Killed in action
Quarter Master Sergeant Edmund John Pitkin; 20293, Royal Artillery; 28 Chinnor Road	Survived
Gunner Thomas Henry Pitkin; 61320, Royal Horse Artillery; 28 Chinnor Road	Survived
Private Harry Plater; DM2/075168, Army Service Corps; 6 Towersey Road	Survived
Private Herbert Plater; 16682, Canadian Infantry; 6 Towersey Road	Survived
Gunner John Plunkett; 282376, Royal Garrison Artillery; Red Cow 3 Aylesbury Road	Survived
Private Harry John Pocock; 4048328, Canadian Infantry 1st Btn; Moreton	Survived
Private William Henry Pollicott; 220531, Army Service Corps; Moorend Lane	Survived
Lieutenant Ernest Marlin Potter MC; Royal Marines HMS Victory; 3 High Street	Survived
Sgt Jack Potter; Queens Own Oxfordshire Hussars; 3 High Street	Survived
Private Frederick Price; 420464, Army Service Corps; 3 Bell Lane	Survived
Bombardier Frederick Price; 64601, Royal Artillery 116th Bty; 8 Church Road	Died of wounds
Private George Price; 59225, Devonshire Regiment; Moorend Lane	Survived
Private Harry Price; 16303, Hampshire Regiment 1st Btn; 7 Windmill Road	Killed in action
Corporal Jack Price; 3405, Oxford & Bucks Light Infantry; 27 East Street	Survived
Seaman Jack Price; J86474, Royal Navy HMS Powerful; 3 Bell Lane	Survived
Stoker Philip Price; S104936, Royal Navy HMS Doris; Moorend Lane	Survived
Stoker William Price; K358, Royal Navy HMS Ark Royal; 8 Church Road	Survived
Private Frederick James Probets; 814948, Canadian Infantry; 39 High Street	Survived
Private Thomas William Probets; Army Service Corps; 13 East Street	Survived
Private Charles Probets; 45335, Oxford & Bucks Light Infantry; Gas Alley East Street	Survived
Private Frederick Probets; 27224, Oxford & Bucks Light Infantry; Gas Alley East Street	Survived
Corporal Harold George Pryce; 013358, Army Ordnance Corps; 108 High Street	Survived
Rifleman Harold Frederick Pullen; 68082, Kings Royal Rifle Corps; Moreton Cottages Moreton	Survived
Rifleman Roland Arthur Pullen; P/1573, Rifle Brigade 16th Btn; Moreton	Died of wounds
Private Bertram W J Purcell; S/2725, Royal Marines; Nelson Street	Survived
Rifleman Hedley Morewood Purser; 41052, Rifle Brigade 11th Btn; 102 High Street	Survived
Gunner Frederick Henry Rawlings; 301258, Royal Garrison Artillery; 13 Bell Lane	Survived
Private Frank Reading; 25828, Royal West Surrey Regiment 10th Btn; 5 Towersey Road	Survived

Private Lewis Rhymes; 7657, Gloucestershire Regiment 1st Btn; Police Station Thame Park Road	Died of wounds
Private E Richardson; Royal Field Artillery; East Street	Survived
Farrier Edwin Richardson; 5905, Army Service Corps; Nelson Street	Survived
Gunner Herbert Richardson; 156617, Royal Artillery; 5 East Street	Killed in action
Private Elisha George Roberts; 466801, Labour Corps; The Castle Thame Park	Survived
Private F Roberts; Army Service Corps; Chinnor Road	Survived
Private George William Roberts; M2/102723, Army Service Corps; 27 Chinnor Road	Survived
Corporal Stephen James Roberts; 29507, Royal Garrison Artillery; 8 Chinnor Road	Killed in action
Sergeant William Edward Roberts; 1498, Queens Own Oxfordshire Hussars; 99 High Street	Died of wounds
Trooper Frank Robinson; 29753, Queens Own Oxfordshire Hussars; 63 Park Street	Survived
Lieutenant James Thomas Robinson; Oxford & Bucks Light Infantry; Bushmead Nelson Street	Survived
Sapper Francis Roe; 55012, Royal Engineers; 4 Bridge Terrace	Survived
Private Arthur Rush; 8866, Oxford & Bucks Light Infantry 2nd Btn; 2 Bell Lane	Died of wounds
Private Thomas Charles Rush; 138958, Canadian Infantry; 2 Towersey Road	Survived
Private James Campbell Russell; 160646, Royal Fusiliers; 26 Chinnor Road	Survived
Private Tom Saunders; 4706, Royal Marines; Wellington Street	Survived
Corporal Arthur R Saw; 312048, Royal Engineers; 37 Chinnor Road	Survived
Private William Henry Saw; M2/333319, Army Service Corps; 21 North Street	Survived
Lieutenant Fred Aubery Lane Sear; Royal Air Force; 125 High Street	Survived
Driver Frederick C Sexton; T3/024544, Army Service Corps; East Street	Survived
Major Donald Patrick Shaw DSO; Dorset Regiment 6th Btn; Lord Williams School Oxford Road	Died of wounds
Captain Edward B Shaw; Indian Army; Lord Williams School Oxford Road	Survived
Private John Boxell Shaw; 9983, Royal Welsh Fusiliers 10th Btn; Queens Road	Killed in action
Sergeant Richard James Shrimpton; 3973, Army Veterinary Corps; Nelson Street	Survived
Private Sidney Augustus Shrimpton; 4700, Royal Fusiliers 9th Btn; 62 High Street	Killed in action
Sergeant Harry John Shrimpton; 8862, Oxford & Bucks Light Infantry 5th Btn; 66 Park Street	Died of wounds
Lieutenant George Ernest Shrimpton; Devonshire Regiment; 30 Upper High Street	Survived
2nd Lieutenant Henry Leonard Shrimpton; MC Royal West Kent Regiment 10th Btn; 30 Upper High St	Survived
Lieutenant John Harvie Shrimpton; Royal Marines; 30 Upper High Street	Survived
Private Frederick Simmonds; Army Veterinary Corps; Park Terrace	Survived
Private W Simmonds; Oxford & Bucks Light Infantry; Park Street	Survived
Leading Seaman Alfred Smith; J14265, Royal Navy HMS Vivid; Priestend	Survived
Private Arthur Smith; Liverpool Scottish; High Street	Survived
Private Edward Bertram Smith; 105110, Machine Gun Corps; 52 High Street	Survived
Private Herbert Philip Smith; M2/098219, Army Service Corps; 5 Wellington Street	Survived
Private William Noel Smith; 1617, Oxf & Bucks Light Infantry 1st/4th Btn; 11 Upper High Street	Killed in action
Rifleman Frank Leslie Soanes; King's Royal Rifle Corps 18th Btn; Half Moon 7 Wellington St	Killed in action
Trooper Reginald Charles Soanes; 29629, City of London Yeomanry; Half Moon 7 Wellington Street	Survived
Petty Officer Sydney James Soanes; 29631, Royal Air Force; Half Moon 7 Wellington Street	Survived
Sergeant Albert Edward Squires; 86310, Royal Field Artillery; 9 Park Street	Survived
Corporal George Squires; 27854, Bedfordshire Regiment 7th Btn; 71 Park Street	Killed in action
Private Benjamin Squires; 22664, Grenadier Guards 2nd Btn; 71 Park Street	Killed in action
Private Joseph Squires; 13804, Machine Gun Corps 20th Coy; 71 Park Street	Died of wounds
Gunner William Benjamin Squires; 59837, Royal Field Artillery; 71 Park Street	Survived
Air Mech William Alfred Alexander Stacey; 211234, Royal Air Force; 33 High Street	Survived
Private Charles Stagg; 13833, Oxford & Bucks Light Infantry; Priestend	Survived
Chief Engineer Alexander William Stark; 1496, Royal Navy; Chinnor Road	Survived
Private Fred Stevens; 189336, Labour Corps 383rd Coy; 85 Park Street	Survived
Trooper Herbert Stevens; 1979, Queens Own Oxfordshire Hussars; 23 Upper High Street	Died of illness
Srgt Maj Herbert Arthur Stockwell MC; Oxford & Bucks Light Infantry 5th Btn; 21 North St	Died of wounds
Private George Stokes; 220903, Royal Army Service Corps; 20 Upper High Street	Survived
Private Richard Ernest Stone; 378482, Army Service Corps; Moorend Lane	Survived
Petty Officer Arthur Stowe; 230956, Royal Air Force; Kings Road	Survived

Sergeant George Stratford; Y/2SR02248, Royal Marines; Croft Road	Survived
Captain John Alexander Summerhayes; Royal Inniskilling Fusiliers; Redholme 78 High Street	Killed in action
Major John Orlando Summerhayes DSO; Royal Army Medical Corps; Redholme 78 High Street	Survived
Driver Stephen John Summersbee; 138835, Army Service Corps; Rooks Lane	Survived
Warrant Officer Arthur Henry Sutton; 1762, East Africa Transport Corp; 1 Buttermarket	Died of illness
Private Edward Henry Oliver Tallett; 346999, Labour Corps 526th Coy; Somerslea, Kings Road	Survived
Private Sidney Thomas Tappin; 10648, Oxford & Bucks Light Infantry 5th Btn; Southern Road	Killed in action
Private Arthur Taylor; 15682, South Wales Borderers 11th Btn; Chinnor Road	Survived
Sergeant Herbert J Taylor; 22063, South Wales Borderers 11th Btn; 53 Park Street	Survived PoW
Gunner John Taylor; 147363, Royal Garrison Artillery; Hampden Cottage Park Street	Survived
Sergeant William Abbott Thomas; S/7198, Army Ordnance Corps; 51 High Street	Survived
Boy 1st class Frank Tickner; J/59090, Royal Navy HMS Vanguard; 42 North Street	Died at sea
Private Frederick James Trafford; 42169, Royal Inniskilling Fusiliers 1st Btn; 6 Park Terrace	Survived PoW
Lieutenant Randolph Richard William Traill; Chaplains Branch; The Prebendal, Long Crendon Road	Survived
Private John Frederick Treble; 136514, Canadian Infantry; 12 Chinnor Road	Survived
Sergeant William Charles Treble; 163704, Canadian Infantry; 12 Chinnor Road	Survived
Private Albert Alexander Trinder; 47527, Essex Regiment 10th Btn; 126 High Street	Killed in action
Trooper Ethelbert Kenelm Valehaden; 15724, 17th Lancers; 8 Priestend	Survived
Private Herbert Harry Vertigen; S/2692, Royal Naval Division 63rd; 26 Queens Road	Survived
CQMS William Frederick Waldram; 200784, Oxford & Bucks Light Infantry 4th Btn; Park Street	Survived
Private Ernest John Walker; 47045, Worcestershire Regiment 16th Btn; 25 Upper High Street	Survived
Private Aubrey J Wall; M2/081951, Army Service Corps; Park Street	Survived
Lance Corporal P Wall; 55 Park Street	Survived
Private John Wall; 081951, Army Service Corps; 55 Park Street	Survived
Private William Arthur Wallington; Oxford & Bucks Light Infantry 5th Btn; 5 Windmill Road	Killed in action
Corporal Donald Hampden Ward; 103252, Royal Engineers; 32 Park Street	Survived
Private Walter Watson; 275505, Oxford & Bucks Light Infantry 3rd Btn; 32 North Street	Survived
Private Alfred John Webb; 66150, Labour Corps; 66 High Street	Survived
Private Edwin Webb; 33872, Royal Defence Corps; Moreton	Survived
Private S G Webb; Oxford & Bucks Light Infantry; The Park Thame Park	Survived
Private John Webster; T4/199533, Army Service Corps; Nelson Street	Survived
Corporal Roy E Welch; 2275, Royal Horse Guards; 8 Upper High Street	Survived
Private Wilfrid Keith Welch; 198, Australian Infantry 5th Reg; 8 Upper High Street	Survived
Private Mark Wells; T/265942, Royal West Surrey Regiment 6th Btn; Greyhound, 44 North Street	Killed in action
Sapper William John Wells; 27665, Royal Engineers; 42 High Street	Survived
Sergeant Cyril Wells; 0434, Wiltshire Regiment 4th Btn; 74 Park Street	Survived
Private Edwin Wells; 83437, Machine Gun Corps; Tythrop Terrace, 117 Wellington Street	Survived
Corporal Walter Wells; 4701, Royal Army Medical Corps; Star & Garter 117 Wellington Street	Survived
Private David Wentworth; 42878, Royal Air Force; 57 Park Street	Survived
Sergeant William Henry Wentworth MM; 15491, Grenadier Guards 3rd Btn; 37 North Street	Died of wounds
Leading Air Mechanic Frederick West; 220718, Royal Air Force; Kings Road	Survived
Air Mechanic Jack Wells West; F11238, Royal Air Force; 25 Park Street	Survived
2nd Lieutenant Ronald James West; Queens West Surrey Regiment; 25 Park Street	Survived
Sergeant William Harold West; 211176, Royal Air Force; 25 Park Street	Survived
Corporal James Benjamin West; 500267, Royal Engineers; 34 Upper High Street	Survived
Air Mechanic Leslie Stacey West; 208469, Royal Air Force; 34 Upper High Street	Survived
Private Frederick White; 13750, Oxford & Bucks Light Infantry 7th Btn; 35 North Street	Survived
Petty Officer H J White; Royal Navy HMS Excellent; 27 Park Street	Survived
Private Herbert White; 647, Oxford & Bucks Light Infantry; 27 Park Street	Survived
Lance Corporal John William White; 62208, Manchester Regiment 2nd Btn; 70 Park Street	Survived
Chief Petty Officer Sylvanus George White DSM; 147690, Royal Navy HMS Attentive II; 64 Park Street	Survived
Private Alfred White; Oxford & Bucks Light Infantry; Priestend	Survived
Corporal John White; SS/98, Army Service Corps; 2 Tythrop Terrace Wellington Street	Survived

Corporal George Frederick White; 94155, Royal Field Artillery; 2 Wellington Street	Survived
Driver Tom White; 5145, Oxford & Bucks Light Infantry; 34 Wellington Street	Survived
Stoker Felix White; 306111, Royal Navy HMS Dolphin; 34 Wellington Street	Survived
Rifleman Edmund Wiley; 625093, London Regiment 1/19th Btn; 30 Wellington Street	Survived
Private Alfred Willis; 44155, Durham Light Infantry 15th Btn;	Killed in action
Private Harry Cooper Wilsdon; G/13020, Middlesex Regiment 13th Btn; East Street	Killed in action
Private Alfred Wilshere; 18608, Hampshire Regiment; Chinnor Road	Survived
Private R G Wilshere; Oxford & Bucks Light Infantry; Chinnor Road	Survived
Staff Sergeant Thomas Arthur Wiltshire; M2/034876, Army Service Corps; Rostrevor, Chinnor Road	Survived
Sergeant F R Wise; Oxford & Bucks Light Infantry; East Street	Survived
Company Sergeant Major Cecil Amos Witney; Oxford & Bucks Light Inf 2nd/4th Btn; Park St	Killed in action
Private Frank Witney; 39239, Highland Light Infantry 2nd Btn; 38 Wellington Street	Survived
Private Walter Witney; M/381126, Army Service Corps; 1 Wellington Street	Survived
Sergeant Charles Wood; 6034, Royal Marines Artillery HMS Malaya; 24 North Street	Died of wounds
Driver Robert Wood; 7566, Royal Engineers; 13 Bell Lane	Survived
Private Sidney Harry Wood; 439425, Canadian Infantry; Park Street	Survived
Sapper William Chinnery Wood; 19369, Royal Engineers; 68 Park Street	Survived
Private Frederick Wright; 9545, Army Veterinary Corps; 3 Church Road	Survived
Private George Henry Wright; 429754, Labour Corps; Moreton	Survived
Lieutenant Charles Wykeham-Martin; Oxford & Bucks Light Infantry; The Park Thame Park	Survived
Captain Aubrey George Wykeham-Musgrave MC; Gloucestershire Yeomanry; Thame Park	Survived
Private Bertie Eustace Charles Yates; 5266, Army Veterinary Corps; 14 Upper High Street	Survived
Corporal Edward John Yates; 17580, Oxford & Bucks Light Infantry; 4 Wellington Street	Survived
Lance Corporal John William Yates; 62208, Manchester Regiment 2nd Btn; 70 Park Street	Survived
Lance Bombadier Joseph Harold Yates; 70725, Royal Garrison Artillery; 6 Park Street	Survived
Corporal Richard Youens; 8811, Royal Army Medical Corps; Priestend	Survived
Private Oliver William Drinkwater Young; 14168, Royal Marines; 23 Chinnor Road	Survived
Private Frederick George Young; 27650, Hampshire Regiment 52nd Btn; Wheatsheaf, 57 North Street	Survived
Corporal Albert Victor Young; Machine Gun Corps 27th Coy; Four Horse Shoes, 47 Park Street	Killed in action
Private William Frederick Young; Oxford & Bucks Light Infantry; Four Horse Shoes, 47 Park Street	Survived

Poems and Quotations

Page 6	Went the Day Well	John Maxwell Edmonds
Page 8	For the Fallen	Lawrence Binyon
Page 14	1914	Wilfred Owen
Page 18	Speech at unveiling of the War Memorial	David Lloyd George
Page 24	Diary note: 4 August 1914	George V
Page 36	In Flanders Fields	John McCrae
Page 36	We Shall Keep The Faith	Moina Michael
Page 60	Attack	Siegfried Sassoon
Page 93	You Come From England	John Maxwell Edmonds
Page 122	Armistice Signal: 11 Nov 1918	GHQ
Page 132	Only a Volunteer	Anon
Page 134	Greetings Postcard	R J P
Page 136	Rendezvous	Alan Seeger
Page 153	Epitaph to those who died at Jutland	Anon
Page 158	1939 Declaration	Neville Chamberlain
Page 162	Air Raid Shelter Notice	Electric Railway Order
Page 188	High Flight	John Gillespie Magee Jr
Page 194	Bombing Statement	Sir Arthur Harris
Page 195	D-Day Dodgers	Hamish Hamilton
Page 198	Blood and Flowers at Monte Cassino	Jarlath Bancroft
Page 202	Malta	George Smith
Page 210	Morning after the Barrage at El Alamein	Bombardier F E Hughes
Page 220	News Reel of Embarkation	Timothy Corsellis
Page 222	Drummer Hodge	Thomas Hardy
Page 228	Fallen Heroes	Cynthia Jones
Page 236	The Soldier	Rupert Brooke
Page 238	Elegy in a Country Courtyard	G K Chesterton

Bibliography

Most of the websites used

Military History
www.forces-war-records.co.uk/
www.nmarchive.com
www.cwgc.org
www.lightbobs.com/
www.unithistories.com/
www.armyservicenumbers.blogspot.co.uk/
www.fleetairarm.com
www.longlongtrail.co.uk

Family History
www.ancestry.co.uk
www.findmypast.co.uk
www.thegenealogist.co.uk
www.dustydocs.com
www.freebmd.org.uk
www.familysearch.org

General
www.thegazette.co.uk
www.nationalarchives.gov.uk/

Published Titles

Title	Author	Publisher
1914-18	David Stevenson	Penguin/Allen Lane
Beneath the Killing Fields	Matthew Leonard	Pen & Sword
Beaumont Hamel	Nigel Cave	Pen & Sword
Bomber Crew	John Sweetman	Abacus
Book of the Somme	Malcolm Brown	Pan
Boy Soldiers of the Great War	Richard van Emden	headline
Catastrophe	Max Hastings	William Collins
Delville Wood	Nigel Cave	Pen & Sword
Desert Rats at War	George Forty	Ian Allen
Destiny in the Desert	Jonathan Dimbleby	Profile Books
Elegy	Andrew Roberts	Head of Zeus
Encyclopaedia of WW2 Aircraft	Paul Eden	Amber
The First World War	Hew Strachan	Simon & Schuster
The First World War	Robin Prior & Trevor Wilson	Cassell
The First Day of the Somme	Martin Middlebrook	Penguin Books
Forgotten Voices of the Great War	Max Arthur	Ebury Press
Gallipoli: Pocket Battlefield Guide	Major & Mrs Holt	Pen & Sword
Gallipoli	Nigel Steel	Pen & Sword
Gallipoli	Peter Hart	Profile Books
The Gallipoli Experience Reconsidered	Peter Liddle	Pen & Sword
The Germans at Beaumont Hamel	Jack Sheldon	Pen & Sword
Great Britain's Great War	Jeremy Paxman	Penguin
The Great War Handbook	Geoff Bridger	Pen & Sword
Hundred Days	Nick Lloyd	Penguin
Mapping the First World War	Peter Chasseaud	Collins
Men Behind the Medals	Graham Pitchfork	Leo Cooper

Title	Author	Publisher
The Old Front Line	Stephen Bull	Casemate
Oxford in the Great War	Malcolm Graham	Pen & Sword
Oxfordshire Remembering 1914-18	Jane Cotter	The History Press
The Phantom Army of Alamein	Rick Stroud	Bloomsbury
Pilots of the Battle of Britain	John G Bentley	Ravette Publishing
RAF Coastal Command Losses of the Second World War Vol 1	Ross McNeill	Midland Publishing
The Salient: Ypres 1914-18	Alan Palmer	Constable
Sanctuary Wood & Hooge	Nigel Cave	Pen & Sword
Somme	Lyn McDonald	Michael Joseph
Somme: Into the Breach	Hugh Sebag-Montefiore	Penguin/Viking
Somme: Pocket Battlefield Guide	Major & Mrs Holt	Pen & Sword
The Somme Battlefield	Martin & Mary Middlebrook	Penguin
A Storm in Flanders	Winston Green	Cassell
The Trench	Trevor Yorke	Countryside Books
Understanding the Somme 1916	Thomas Scotland & Steven Heys	Helion
The Western Front	Richard Holmes	BBC Books
The Wipers Times	Sherwood Foresters	
Ypres Salient: Pocket Battlefield Guide	Major & Mrs Holt	Pen & Sword

Thame Remembers